CAPTAIN'S LOG...

Patrick Stewart interviewed
by Ian Spelling

Patrick Stewart disappears swiftly into the New York City skyline.

It's a bizarre sight. Trekkers are used to seeing Stewart's *Star Trek: The Next Generation* alter-ego, Captain Jean-Luc Picard, whisking about in the *U.S.S. Enterprise NCC-1701-E* or beaming from one place to another via the transporter. But on this day, even though Stewart sports full Starfleet regalia, he is pedalling into the distance on a rather ordinary 20th Century bicycle, and that Manhattan skyline is nothing but a giant set, the streets of the Big Apple as seen on the Paramount Pictures backlot in Hollywood. And Stewart, after an interview in his trailer, is returning to the set of *Star Trek: First Contact.*

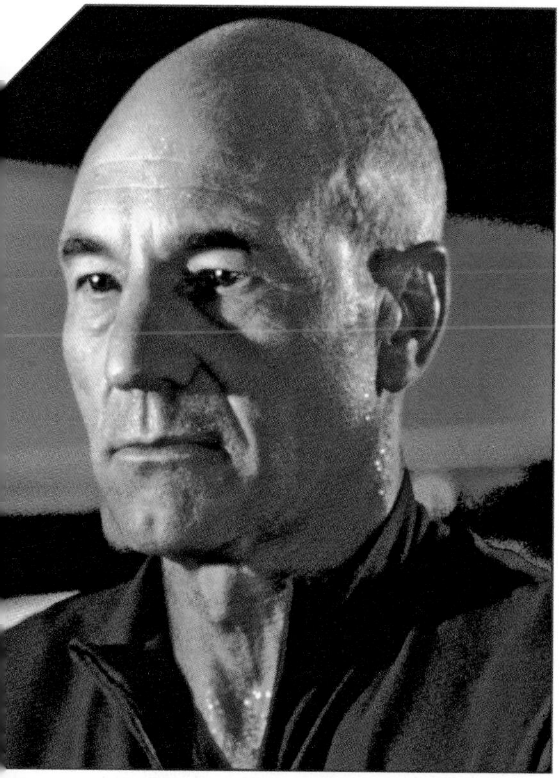

Such a great, ironically appropriate coda to the Stewart interview is his exit by bike that it makes perfect sense to start an article about Stewart with the anecdote. In moments, Stewart will be back before the camera, taking his cues from director Jonathan Frakes, just as he was about an hour earlier. It was then that Stewart shared the set with Michael Dorn, Marina Sirtis, Frakes, Brent Spiner and Gates McFadden on one of the rare *Star Trek: First Contact* production days in which almost the entire cast was working at the same time. It was moments after Frakes called "Cut" on a scene in which Worf arrives on the *Enterprise-E* from an embattled *U.S.S. Defiant* that Stewart strode over to his trailer to talk. "This is proving to be as good an experience as I hoped it would be and an even better one in one particular instance, and that is the work we are doing here with Jonathan as our director," Stewart says earnestly as he juggles lunch, an interview and some paternal concern about his cat, Bela, who is a bit under the weather. "It's been very nice so far to be back here with everyone, to be playing Picard once again, but I am most pleased that Jonathan earned the job and that he has so heartily embraced the task.

"He is bringing everything he learned while he was acting and directing episodes of *Star Trek: The Next Generation* to *Star Trek: First Contact*, and it is paying off, for us and for Jonathan. One can see that, given the scale of this movie, a director – and a first-time director at that – might have been overwhelmed by it all. On the contrary, Jonathan stands so tall while he's directing, literally and figuratively. I had a visitor on the set the other day and they said, 'This is amazing. I have never seen the director of a movie this complicated appear to be as relaxed and at ease as Jonathan is.' He's really doing a wonderful job of it. It's thrilling to be here – as we were when Jonathan directed his first episode of the

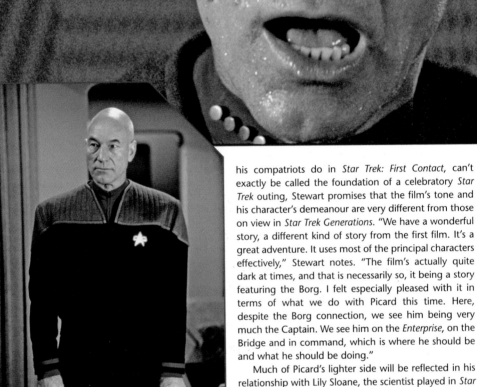

television series – for what I think is going to be a very grand directing career for Jonathan."

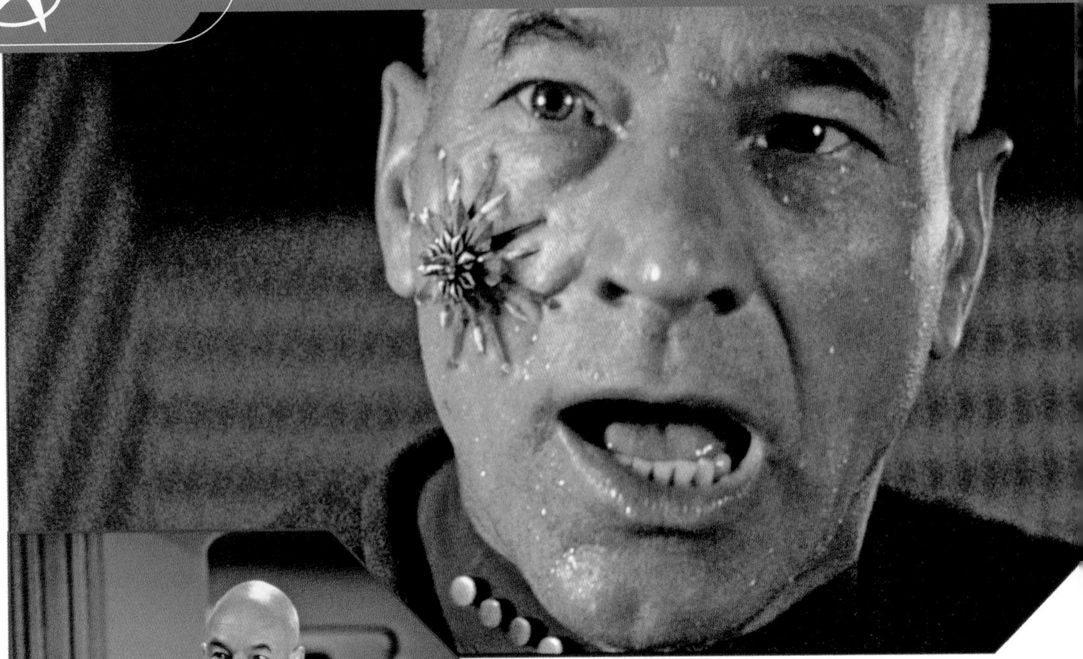

Stewart is equally enthusiastic about *Star Trek: First Contact* as a whole. While he ultimately liked *Star Trek Generations* and felt the David Carson-directed film did a reasonably good job of passing the torch from the original *Star Trek* crew to that of *Star Trek: The Next Generation*, he feels it was a dark film, one in which too much time was spent focusing on a Picard who was noticeably distracted and brooding. The captain was that way, understandably so, because he was surrounded by death. After all, we learnt that his brother and nephew had died senselessly in the opening reels. Captain Kirk (William Shatner) perished while fighting Soran (Malcolm McDowell) alongside him. And the *U.S.S. Enterprise-D* went down in a blazing ball of flames.

Although battling the dreaded Borg, as Picard and

his compatriots do in *Star Trek: First Contact*, can't exactly be called the foundation of a celebratory *Star Trek* outing, Stewart promises that the film's tone and his character's demeanour are very different from those on view in *Star Trek Generations*. "We have a wonderful story, a different kind of story from the first film. It's a great adventure. It uses most of the principal characters effectively," Stewart notes. "The film's actually quite dark at times, and that is necessarily so, it being a story featuring the Borg. I felt especially pleased with it in terms of what we do with Picard this time. Here, despite the Borg connection, we see him being very much the Captain. We see him on the *Enterprise*, on the Bridge and in command, which is where he should be and what he should be doing."

Much of Picard's lighter side will be reflected in his relationship with Lily Sloane, the scientist played in *Star Trek: First Contact* by Alfre Woodard. Sloane is the associate of Zefram Cochrane (James Cromwell), and it is she who winds up on the *U.S.S. Enterprise-E* like Alice in Wonderland. Stewart won't go so far as to describe their relationship as a romance, but he reveals that there is a "definite attraction and appeal that grows out of the experiences they share together." It was Stewart who initially suggested to the film's producers that a black actress be cast as Sloane, determined to counter present-day racism with some 24th Century-style acceptance. "Racism is a reality, I suppose. But it is not part of my universe," he insists. "This was one of my reasons, from the beginning, for suggesting a black actress for Lily: It's absolutely at the heart of what *Star Trek* is all about, because I don't see it as an issue. I see in Lily a tremendously attractive, intelligent woman being played by a tremendously attractive, intelligent woman and a brilliant actress."

Ultimately, Stewart sounds happy that he has

STAR TREK
THE NEXT GENERATION™

THE HERO FACTOR

MICHAEL JAN FRIEDMAN

PABLO MARCOS

TITAN BOOKS

STAR TREK: THE NEXT GENERATION –
THE HERO FACTOR

ISBN 1 84576 153 7

Published by Titan Books
A division of Titan Publishing Group Ltd.
144 Southwark St
London SE1 0UP

This book collects issues #1–6 of *Star Trek: The Next Generation* (ongoing), originally published in the USA by DC Comics.

A CIP catalogue record for this title is available from the British Library.

This edition first published: September 2005
2 4 6 8 10 9 7 5 3 1

Printed in Italy.

Other titles of interest available from Titan Books:

Star Trek: To Boldly Go (ISBN: 1 84576 084 0)
Alien Legion: On the Edge (ISBN: 1 84023 765 1)
Alien Legion: Tenants of Hell (ISBN: 1 84023 811 9)
Battlestar Galactica: Saga of a Star World (ISBN: 1 84023 930 1)
Battlestar Galactica: The Memory Machine (ISBN: 1 84023 945 X)

What did you think of this book?
We love to hear from our readers.
Please email us at: readerfeedback@titanemail.com,
or write to us at the above address.

www.titanbooks.com

returned to the character that has given him financial security, made him a star and allowed him to pursue any number of other exciting projects outside the *Star Trek* galaxy. Since *Star Trek Generations*, Stewart has hardly slowed down to catch his breath. He sashayed through a wonderful part as a gay man in the Paul Rudnick comedy, *Jeffrey*, gave *Party of Five* star Neve Campbell the creeps in *The Canterville Ghost,* and played a dance instructor in a film entitled *Let It Be Me*, with Jennifer Beals, Leslie Caron and Campbell Scott. He has hosted a well-received evening of the famous US comedy show *Saturday Night Live* in which, yes, he roasted *ST:TNG* to a nice crisp, lent his unmistakable voice to a wide variety of television commercials and educational CD-ROM games, and even turned up on the children's programme, *Sesame Street*, to promote the virtues of the letter 'B'.

The actor also took to the stage in the summer of 1995 as a fierce Prospero in a production of *The Tempest*. Initially a free, outdoor show in New York's famed Central Park (as part of its annual Shakespeare Festival), *The Tempest* proved so popular that it was transferred to Broadway for a sold-out run of several months. Clearly, Stewart is as proud of *The Tempest* as he could possibly be. "The experience was as good as any I've ever had," he enthuses. "It was simply an exhilarating experience. It was the first show to transfer from the Park to Broadway in, I think, eighteen years. The show before it was *The Pirates of Penzance*. I don't know how long it had been since a Shakespeare

production had transferred. Certainly, it was a number of years before a US production of Shakespeare had played on Broadway. I've actually been harassing [*Tempest* director] George C Wolfe about another project. It's not *Richard III*, which, if you look closely at *Star Trek: First Contact*, is in Picard's ready room [in a glass case]. It would be one of the tragedies."

As if all that weren't enough, Stewart has a full slate of upcoming films on the way, including a thriller, *Safe House*, and a comedy, *Smart Alec* [Editor's note: the movie was eventually released under the title

Masterminds]. "I play an ex-DIA agent in *Safe House*," Stewart reveals, "DIA being the Defense Intelligence Agency, who has barricaded himself inside his Hollywood Hills home using the latest security technology that can be found. He believes that his life has been threatened by a man who was once his boss, an admiral who is now running for President of the United States. The admiral is killing off all of the people who used to work for him and who may have dirt on him.

"And I have a lot of dirt on him for things he did while he was with the DIA. My character is the last guy alive, but no one believes him because he is in the early stages of Alzheimer's Disease. Everyone thinks his paranoia is part of the disease. So, as the actual danger to his life gets close, his ability to deal with the threat, with anything around him, gets worse and worse. We don't have a distributor for the film yet, but I think it may come out very, very well."

Stewart has also completed principal photography on *Smart Alec*, a comedy that was shot on location in Canada immediately after *Star Trek: First Contact* wrapped up. "It's an action-comedy and I get to play a luminously unpleasant character," Stewart says, smiling broadly. "The major conflict is the competition between this super criminal that I play and a teenager [played by Vincent Kartheiser, who went on to play the role of Connor, the vampire's son in *Angel*], who was in the movie *Alaska*. He's a wonderful young talent. The best way I can describe the film is to say that it will be a little like *Home Alone* in spirit and in its comedy."

These days, Stewart seems to be doing rather well for himself. He lives in Los Angeles most of the time, but maintains a residence in London. He recently sang at the Hollywood Bowl and will be taking to the stage come December in a limited-run Los Angeles production of his popular one-man show, Charles Dickens' *A Christmas Carol*. He hopes to direct a small film in the future, perhaps even a film version of *The Merchant of Venice* in the style of Sir Ian McKellan's *Richard III*.

So positive have Stewart's experiences away from *Star Trek: The Next Generation* been that he is actually looking forward to reprising his role as Jean-Luc Picard every few years in future films. Indeed, *Star Trek: The Next Generation* and Picard have not, as Stewart once feared like some fear the plague, stood in the way of his pursuing other opportunities, other roles that allow him to fully express himself as an actor.

"I was absolutely determined to be in a state of preparedness in my career as an actor to move on after *Star Trek: The Next Generation* went off the air, and I think I was successful in doing that," Patrick Stewart says as the conversation comes to a close. "I have always said I would not mind coming back to *Star Trek* and to Picard as long as I had the opportunity to do other things.

"I still feel that way."

And with that, Stewart takes one last bite of his salad, pets his beloved Bela goodbye for now, and hops on that bicycle which will shuttle him back to the *U.S.S. Enterprise-E* bridge.

It really is quite a sight.

[Editor's note: This interview first appeared in *Star Trek Monthly* #22, cover date December 1996, published in the UK by Titan Magazines. *Star Trek: First Contact* was released in 1996.]

THE DATA FILE

Brent Spiner interviewed
by Joe Nazzaro and Ian Spelling

For Brent Spiner, the sixth season of *Star Trek: The Next Generation* saw his character of Data moving slowly but steadily along the path towards humanity. In *The Quality of Life* (directed by co-star Jonathan Frakes), the inquisitive android explored the nature and definition of mechanical life, even at the risk of his own career. In *Birthright* Part One, a dormant program in his brain was activated, causing dream-like hallucinations, in which he saw a youthful version of his creator, Dr Soong. Finally, in *Descent* Part One, the android experienced his first emotions: anger, and pleasure at the death of one of the enemy Borg. It was a busy year in the development of Data.

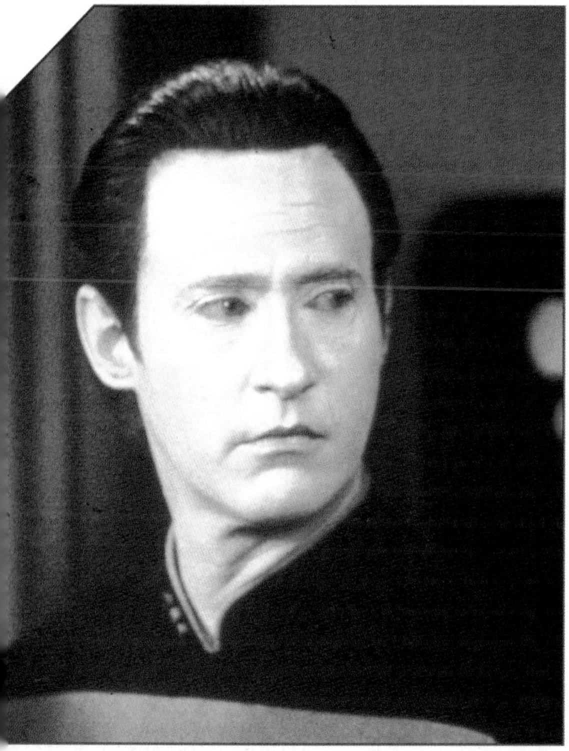

While *Star Trek: The Next Generation* moved into its seventh and final season before making the jump into feature films, across the Paramount Pictures lot, its sister series *Star Trek: Deep Space Nine* was in its sophomore outing in syndication. The parallels weren't lost on Spiner at the time (who remembered another group of actors trying to bring a new *Star Trek* series to television just a few years ago).

"I may be wrong, because I haven't spoken to all of them," he commented, as to whether or not he has discussed the plusses and minuses of a career in outer space with the new kids on the block, "but I would think their reluctance would simply be doing series television period. That was always my reluctance.

"I wasn't sure about taking this job initially, because I didn't want to be in a series. However, it's much better going into a show like *Star Trek* – to be in an honourable series rather than a piece of fluff. With *Star Trek*, you can be sure that's going to be gratifying in terms of ideas and concepts and all sorts of possibilities for the future."

With then just six years of *Star Trek: The Next Generation* under his Starfleet belt, Spiner was proud of the character he helped create. For Spiner, the key to Data's believability is playing him absolutely straight, even in humorous situations. "He's never intentionally funny," the actor insisted, prior to events in the first feature film which saw his character finally install the emotion chip created by his father, Doctor Noonien Soong. "I think *The Outrageous Okona* was his only attempt at being funny. We may have tried a line or two somewhere in the 150-odd episodes we've done now, but I can't remember any of them at this point.

"Data's humour always comes out of the situations, and out of the character, but it's actually the juxtaposition of Data and his way of dealing with a straight situation that creates humour."

Spiner is pleased with the development of Data over the years. "I was particularly pleased with the sixth season.

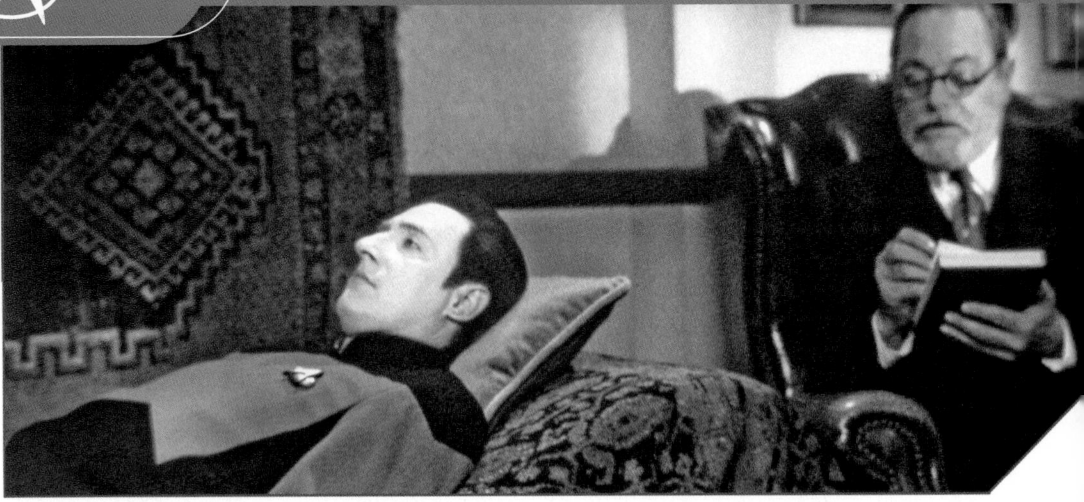

It was one of the best years we've had. Most of the actors, I think, have a preference for our first year or two, when we were exploring a little bit more and trying to find our characters. Some of our best episodes took place during the third, fourth and fifth years, but just as a general feeling over an entire season, our sixth was the best. It felt more like the first and second series did.

"We had a new writing staff – these guys had written for us before, but when [Executive Producer] Jeri Taylor took over, she gave these guys, who were very young, the opportunity to just write. As a result, we had some really interesting episodes and, in general, a more interesting year than we'd had in a while."

As to further explorations of his android alter-ego, "I just like to leave that up to the writers at this point, but I really like the way things are proceeding. It was Brannon Braga's idea to give Data a dream program [*Birthright* Part One]. I thought that was inspired. It was about the most interesting thing I've had to do in a couple of years, as far as developing the character itself was concerned. In terms of expanding on the character and exploring his possibilities, I thought Brannon's idea was brilliant.

"The idea of pursuing emotion was also interesting to me. In *Descent* Part One, they really pushed it further and that's basically Ron Moore who wrote that. Hopefully, we'll see more of that kind of development."

The actor's distinctive gold make-up is Data's trademark, so much so that Spiner titled his first album *Ol' Yellow Eyes is Back*. How important is the actual physical appearance to Spiner's playing the role? "I don't feel differently because I'm wearing this make-up. It was important when I was playing Dr Soong [in *Brothers*], because it wasn't until I saw the make-up on my face that I knew who my character was. Sitting there in the make-up chair, looking in the mirror at this man who was not me, I had a better understanding of Soong than I did internally up until then. As Data, it's just make-up. The character is someone I could turn on without it.

"As an actor, I've changed my appearance many times and I think that's important when it's specific to a particular role. The next time out, I'll be a different character and I won't look like this anymore, but for now it's a benefit rather than a detriment."

While Spiner may not need the gold make-up and contact lenses to get into the proper frame of mind, he guards his character's reality carefully. Photographers are allowed to take pictures of Spiner before getting into make-up, or after the transformation is complete, but in-between photos are strictly off limits. "It seems that since we first began doing the series," explains the actor, "the whole idea of putting on the make-up was creating illusion. We were trying to create the illusion that I was an android, but systematically from day one, the public relations angle has been, 'Let's go behind the scenes and show how it's done.' That means there's no illusion anymore. I become just another guy in make-up. It's the magic: once you know how the trick is done, it's not interesting anymore."

Added to the daily make-up are the occasional electronic effects. On any given week, Spiner found the back, front or top of his head opened up, revealing rows of blinking lights within. While these FX may take time to set up, the actor doesn't find them particularly difficult. "They're just time-consuming. Whenever they do something like open my neck, or the back of my head, everything just stops for however long it takes to set it up. It's not any more uncomfortable than it normally is."

Asked about forthcoming feature films, Spiner, a long-time film buff, has strong views on the matter. "Every actor wants to be in features," he elaborates, "I don't think there's anyone in the business who doesn't, but I think, for me to say at this point, 'When this is over, I want to do features,' is stupid. I've always wanted to – everybody does – but opportunities to do that are very, very limited.

"Television, oddly enough, may be the only form of show business that actually looks out for its own, in a way. Once someone has had a hit series, you can be pretty sure you'll see that person again in another series somewhere down the road. In film, you're only as good as your last feature, or at least your last two pictures. If they don't make money, then you'll never see that person again, or at least not for another ten to fifteen years."

Spiner's far-off future, now his work *has* spread into

feature films, may include more stage work. The actor had (and has) his own views on working in theatre. "I would like to keep doing stage work and whatever film or television I can do until I'm somewhere in my 100s," he grins, obviously relishing the idea of working into his dotage.

Spiner returns to the subject of *Star Trek: The Next Generation*, and its ever-increasing group of actors/directors. The first of Spiner's co-stars to helm an episode was Jonathan Frakes, who helped bring *The Offspring* to life during the third season and went on to direct some of the series' finest episodes, including *Reunion*, *The Drumhead*, *The Quality of Life* and *The Chase*.

A year later, Patrick Stewart picked up the director's baton, with *In Theory*, and followed it up with *Hero Worship* and *A Fistful of Datas*, one of Spiner's favourite episodes. LeVar Burton's freshman outing, *Second Chances*, was regarded as one of the sixth season's most sensitively handled segments.

After Frakes, Stewart and Burton, Spiner admits that he too would like to try his hand – although directing *Star Trek* held no appeal. "I think I would like to direct one day, I just don't think I would particularly like directing an action-adventure. It's not really my field. I would prefer directing comedy because I would have more skill with it."

Talking of *Star Trek*, with another season then still to be recorded, Spiner had some strong views on how the show is put together. "I feel in a way, that at this point all of us direct almost every episode. Most of the directors we've had are much more accessible in terms of our suggesting a possible shot. Even though I haven't broken a script down, and done a shot list, and said, 'Action!' out loud, I feel I've absorbed a lot of information that would serve me well if I was going to direct.

"I really like to work with directors like Rick Kolbe [*Darmok*], Cliff Bole [*Conspiracy*] and Les Landau [*Family*]. They know the show, they trust us, and they don't give us some stupid subtext that we thought of four years ago. That's much easier than working with someone who, having just seen the show for the first time, or maybe just a few episodes, has this brainstorm, not knowing that in episode #93, we already solved that problem.

"Occasionally, someone will come in and infuse new energy into the show," Spiner quickly admits. "It's particularly fun for me, aside from those directors I've already mentioned, when Jonathan or Patrick or LeVar directs. I was very excited about LeVar directing an episode, because when one of us directs, the cast and crew really get behind him, and that creates a new, exciting energy. I enjoyed watching that process as it happens, but bringing in a director who has done a thousand cop shows in his life – it's generally fine, and it usually works out, but it's not a particularly exciting proposition."

Of the more than three dozen directors he has worked with on *Star Trek: The Next Generation*, Spiner has no trouble choosing a personal favourite. "We've had some really good directors on the show, but my single favourite director is Jonathan Frakes. It's not because he's a member of the cast or because he's my friend; I think Jonathan is a genuinely talented director. I think he will be a director, period, because he's really got 'it'.

"If you spoke to anyone in the cast they would say that Jonathan is our favourite director, and it's not just about our association with him. It's his style as a director. Ask the crew; they'll also tell you he's their favourite director, because he's efficient, and works both sides of a camera very well. He doesn't neglect the acting at all. I think it's his experience as an actor that makes him a sensitive director and able to motivate everything we do. If he doesn't like what you're doing, he'll find a way to get you to do it, but that method of making it happen is very delicate and provocative.

"Every time I hear that Jonathan is directing a show, I'm always excited about it because I know it's going to be great. He has taken scripts on the page and turned them into really good episodes, not just from the acting standpoint, but because he's so imaginative with the camera."

He points to *The Offspring* as the perfect example of Frakes' directorial style. "In that and subsequent stories, he's not afraid of shooting a big master [establishing] shot that says it all. It's a big risk, but Jonathan has taken it more often than not. The shot has been so well designed that there's no question about it."

Spiner is reminded of a moment during the lensing of *Lessons* when a complicated music recital scene was shot in the Observation Lounge. While director Robert Weimer was coaching Spiner and actress Wendy Hughes in the handling of their respective musical instruments, Frakes stood quietly in the background, studying the set's layout.

"One of the reasons for that was because he was directing the next episode [*The Chase*], and he was

looking at the room thinking, 'Where can I put my camera that nobody has ever put it before?'

"You'll notice in any of Jonathan's episodes, whenever we're in the Observation Lounge, which is a very difficult room to shoot in, that room looks different every time you see it, whereas it always looks the same in almost every other director's shows. He has gotten some wonderful shots in there which no one else has found."

Working on the *U.S.S. Enterprise NCC-1701-D* has provided some unique experiences. Filming Professor Stephen Hawking's poker-playing cameo in *Descent Part One*, Spiner notes, was thrilling. "It's not every day that you have probably the smartest man in the universe sitting across from you, actually playing a scene from *Star Trek: The Next Generation*. But there he was, and by his own choice. He asked to appear on the show.

"I spoke with Hawking a couple of times, but we actually did more communicating through eye contact. He seemed to say a lot in silence, if you can understand what I mean. He has this incredible computer with a menu of words that speaks sentences for him. But it does take a while and I really didn't think I could come up with anything worthy enough for him to spend his time trying to scan through his computer to answer me."

The actor's favourite episodes are no surprise. "In general, I like the ones that feature the character of Data," he notes. "I think almost everyone in the cast will say their favourite episode in the entire experience so far has been *The Offspring*, Jonathan's first directorial effort. It was also a wonderful script from René Echeverria. It's *Star Trek* at its very best and it was my personal favourite.

"There have been many good episodes. *Measure of a Man* was a really good episode, too. I have episodes that I particularly like because of what I got to do, but which I don't necessarily think are among our better episodes as wholes. I just like what they allowed me to do."

Spiner now attends the occasional SF convention, which he considers part of the job of playing Data. It's a duty that he doesn't mind. "The response and the experience have always been pleasant," he raves. "The only downside to that is the exhaustion of wrapping up at midnight on Friday, getting up at 5am Saturday, getting on a plane and flying across the country, getting back at 11pm Sunday, and then coming in at 5.45 the next morning. It's exhausting, but the experience is still very pleasant."

Although there are Brent Spiner fan clubs, the actor hasn't sanctioned any specific organisations. "I don't disapprove of it at all," he declares. "If anyone wants to do that, it's their business. I appreciate the fans, and I always have, but I feel really silly sanctioning something where people would gather to celebrate me. That just feels a little odd to me. If people want to reach me they can write to me at Paramount Pictures. Everything will eventually get to me."

When this interview was conducted the actor had another season of *Star Trek: The Next Generation* still to finish, and a film waiting in the wings. But he was in no hurry to think about what lies beyond. After all, originally, he didn't expect it all to last this long. "To be honest, I thought we would be on for a year because it wouldn't be popular, wouldn't catch on. The original show was legendary and I just didn't see any real possibility for us. I remember Leonard Nimoy saying, 'It's very difficult to catch lightning in a bottle.' It's even harder to catch lightning a second time. Oddly enough, they seem to have done it a third time now with *Star Trek: Deep Space Nine*."

Spiner and his fellow cast members get along very well, often spending time together when they aren't shooting. "We all really do like each other, which has been the best thing about the whole experience. I get to work every day with people I really like. I think that's quite unique, particularly in television. There's so much pressure and the hours are so gruelling.

"When and if the time comes that I'm not doing *Star Trek: The Next Generation*, I think the thing I will miss most and think about most are my friends from the show." But Spiner has plenty of time left, we hope, playing a certain gold-skinned android. "This is my fifteen minutes," he jokes, "and right now, I'm around minute seven or eight. I intend to use all fifteen!"

[Editor's note: This interview first appeared in *Star Trek Monthly* #3, cover dated May 1995, published in the UK by Titan magazines. The interview was conducted during *Star Trek: The Next Generation*'s seventh and final season.]

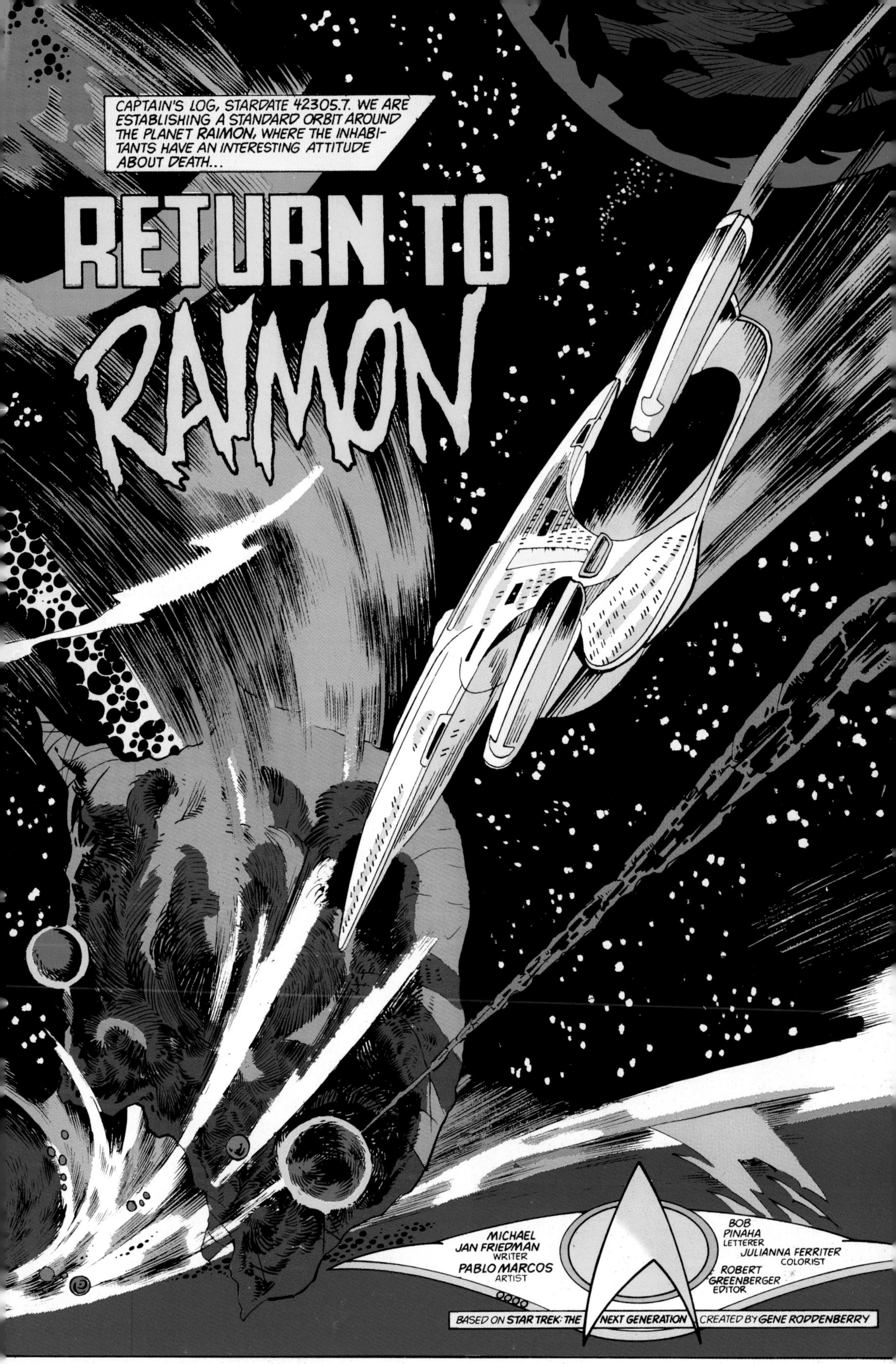

CAPTAIN'S LOG, STARDATE 42305.7. WE ARE ESTABLISHING A STANDARD ORBIT AROUND THE PLANET RAIMON, WHERE THE INHABITANTS HAVE AN INTERESTING ATTITUDE ABOUT DEATH...
RETURN TO RAIMON
MICHAEL JAN FRIEDMAN WRITER
PABLO MARCOS ARTIST
BOB PINAHA LETTERER
JULIANNA FERRITER COLORIST
ROBERT GREENBERGER EDITOR
BASED ON STAR TREK: THE NEXT GENERATION CREATED BY GENE RODDENBERRY

WHAT'S MORE, THE EVENT IS ANYTHING BUT SOLEMN. IN FACT, IT'S A FAIRLY *EXTRAVAGANT* CELEBRATION-- WITH THE DYING ONE IN ATTENDANCE AS GUEST OF HONOR.

WHEN A RAIMONIAN LEARNS THAT HIS DEATH IS IMMINENT, HE CALLS FOR A GATHERING OF HIS PEERS TO MARK THE EVENT. BUT THE GATHERING TAKES PLACE *BEFORE* HIS DEMISE-- NOT AFTERWARD AS IN MOST CULTURES.

THE PRIMARCH OF RAIMON, THE MOST IMPORTANT POLITICAL FIGURE ON THE PLANET, HAS CALLED FOR HIS DEATH CELEBRATION. AS IS CUSTOMARY, IT WILL CULMINATE IN A PUBLIC READING OF HIS LAST WILL AND TESTAMENT.

SINCE THE FEDERATION HAS LONG ENJOYED A MINING TREATY WITH RAIMON, THANKS TO THE INDULGENCE OF THE PRIMARCH AND HIS FORE-BEARS, WE HAVE BEEN ASKED TO SEND A PARTY OF REPRESENTA-TIVES TO THE CELEBRATION.

AND OF COURSE, TO THE READING OF THE PRIMARCH'S WILL AS WELL.

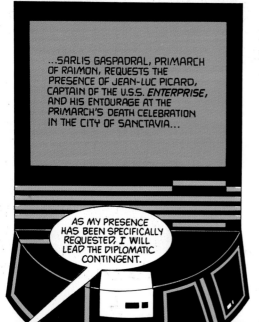

...SARLIS GASPADRAL, PRIMARCH OF RAIMON, REQUESTS THE PRESENCE OF JEAN-LUC PICARD, CAPTAIN OF THE U.S.S. *ENTERPRISE*, AND HIS ENTOURAGE AT THE PRIMARCH'S DEATH CELEBRATION IN THE CITY OF SANCTAVIA...

AS MY PRESENCE HAS BEEN SPECIFICALLY REQUESTED, I WILL LEAD THE DIPLOMATIC CONTINGENT.

LOG ENTRY COMPLETE. PICARD OUT.

2

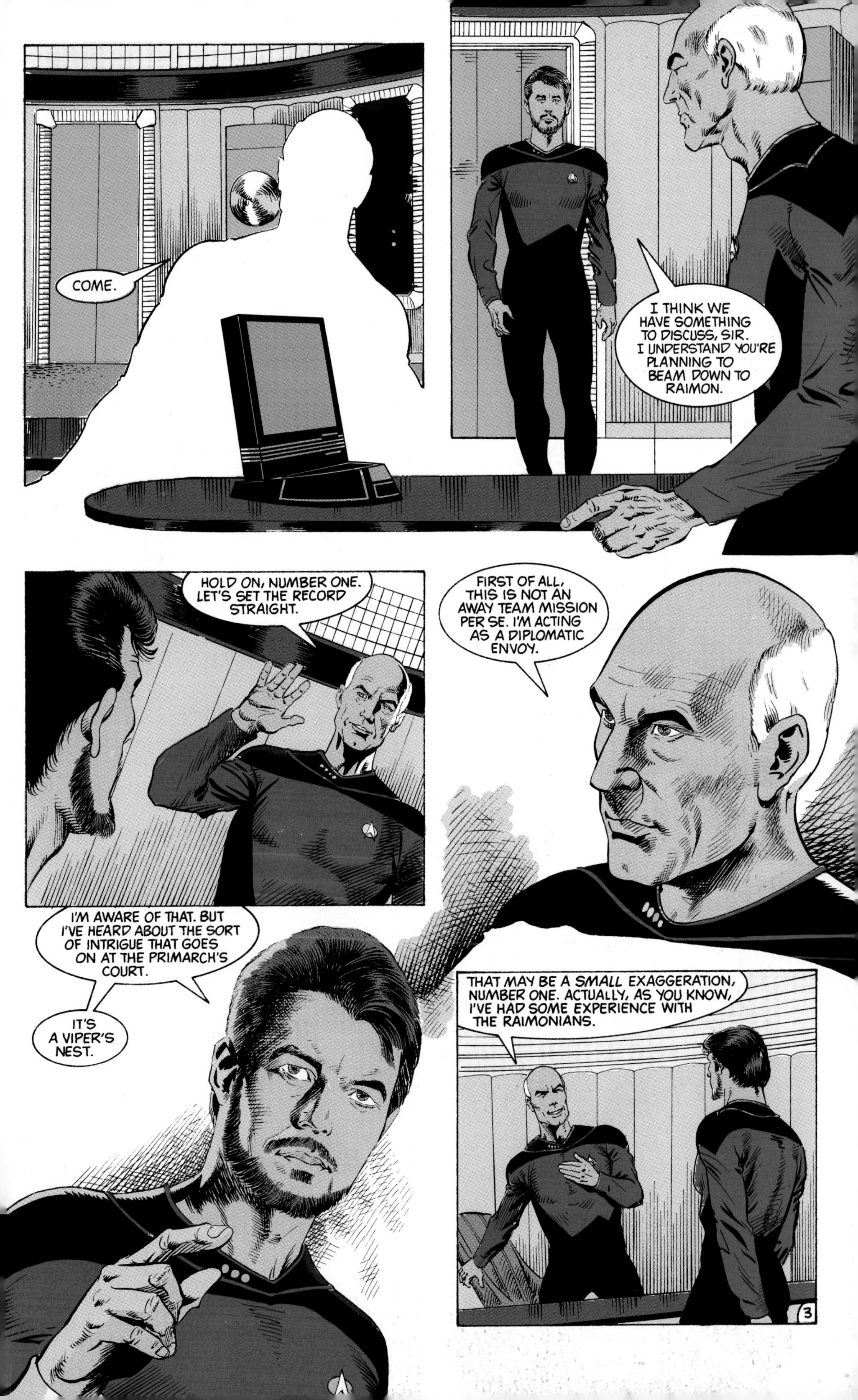
COME.
I THINK WE HAVE SOMETHING TO DISCUSS, SIR. I UNDERSTAND YOU'RE PLANNING TO BEAM DOWN TO RAIMON.
HOLD ON, NUMBER ONE. LET'S SET THE RECORD STRAIGHT.
FIRST OF ALL, THIS IS NOT AN AWAY TEAM MISSION PER SE. I'M ACTING AS A DIPLOMATIC ENVOY.
I'M AWARE OF THAT. BUT I'VE HEARD ABOUT THE SORT OF INTRIGUE THAT GOES ON AT THE PRIMARCH'S COURT.
IT'S A VIPER'S NEST.
THAT MAY BE A *SMALL* EXAGGERATION, NUMBER ONE. ACTUALLY, AS YOU KNOW, I'VE HAD SOME EXPERIENCE WITH THE RAIMONIANS.
3

I'M AWARE OF THAT TOO. YOU WERE THE FEDERATION'S ENVOY TO THE DEATH CELEBRATION OF THE PREVIOUS PRIMARCH--THE CURRENT PRIMARCH'S FATHER.

APPARENTLY, YOUR PRESENCE THERE WAS... MEMORABLE.

LET'S JUST SAY I EMBRACED THE SPIRIT OF THE PLACE, AND ESTABLISHED A GOOD RAPPORT WITH THE ROYAL FAMILY.

IN ANY CASE, I CAN'T REFUSE TO GO. THE PRIMARCH HAS MADE A POINT OF REQUESTING THAT I ATTEND *PERSONALLY*. IF ANYONE ELSE SHOWED UP IN MY PLACE, IT WOULD BE CONSIDERED AN INSULT.

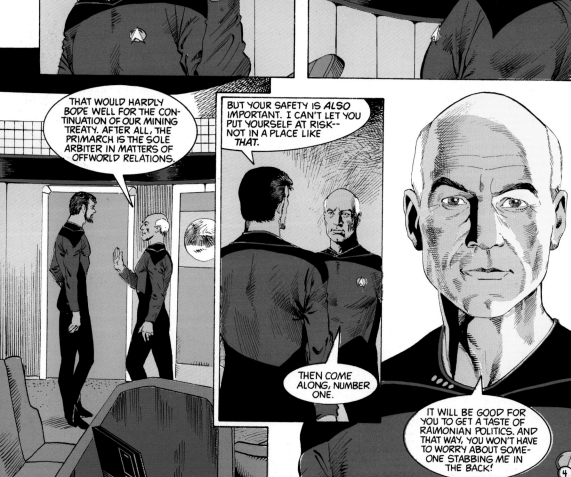

THAT WOULD HARDLY BODE WELL FOR THE CONTINUATION OF OUR MINING TREATY. AFTER ALL, THE PRIMARCH IS THE SOLE ARBITER IN MATTERS OF OFFWORLD RELATIONS.

BUT YOUR SAFETY IS *ALSO* IMPORTANT. I CAN'T LET YOU PUT YOURSELF AT RISK-- NOT IN A PLACE LIKE *THAT*.

THEN COME ALONG, NUMBER ONE.

IT WILL BE GOOD FOR YOU TO GET A TASTE OF RAIMONIAN POLITICS. AND THAT WAY, YOU WON'T HAVE TO WORRY ABOUT SOMEONE STABBING ME IN THE BACK!

4

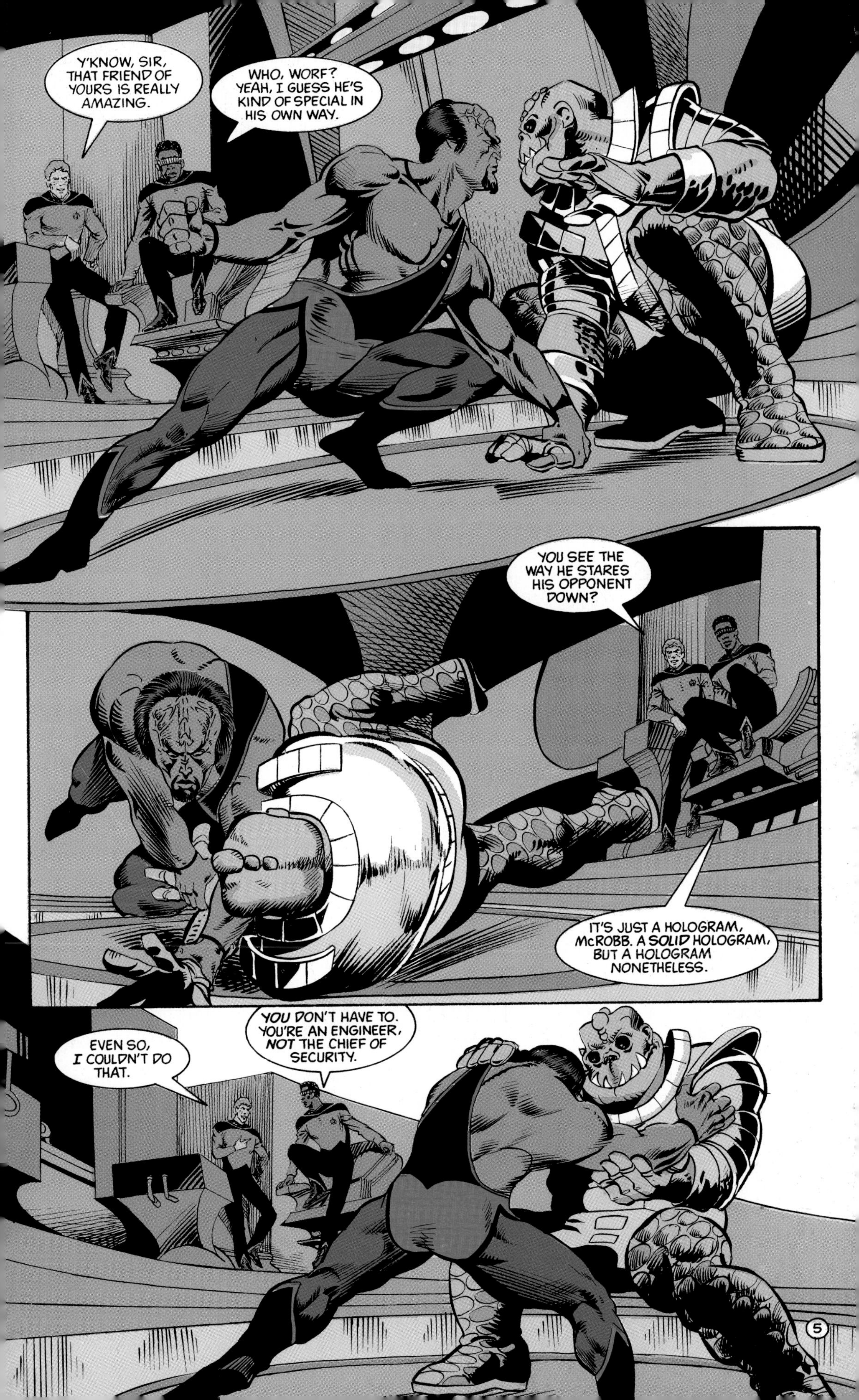
Y'KNOW, SIR, THAT FRIEND OF YOURS IS REALLY AMAZING.
WHO, WORF? YEAH, I GUESS HE'S KIND OF SPECIAL IN HIS OWN WAY.
YOU SEE THE WAY HE STARES HIS OPPONENT DOWN?
IT'S JUST A HOLOGRAM, McROBB. A SOLID HOLOGRAM, BUT A HOLOGRAM NONETHELESS.
EVEN SO, I COULDN'T DO THAT.
YOU DON'T HAVE TO. YOU'RE AN ENGINEER, NOT THE CHIEF OF SECURITY.

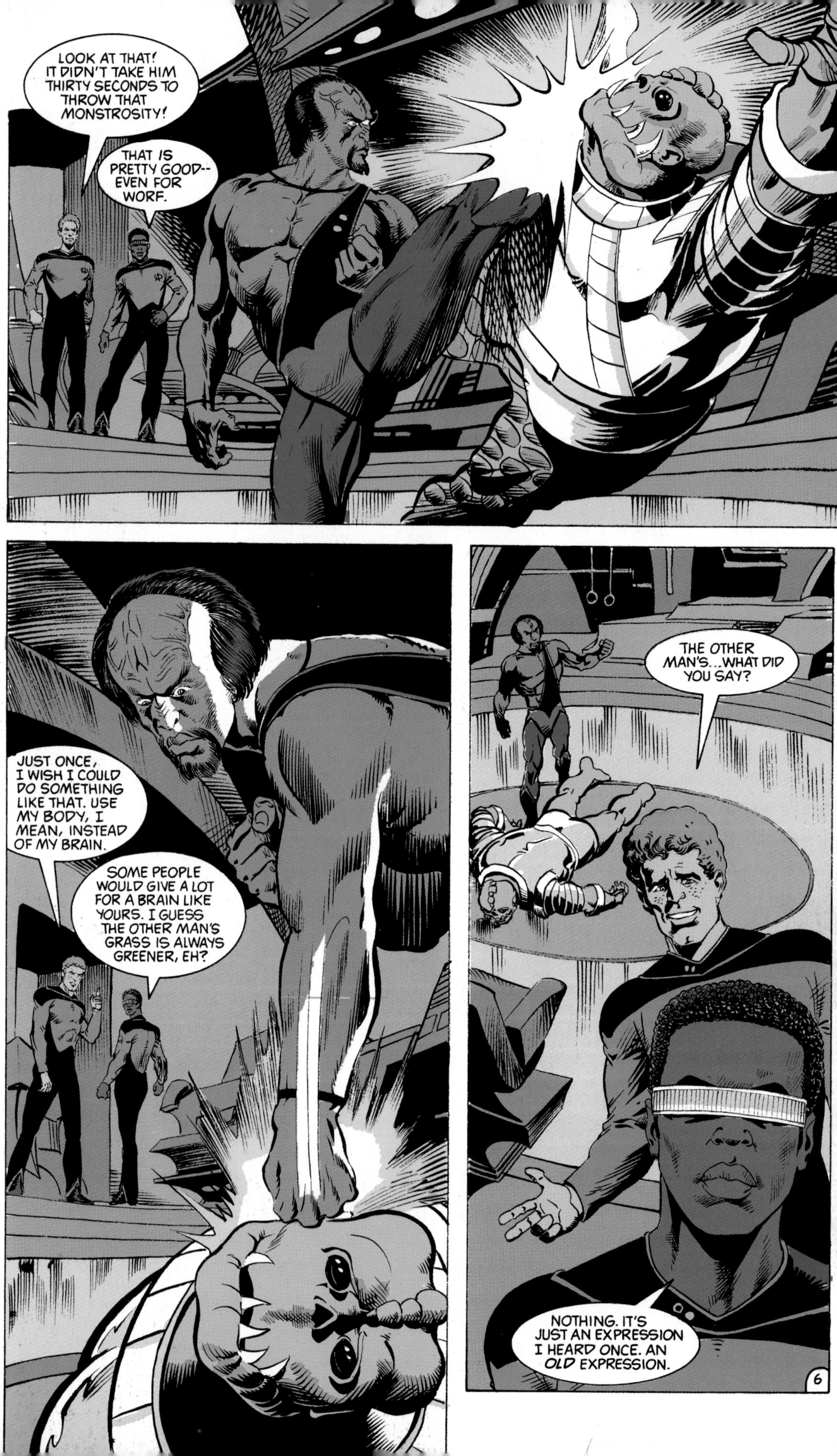
LOOK AT THAT! IT DIDN'T TAKE HIM THIRTY SECONDS TO THROW THAT MONSTROSITY!
THAT IS PRETTY GOOD-- EVEN FOR WORF.
JUST ONCE, I WISH I COULD DO SOMETHING LIKE THAT. USE MY BODY, I MEAN, INSTEAD OF MY BRAIN.
SOME PEOPLE WOULD GIVE A LOT FOR A BRAIN LIKE YOURS. I GUESS THE OTHER MAN'S GRASS IS ALWAYS GREENER, EH?
THE OTHER MAN'S...WHAT DID YOU SAY?
NOTHING. IT'S JUST AN EXPRESSION I HEARD ONCE. AN OLD EXPRESSION.
6

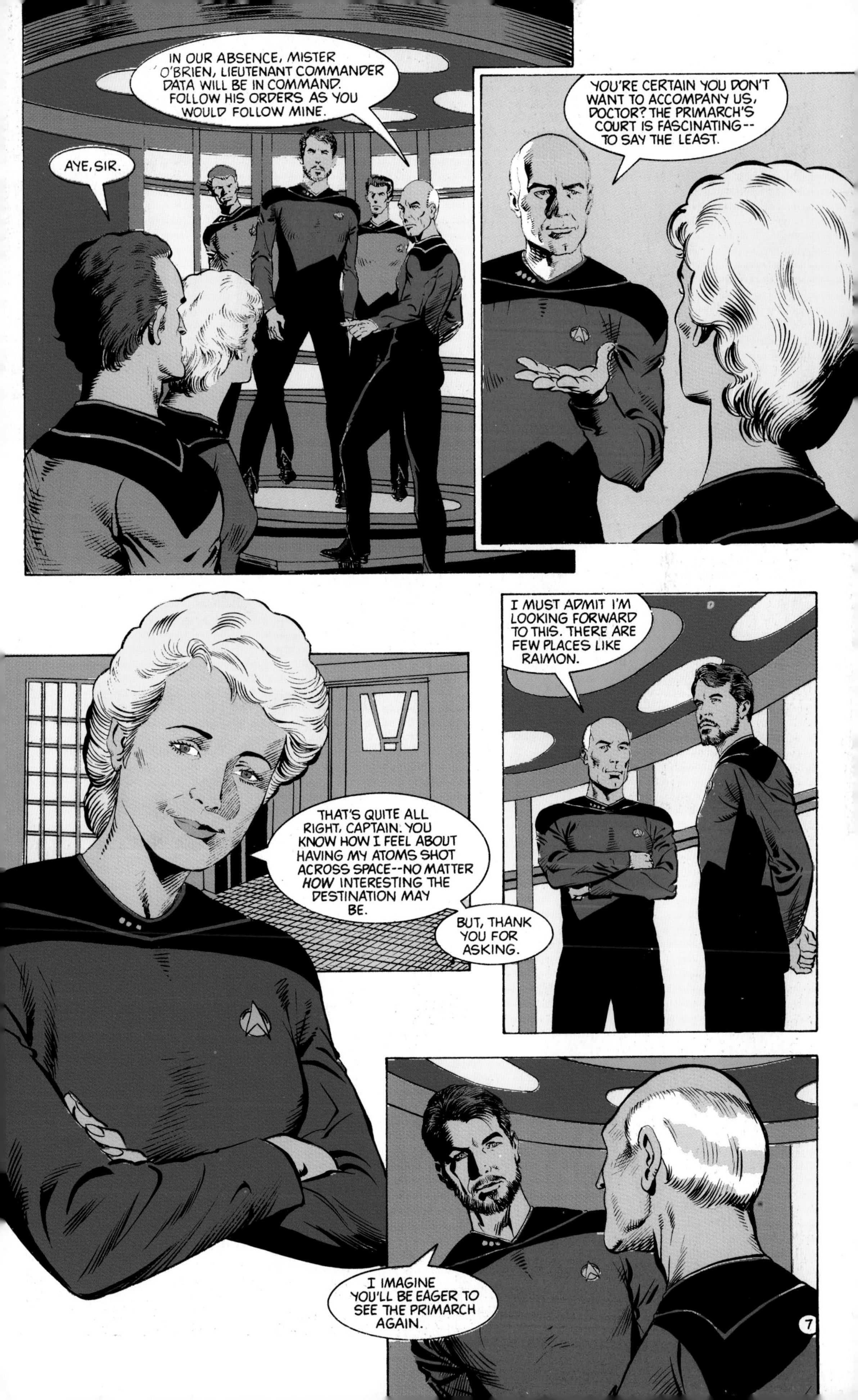

IN OUR ABSENCE, MISTER O'BRIEN, LIEUTENANT COMMANDER DATA WILL BE IN COMMAND. FOLLOW HIS ORDERS AS YOU WOULD FOLLOW MINE.
AYE, SIR.
YOU'RE CERTAIN YOU DON'T WANT TO ACCOMPANY US, DOCTOR? THE PRIMARCH'S COURT IS FASCINATING-- TO SAY THE LEAST.
THAT'S QUITE ALL RIGHT, CAPTAIN. YOU KNOW HOW I FEEL ABOUT HAVING MY ATOMS SHOT ACROSS SPACE--NO MATTER *HOW* INTERESTING THE DESTINATION MAY BE.
BUT, THANK YOU FOR ASKING.
I MUST ADMIT I'M LOOKING FORWARD TO THIS. THERE ARE FEW PLACES LIKE RAIMON.
I IMAGINE YOU'LL BE EAGER TO SEE THE PRIMARCH AGAIN.
7

I'D LIKE TO SEE HIM AGAIN, YES. BUT IT IS NOT AS IF WE WERE THE BEST OF FRIENDS.

READY WHEN YOU ARE, SIR.

THANK YOU, MISTER O'BRIEN.

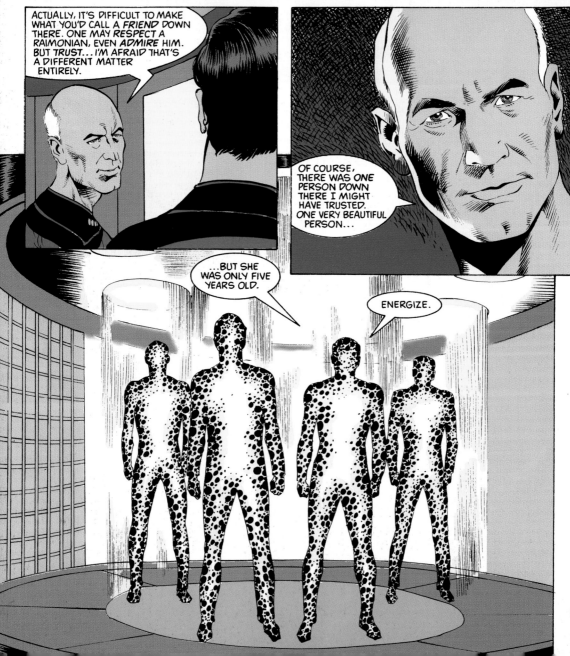

ACTUALLY, IT'S DIFFICULT TO MAKE WHAT YOU'D CALL A FRIEND DOWN THERE. ONE MAY RESPECT A RAIMONIAN, EVEN ADMIRE HIM. BUT TRUST... I'M AFRAID THAT'S A DIFFERENT MATTER ENTIRELY.

OF COURSE, THERE WAS ONE PERSON DOWN THERE I MIGHT HAVE TRUSTED. ONE VERY BEAUTIFUL PERSON...

...BUT SHE WAS ONLY FIVE YEARS OLD.

ENERGIZE.

8

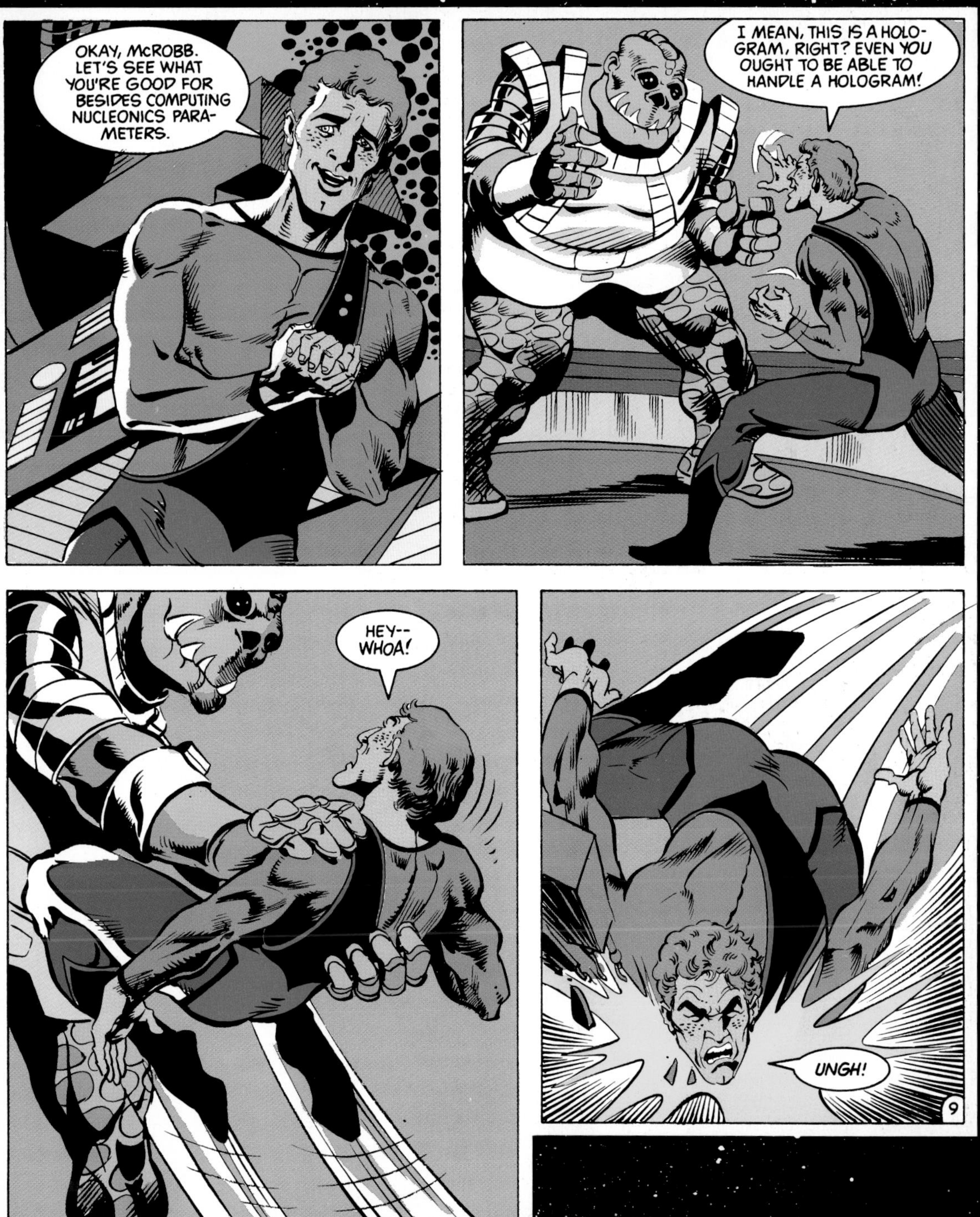
OKAY, McROBB. LET'S SEE WHAT YOU'RE GOOD FOR BESIDES COMPUTING NUCLEONICS PARAMETERS.
I MEAN, THIS IS A HOLOGRAM, RIGHT? EVEN YOU OUGHT TO BE ABLE TO HANDLE A HOLOGRAM!
HEY-- WHOA!
UNGH!
9

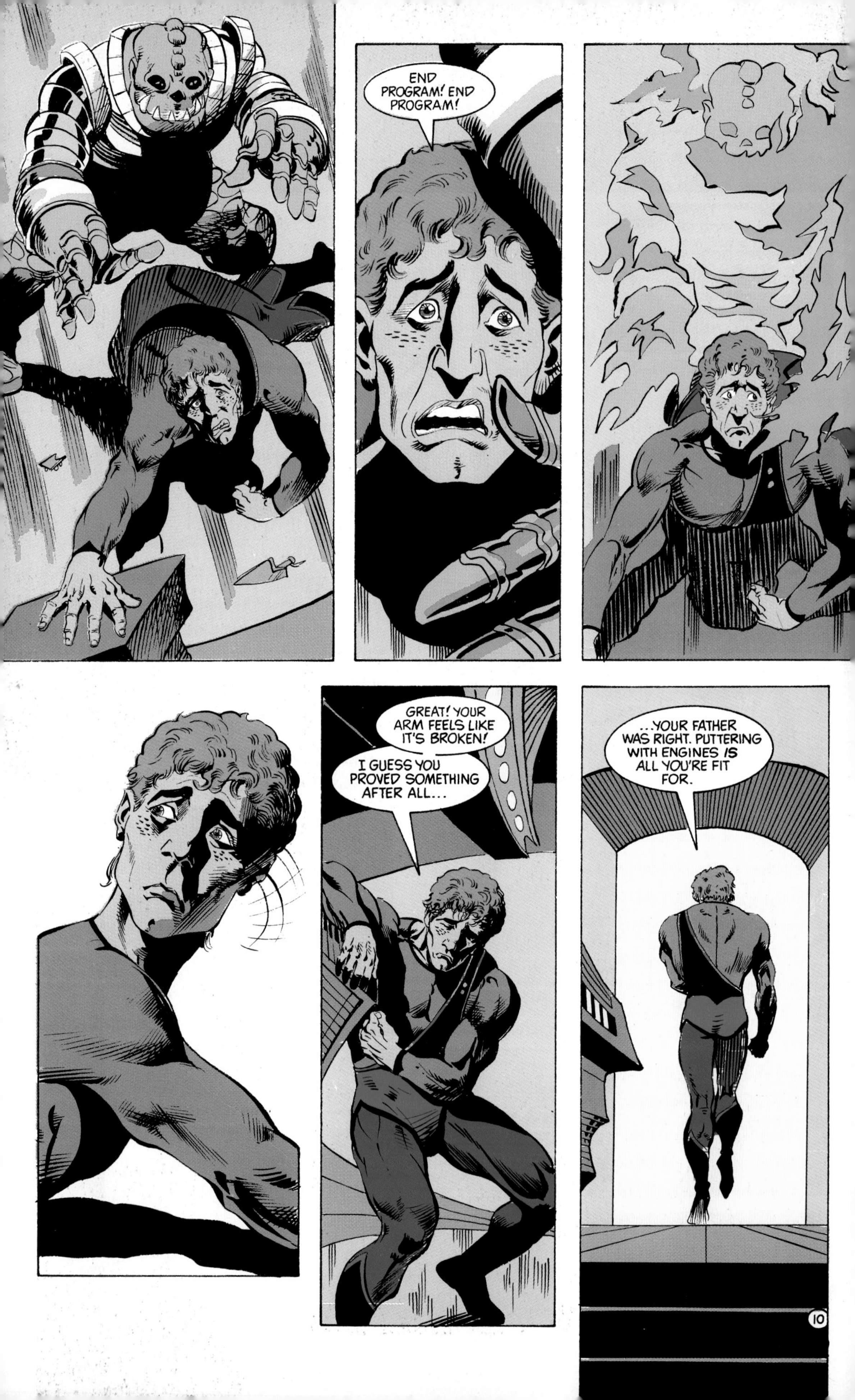

END PROGRAM! END PROGRAM!
GREAT! YOUR ARM FEELS LIKE IT'S BROKEN!
I GUESS YOU PROVED SOMETHING AFTER ALL...
...YOUR FATHER WAS RIGHT. PUTTERING WITH ENGINES IS ALL YOU'RE FIT FOR.

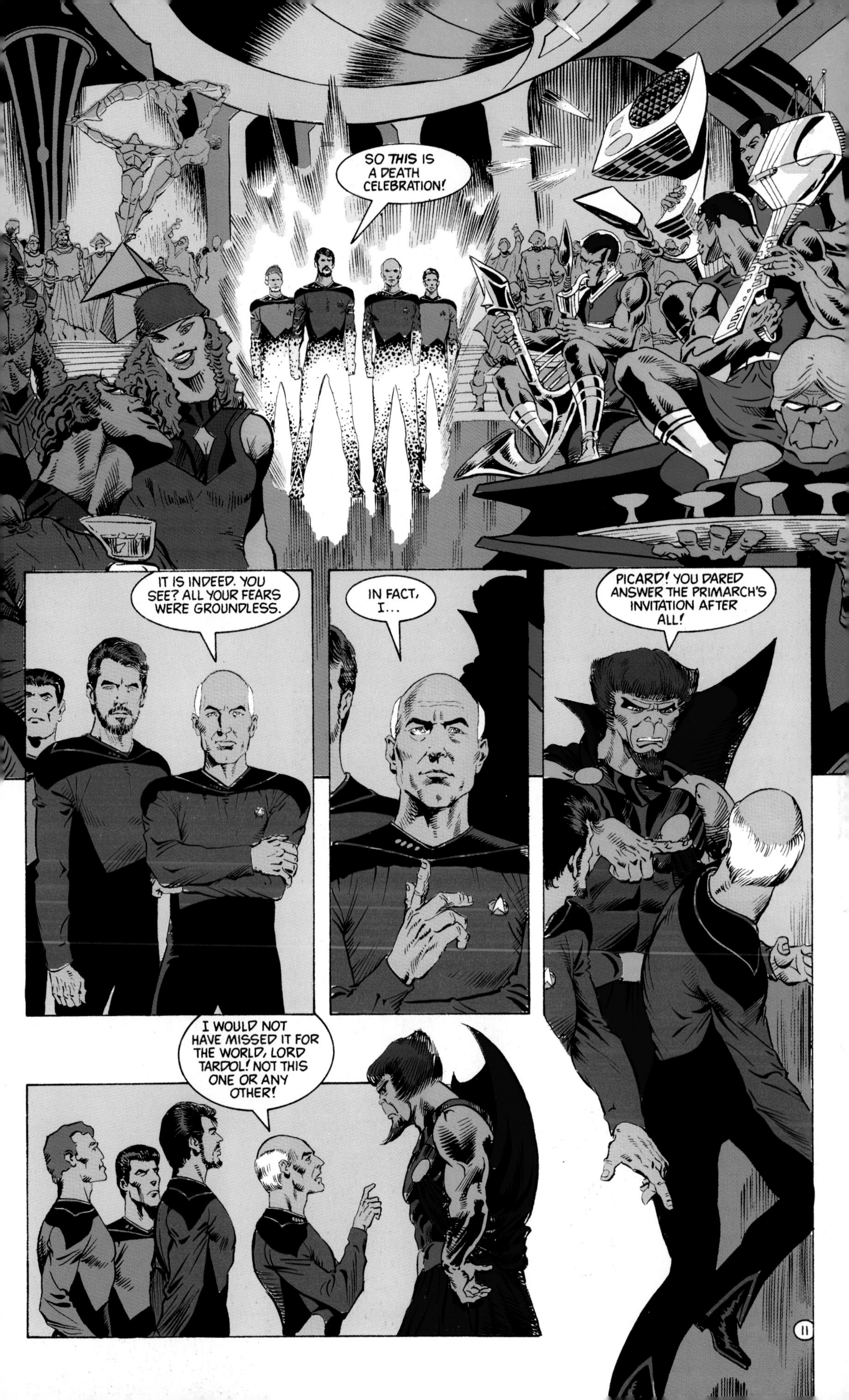
SO THIS IS A DEATH CELEBRATION!
IT IS INDEED. YOU SEE? ALL YOUR FEARS WERE GROUNDLESS.
IN FACT, I...
PICARD! YOU DARED ANSWER THE PRIMARCH'S INVITATION AFTER ALL!
I WOULD NOT HAVE MISSED IT FOR THE WORLD, LORD TARDOL! NOT THIS ONE OR ANY OTHER!

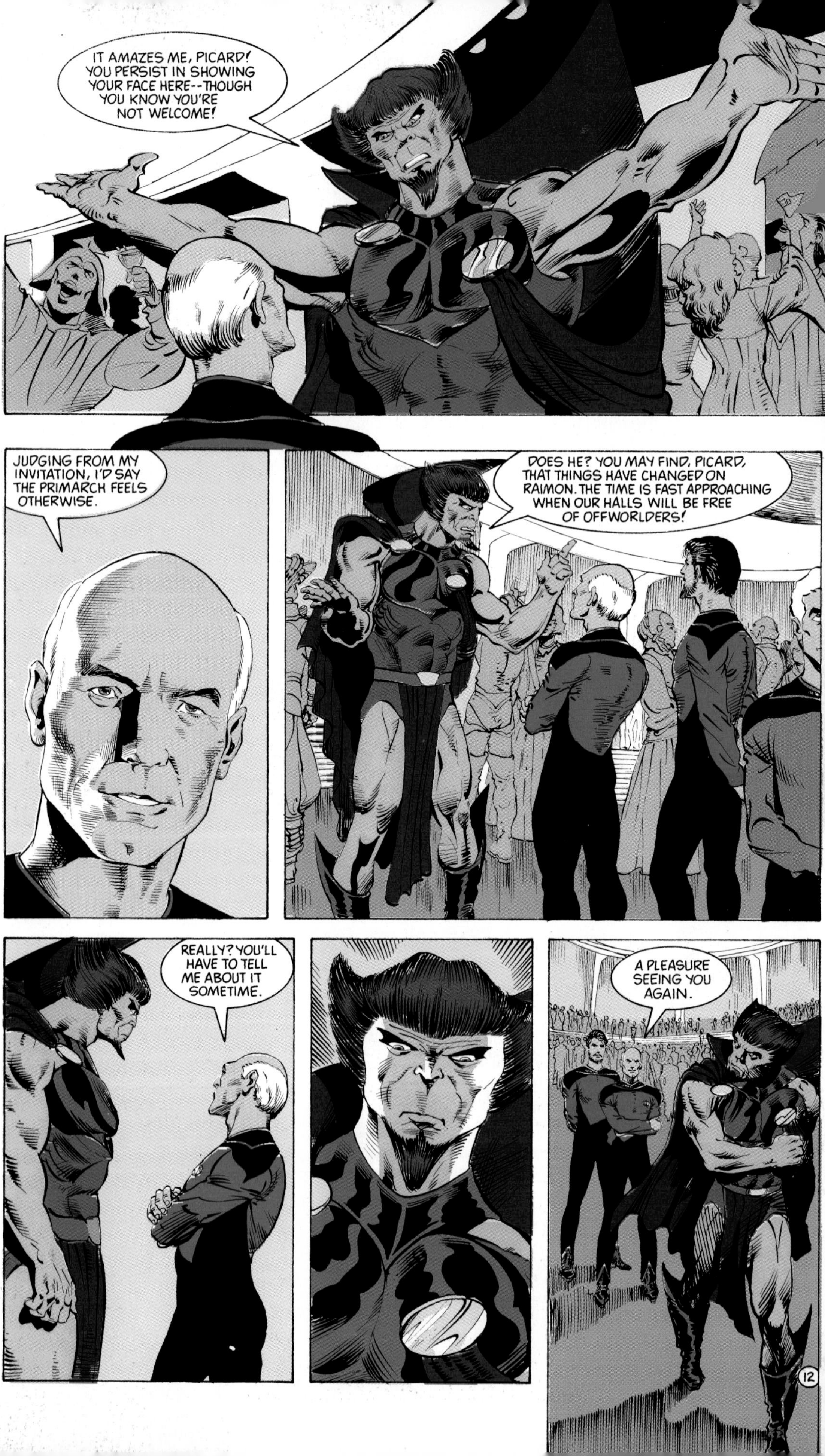
IT AMAZES ME, PICARD! YOU PERSIST IN SHOWING YOUR FACE HERE--THOUGH YOU KNOW YOU'RE NOT WELCOME!
JUDGING FROM MY INVITATION, I'D SAY THE PRIMARCH FEELS OTHERWISE.
DOES HE? YOU MAY FIND, PICARD, THAT THINGS HAVE CHANGED ON RAIMON. THE TIME IS FAST APPROACHING WHEN OUR HALLS WILL BE FREE OF OFFWORLDERS!
REALLY? YOU'LL HAVE TO TELL ME ABOUT IT SOMETIME.
A PLEASURE SEEING YOU AGAIN.
12

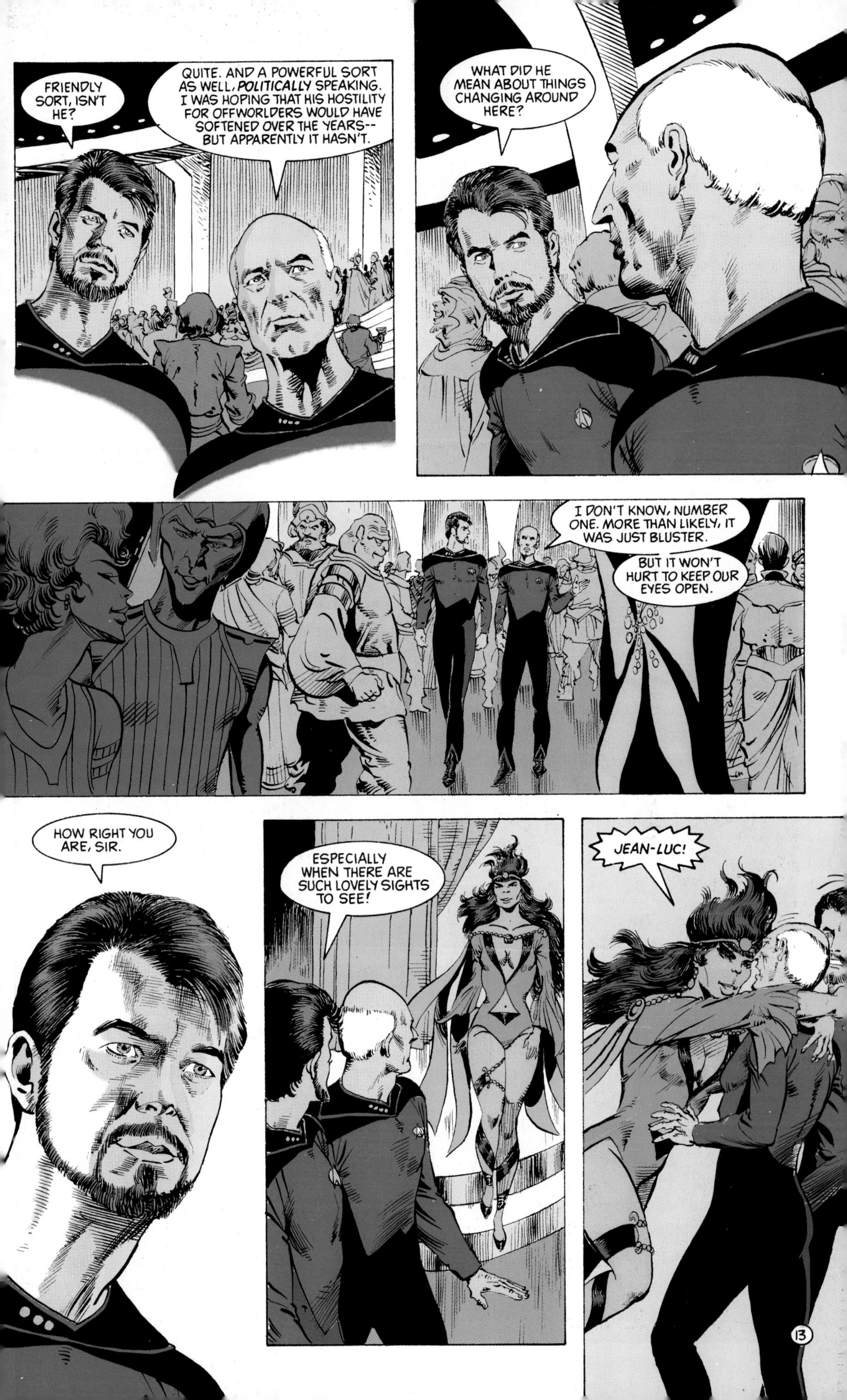

FRIENDLY SORT, ISN'T HE?
QUITE. AND A POWERFUL SORT AS WELL, POLITICALLY SPEAKING. I WAS HOPING THAT HIS HOSTILITY FOR OFFWORLDERS WOULD HAVE SOFTENED OVER THE YEARS-- BUT APPARENTLY IT HASN'T.
WHAT DID HE MEAN ABOUT THINGS CHANGING AROUND HERE?
I DON'T KNOW, NUMBER ONE. MORE THAN LIKELY, IT WAS JUST BLUSTER.
BUT IT WON'T HURT TO KEEP OUR EYES OPEN.
HOW RIGHT YOU ARE, SIR.
ESPECIALLY WHEN THERE ARE SUCH LOVELY SIGHTS TO SEE!
JEAN-LUC!

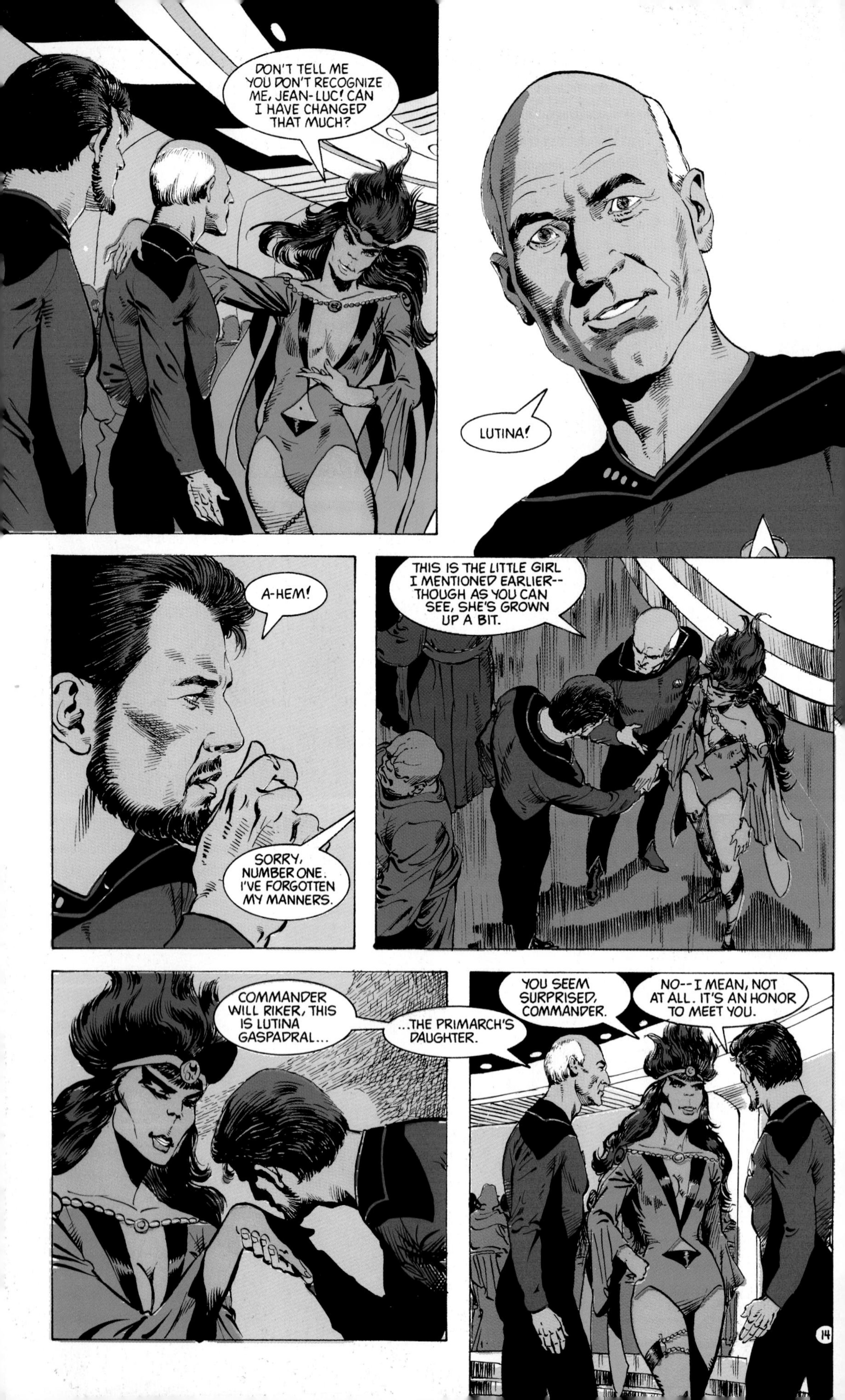
DON'T TELL ME YOU DON'T RECOGNIZE ME, JEAN-LUC! CAN I HAVE CHANGED THAT MUCH?
LUTINA!
A-HEM!
SORRY, NUMBER ONE. I'VE FORGOTTEN MY MANNERS.
THIS IS THE LITTLE GIRL I MENTIONED EARLIER-- THOUGH AS YOU CAN SEE, SHE'S GROWN UP A BIT.
COMMANDER WILL RIKER, THIS IS LUTINA GASPADRAL...
...THE PRIMARCH'S DAUGHTER.
YOU SEEM SURPRISED, COMMANDER.
NO-- I MEAN, NOT AT ALL. IT'S AN HONOR TO MEET YOU.
14

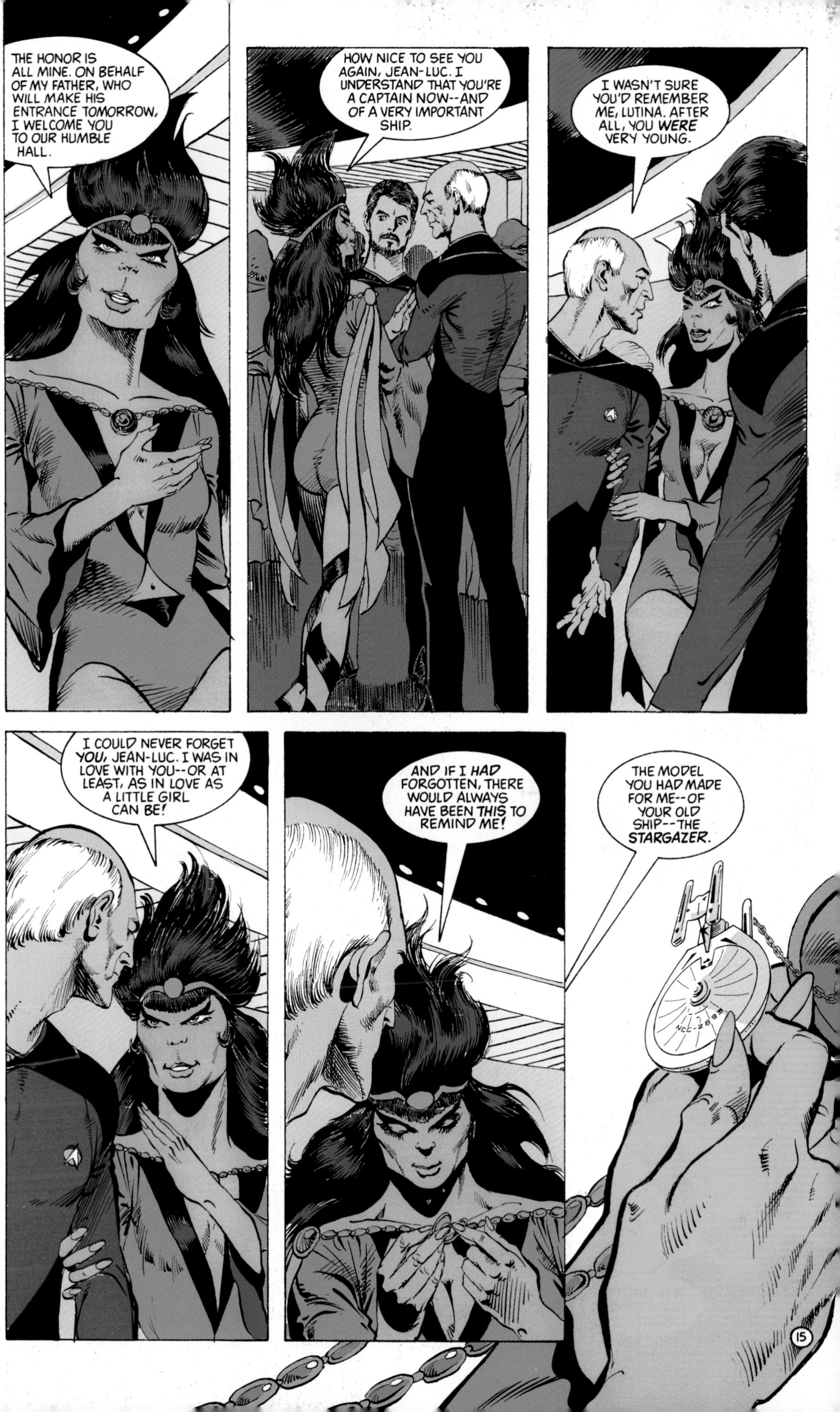
THE HONOR IS ALL MINE. ON BEHALF OF MY FATHER, WHO WILL MAKE HIS ENTRANCE TOMORROW, I WELCOME YOU TO OUR HUMBLE HALL.
HOW NICE TO SEE YOU AGAIN, JEAN-LUC. I UNDERSTAND THAT YOU'RE A CAPTAIN NOW--AND OF A VERY IMPORTANT SHIP.
I WASN'T SURE YOU'D REMEMBER ME, LUTINA. AFTER ALL, YOU WERE VERY YOUNG.
I COULD NEVER FORGET YOU, JEAN-LUC. I WAS IN LOVE WITH YOU--OR AT LEAST, AS IN LOVE AS A LITTLE GIRL CAN BE!
AND IF I HAD FORGOTTEN, THERE WOULD ALWAYS HAVE BEEN THIS TO REMIND ME!
THE MODEL YOU HAD MADE FOR ME--OF YOUR OLD SHIP--THE STARGAZER.
NCC-2893

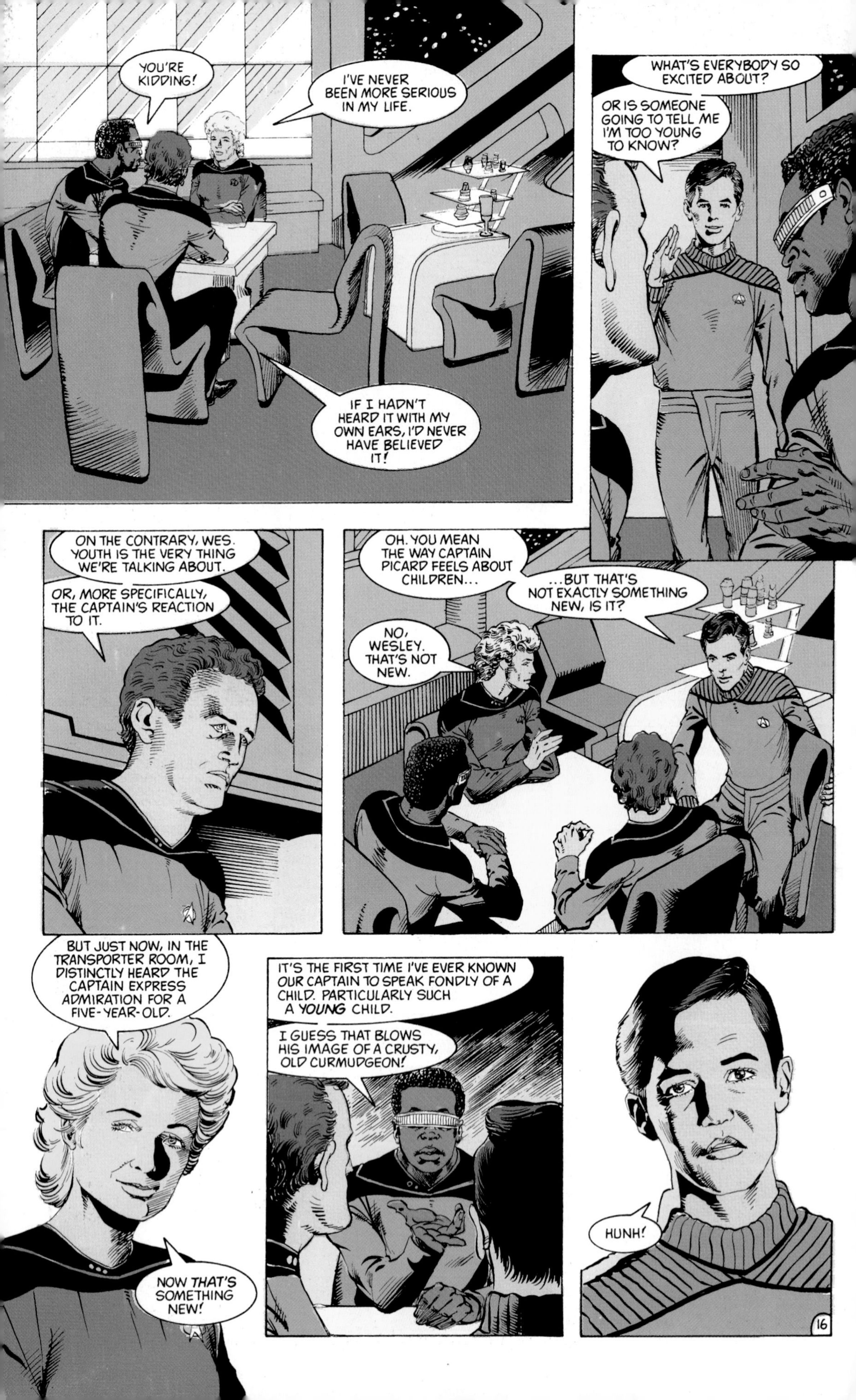
YOU'RE KIDDING!
I'VE NEVER BEEN MORE SERIOUS IN MY LIFE.
IF I HADN'T HEARD IT WITH MY OWN EARS, I'D NEVER HAVE BELIEVED IT!
WHAT'S EVERYBODY SO EXCITED ABOUT?
OR IS SOMEONE GOING TO TELL ME I'M TOO YOUNG TO KNOW?
ON THE CONTRARY, WES. YOUTH IS THE VERY THING WE'RE TALKING ABOUT.
OR, MORE SPECIFICALLY, THE CAPTAIN'S REACTION TO IT.
OH. YOU MEAN THE WAY CAPTAIN PICARD FEELS ABOUT CHILDREN...
...BUT THAT'S NOT EXACTLY SOMETHING NEW, IS IT?
NO, WESLEY. THAT'S NOT NEW.
BUT JUST NOW, IN THE TRANSPORTER ROOM, I DISTINCTLY HEARD THE CAPTAIN EXPRESS ADMIRATION FOR A FIVE-YEAR-OLD.
NOW *THAT'S* SOMETHING NEW!
IT'S THE FIRST TIME I'VE EVER KNOWN OUR CAPTAIN TO SPEAK FONDLY OF A CHILD. PARTICULARLY SUCH A *YOUNG* CHILD.
I GUESS THAT BLOWS HIS IMAGE OF A CRUSTY, OLD CURMUDGEON!
HUNH!
16

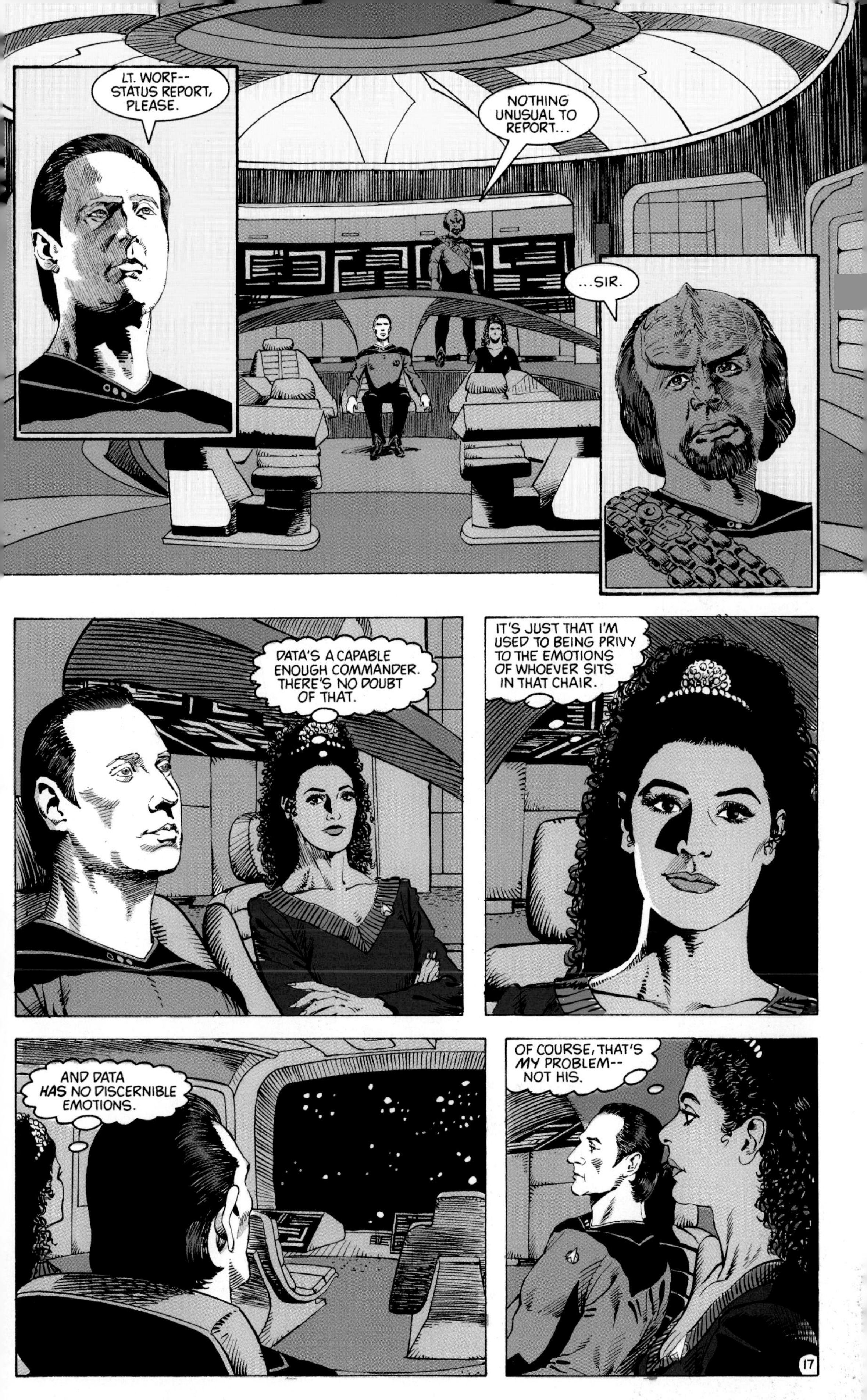
LT. WORF--
STATUS REPORT,
PLEASE.
NOTHING
UNUSUAL TO
REPORT...
...SIR.
DATA'S A CAPABLE
ENOUGH COMMANDER.
THERE'S NO DOUBT
OF THAT.
IT'S JUST THAT I'M
USED TO BEING PRIVY
TO THE EMOTIONS
OF WHOEVER SITS
IN THAT CHAIR.
AND DATA
HAS NO DISCERNIBLE
EMOTIONS.
OF COURSE, THAT'S
MY PROBLEM--
NOT HIS.
17

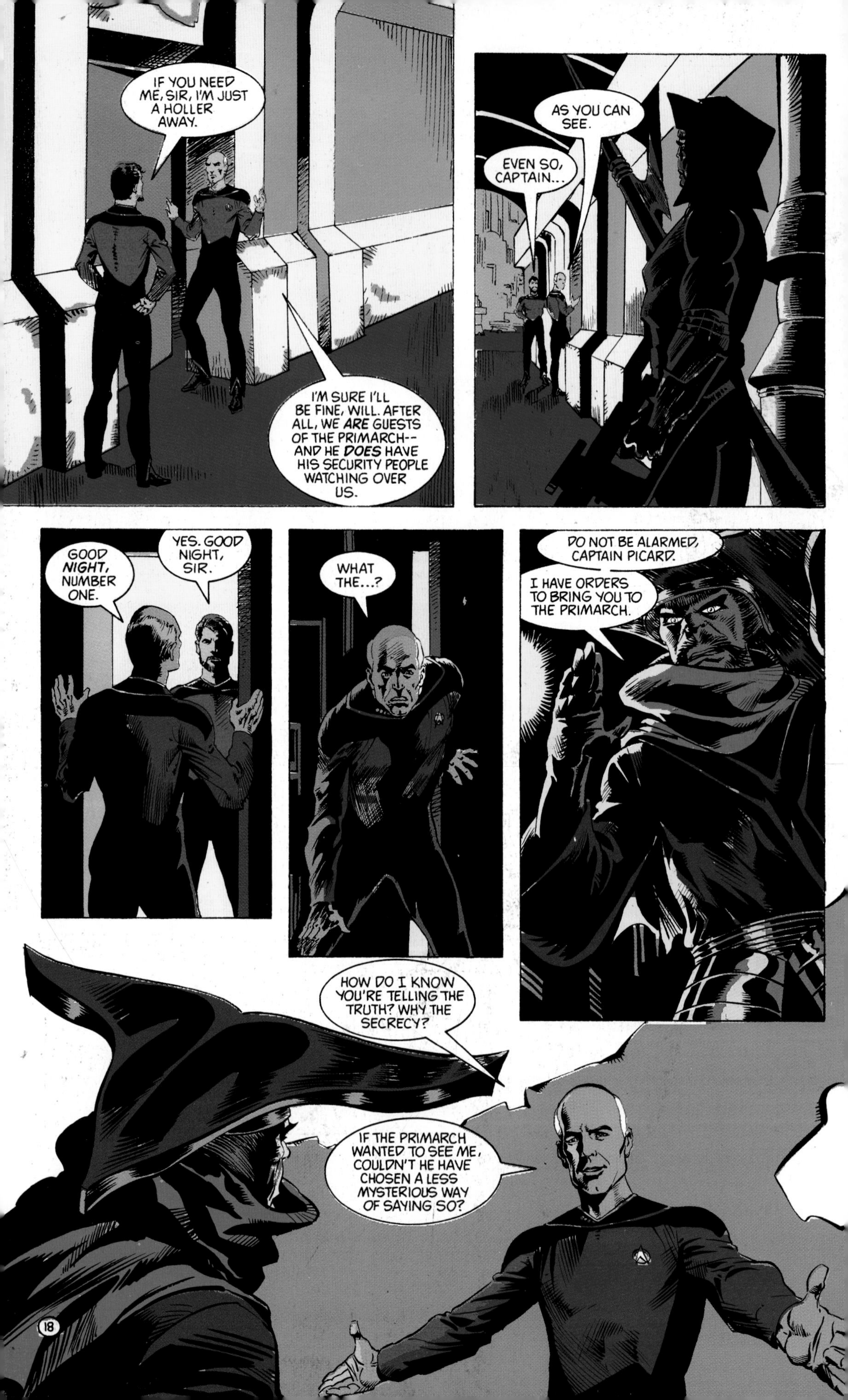

IF YOU NEED ME, SIR, I'M JUST A HOLLER AWAY.
I'M SURE I'LL BE FINE, WILL. AFTER ALL, WE ARE GUESTS OF THE PRIMARCH-- AND HE DOES HAVE HIS SECURITY PEOPLE WATCHING OVER US.
AS YOU CAN SEE.
EVEN SO, CAPTAIN...
GOOD NIGHT, NUMBER ONE.
YES. GOOD NIGHT, SIR.
WHAT THE...?
DO NOT BE ALARMED, CAPTAIN PICARD.
I HAVE ORDERS TO BRING YOU TO THE PRIMARCH.
HOW DO I KNOW YOU'RE TELLING THE TRUTH? WHY THE SECRECY?
IF THE PRIMARCH WANTED TO SEE ME, COULDN'T HE HAVE CHOSEN A LESS MYSTERIOUS WAY OF SAYING SO?

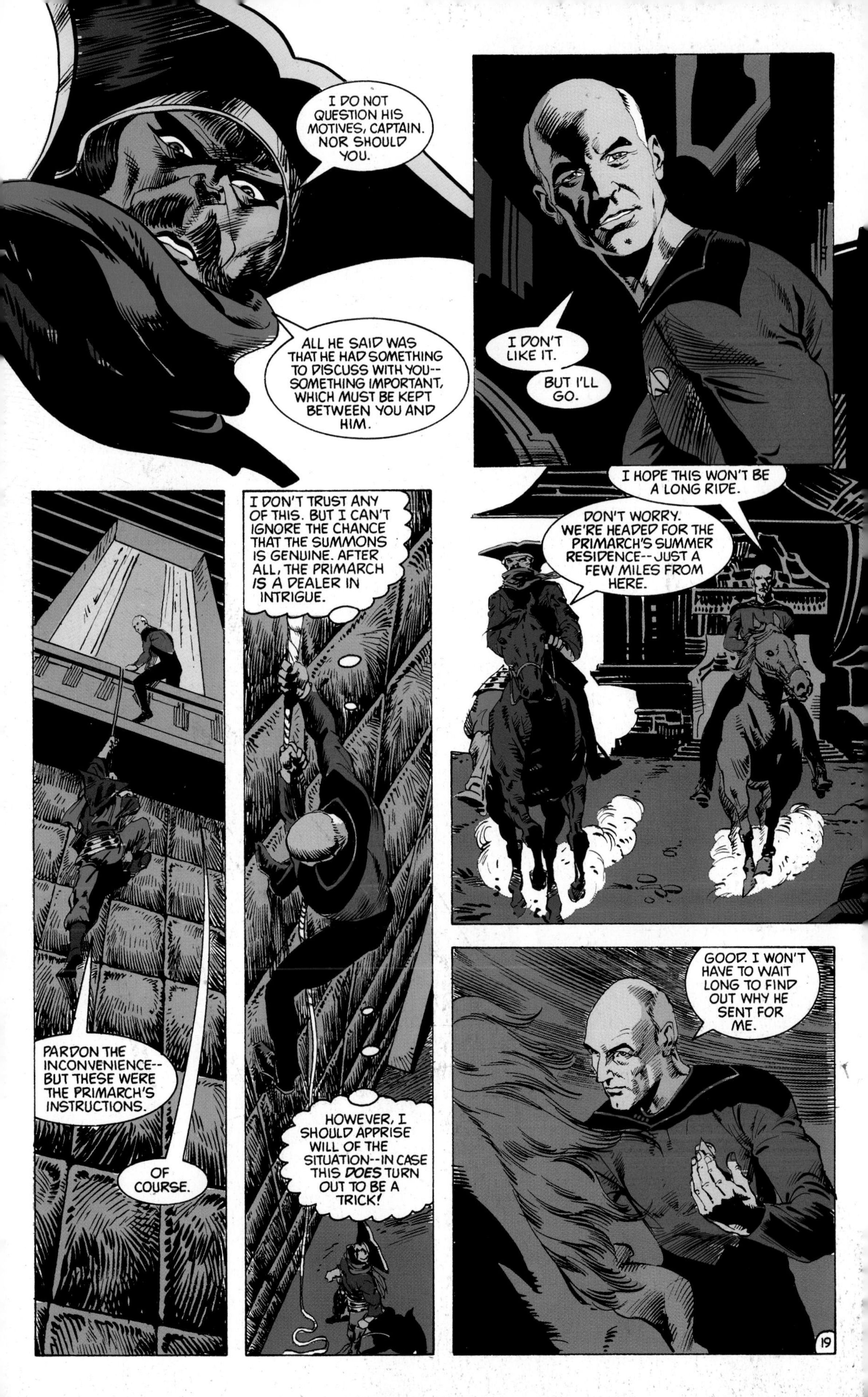

I DO NOT QUESTION HIS MOTIVES, CAPTAIN. NOR SHOULD YOU.
ALL HE SAID WAS THAT HE HAD SOMETHING TO DISCUSS WITH YOU-- SOMETHING IMPORTANT, WHICH MUST BE KEPT BETWEEN YOU AND HIM.
I DON'T LIKE IT.
BUT I'LL GO.
PARDON THE INCONVENIENCE-- BUT THESE WERE THE PRIMARCH'S INSTRUCTIONS.
OF COURSE.
I DON'T TRUST ANY OF THIS. BUT I CAN'T IGNORE THE CHANCE THAT THE SUMMONS IS GENUINE. AFTER ALL, THE PRIMARCH *IS* A DEALER IN INTRIGUE.
HOWEVER, I SHOULD APPRISE WILL OF THE SITUATION--IN CASE THIS *DOES* TURN OUT TO BE A TRICK!
I HOPE THIS WON'T BE A LONG RIDE.
DON'T WORRY. WE'RE HEADED FOR THE PRIMARCH'S SUMMER RESIDENCE--JUST A FEW MILES FROM HERE.
GOOD. I WON'T HAVE TO WAIT LONG TO FIND OUT WHY HE SENT FOR ME.

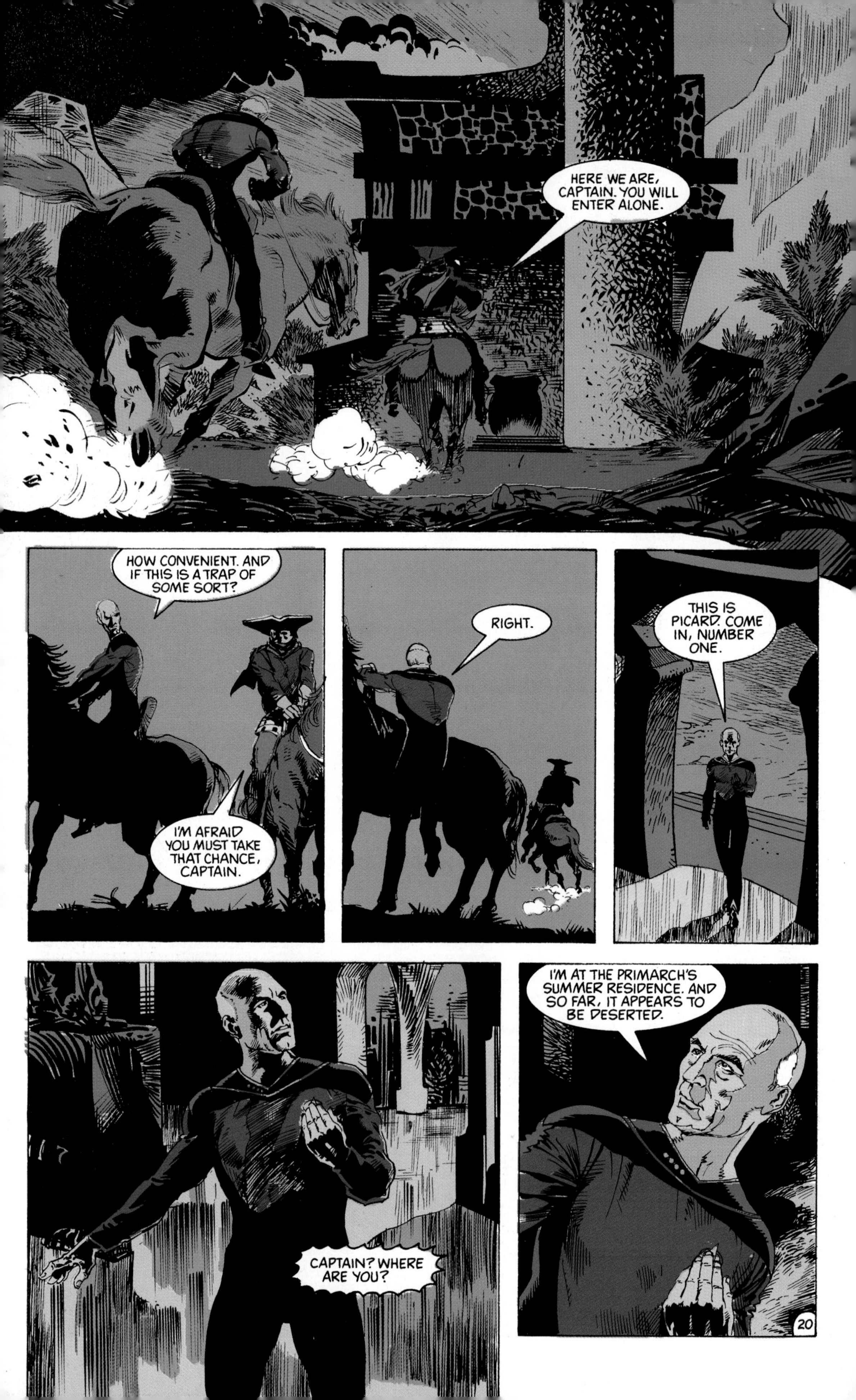
HERE WE ARE, CAPTAIN. YOU WILL ENTER ALONE.
HOW CONVENIENT. AND IF THIS IS A TRAP OF SOME SORT?
I'M AFRAID YOU MUST TAKE THAT CHANCE, CAPTAIN.
RIGHT.
THIS IS PICARD. COME IN, NUMBER ONE.
CAPTAIN? WHERE ARE YOU?
I'M AT THE PRIMARCH'S SUMMER RESIDENCE. AND SO FAR, IT APPEARS TO BE DESERTED.
20

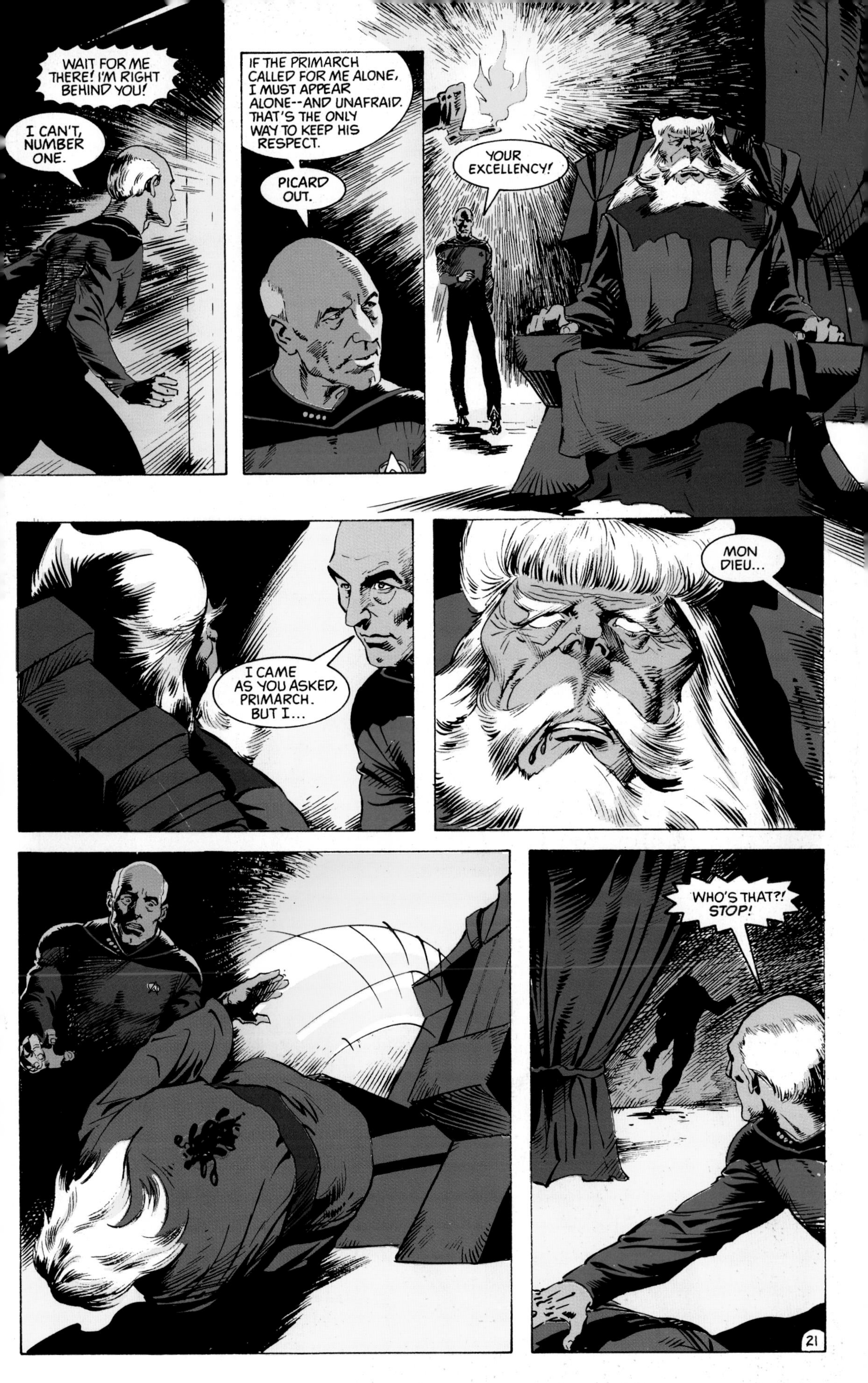
WAIT FOR ME THERE! I'M RIGHT BEHIND YOU!
I CAN'T, NUMBER ONE.
IF THE PRIMARCH CALLED FOR ME ALONE, I MUST APPEAR ALONE--AND UNAFRAID. THAT'S THE ONLY WAY TO KEEP HIS RESPECT.
PICARD OUT.
YOUR EXCELLENCY!
I CAME AS YOU ASKED, PRIMARCH. BUT I...
MON DIEU...
WHO'S THAT?! STOP!

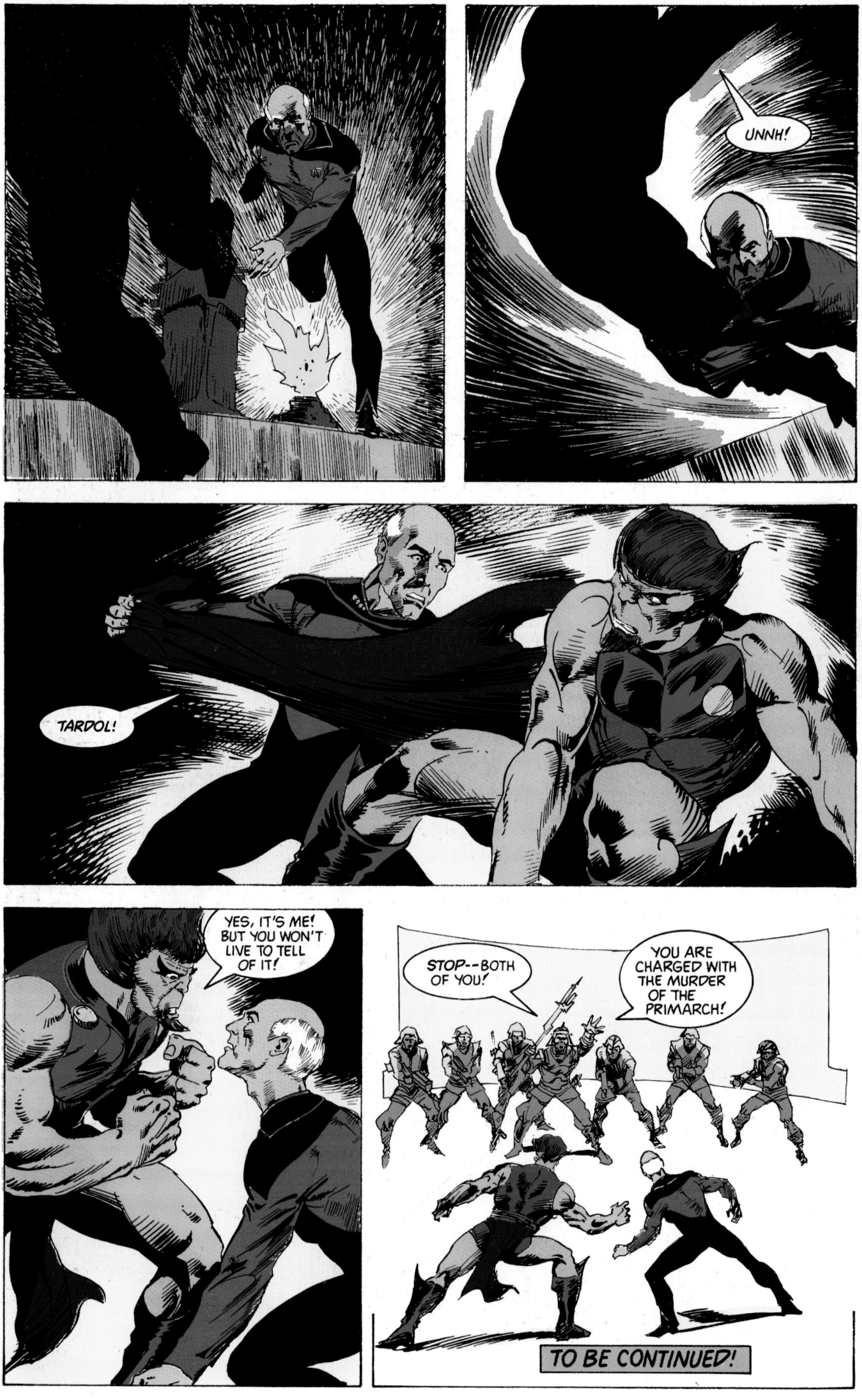
UNNH!
TARDOL!
YES, IT'S ME! BUT YOU WON'T LIVE TO TELL OF IT!
STOP--BOTH OF YOU!
YOU ARE CHARGED WITH THE MURDER OF THE PRIMARCH!
TO BE CONTINUED!

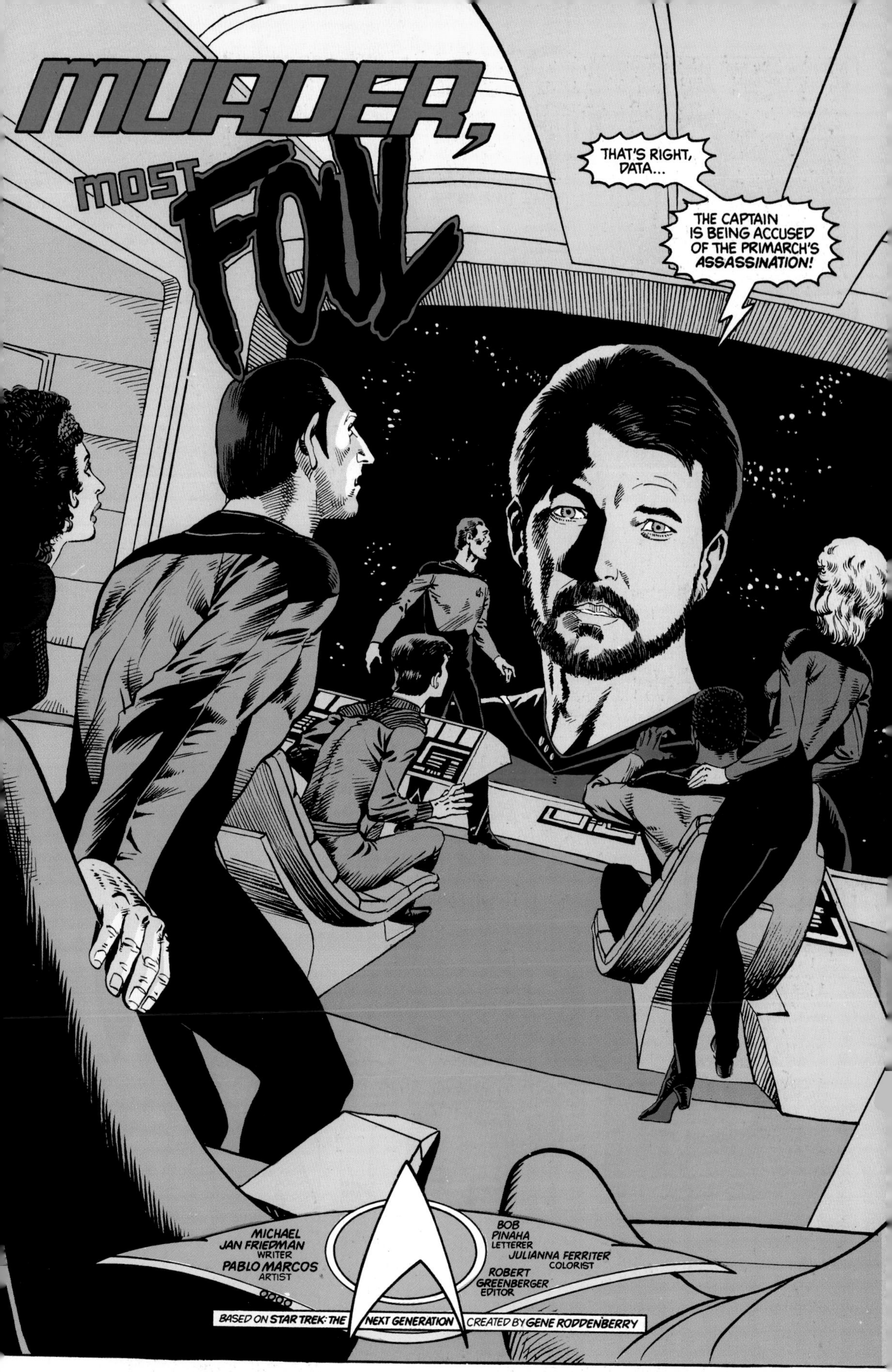
MURDER, MOST FOUL
THAT'S RIGHT, DATA...
THE CAPTAIN IS BEING ACCUSED OF THE PRIMARCH'S ASSASSINATION!
MICHAEL JAN FRIEDMAN WRITER
PABLO MARCOS ARTIST
BOB PINAHA LETTERER
JULIANNA FERRITER COLORIST
ROBERT GREENBERGER EDITOR
BASED ON STAR TREK: THE NEXT GENERATION CREATED BY GENE RODDENBERRY

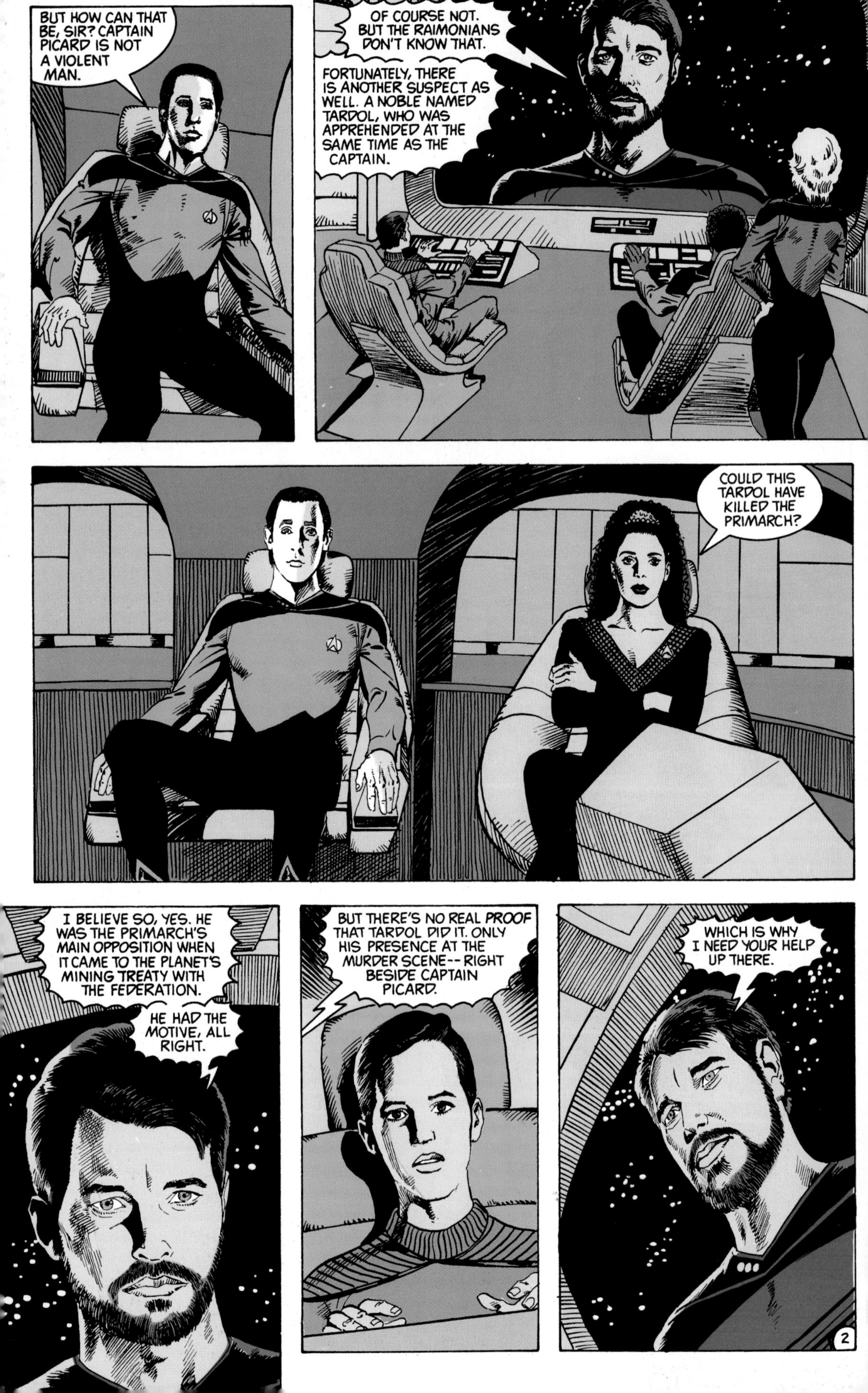
BUT HOW CAN THAT BE, SIR? CAPTAIN PICARD IS NOT A VIOLENT MAN.
OF COURSE NOT. BUT THE RAIMONIANS DON'T KNOW THAT.
FORTUNATELY, THERE IS ANOTHER SUSPECT AS WELL. A NOBLE NAMED TARDOL, WHO WAS APPREHENDED AT THE SAME TIME AS THE CAPTAIN.
COULD THIS TARDOL HAVE KILLED THE PRIMARCH?
I BELIEVE SO, YES. HE WAS THE PRIMARCH'S MAIN OPPOSITION WHEN IT CAME TO THE PLANET'S MINING TREATY WITH THE FEDERATION.
HE HAD THE MOTIVE, ALL RIGHT.
BUT THERE'S NO REAL *PROOF* THAT TARDOL DID IT. ONLY HIS PRESENCE AT THE MURDER SCENE-- RIGHT BESIDE CAPTAIN PICARD.
WHICH IS WHY I NEED YOUR HELP UP THERE.
2

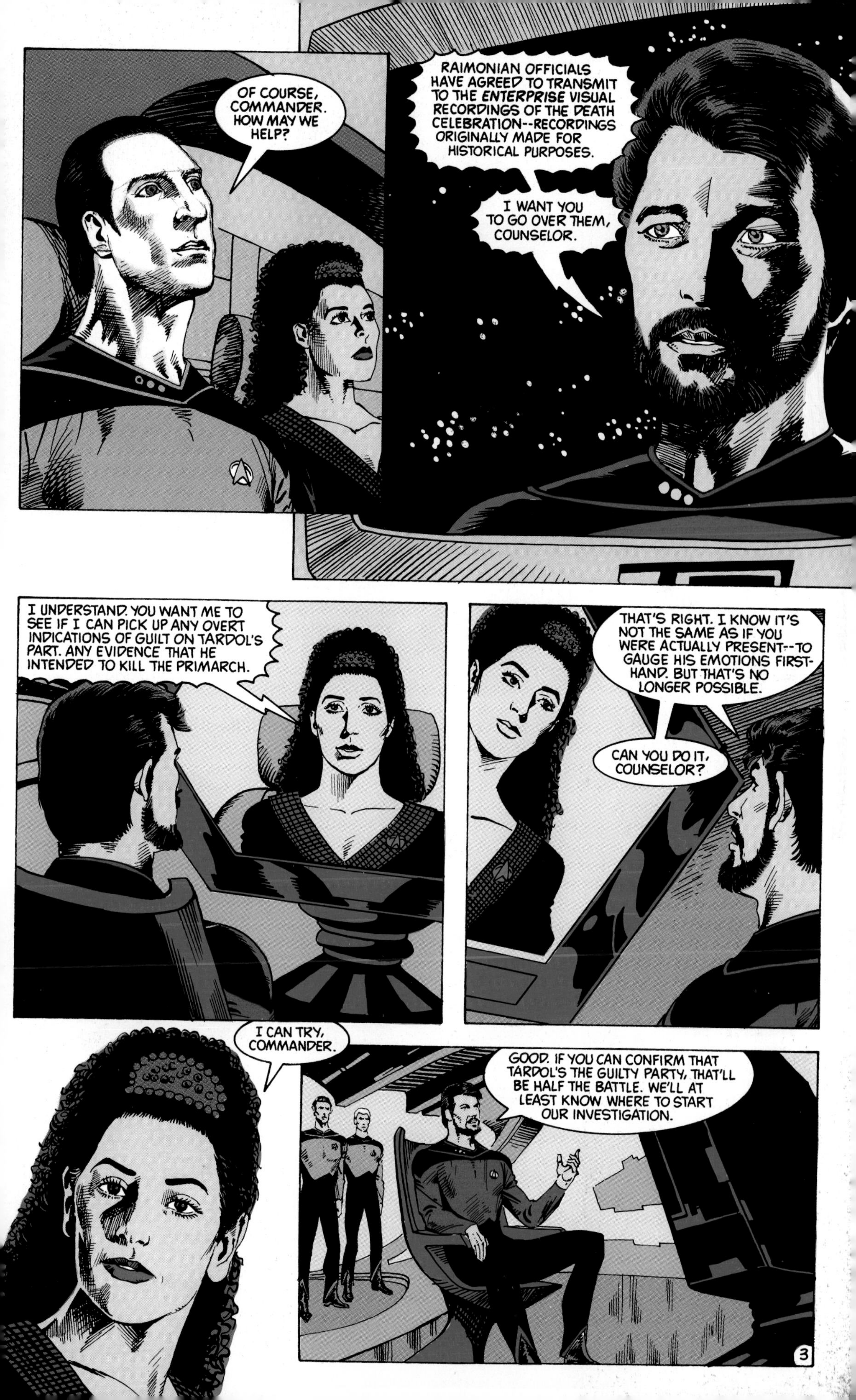
OF COURSE, COMMANDER. HOW MAY WE HELP?
RAIMONIAN OFFICIALS HAVE AGREED TO TRANSMIT TO THE ENTERPRISE VISUAL RECORDINGS OF THE DEATH CELEBRATION--RECORDINGS ORIGINALLY MADE FOR HISTORICAL PURPOSES.
I WANT YOU TO GO OVER THEM, COUNSELOR.
I UNDERSTAND. YOU WANT ME TO SEE IF I CAN PICK UP ANY OVERT INDICATIONS OF GUILT ON TARDOL'S PART. ANY EVIDENCE THAT HE INTENDED TO KILL THE PRIMARCH.
THAT'S RIGHT. I KNOW IT'S NOT THE SAME AS IF YOU WERE ACTUALLY PRESENT--TO GAUGE HIS EMOTIONS FIRST-HAND. BUT THAT'S NO LONGER POSSIBLE.
CAN YOU DO IT, COUNSELOR?
I CAN TRY, COMMANDER.
GOOD. IF YOU CAN CONFIRM THAT TARDOL'S THE GUILTY PARTY, THAT'LL BE HALF THE BATTLE. WE'LL AT LEAST KNOW WHERE TO START OUR INVESTIGATION.
3

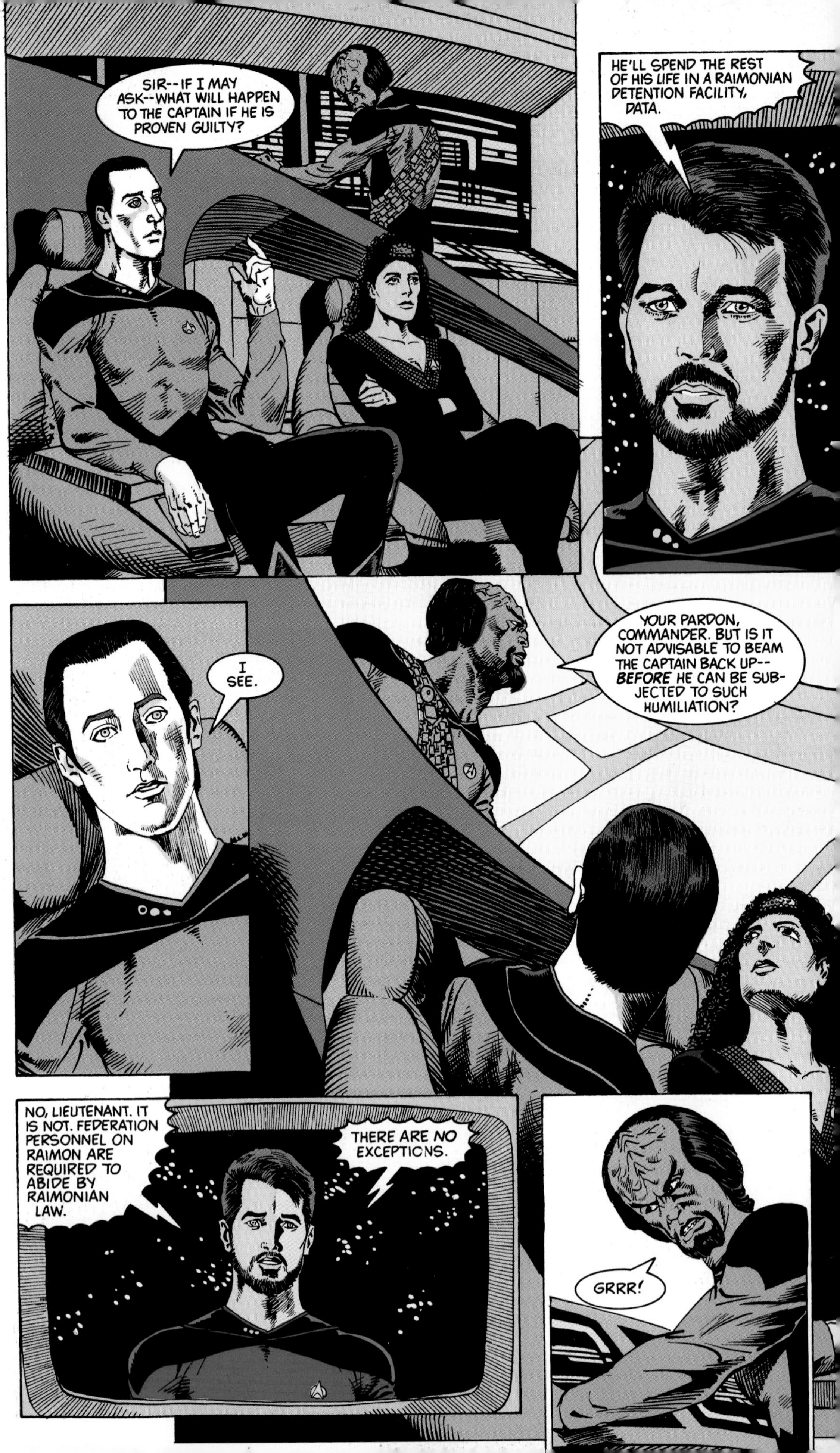
SIR--IF I MAY ASK--WHAT WILL HAPPEN TO THE CAPTAIN IF HE IS PROVEN GUILTY?
HE'LL SPEND THE REST OF HIS LIFE IN A RAIMONIAN DETENTION FACILITY, DATA.
I SEE.
YOUR PARDON, COMMANDER. BUT IS IT NOT ADVISABLE TO BEAM THE CAPTAIN BACK UP-- *BEFORE* HE CAN BE SUBJECTED TO SUCH HUMILIATION?
NO, LIEUTENANT. IT IS NOT. FEDERATION PERSONNEL ON RAIMON ARE REQUIRED TO ABIDE BY RAIMONIAN LAW.
THERE ARE *NO* EXCEPTIONS.
GRRR!

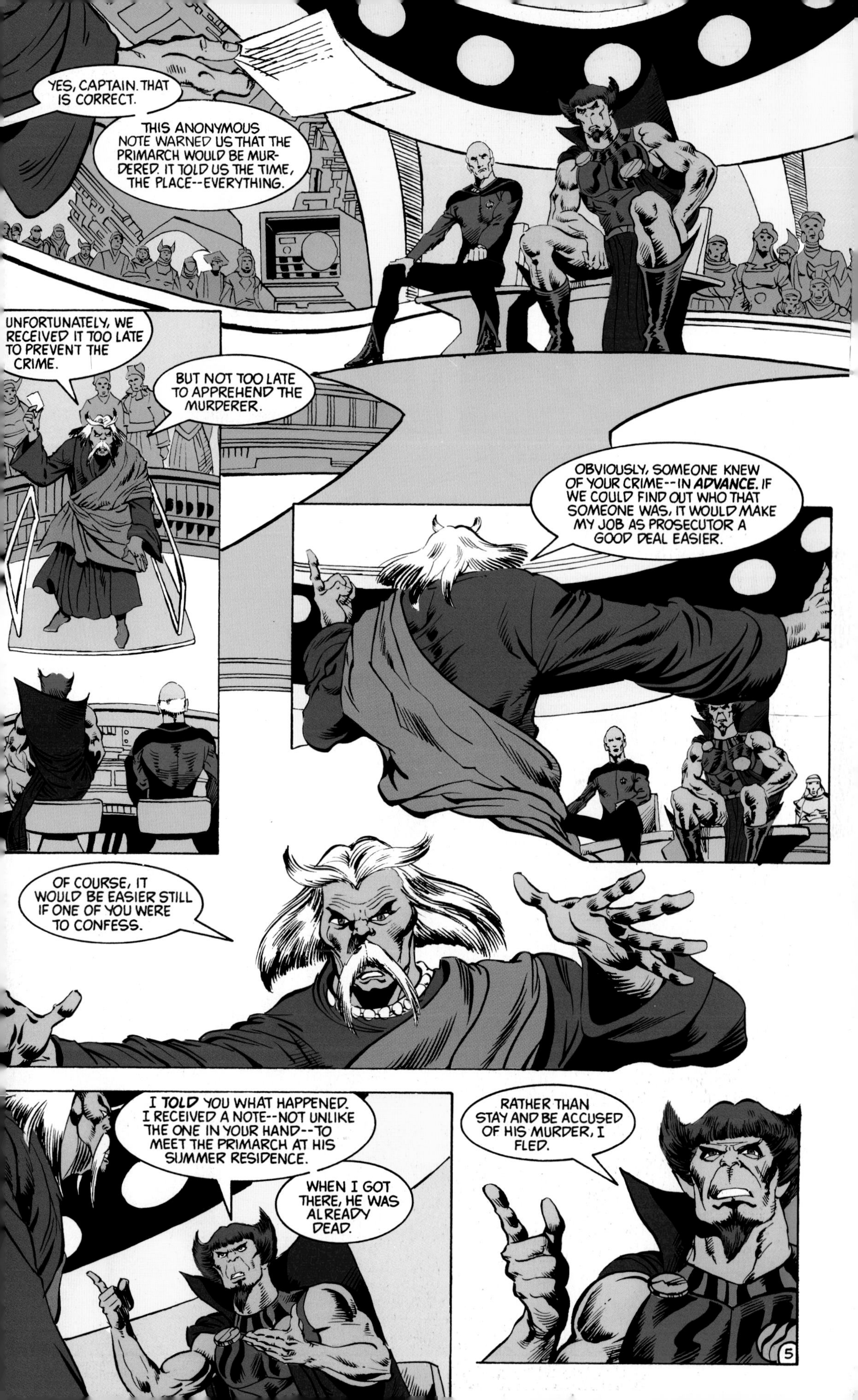
YES, CAPTAIN. THAT IS CORRECT.
THIS ANONYMOUS NOTE WARNED US THAT THE PRIMARCH WOULD BE MUR-DERED. IT TOLD US THE TIME, THE PLACE--EVERYTHING.
UNFORTUNATELY, WE RECEIVED IT TOO LATE TO PREVENT THE CRIME.
BUT NOT TOO LATE TO APPREHEND THE MURDERER.
OBVIOUSLY, SOMEONE KNEW OF YOUR CRIME--IN ADVANCE. IF WE COULD FIND OUT WHO THAT SOMEONE WAS, IT WOULD MAKE MY JOB AS PROSECUTOR A GOOD DEAL EASIER.
OF COURSE, IT WOULD BE EASIER STILL IF ONE OF YOU WERE TO CONFESS.
I TOLD YOU WHAT HAPPENED. I RECEIVED A NOTE--NOT UNLIKE THE ONE IN YOUR HAND--TO MEET THE PRIMARCH AT HIS SUMMER RESIDENCE.
WHEN I GOT THERE, HE WAS ALREADY DEAD.
RATHER THAN STAY AND BE ACCUSED OF HIS MURDER, I FLED.

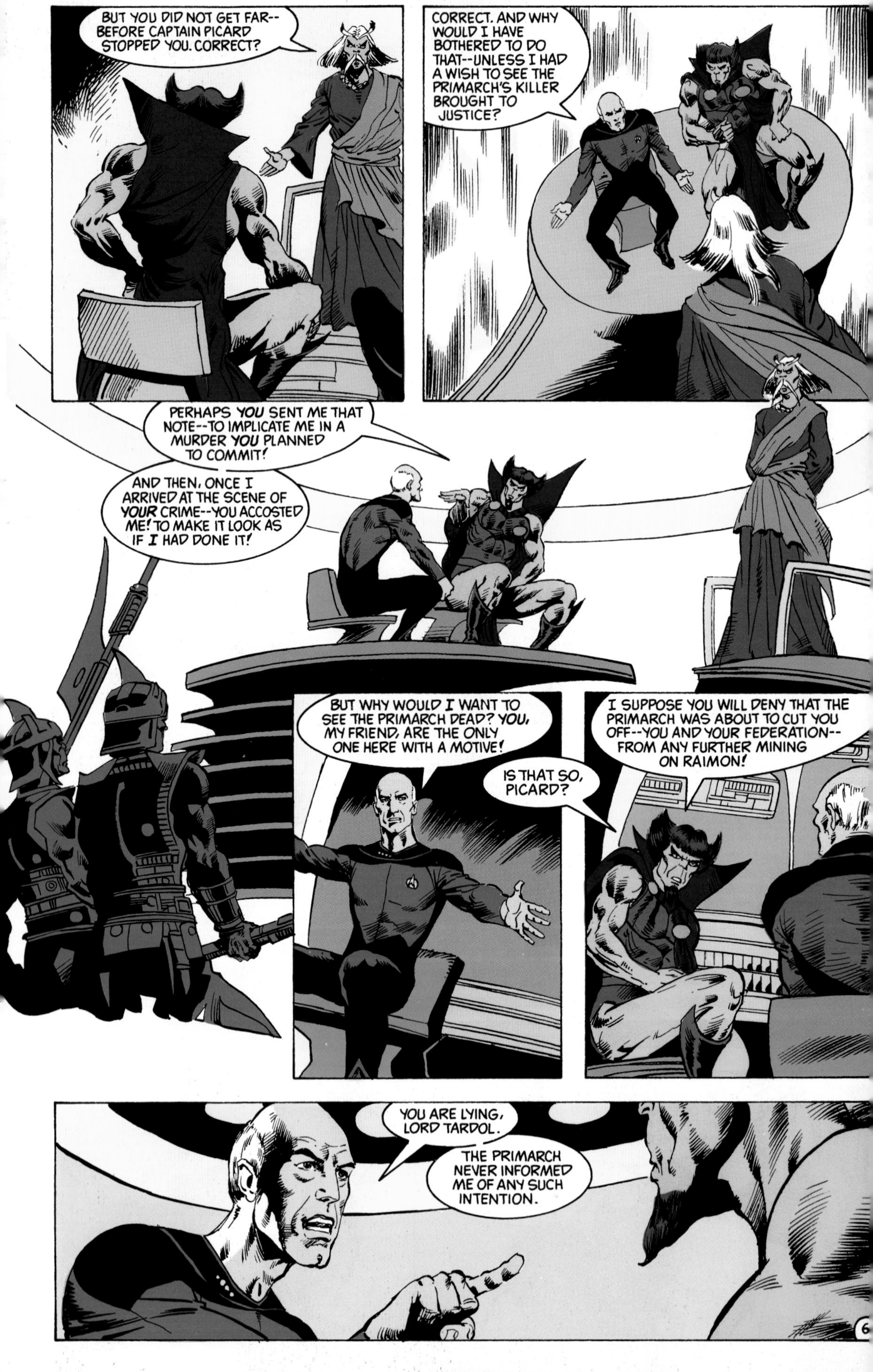
BUT YOU DID NOT GET FAR-- BEFORE CAPTAIN PICARD STOPPED YOU. CORRECT?
CORRECT. AND WHY WOULD I HAVE BOTHERED TO DO THAT--UNLESS I HAD A WISH TO SEE THE PRIMARCH'S KILLER BROUGHT TO JUSTICE?
PERHAPS YOU SENT ME THAT NOTE--TO IMPLICATE ME IN A MURDER YOU PLANNED TO COMMIT!
AND THEN, ONCE I ARRIVED AT THE SCENE OF YOUR CRIME--YOU ACCOSTED ME! TO MAKE IT LOOK AS IF I HAD DONE IT!
BUT WHY WOULD I WANT TO SEE THE PRIMARCH DEAD? YOU, MY FRIEND, ARE THE ONLY ONE HERE WITH A MOTIVE!
I SUPPOSE YOU WILL DENY THAT THE PRIMARCH WAS ABOUT TO CUT YOU OFF--YOU AND YOUR FEDERATION-- FROM ANY FURTHER MINING ON RAIMON!
IS THAT SO, PICARD?
YOU ARE LYING, LORD TARDOL.
THE PRIMARCH NEVER INFORMED ME OF ANY SUCH INTENTION.

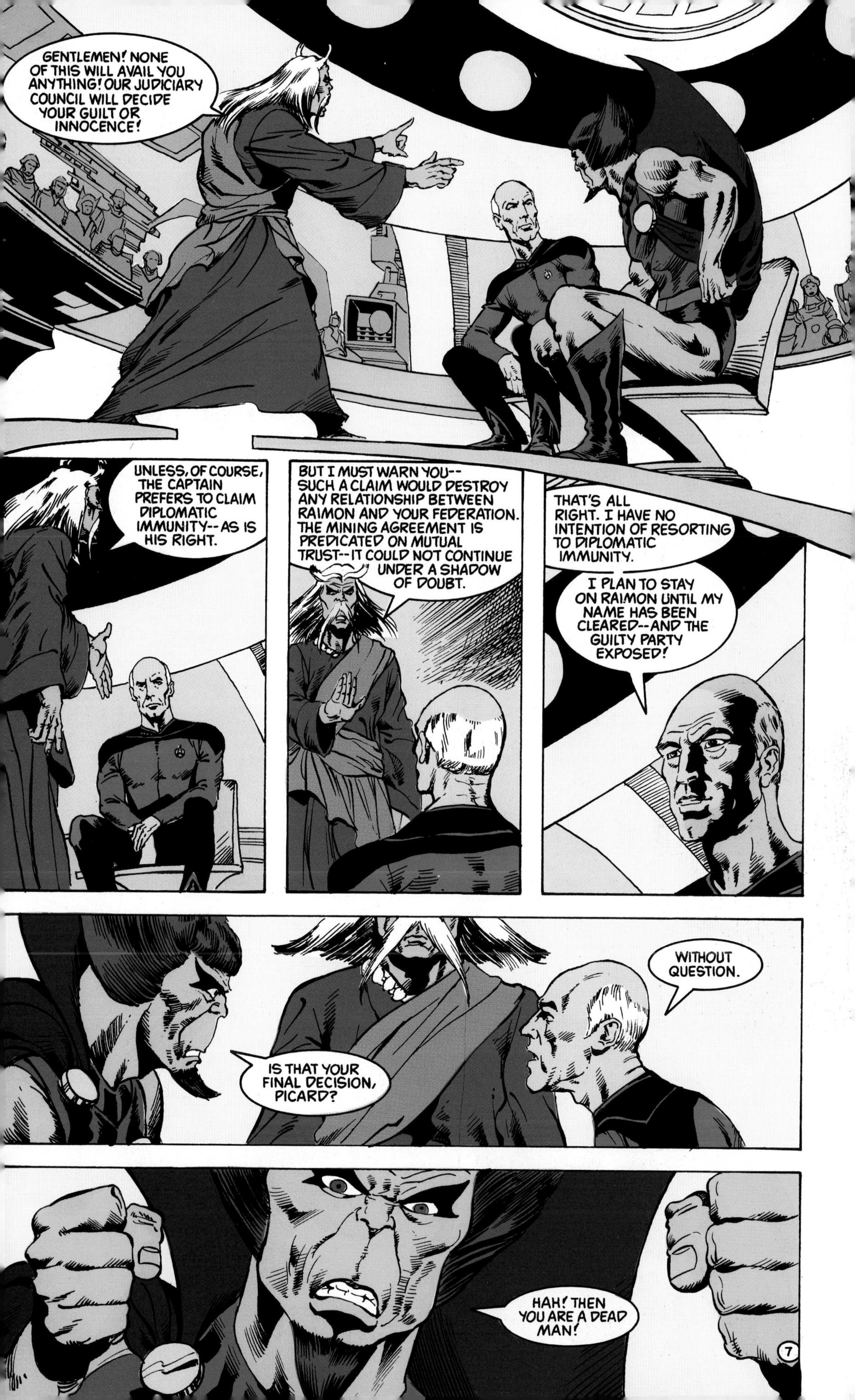
GENTLEMEN! NONE OF THIS WILL AVAIL YOU ANYTHING! OUR JUDICIARY COUNCIL WILL DECIDE YOUR GUILT OR INNOCENCE!
UNLESS, OF COURSE, THE CAPTAIN PREFERS TO CLAIM DIPLOMATIC IMMUNITY--AS IS HIS RIGHT.
BUT I MUST WARN YOU--SUCH A CLAIM WOULD DESTROY ANY RELATIONSHIP BETWEEN RAIMON AND YOUR FEDERATION. THE MINING AGREEMENT IS PREDICATED ON MUTUAL TRUST--IT COULD NOT CONTINUE UNDER A SHADOW OF DOUBT.
THAT'S ALL RIGHT. I HAVE NO INTENTION OF RESORTING TO DIPLOMATIC IMMUNITY.
I PLAN TO STAY ON RAIMON UNTIL MY NAME HAS BEEN CLEARED--AND THE GUILTY PARTY EXPOSED!
IS THAT YOUR FINAL DECISION, PICARD?
WITHOUT QUESTION.
HAH! THEN YOU ARE A DEAD MAN!
7

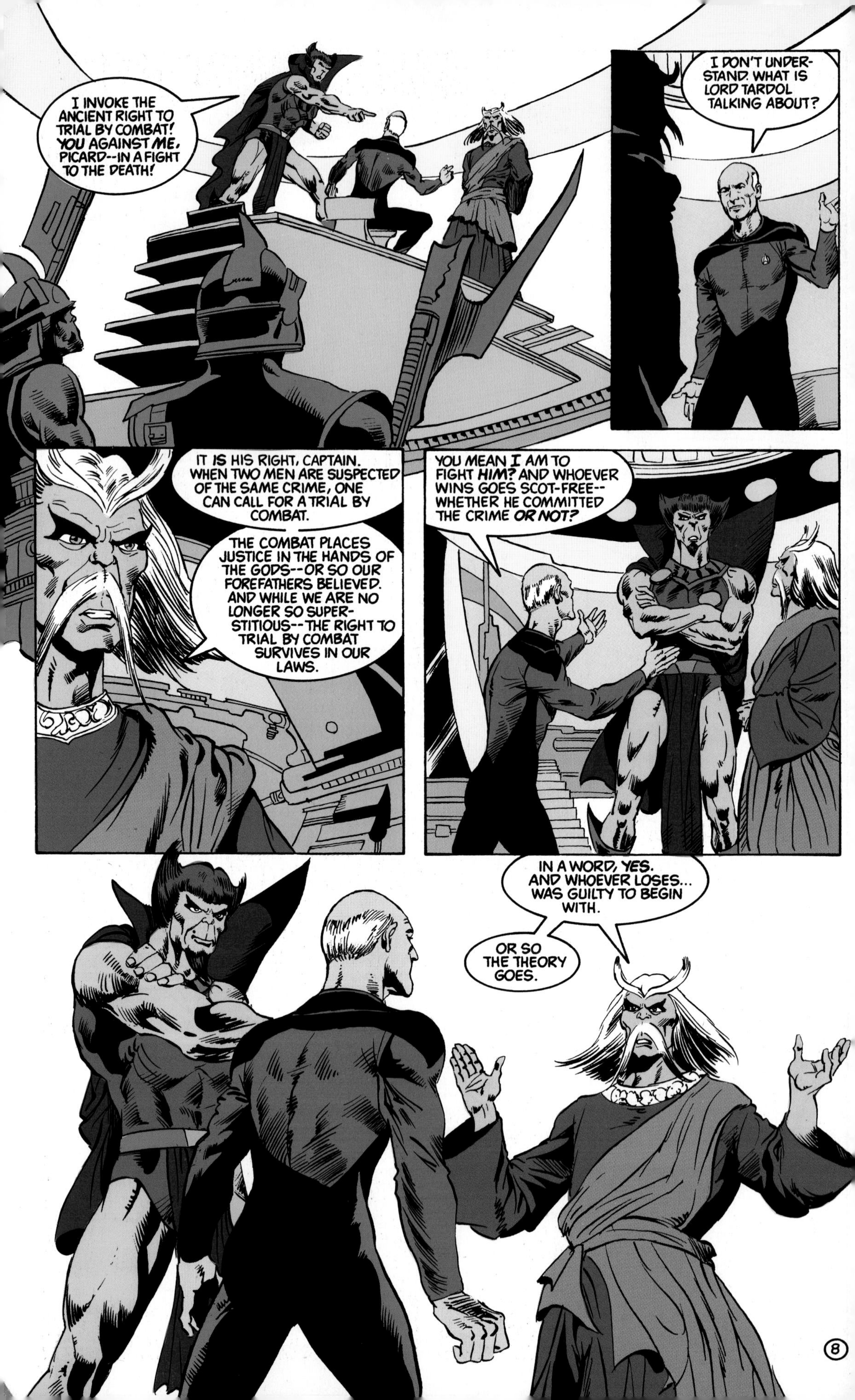
I INVOKE THE ANCIENT RIGHT TO TRIAL BY COMBAT! YOU AGAINST ME, PICARD--IN A FIGHT TO THE DEATH!
I DON'T UNDER-STAND. WHAT IS LORD TARDOL TALKING ABOUT?
IT IS HIS RIGHT, CAPTAIN. WHEN TWO MEN ARE SUSPECTED OF THE SAME CRIME, ONE CAN CALL FOR A TRIAL BY COMBAT.
THE COMBAT PLACES JUSTICE IN THE HANDS OF THE GODS--OR SO OUR FOREFATHERS BELIEVED. AND WHILE WE ARE NO LONGER SO SUPER-STITIOUS--THE RIGHT TO TRIAL BY COMBAT SURVIVES IN OUR LAWS.
YOU MEAN I AM TO FIGHT HIM? AND WHOEVER WINS GOES SCOT-FREE--WHETHER HE COMMITTED THE CRIME OR NOT?
IN A WORD, YES. AND WHOEVER LOSES... WAS GUILTY TO BEGIN WITH.
OR SO THE THEORY GOES.

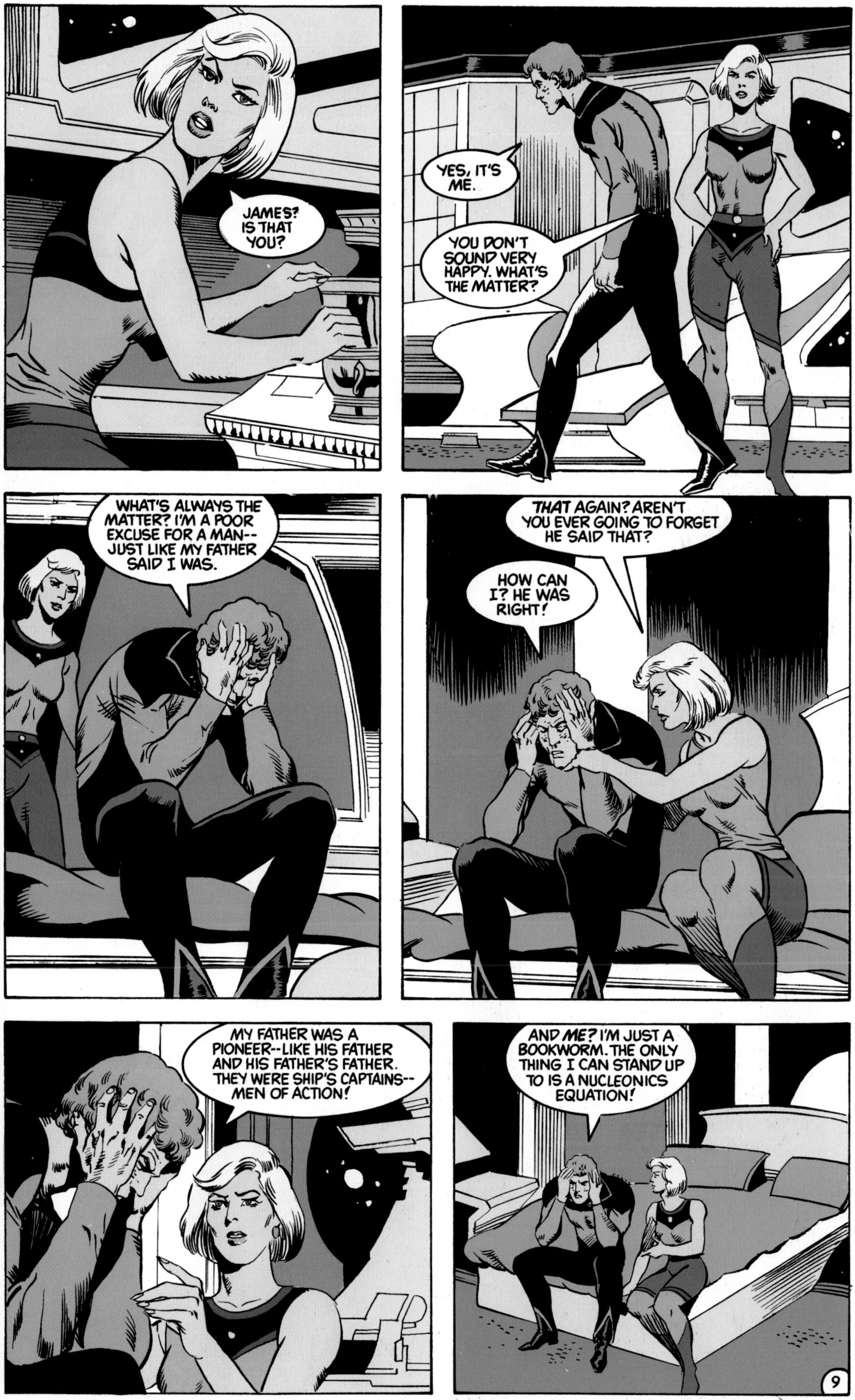
JAMES? IS THAT YOU?
YES, IT'S ME.
YOU DON'T SOUND VERY HAPPY. WHAT'S THE MATTER?
WHAT'S ALWAYS THE MATTER? I'M A POOR EXCUSE FOR A MAN--JUST LIKE MY FATHER SAID I WAS.
THAT AGAIN? AREN'T YOU EVER GOING TO FORGET HE SAID THAT?
HOW CAN I? HE WAS RIGHT!
MY FATHER WAS A PIONEER--LIKE HIS FATHER AND HIS FATHER'S FATHER. THEY WERE SHIP'S CAPTAINS--MEN OF ACTION!
AND ME? I'M JUST A BOOKWORM. THE ONLY THING I CAN STAND UP TO IS A NUCLEONICS EQUATION!
9

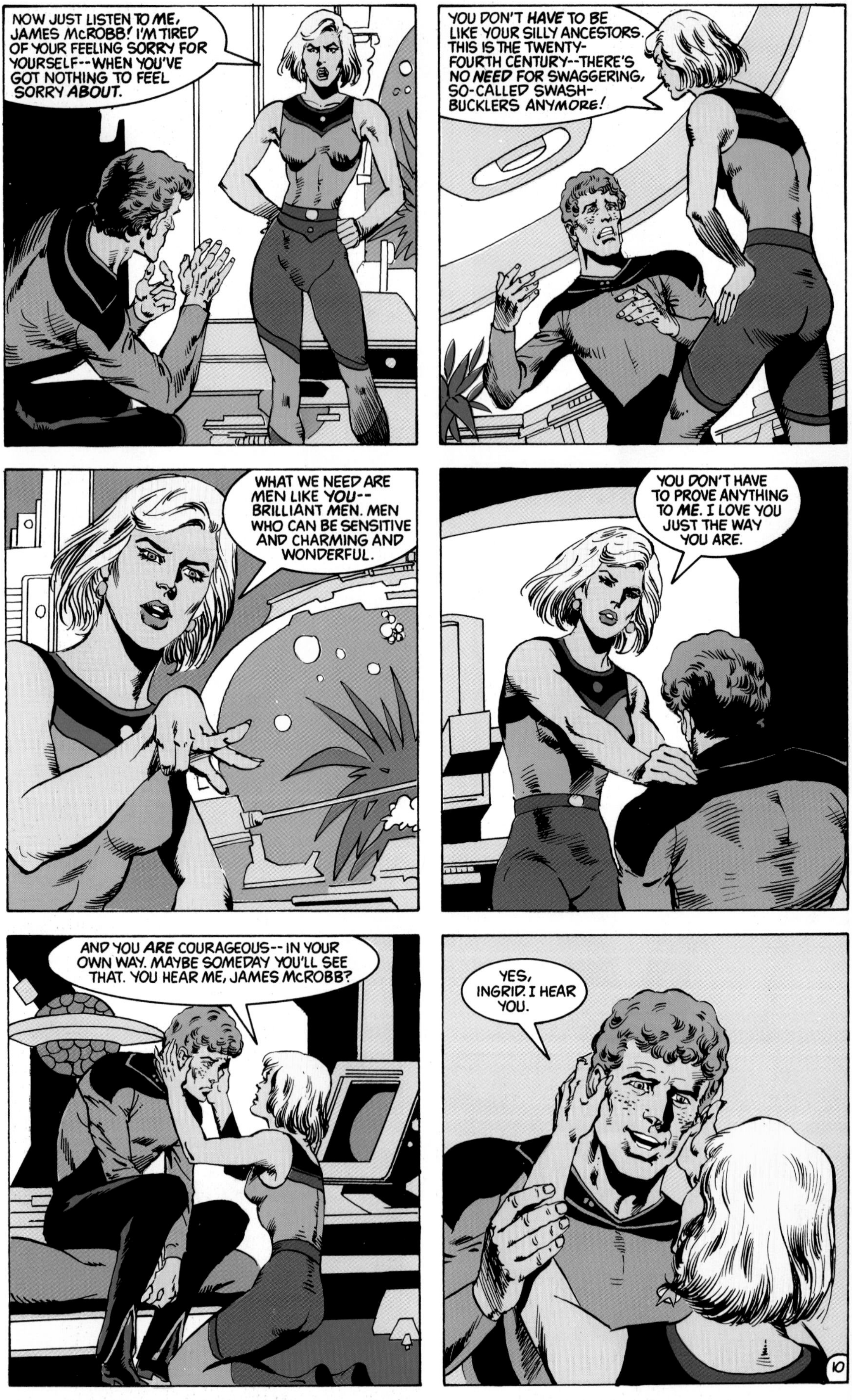
NOW JUST LISTEN TO ME, JAMES McROBB! I'M TIRED OF YOUR FEELING SORRY FOR YOURSELF--WHEN YOU'VE GOT NOTHING TO FEEL SORRY ABOUT.
YOU DON'T HAVE TO BE LIKE YOUR SILLY ANCESTORS. THIS IS THE TWENTY-FOURTH CENTURY--THERE'S NO NEED FOR SWAGGERING, SO-CALLED SWASH-BUCKLERS ANYMORE!
WHAT WE NEED ARE MEN LIKE YOU--BRILLIANT MEN. MEN WHO CAN BE SENSITIVE AND CHARMING AND WONDERFUL.
YOU DON'T HAVE TO PROVE ANYTHING TO ME. I LOVE YOU JUST THE WAY YOU ARE.
AND YOU ARE COURAGEOUS--IN YOUR OWN WAY. MAYBE SOMEDAY YOU'LL SEE THAT. YOU HEAR ME, JAMES McROBB?
YES, INGRID. I HEAR YOU.
10

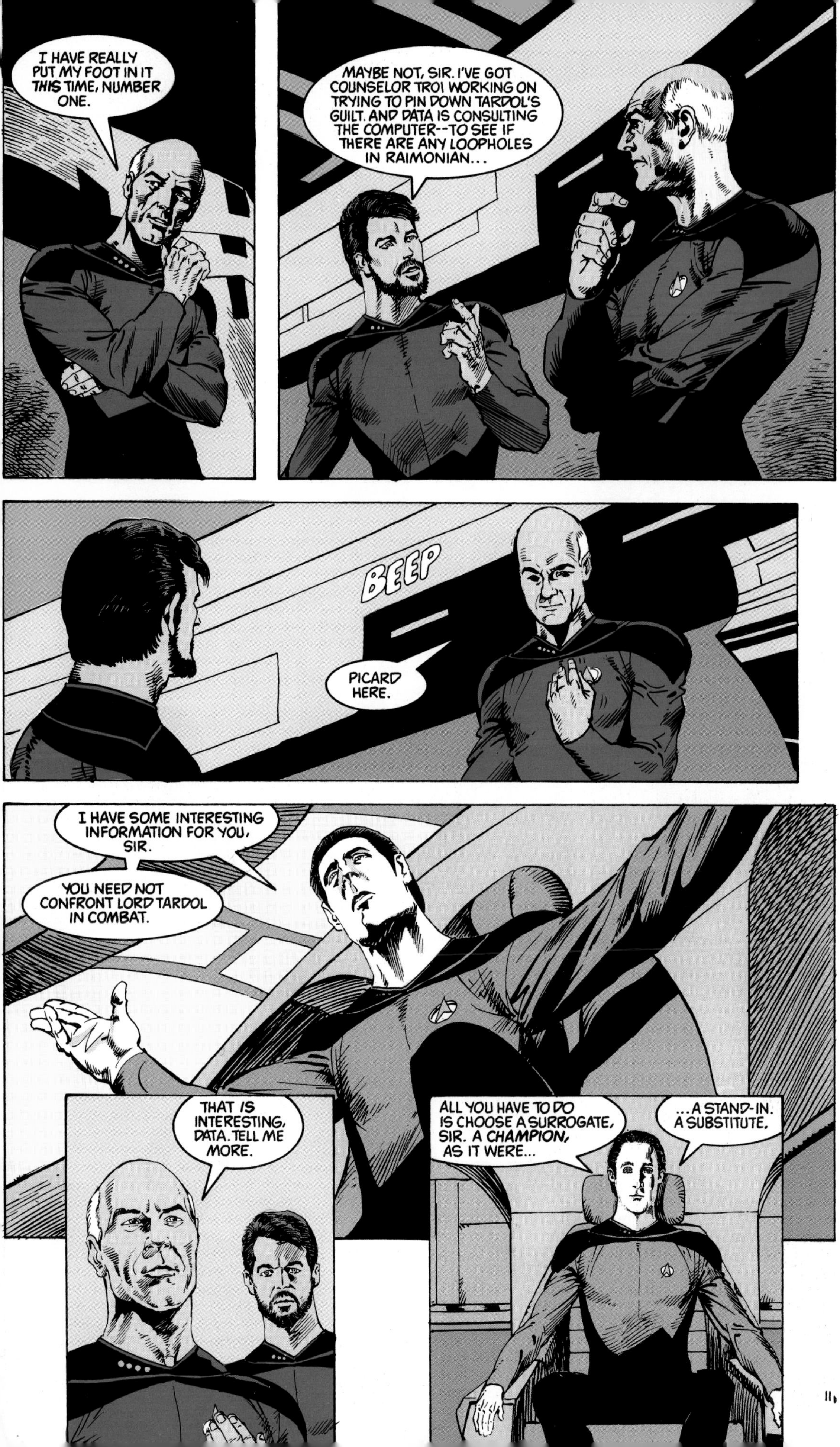
I HAVE REALLY PUT MY FOOT IN IT THIS TIME, NUMBER ONE.
MAYBE NOT, SIR. I'VE GOT COUNSELOR TROI WORKING ON TRYING TO PIN DOWN TARDOL'S GUILT. AND DATA IS CONSULTING THE COMPUTER--TO SEE IF THERE ARE ANY LOOPHOLES IN RAIMONIAN...
BEEP
PICARD HERE.
I HAVE SOME INTERESTING INFORMATION FOR YOU, SIR.
YOU NEED NOT CONFRONT LORD TARDOL IN COMBAT.
THAT IS INTERESTING, DATA. TELL ME MORE.
ALL YOU HAVE TO DO IS CHOOSE A SURROGATE, SIR. A CHAMPION, AS IT WERE...
...A STAND-IN. A SUBSTITUTE.

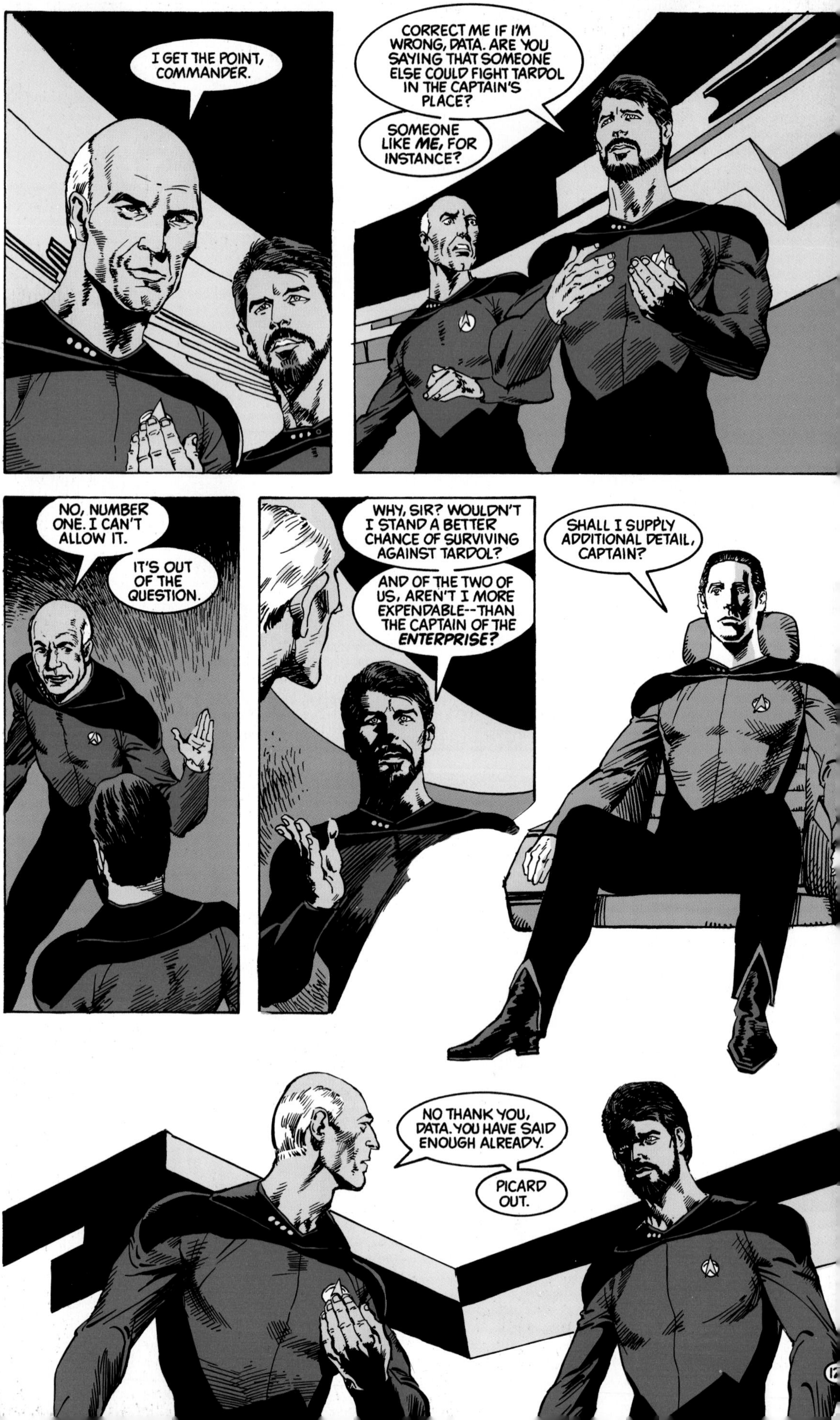
I GET THE POINT, COMMANDER.
CORRECT ME IF I'M WRONG, DATA. ARE YOU SAYING THAT SOMEONE ELSE COULD FIGHT TARDOL IN THE CAPTAIN'S PLACE?
SOMEONE LIKE ME, FOR INSTANCE?
NO, NUMBER ONE. I CAN'T ALLOW IT.
IT'S OUT OF THE QUESTION.
WHY, SIR? WOULDN'T I STAND A BETTER CHANCE OF SURVIVING AGAINST TARDOL?
AND OF THE TWO OF US, AREN'T I MORE EXPENDABLE--THAN THE CAPTAIN OF THE ENTERPRISE?
SHALL I SUPPLY ADDITIONAL DETAIL, CAPTAIN?
NO THANK YOU, DATA. YOU HAVE SAID ENOUGH ALREADY.
PICARD OUT.

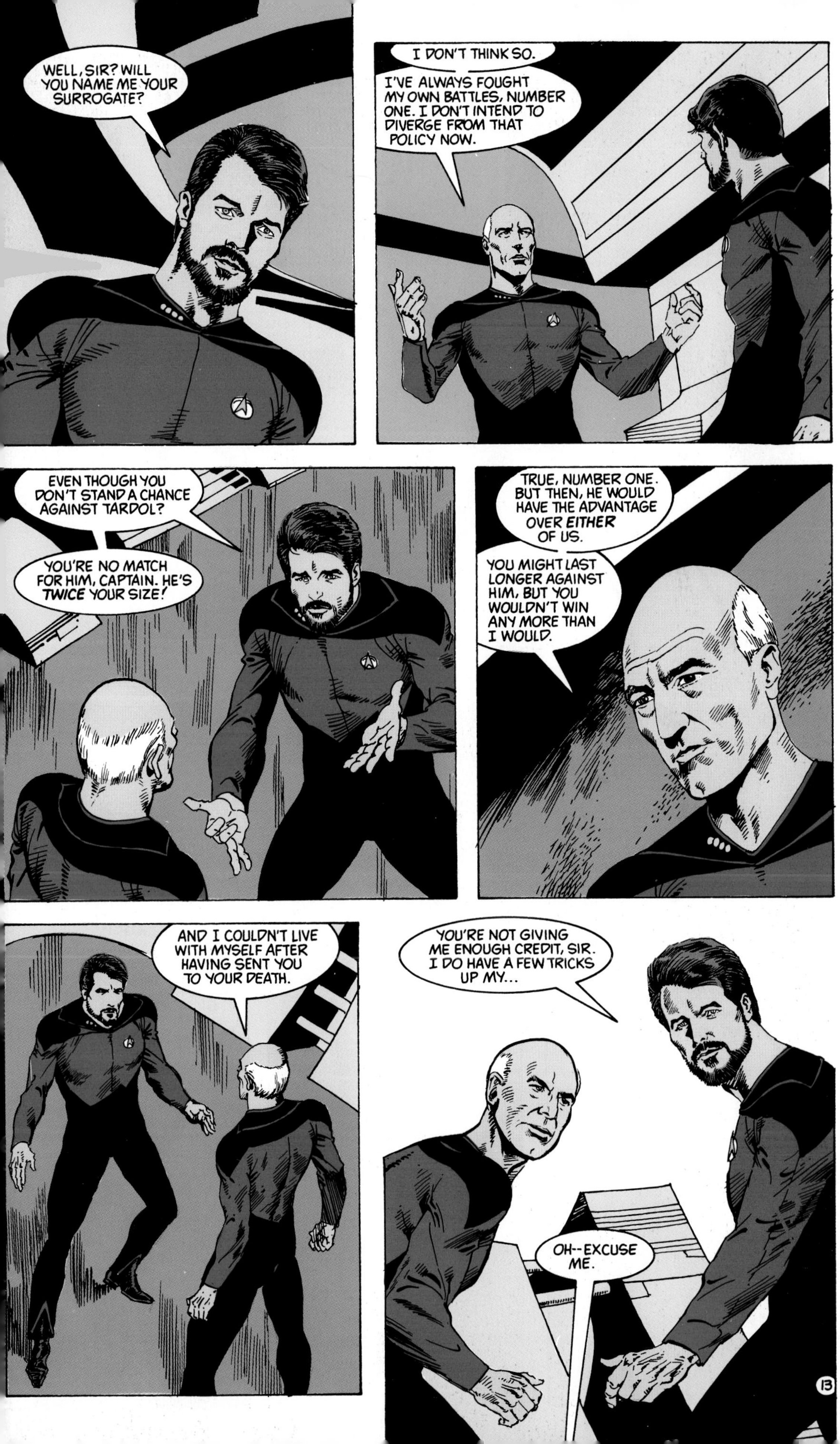

WELL, SIR? WILL YOU NAME ME YOUR SURROGATE?
I DON'T THINK SO.
I'VE ALWAYS FOUGHT MY OWN BATTLES, NUMBER ONE. I DON'T INTEND TO DIVERGE FROM THAT POLICY NOW.
EVEN THOUGH YOU DON'T STAND A CHANCE AGAINST TARDOL?
YOU'RE NO MATCH FOR HIM, CAPTAIN. HE'S TWICE YOUR SIZE!
TRUE, NUMBER ONE. BUT THEN, HE WOULD HAVE THE ADVANTAGE OVER EITHER OF US.
YOU MIGHT LAST LONGER AGAINST HIM, BUT YOU WOULDN'T WIN ANY MORE THAN I WOULD.
AND I COULDN'T LIVE WITH MYSELF AFTER HAVING SENT YOU TO YOUR DEATH.
YOU'RE NOT GIVING ME ENOUGH CREDIT, SIR. I DO HAVE A FEW TRICKS UP MY...
OH--EXCUSE ME.
13

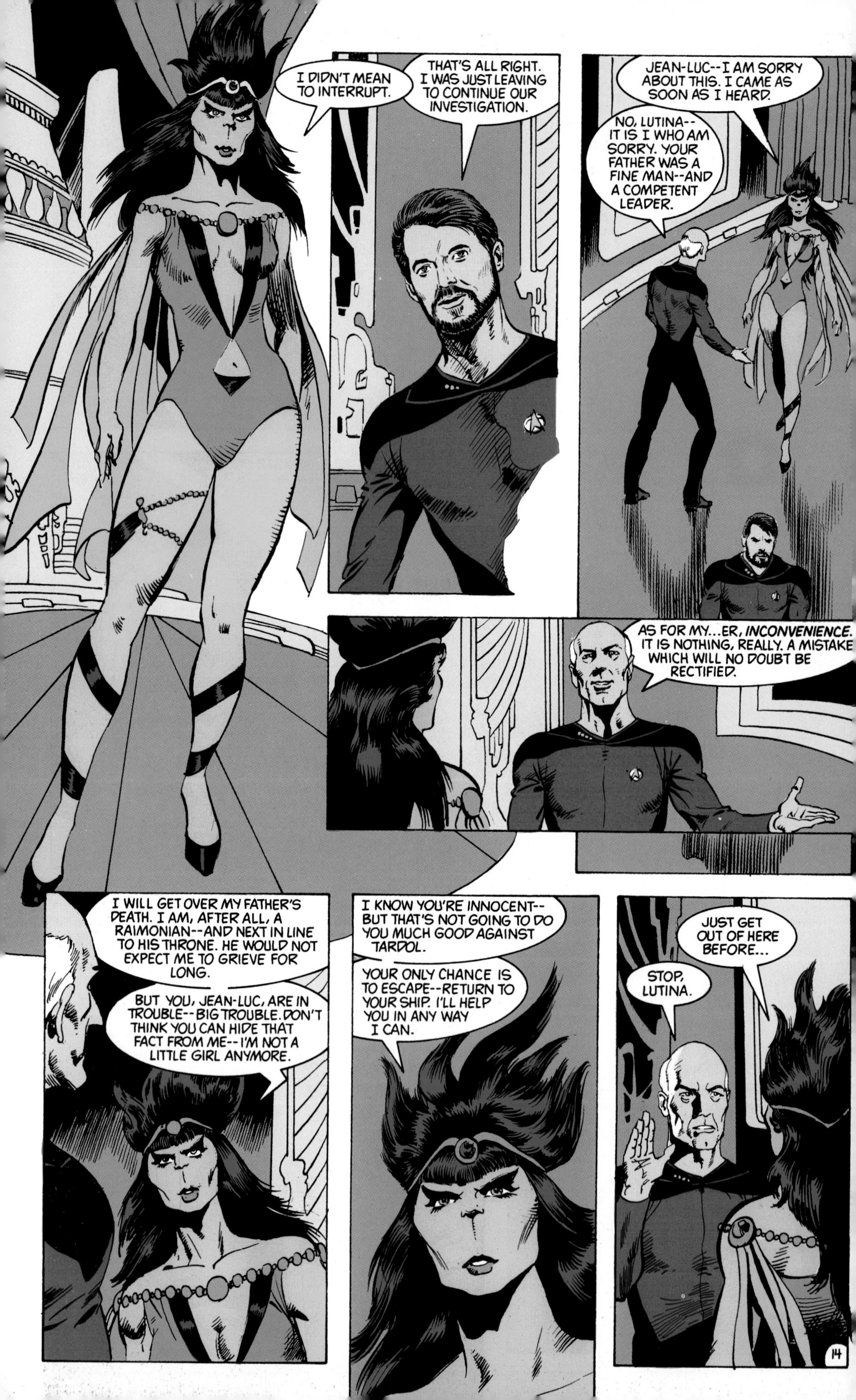
I DIDN'T MEAN TO INTERRUPT.
THAT'S ALL RIGHT. I WAS JUST LEAVING TO CONTINUE OUR INVESTIGATION.
JEAN-LUC--I AM SORRY ABOUT THIS. I CAME AS SOON AS I HEARD.
NO, LUTINA-- IT IS I WHO AM SORRY. YOUR FATHER WAS A FINE MAN--AND A COMPETENT LEADER.
AS FOR MY...ER, *INCONVENIENCE.* IT IS NOTHING, REALLY. A MISTAKE WHICH WILL NO DOUBT BE RECTIFIED.
I WILL GET OVER MY FATHER'S DEATH. I AM, AFTER ALL, A RAIMONIAN--AND NEXT IN LINE TO HIS THRONE. HE WOULD NOT EXPECT ME TO GRIEVE FOR LONG.
BUT YOU, JEAN-LUC, ARE IN TROUBLE--BIG TROUBLE. DON'T THINK YOU CAN HIDE THAT FACT FROM ME--I'M NOT A LITTLE GIRL ANYMORE.
I KNOW YOU'RE INNOCENT-- BUT THAT'S NOT GOING TO DO YOU MUCH GOOD AGAINST TARDOL.
YOUR ONLY CHANCE IS TO ESCAPE--RETURN TO YOUR SHIP. I'LL HELP YOU IN ANY WAY I CAN.
JUST GET OUT OF HERE BEFORE...
STOP, LUTINA.
14

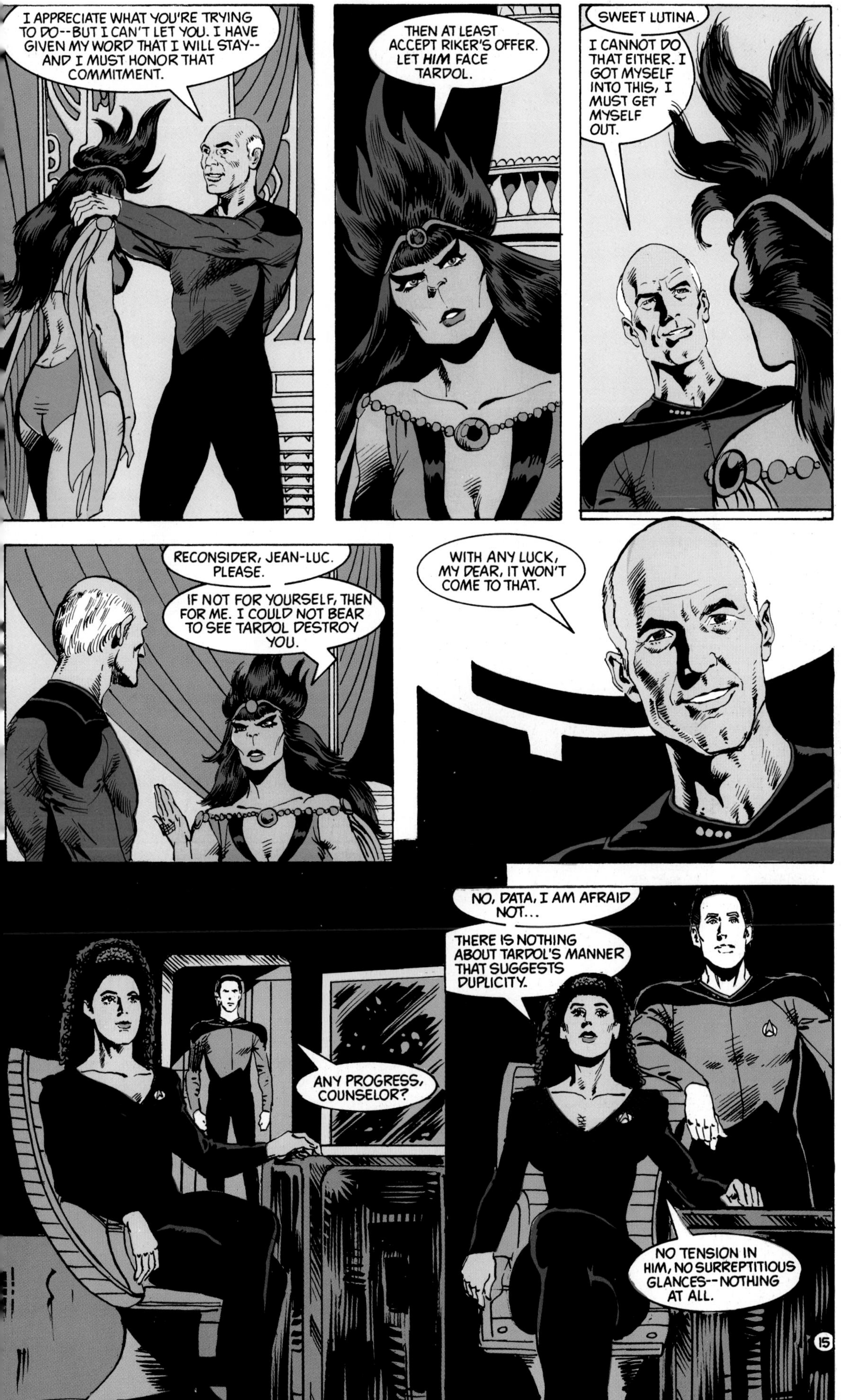
I APPRECIATE WHAT YOU'RE TRYING TO DO--BUT I CAN'T LET YOU. I HAVE GIVEN MY WORD THAT I WILL STAY--AND I MUST HONOR THAT COMMITMENT.
THEN AT LEAST ACCEPT RIKER'S OFFER. LET HIM FACE TARDOL.
SWEET LUTINA.
I CANNOT DO THAT EITHER. I GOT MYSELF INTO THIS, I MUST GET MYSELF OUT.
RECONSIDER, JEAN-LUC. PLEASE.
IF NOT FOR YOURSELF, THEN FOR ME. I COULD NOT BEAR TO SEE TARDOL DESTROY YOU.
WITH ANY LUCK, MY DEAR, IT WON'T COME TO THAT.
ANY PROGRESS, COUNSELOR?
NO, DATA, I AM AFRAID NOT...
THERE IS NOTHING ABOUT TARDOL'S MANNER THAT SUGGESTS DUPLICITY.
NO TENSION IN HIM, NO SURREPTITIOUS GLANCES--NOTHING AT ALL.

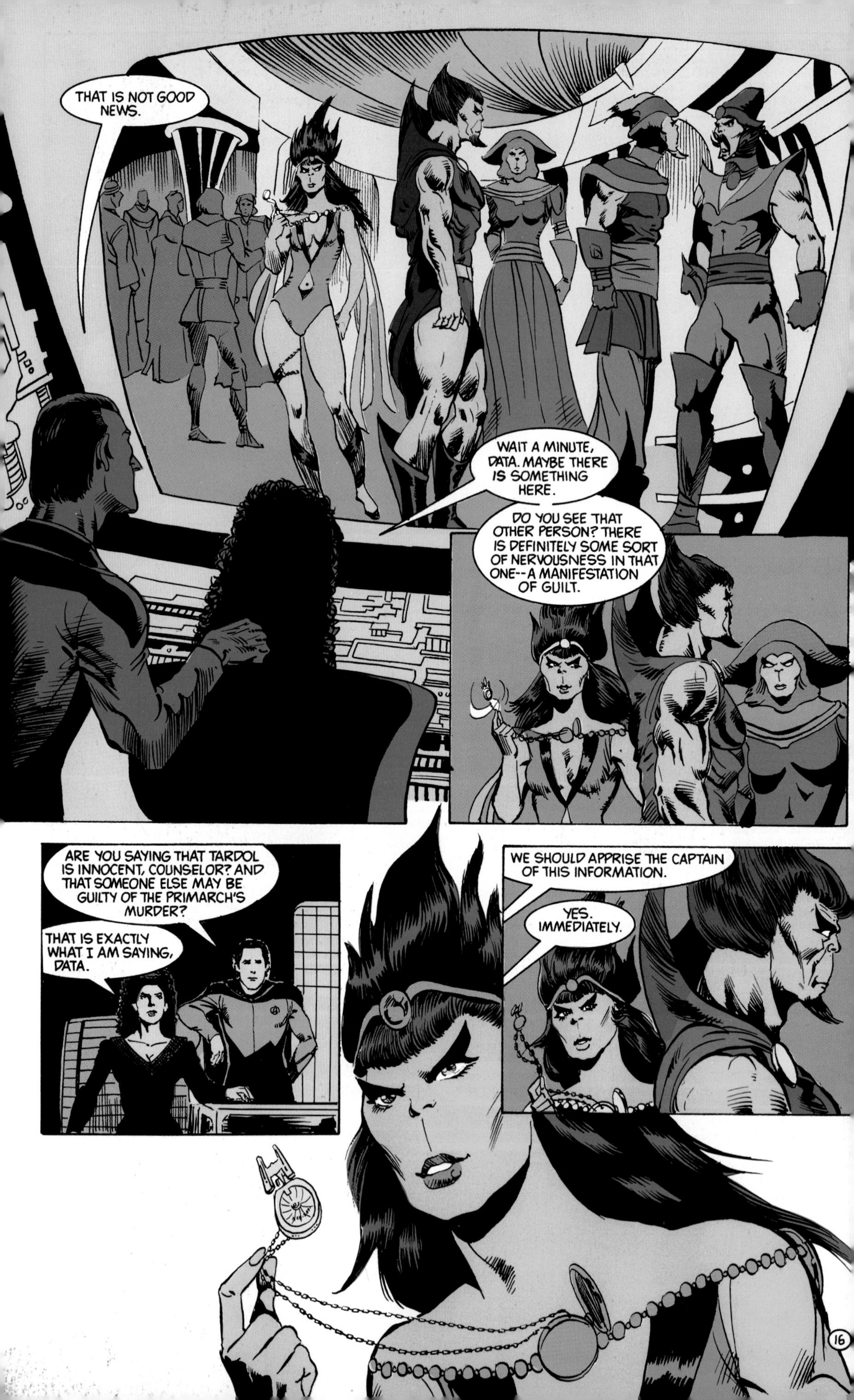
THAT IS NOT GOOD NEWS.
WAIT A MINUTE, DATA. MAYBE THERE IS SOMETHING HERE.
DO YOU SEE THAT OTHER PERSON? THERE IS DEFINITELY SOME SORT OF NERVOUSNESS IN THAT ONE--A MANIFESTATION OF GUILT.
ARE YOU SAYING THAT TARDOL IS INNOCENT, COUNSELOR? AND THAT SOMEONE ELSE MAY BE GUILTY OF THE PRIMARCH'S MURDER?
THAT IS EXACTLY WHAT I AM SAYING, DATA.
WE SHOULD APPRISE THE CAPTAIN OF THIS INFORMATION.
YES. IMMEDIATELY.

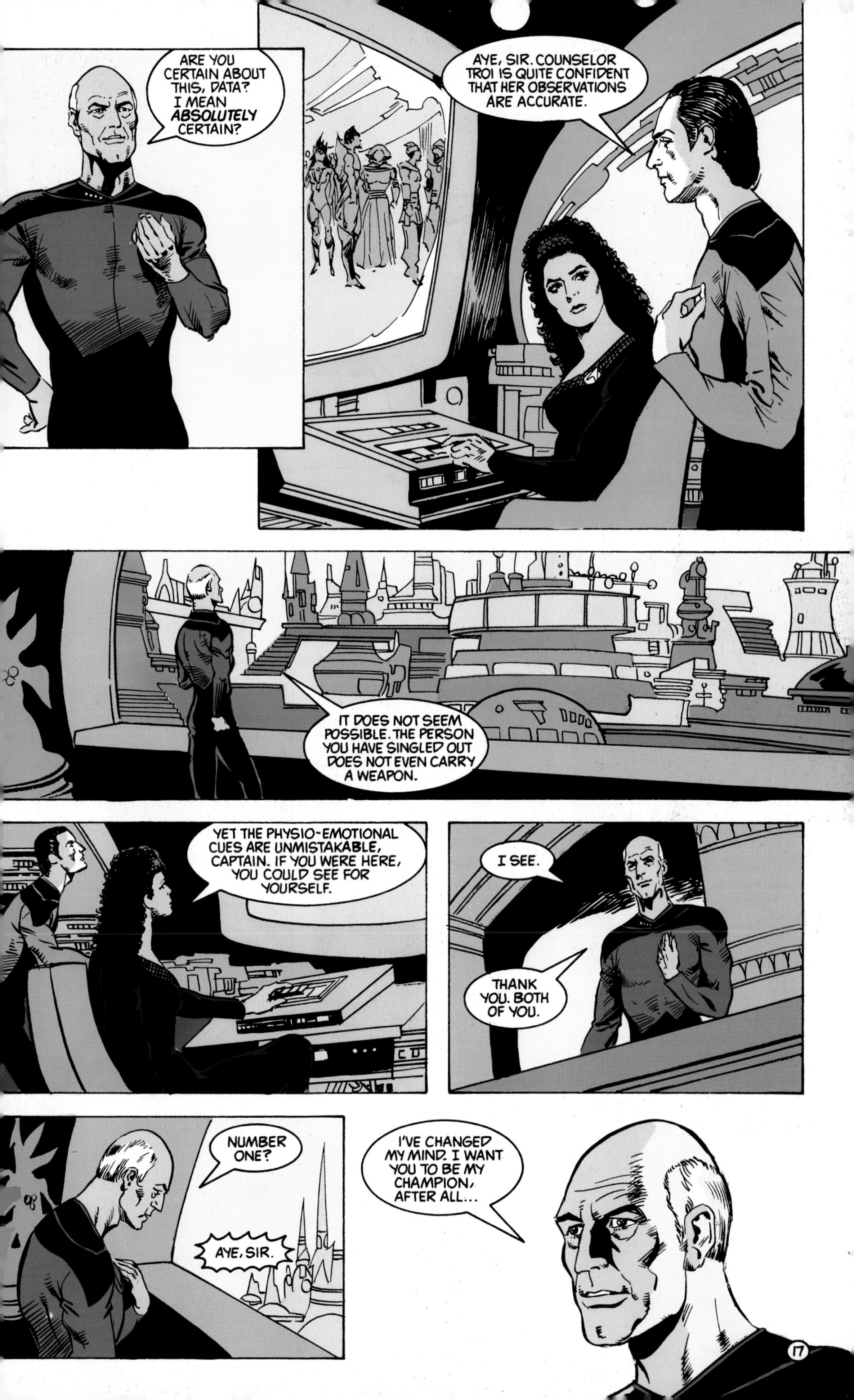
ARE YOU CERTAIN ABOUT THIS, DATA? I MEAN ABSOLUTELY CERTAIN?
AYE, SIR. COUNSELOR TROI IS QUITE CONFIDENT THAT HER OBSERVATIONS ARE ACCURATE.
IT DOES NOT SEEM POSSIBLE. THE PERSON YOU HAVE SINGLED OUT DOES NOT EVEN CARRY A WEAPON.
YET THE PHYSIO-EMOTIONAL CUES ARE UNMISTAKABLE, CAPTAIN. IF YOU WERE HERE, YOU COULD SEE FOR YOURSELF.
I SEE.
THANK YOU. BOTH OF YOU.
NUMBER ONE?
AYE, SIR.
I'VE CHANGED MY MIND. I WANT YOU TO BE MY CHAMPION, AFTER ALL...

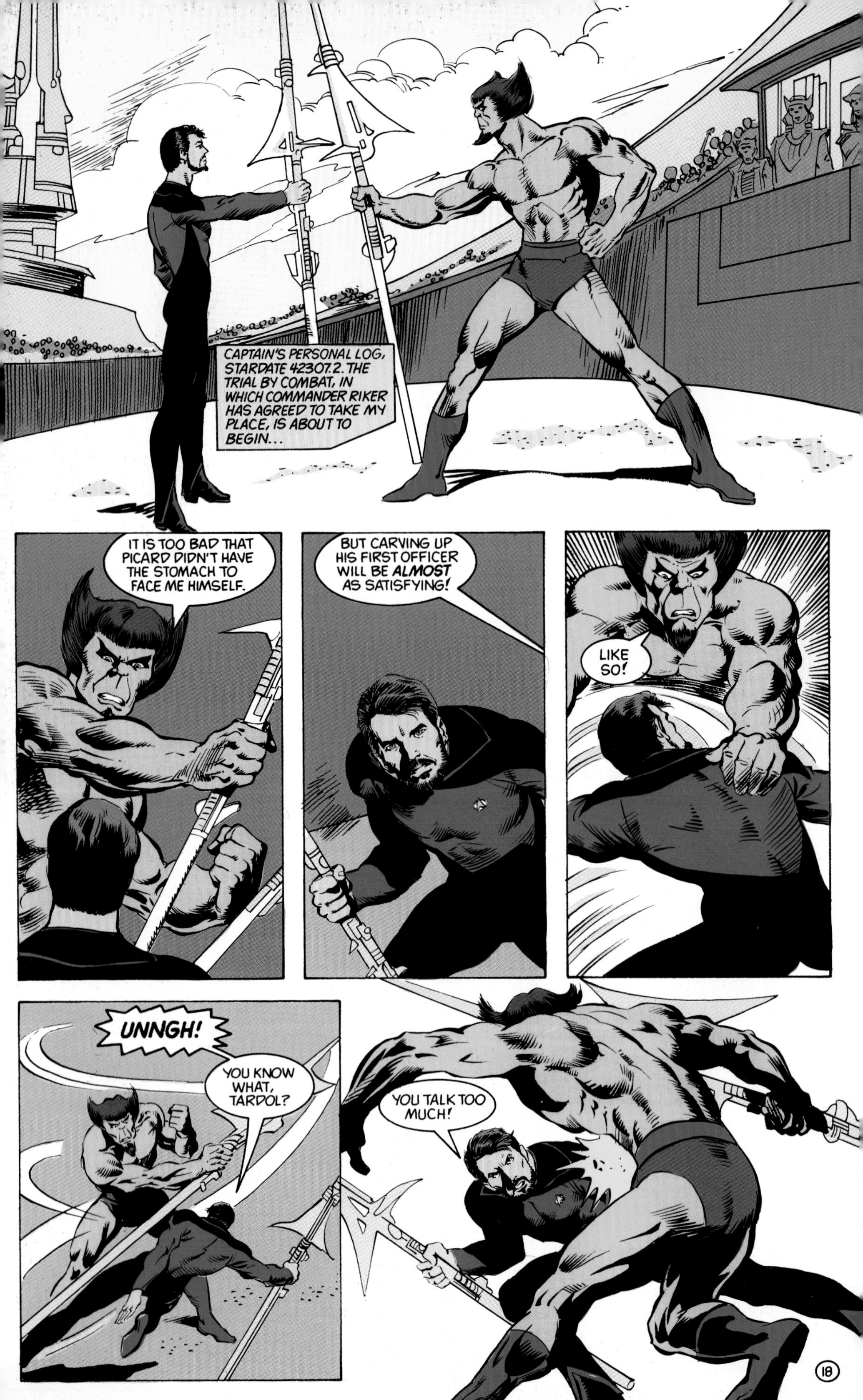

CAPTAIN'S PERSONAL LOG, STARDATE 42307.2. THE TRIAL BY COMBAT, IN WHICH COMMANDER RIKER HAS AGREED TO TAKE MY PLACE, IS ABOUT TO BEGIN...
IT IS TOO BAD THAT PICARD DIDN'T HAVE THE STOMACH TO FACE ME HIMSELF.
BUT CARVING UP HIS FIRST OFFICER WILL BE ALMOST AS SATISFYING!
LIKE SO!
UNNGH!
YOU KNOW WHAT, TARDOL?
YOU TALK TOO MUCH!

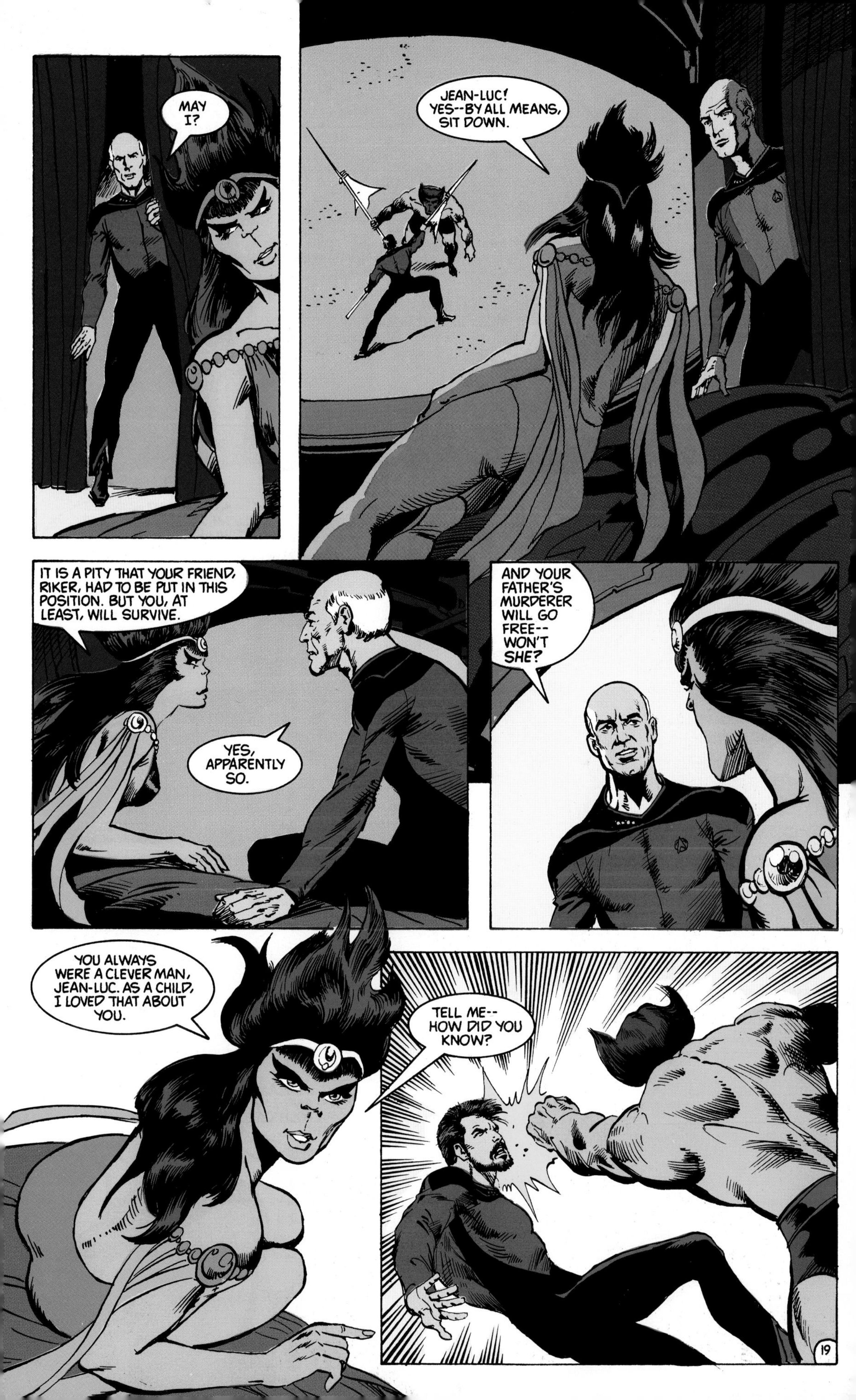
MAY I?
JEAN-LUC! YES--BY ALL MEANS, SIT DOWN.
IT IS A PITY THAT YOUR FRIEND, RIKER, HAD TO BE PUT IN THIS POSITION. BUT YOU, AT LEAST, WILL SURVIVE.
YES, APPARENTLY SO.
AND YOUR FATHER'S MURDERER WILL GO FREE-- WON'T SHE?
YOU ALWAYS WERE A CLEVER MAN, JEAN-LUC. AS A CHILD, I LOVED THAT ABOUT YOU.
TELL ME-- HOW DID YOU KNOW?

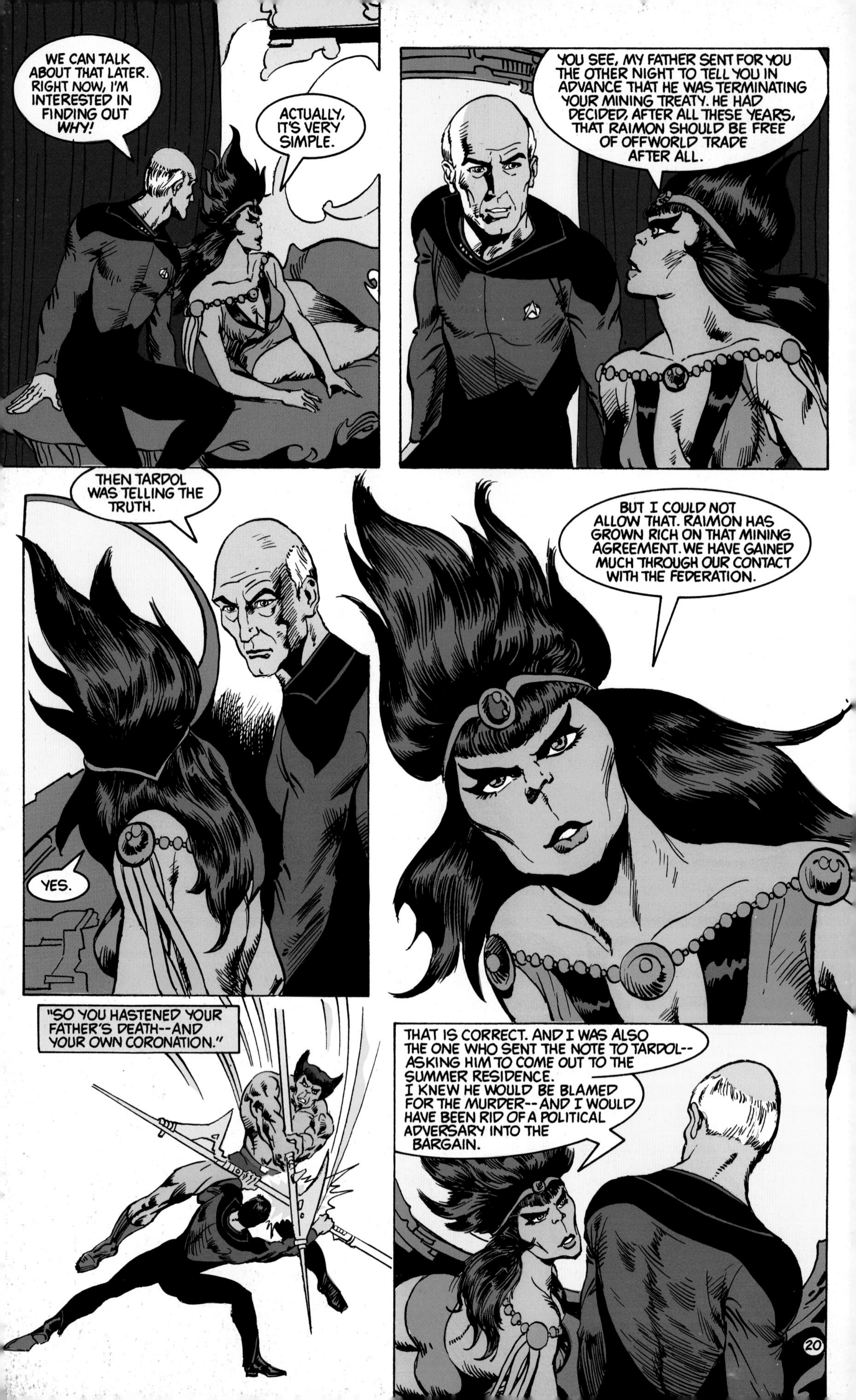
WE CAN TALK ABOUT THAT LATER. RIGHT NOW, I'M INTERESTED IN FINDING OUT WHY!
ACTUALLY, IT'S VERY SIMPLE.
YOU SEE, MY FATHER SENT FOR YOU THE OTHER NIGHT TO TELL YOU IN ADVANCE THAT HE WAS TERMINATING YOUR MINING TREATY. HE HAD DECIDED, AFTER ALL THESE YEARS, THAT RAIMON SHOULD BE FREE OF OFFWORLD TRADE AFTER ALL.
THEN TARDOL WAS TELLING THE TRUTH.
YES.
BUT I COULD NOT ALLOW THAT. RAIMON HAS GROWN RICH ON THAT MINING AGREEMENT. WE HAVE GAINED MUCH THROUGH OUR CONTACT WITH THE FEDERATION.
"SO YOU HASTENED YOUR FATHER'S DEATH--AND YOUR OWN CORONATION."
THAT IS CORRECT. AND I WAS ALSO THE ONE WHO SENT THE NOTE TO TARDOL--ASKING HIM TO COME OUT TO THE SUMMER RESIDENCE.
I KNEW HE WOULD BE BLAMED FOR THE MURDER--AND I WOULD HAVE BEEN RID OF A POLITICAL ADVERSARY INTO THE BARGAIN.
20

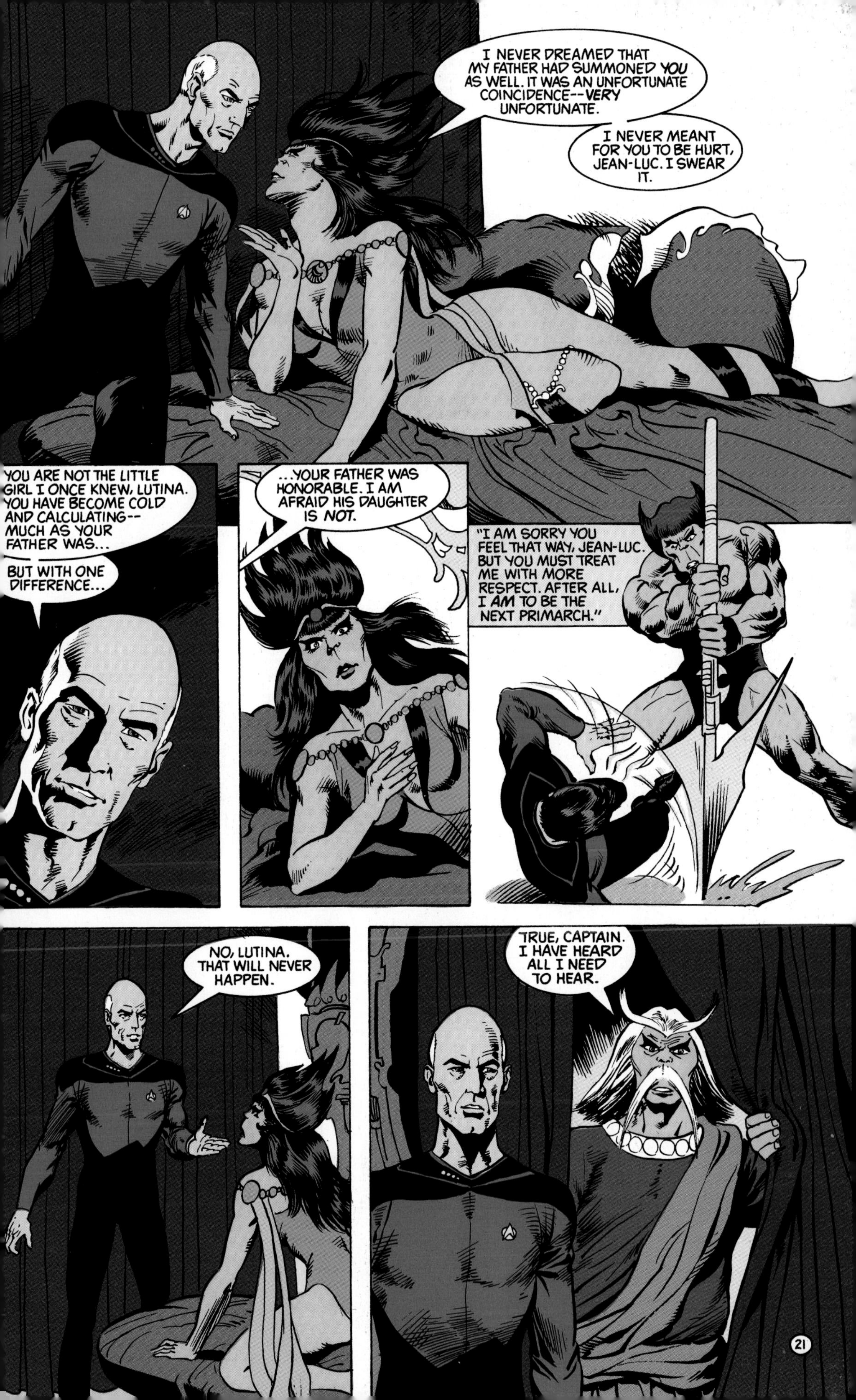
I NEVER DREAMED THAT MY FATHER HAD SUMMONED YOU AS WELL. IT WAS AN UNFORTUNATE COINCIDENCE--VERY UNFORTUNATE.
I NEVER MEANT FOR YOU TO BE HURT, JEAN-LUC. I SWEAR IT.
YOU ARE NOT THE LITTLE GIRL I ONCE KNEW, LUTINA. YOU HAVE BECOME COLD AND CALCULATING--MUCH AS YOUR FATHER WAS...
BUT WITH ONE DIFFERENCE...
...YOUR FATHER WAS HONORABLE. I AM AFRAID HIS DAUGHTER IS NOT.
"I AM SORRY YOU FEEL THAT WAY, JEAN-LUC. BUT YOU MUST TREAT ME WITH MORE RESPECT. AFTER ALL, I AM TO BE THE NEXT PRIMARCH."
NO, LUTINA. THAT WILL NEVER HAPPEN.
TRUE, CAPTAIN. I HAVE HEARD ALL I NEED TO HEAR.

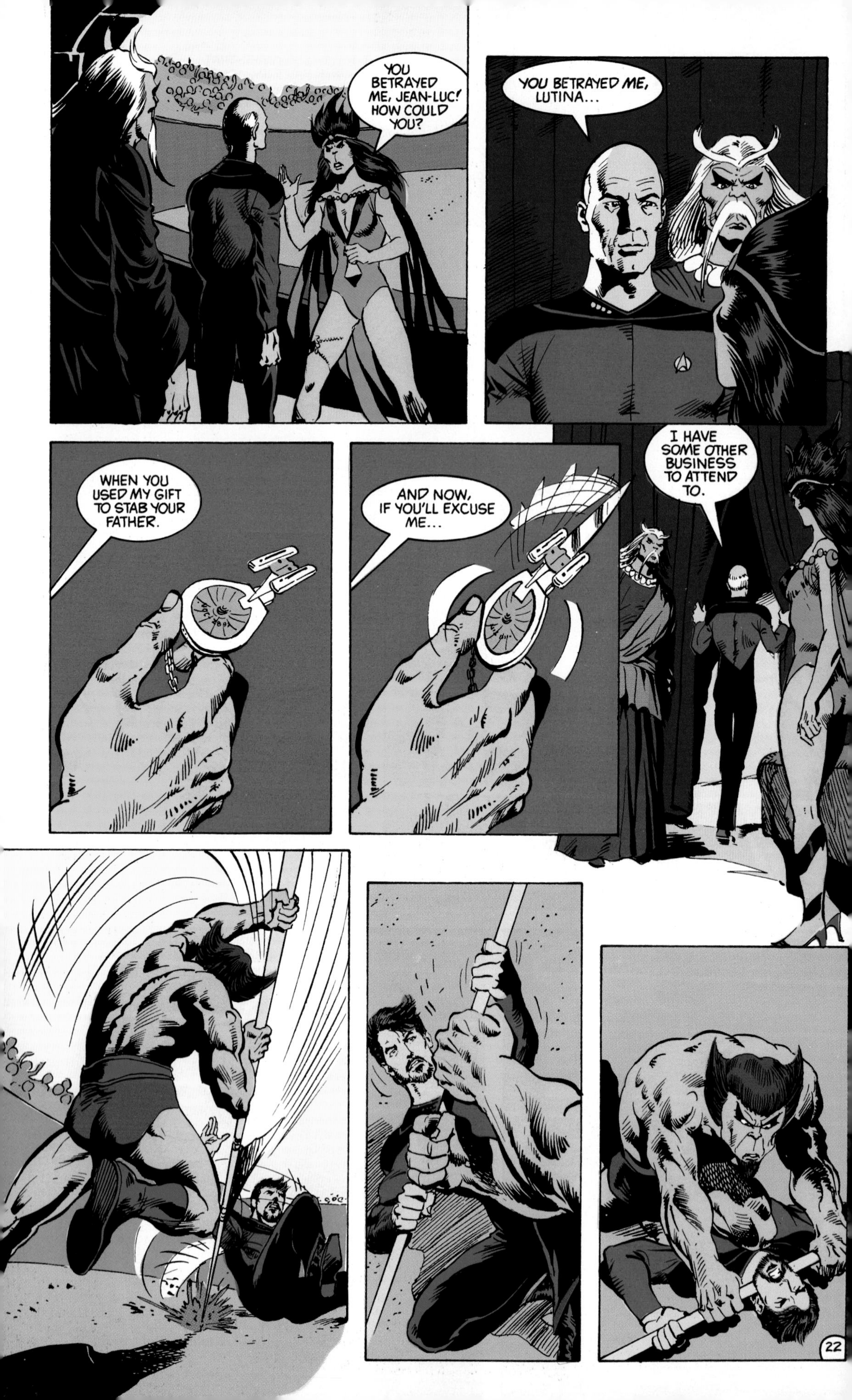
YOU BETRAYED ME, JEAN-LUC! HOW COULD YOU?
YOU BETRAYED *ME*, LUTINA...
WHEN YOU USED MY GIFT TO STAB YOUR FATHER.
AND NOW, IF YOU'LL EXCUSE ME...
I HAVE SOME OTHER BUSINESS TO ATTEND TO.

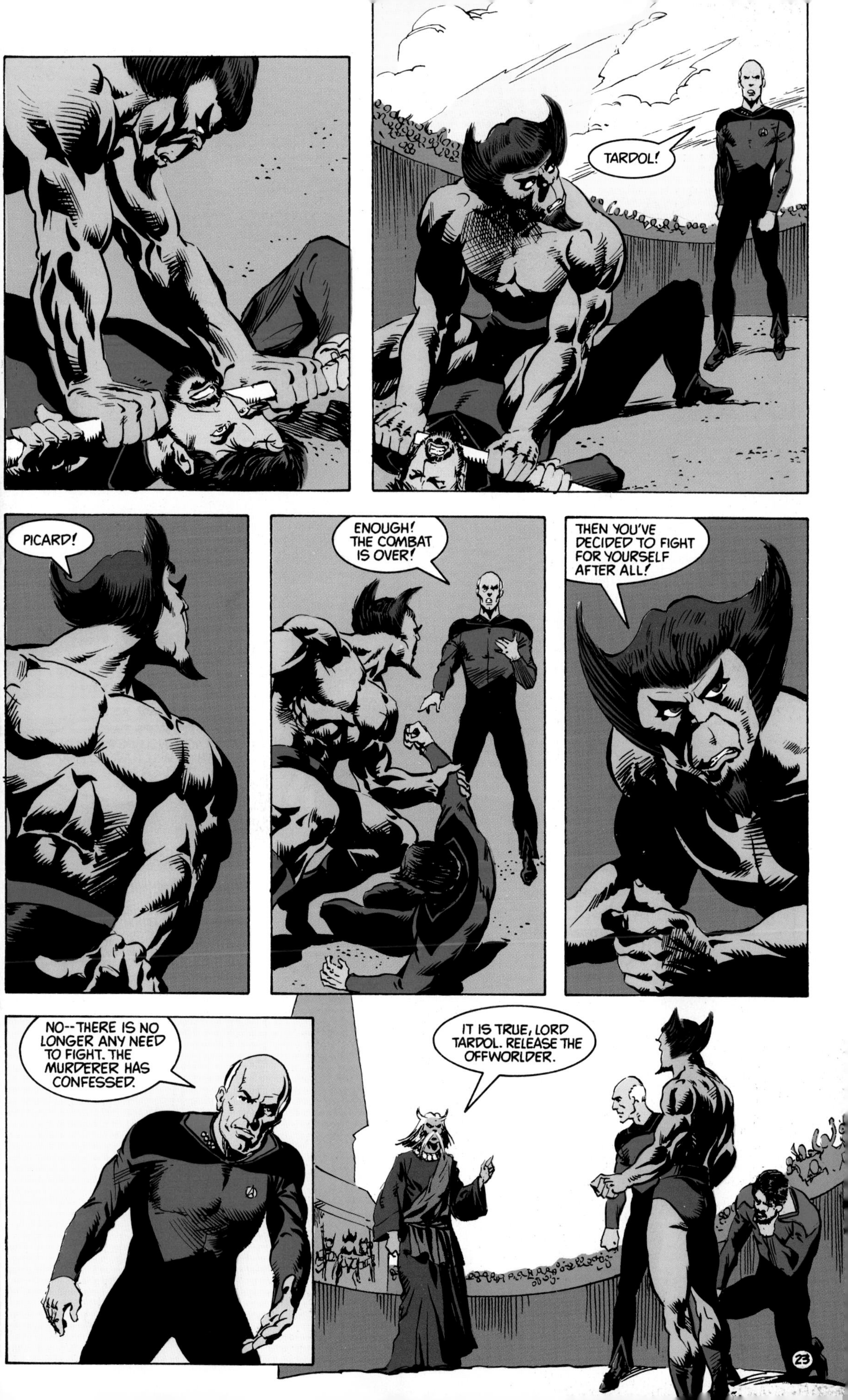

TARDOL!
PICARD!
ENOUGH! THE COMBAT IS OVER!
THEN YOU'VE DECIDED TO FIGHT FOR YOURSELF AFTER ALL!
NO--THERE IS NO LONGER ANY NEED TO FIGHT. THE MURDERER HAS CONFESSED.
IT IS TRUE, LORD TARDOL. RELEASE THE OFFWORLDER.

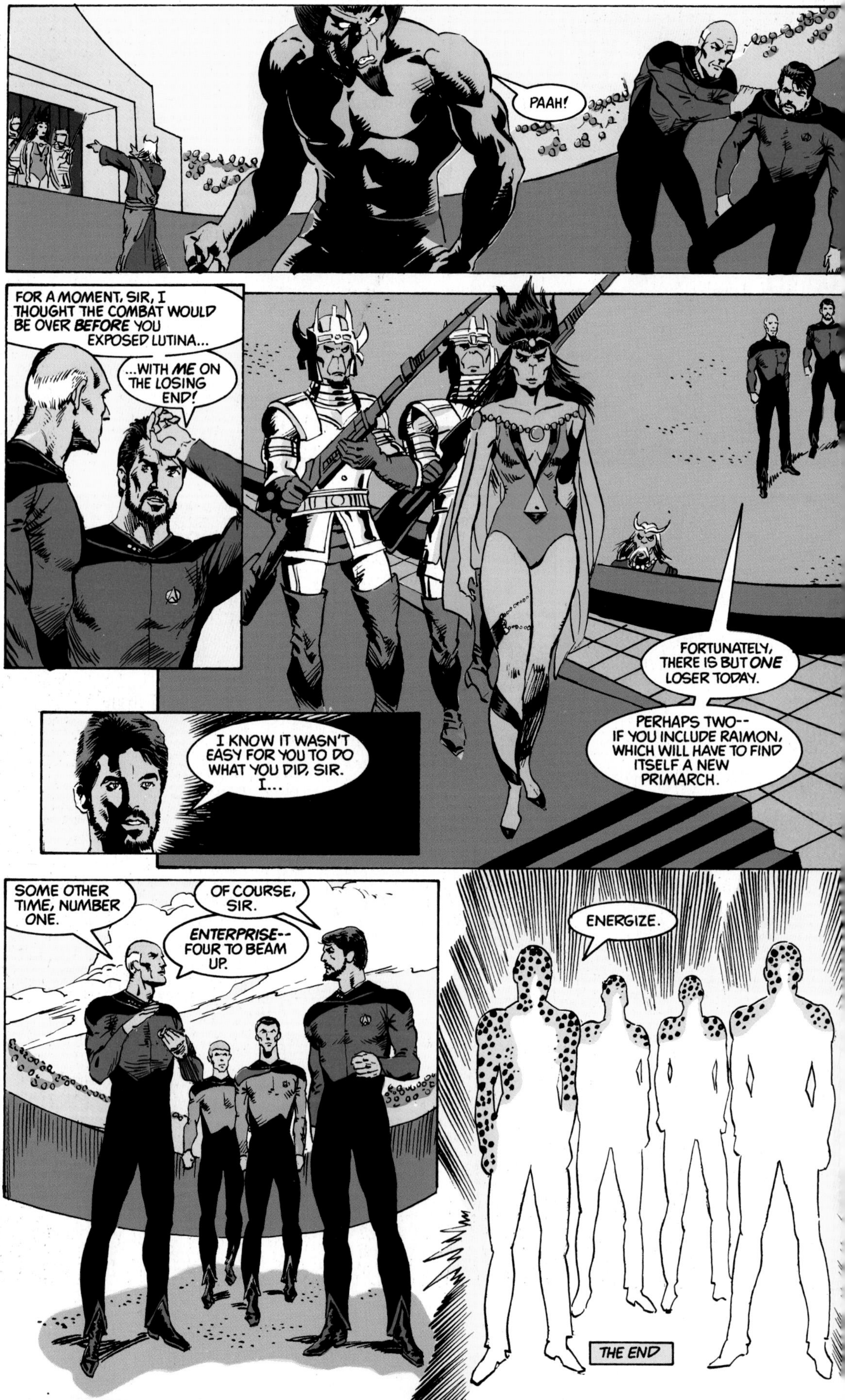
PAAH!
FOR A MOMENT, SIR, I THOUGHT THE COMBAT WOULD BE OVER BEFORE YOU EXPOSED LUTINA...
...WITH ME ON THE LOSING END!
FORTUNATELY, THERE IS BUT ONE LOSER TODAY.
PERHAPS TWO-- IF YOU INCLUDE RAIMON, WHICH WILL HAVE TO FIND ITSELF A NEW PRIMARCH.
I KNOW IT WASN'T EASY FOR YOU TO DO WHAT YOU DID, SIR. I...
SOME OTHER TIME, NUMBER ONE.
OF COURSE, SIR.
ENTERPRISE-- FOUR TO BEAM UP.
ENERGIZE.
THE END

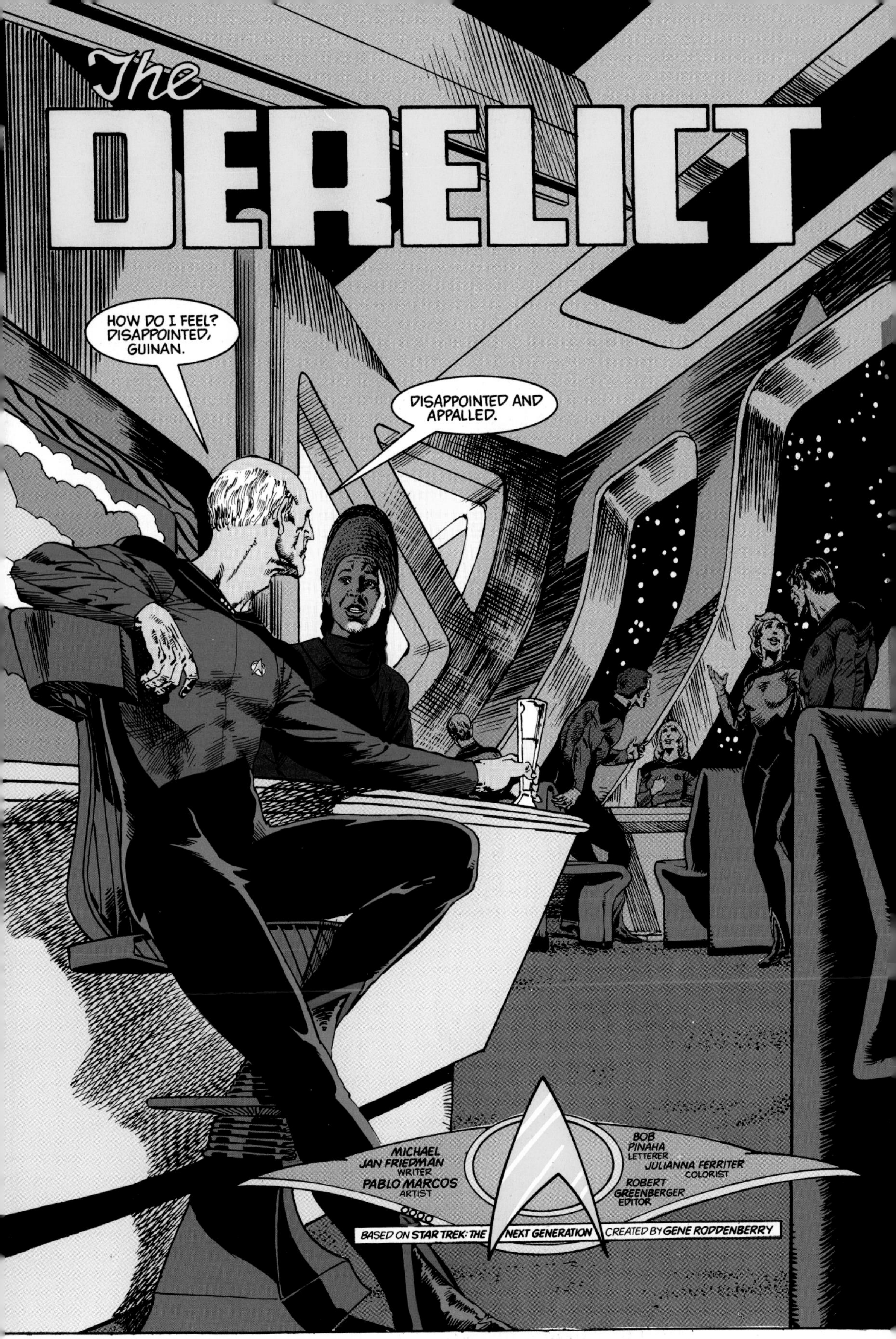
The
DERELICT
HOW DO I FEEL? DISAPPOINTED, GUINAN.
DISAPPOINTED AND APPALLED.
MICHAEL JAN FRIEDMAN WRITER
PABLO MARCOS ARTIST
BOB PINAHA LETTERER
JULIANNA FERRITER COLORIST
ROBERT GREENBERGER EDITOR
BASED ON STAR TREK: THE NEXT GENERATION CREATED BY GENE RODDENBERRY

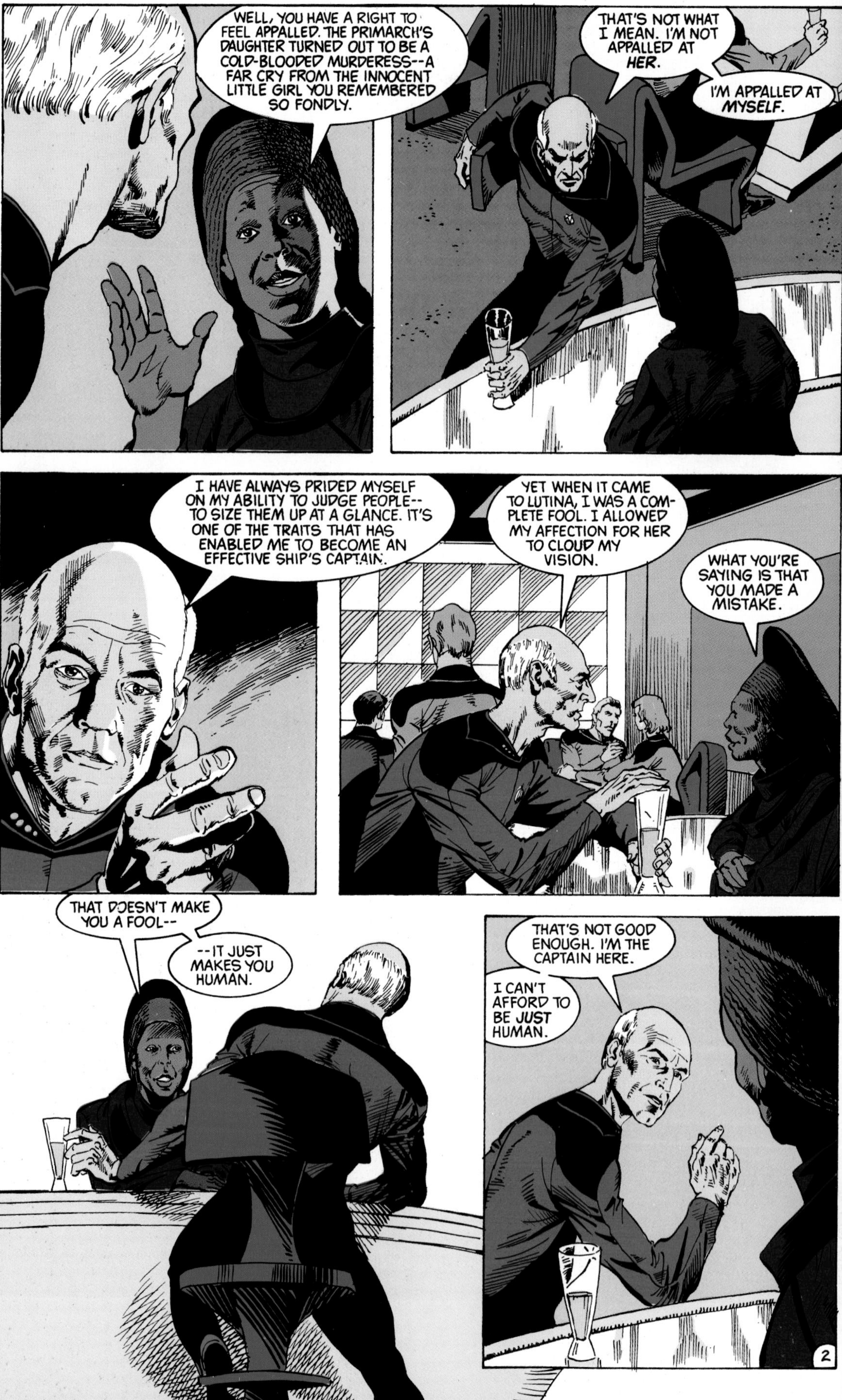
WELL, YOU HAVE A RIGHT TO FEEL APPALLED. THE PRIMARCH'S DAUGHTER TURNED OUT TO BE A COLD-BLOODED MURDERESS--A FAR CRY FROM THE INNOCENT LITTLE GIRL YOU REMEMBERED SO FONDLY.
THAT'S NOT WHAT I MEAN. I'M NOT APPALLED AT **HER**.
I'M APPALLED AT **MYSELF**.
I HAVE ALWAYS PRIDED MYSELF ON MY ABILITY TO JUDGE PEOPLE--TO SIZE THEM UP AT A GLANCE. IT'S ONE OF THE TRAITS THAT HAS ENABLED ME TO BECOME AN EFFECTIVE SHIP'S CAPTAIN.
YET WHEN IT CAME TO LUTINA, I WAS A COMPLETE FOOL. I ALLOWED MY AFFECTION FOR HER TO CLOUD MY VISION.
WHAT YOU'RE SAYING IS THAT YOU MADE A MISTAKE.
THAT DOESN'T MAKE YOU A FOOL--
--IT JUST MAKES YOU HUMAN.
THAT'S NOT GOOD ENOUGH. I'M THE CAPTAIN HERE.
I CAN'T AFFORD TO BE **JUST** HUMAN.
2

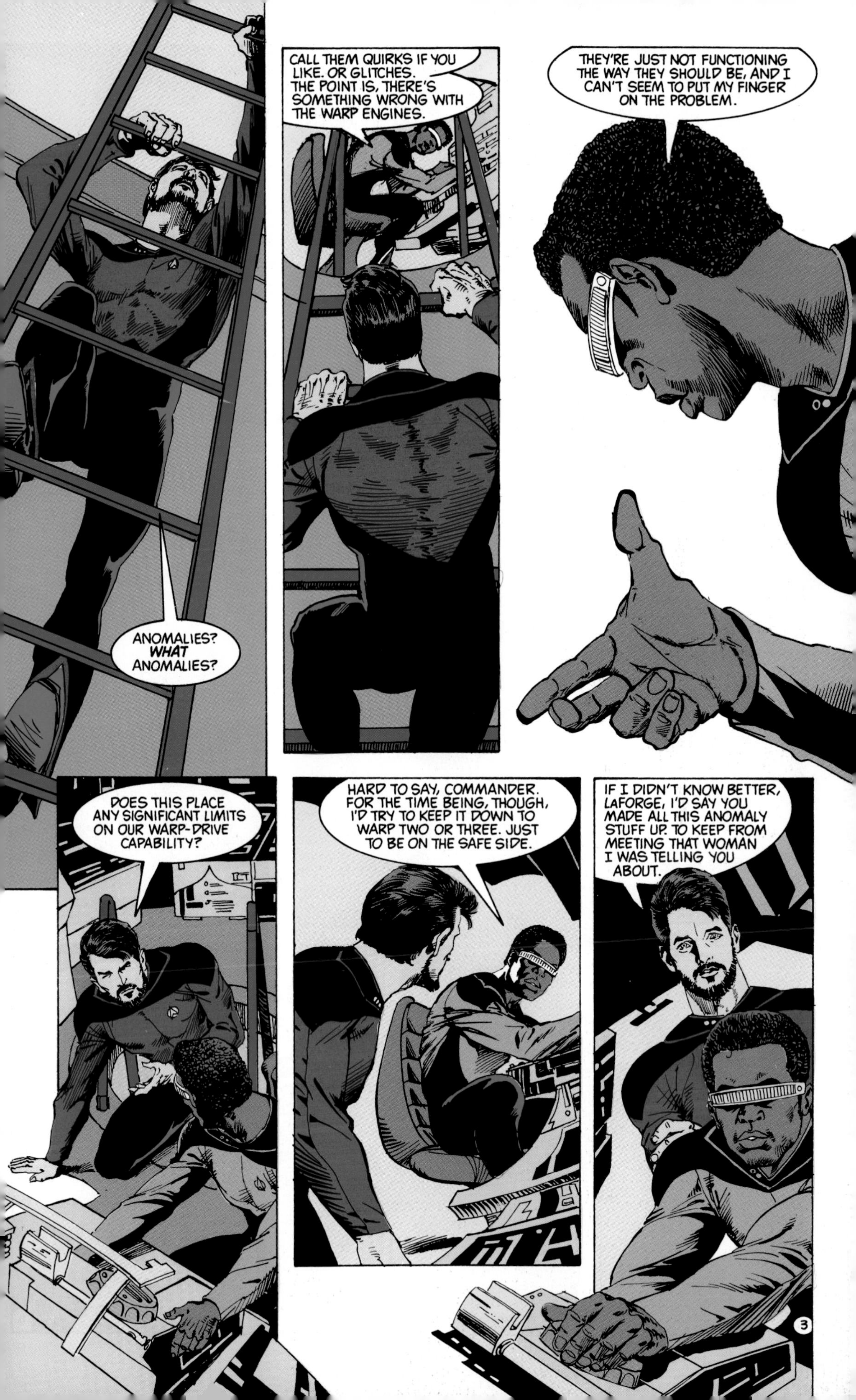
ANOMALIES? WHAT ANOMALIES?
CALL THEM QUIRKS IF YOU LIKE. OR GLITCHES. THE POINT IS, THERE'S SOMETHING WRONG WITH THE WARP ENGINES.
THEY'RE JUST NOT FUNCTIONING THE WAY THEY SHOULD BE, AND I CAN'T SEEM TO PUT MY FINGER ON THE PROBLEM.
DOES THIS PLACE ANY SIGNIFICANT LIMITS ON OUR WARP-DRIVE CAPABILITY?
HARD TO SAY, COMMANDER. FOR THE TIME BEING, THOUGH, I'D TRY TO KEEP IT DOWN TO WARP TWO OR THREE. JUST TO BE ON THE SAFE SIDE.
IF I DIDN'T KNOW BETTER, LAFORGE, I'D SAY YOU MADE ALL THIS ANOMALY STUFF UP. TO KEEP FROM MEETING THAT WOMAN I WAS TELLING YOU ABOUT.

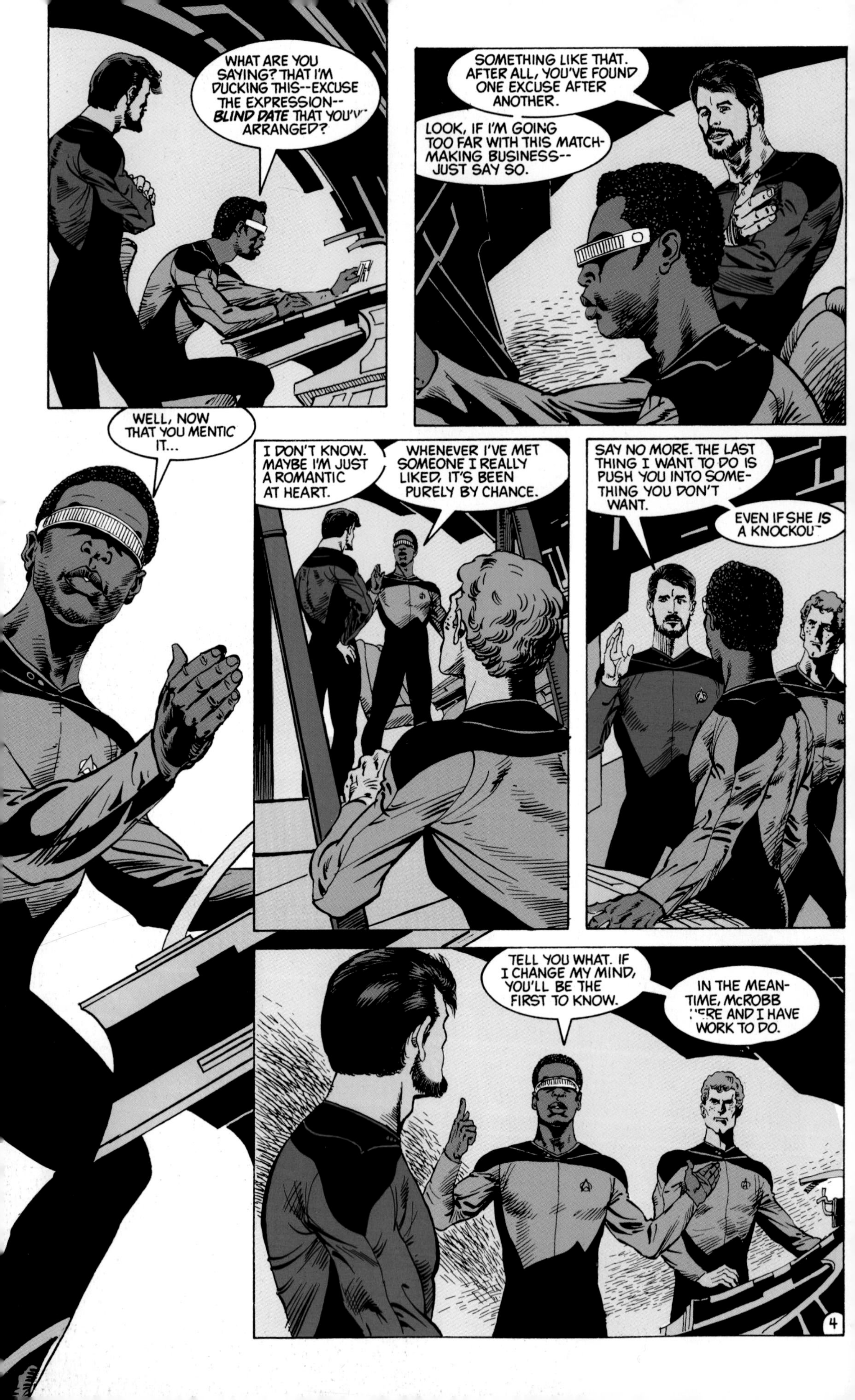
WHAT ARE YOU SAYING? THAT I'M DUCKING THIS--EXCUSE THE EXPRESSION-- *BLIND DATE* THAT YOU'V ARRANGED?
SOMETHING LIKE THAT. AFTER ALL, YOU'VE FOUND ONE EXCUSE AFTER ANOTHER.
LOOK, IF I'M GOING TOO FAR WITH THIS MATCH-MAKING BUSINESS-- JUST SAY SO.
WELL, NOW THAT YOU MENTIC IT...
I DON'T KNOW. MAYBE I'M JUST A ROMANTIC AT HEART.
WHENEVER I'VE MET SOMEONE I REALLY LIKED, IT'S BEEN PURELY BY CHANCE.
SAY NO MORE. THE LAST THING I WANT TO DO IS PUSH YOU INTO SOME-THING YOU DON'T WANT.
EVEN IF SHE *IS* A KNOCKOU
TELL YOU WHAT. IF I CHANGE MY MIND, YOU'LL BE THE FIRST TO KNOW.
IN THE MEAN-TIME, McROBB HERE AND I HAVE WORK TO DO.

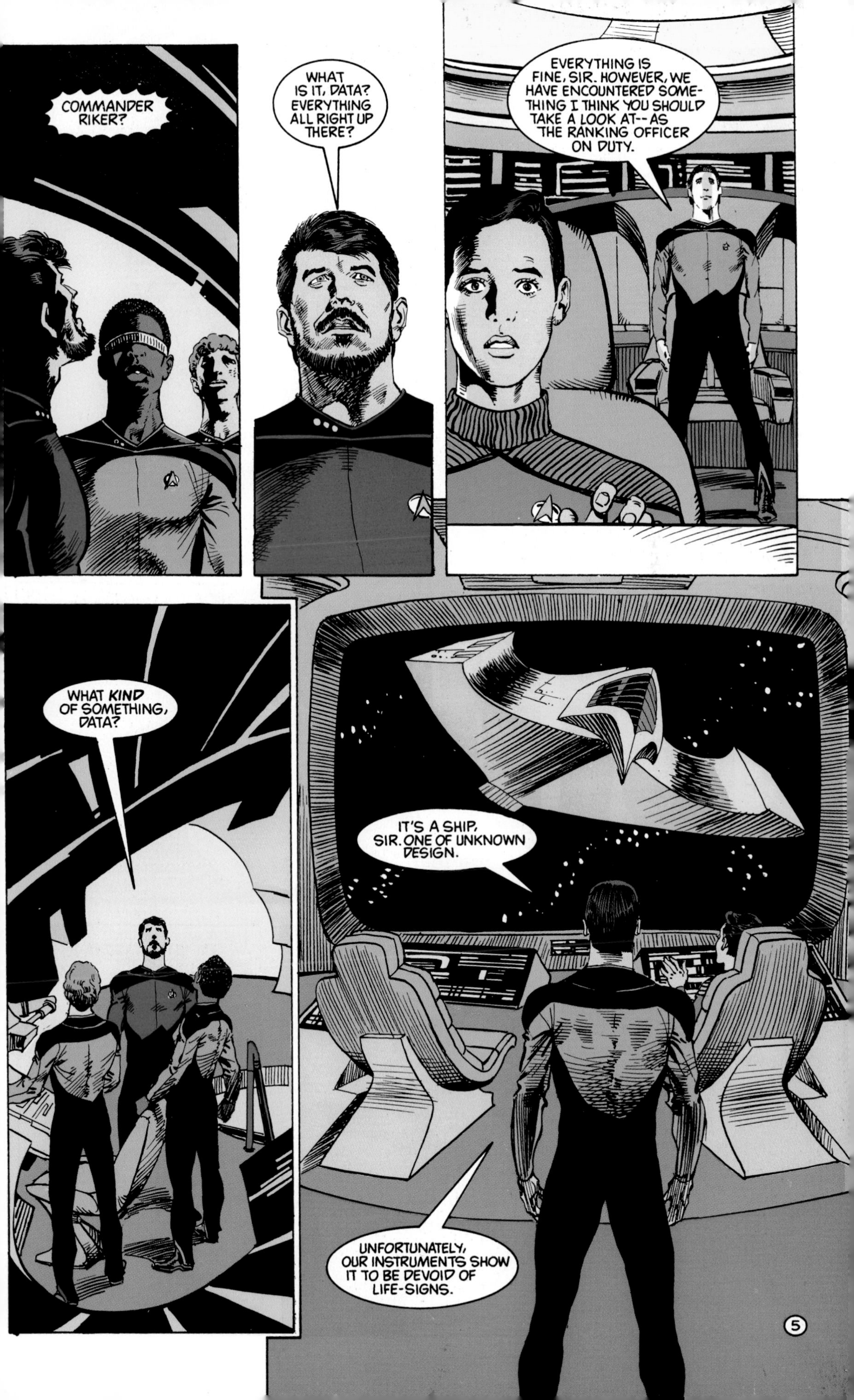
COMMANDER RIKER?
WHAT IS IT, DATA? EVERYTHING ALL RIGHT UP THERE?
EVERYTHING IS FINE, SIR. HOWEVER, WE HAVE ENCOUNTERED SOMETHING I THINK YOU SHOULD TAKE A LOOK AT-- AS THE RANKING OFFICER ON DUTY.
WHAT KIND OF SOMETHING, DATA?
IT'S A SHIP, SIR. ONE OF UNKNOWN DESIGN.
UNFORTUNATELY, OUR INSTRUMENTS SHOW IT TO BE DEVOID OF LIFE-SIGNS.
5

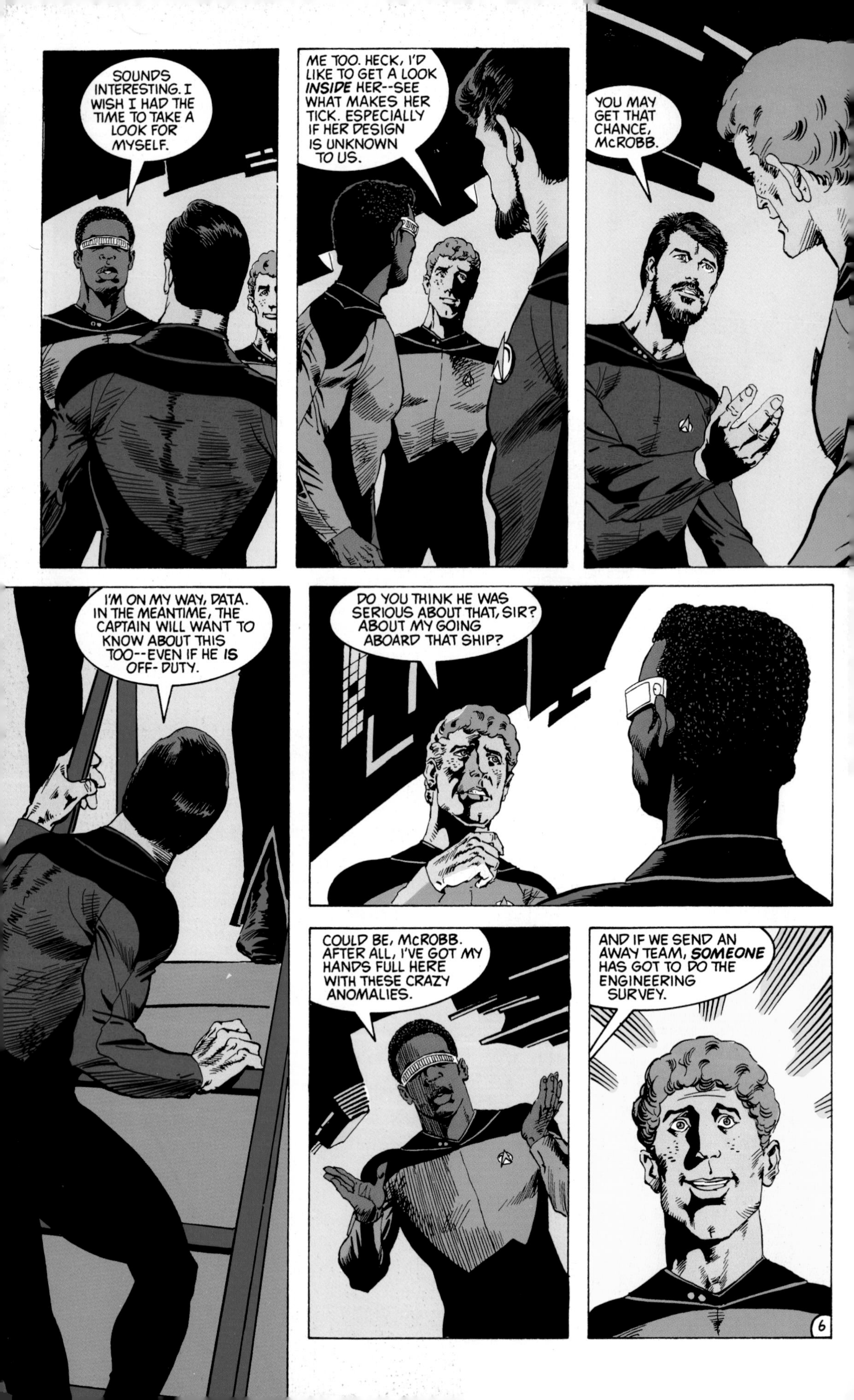
SOUNDS INTERESTING. I WISH I HAD THE TIME TO TAKE A LOOK FOR MYSELF.
ME TOO. HECK, I'D LIKE TO GET A LOOK INSIDE HER--SEE WHAT MAKES HER TICK. ESPECIALLY IF HER DESIGN IS UNKNOWN TO US.
YOU MAY GET THAT CHANCE, McROBB.
I'M ON MY WAY, DATA. IN THE MEANTIME, THE CAPTAIN WILL WANT TO KNOW ABOUT THIS TOO--EVEN IF HE IS OFF-DUTY.
DO YOU THINK HE WAS SERIOUS ABOUT THAT, SIR? ABOUT MY GOING ABOARD THAT SHIP?
COULD BE, McROBB. AFTER ALL, I'VE GOT MY HANDS FULL HERE WITH THESE CRAZY ANOMALIES.
AND IF WE SEND AN AWAY TEAM, SOMEONE HAS GOT TO DO THE ENGINEERING SURVEY.
6

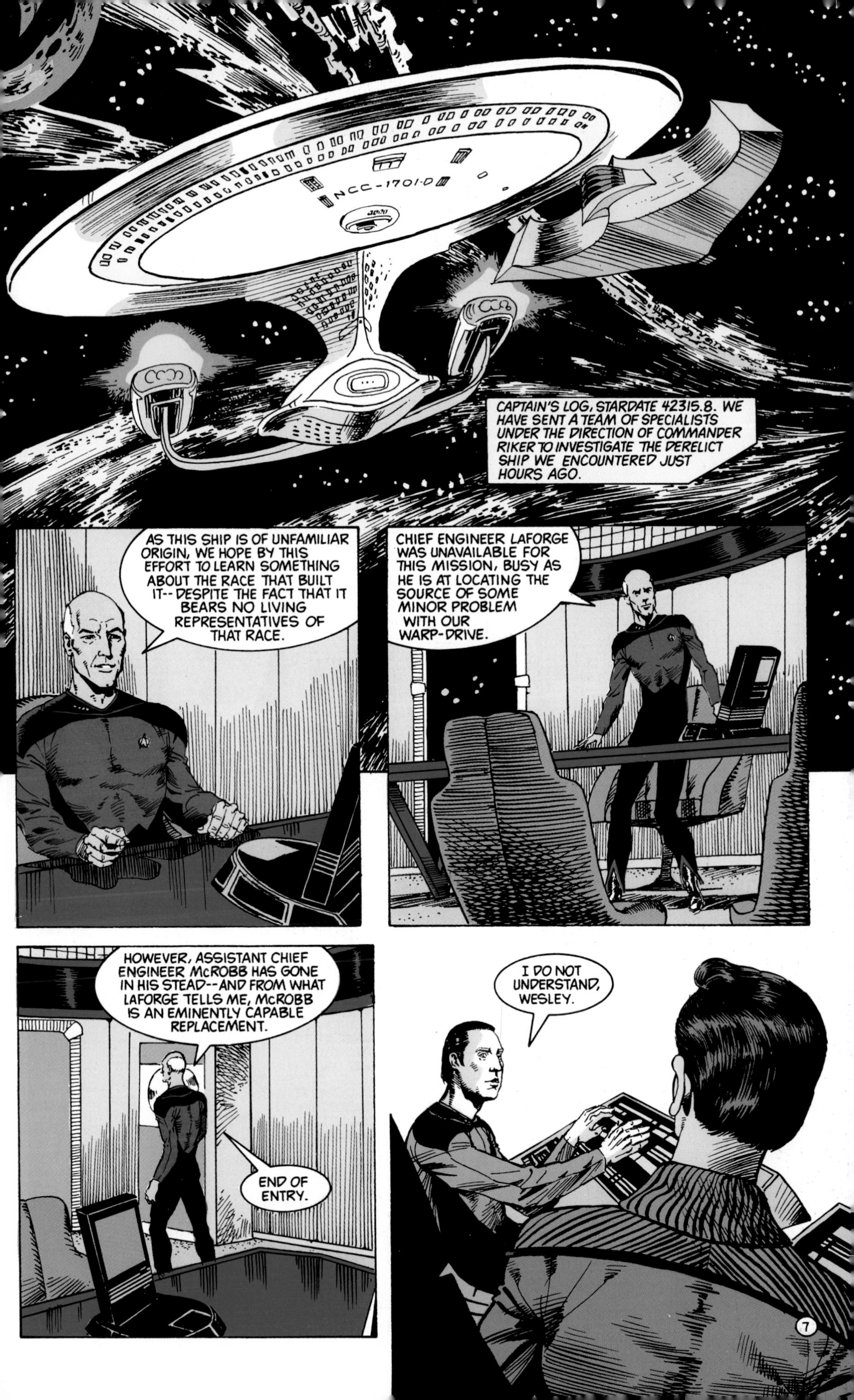

CAPTAIN'S LOG, STARDATE 42315.8. WE HAVE SENT A TEAM OF SPECIALISTS UNDER THE DIRECTION OF COMMANDER RIKER TO INVESTIGATE THE DERELICT SHIP WE ENCOUNTERED JUST HOURS AGO.
AS THIS SHIP IS OF UNFAMILIAR ORIGIN, WE HOPE BY THIS EFFORT TO LEARN SOMETHING ABOUT THE RACE THAT BUILT IT-- DESPITE THE FACT THAT IT BEARS NO LIVING REPRESENTATIVES OF THAT RACE.
CHIEF ENGINEER LAFORGE WAS UNAVAILABLE FOR THIS MISSION, BUSY AS HE IS AT LOCATING THE SOURCE OF SOME MINOR PROBLEM WITH OUR WARP-DRIVE.
HOWEVER, ASSISTANT CHIEF ENGINEER McROBB HAS GONE IN HIS STEAD--AND FROM WHAT LAFORGE TELLS ME, McROBB IS AN EMINENTLY CAPABLE REPLACEMENT.
END OF ENTRY.
I DO NOT UNDERSTAND, WESLEY.

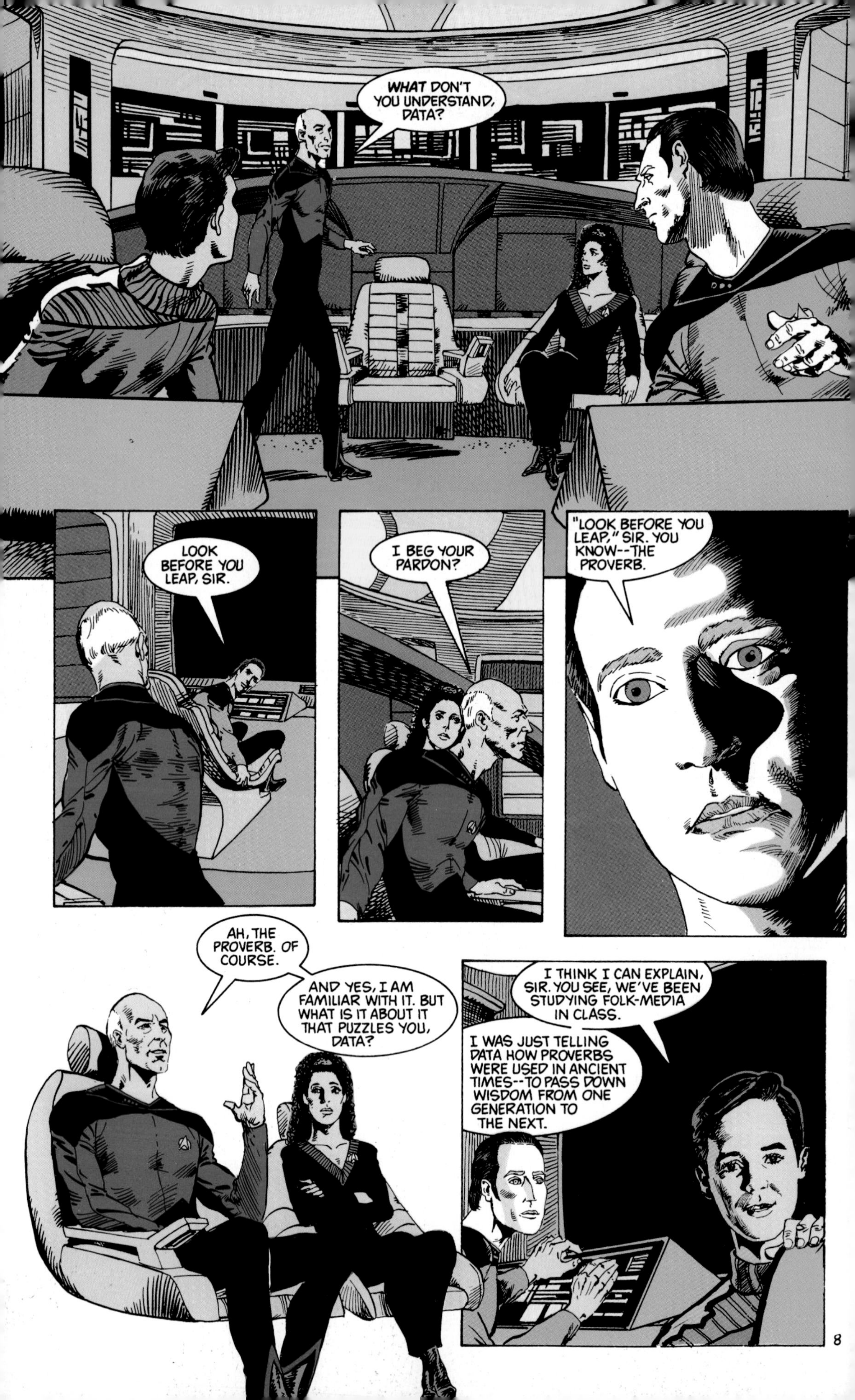
WHAT DON'T YOU UNDERSTAND, DATA?
LOOK BEFORE YOU LEAP, SIR.
I BEG YOUR PARDON?
"LOOK BEFORE YOU LEAP," SIR. YOU KNOW--THE PROVERB.
AH, THE PROVERB. OF COURSE.
AND YES, I AM FAMILIAR WITH IT. BUT WHAT IS IT ABOUT IT THAT PUZZLES YOU, DATA?
I THINK I CAN EXPLAIN, SIR. YOU SEE, WE'VE BEEN STUDYING FOLK-MEDIA IN CLASS.
I WAS JUST TELLING DATA HOW PROVERBS WERE USED IN ANCIENT TIMES--TO PASS DOWN WISDOM FROM ONE GENERATION TO THE NEXT.

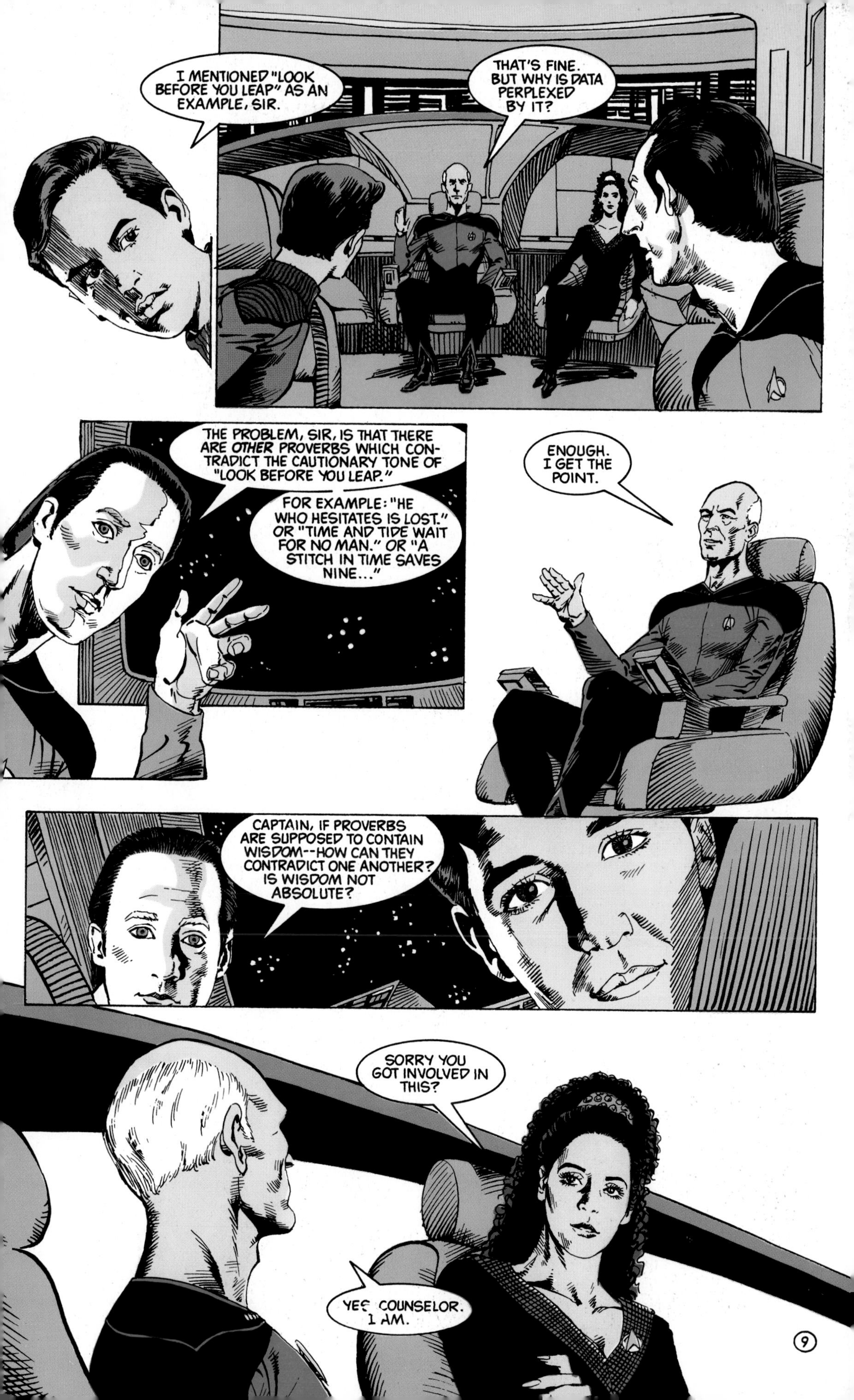
I MENTIONED "LOOK BEFORE YOU LEAP" AS AN EXAMPLE, SIR.
THAT'S FINE. BUT WHY IS DATA PERPLEXED BY IT?
THE PROBLEM, SIR, IS THAT THERE ARE *OTHER* PROVERBS WHICH CONTRADICT THE CAUTIONARY TONE OF "LOOK BEFORE YOU LEAP."
FOR EXAMPLE: "HE WHO HESITATES IS LOST." OR "TIME AND TIDE WAIT FOR NO MAN." OR "A STITCH IN TIME SAVES NINE..."
ENOUGH. I GET THE POINT.
CAPTAIN, IF PROVERBS ARE SUPPOSED TO CONTAIN WISDOM--HOW CAN THEY CONTRADICT ONE ANOTHER? IS WISDOM NOT ABSOLUTE?
SORRY YOU GOT INVOLVED IN THIS?
YES, COUNSELOR. I AM.

HMM. OUR SENSOR READINGS WERE RIGHT ON TARGET.

THERE ARE NO SIGNS OF LIFE HERE-- NONE AT ALL.

THAT'S TOO BAD. DO ANY EXPLANATIONS JUMP OUT AT YOU, DOCTOR?

I'M AFRAID NOT. THERE ARE NO TOXINS PRESENT, NO SIGNIFICANT LEVELS OF RADIATION.

OF COURSE, SINCE WE DON'T KNOW ANYTHING ABOUT THE INHABITANTS, IT'S HARD TO GUESS WHAT MIGHT HAVE BEEN HARMFUL TO THEM.

NO DAMAGE THAT I CAN SEE, COMMANDER. IF THERE WAS AN ACCIDENT, IT TOOK PLACE ELSEWHERE ON THE SHIP.

THERE MAY NOT BE ANY LIFE HERE, BUT THIS SHIP IS FAR FROM DEAD. I'M GETTING AN ENERGY-SOURCE READING FROM FARTHER FORWARD.

I WONDER WHY WE DIDN'T PICK THAT UP BACK ON THE ENTERPRISE?

MISTER RIKER! I'VE FOUND THE ENTRANCE TO THE NEXT COMPARTMENT, SIR!

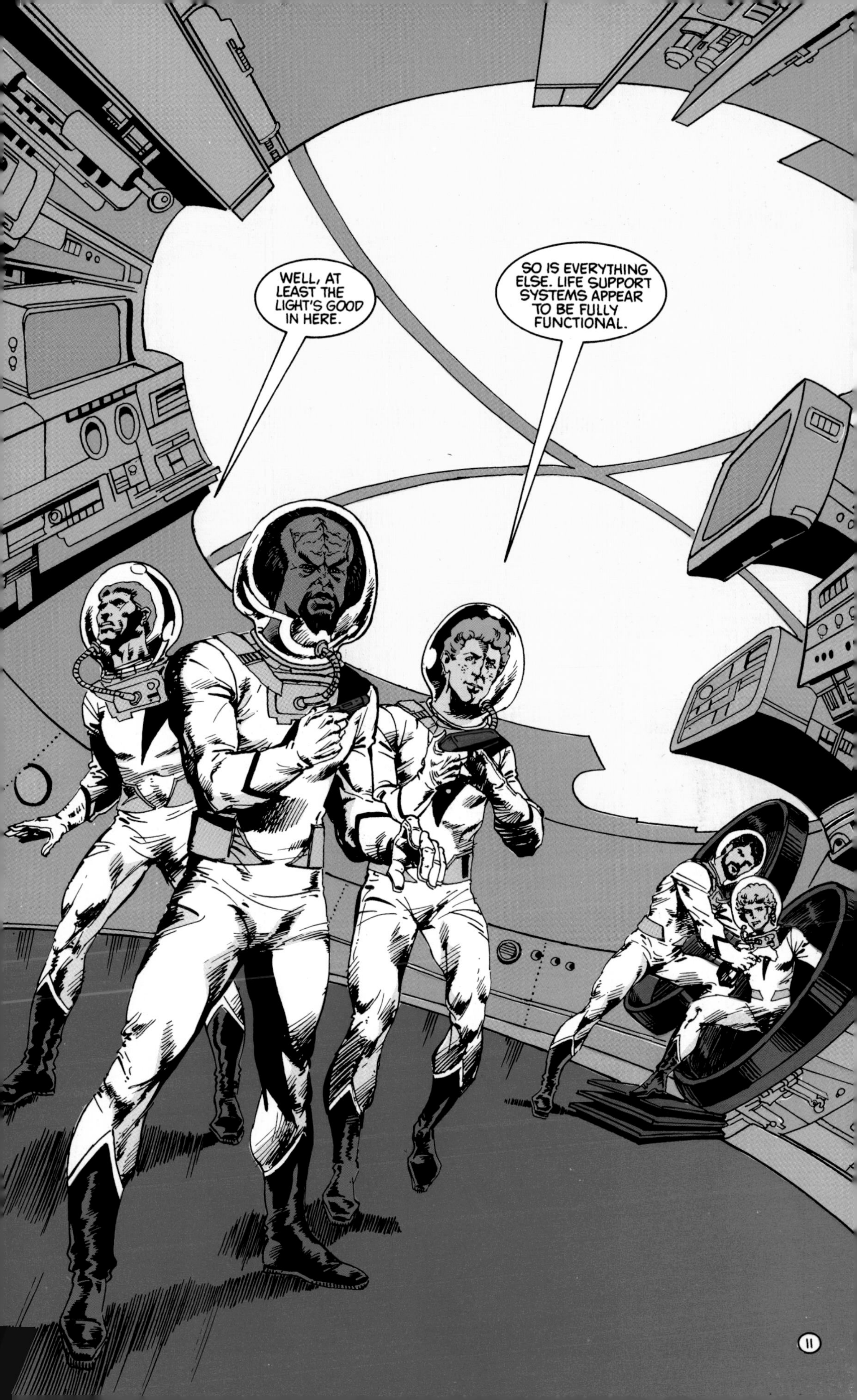
WELL, AT LEAST THE LIGHT'S GOOD IN HERE.
SO IS EVERYTHING ELSE. LIFE SUPPORT SYSTEMS APPEAR TO BE FULLY FUNCTIONAL.

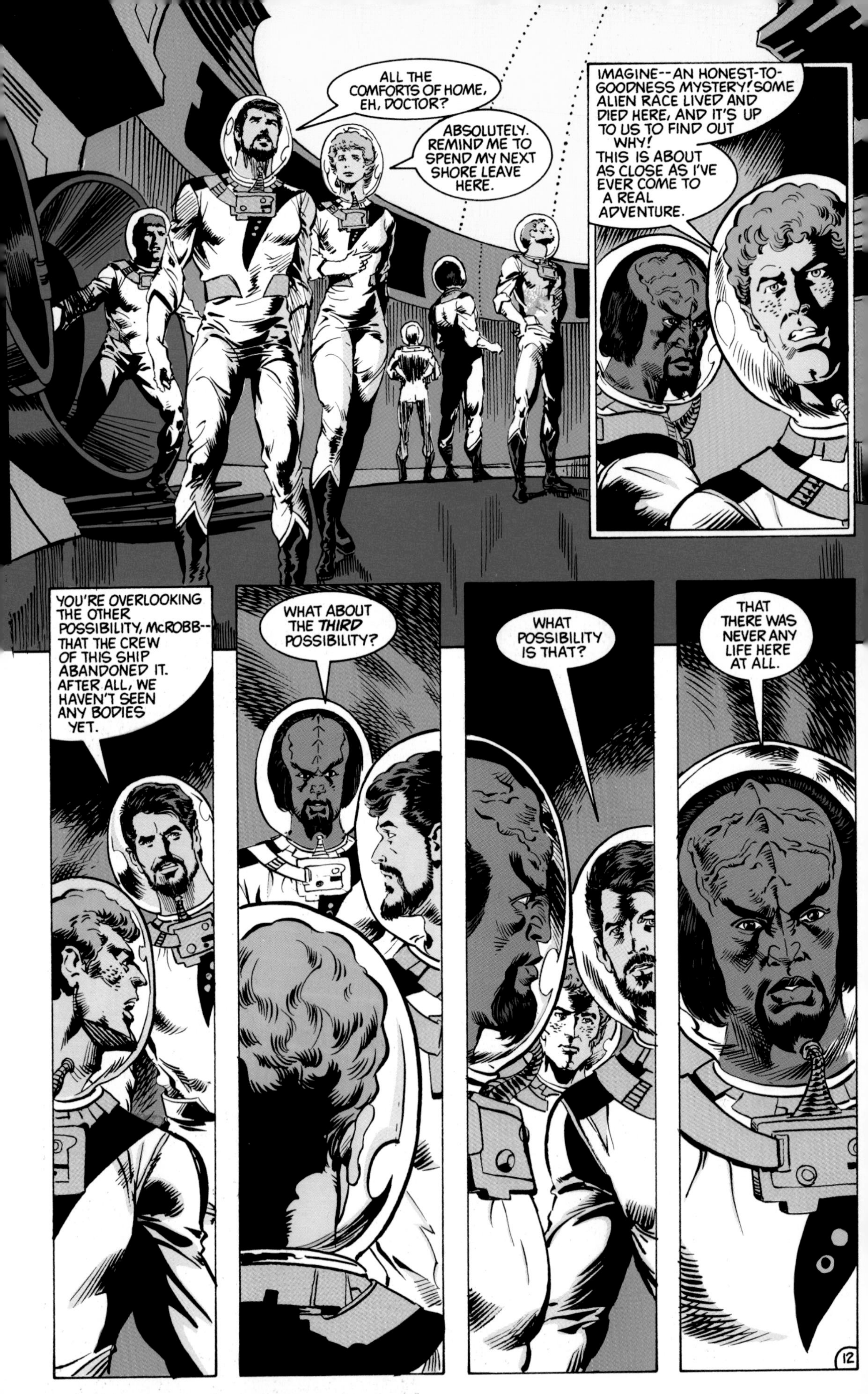
ALL THE COMFORTS OF HOME, EH, DOCTOR?
ABSOLUTELY. REMIND ME TO SPEND MY NEXT SHORE LEAVE HERE.
IMAGINE--AN HONEST-TO-GOODNESS MYSTERY! SOME ALIEN RACE LIVED AND DIED HERE, AND IT'S UP TO US TO FIND OUT WHY!
THIS IS ABOUT AS CLOSE AS I'VE EVER COME TO A REAL ADVENTURE.
YOU'RE OVERLOOKING THE OTHER POSSIBILITY, McROBB--THAT THE CREW OF THIS SHIP ABANDONED IT. AFTER ALL, WE HAVEN'T SEEN ANY BODIES YET.
WHAT ABOUT THE *THIRD* POSSIBILITY?
WHAT POSSIBILITY IS THAT?
THAT THERE WAS NEVER ANY LIFE HERE AT ALL.
12

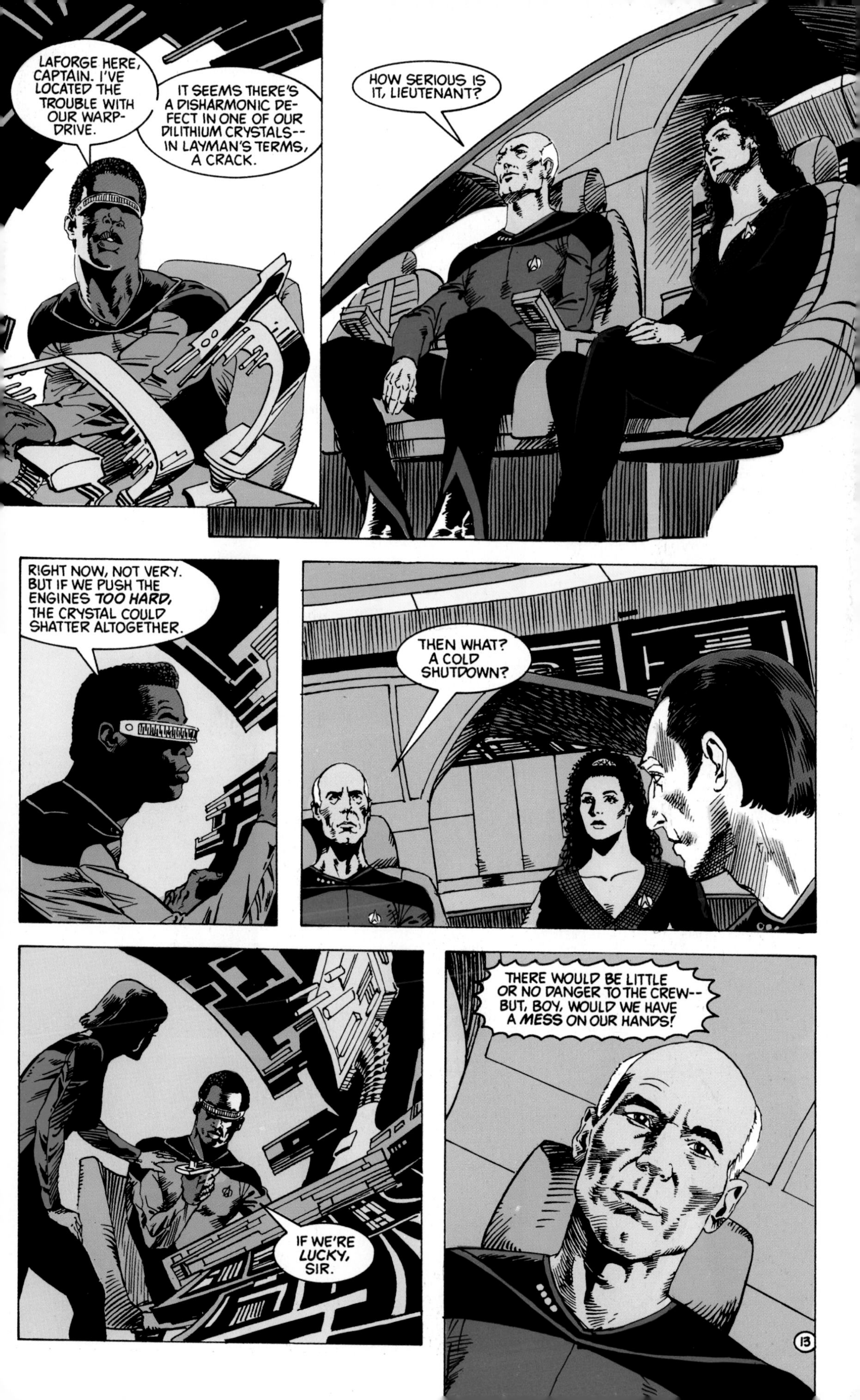
LAFORGE HERE, CAPTAIN. I'VE LOCATED THE TROUBLE WITH OUR WARP-DRIVE.
IT SEEMS THERE'S A DISHARMONIC DEFECT IN ONE OF OUR DILITHIUM CRYSTALS-- IN LAYMAN'S TERMS, A CRACK.
HOW SERIOUS IS IT, LIEUTENANT?
RIGHT NOW, NOT VERY. BUT IF WE PUSH THE ENGINES *TOO HARD,* THE CRYSTAL COULD SHATTER ALTOGETHER.
THEN WHAT? A COLD SHUTDOWN?
IF WE'RE *LUCKY,* SIR.
THERE WOULD BE LITTLE OR NO DANGER TO THE CREW-- BUT, BOY, WOULD WE HAVE A *MESS* ON OUR HANDS!
13

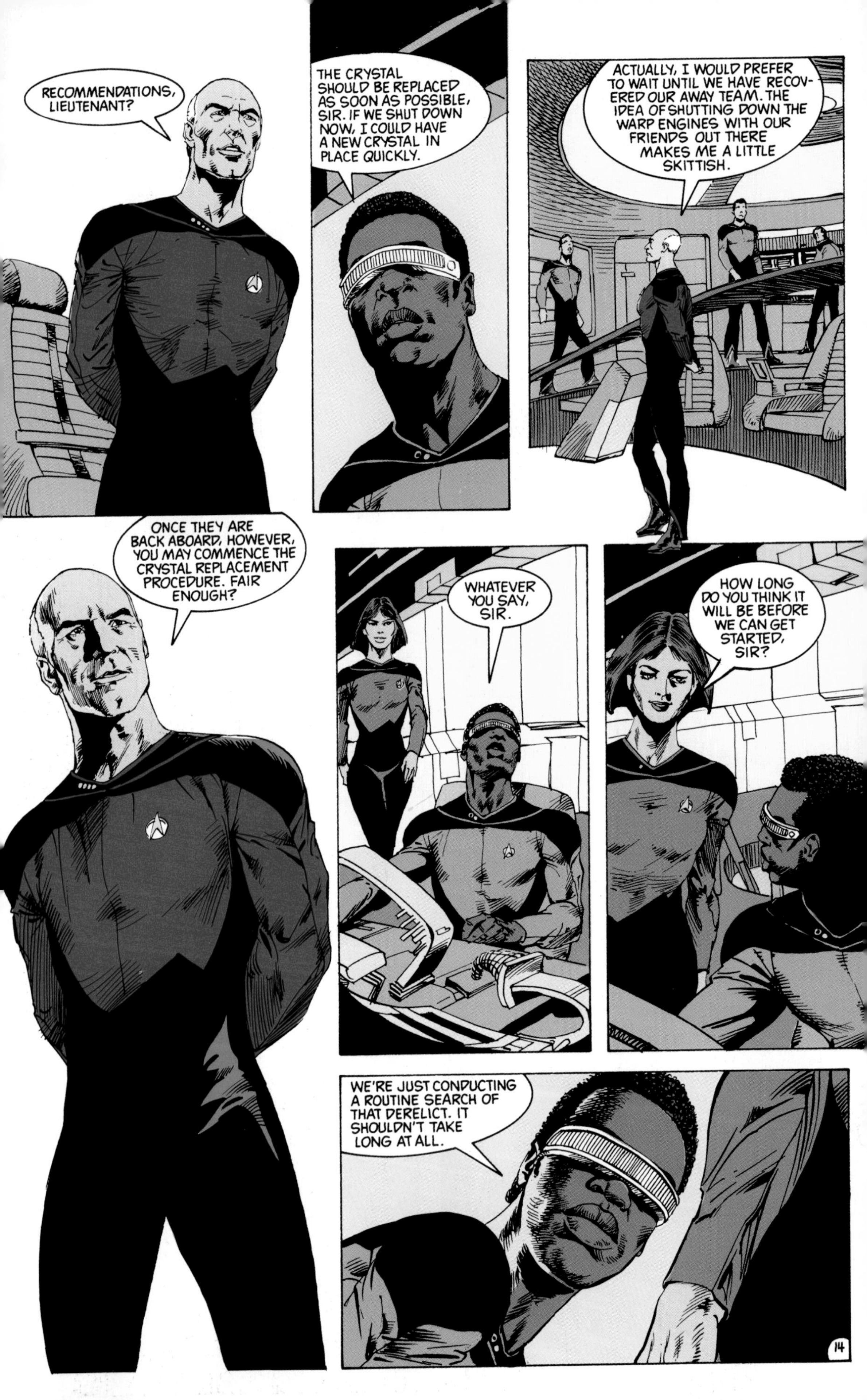
RECOMMENDATIONS, LIEUTENANT?
THE CRYSTAL SHOULD BE REPLACED AS SOON AS POSSIBLE, SIR. IF WE SHUT DOWN NOW, I COULD HAVE A NEW CRYSTAL IN PLACE QUICKLY.
ACTUALLY, I WOULD PREFER TO WAIT UNTIL WE HAVE RECOVERED OUR AWAY TEAM. THE IDEA OF SHUTTING DOWN THE WARP ENGINES WITH OUR FRIENDS OUT THERE MAKES ME A LITTLE SKITTISH.
ONCE THEY ARE BACK ABOARD, HOWEVER, YOU MAY COMMENCE THE CRYSTAL REPLACEMENT PROCEDURE. FAIR ENOUGH?
WHATEVER YOU SAY, SIR.
HOW LONG DO YOU THINK IT WILL BE BEFORE WE CAN GET STARTED, SIR?
WE'RE JUST CONDUCTING A ROUTINE SEARCH OF THAT DERELICT. IT SHOULDN'T TAKE LONG AT ALL.
14

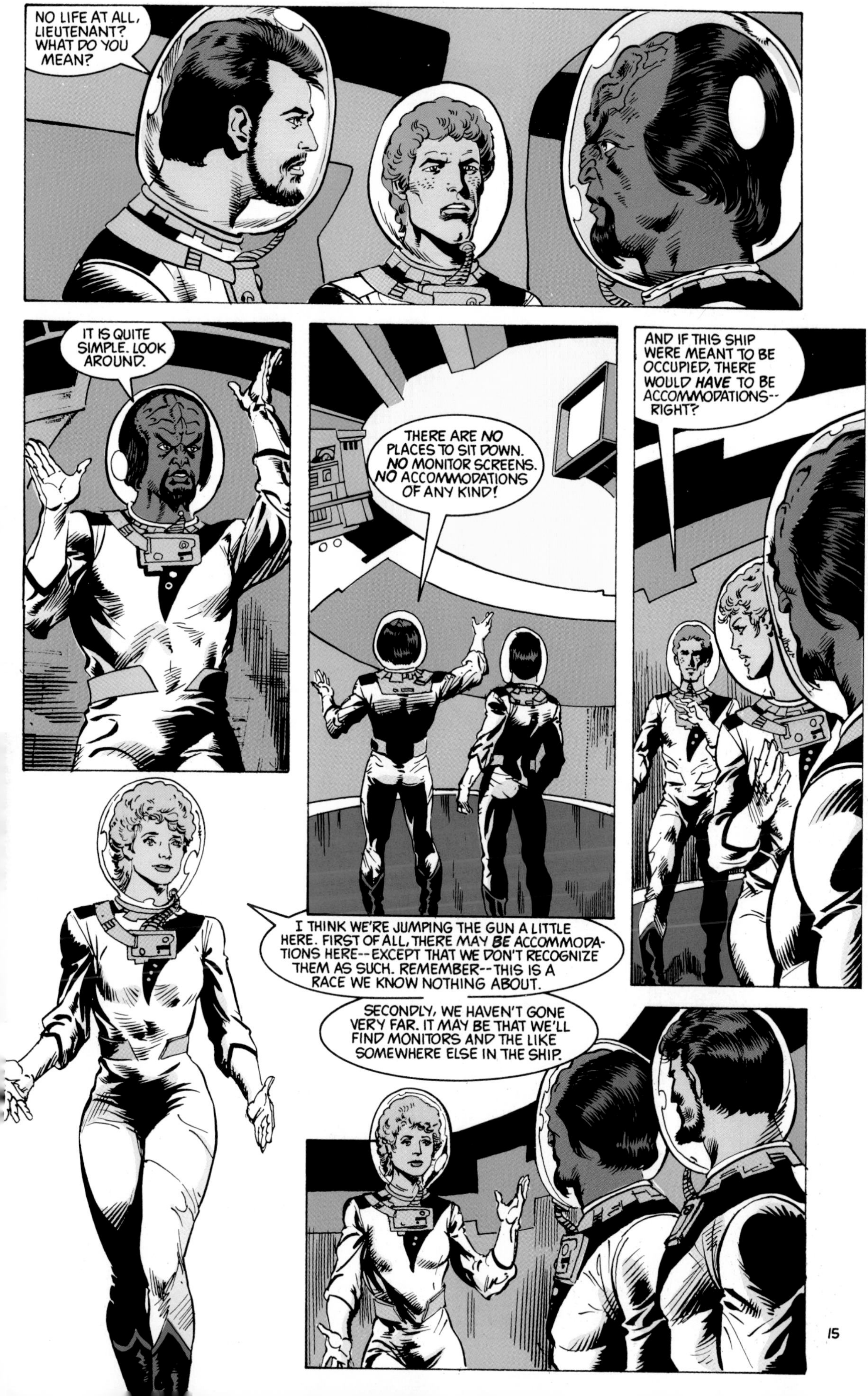
NO LIFE AT ALL, LIEUTENANT? WHAT DO YOU MEAN?
IT IS QUITE SIMPLE. LOOK AROUND.
THERE ARE NO PLACES TO SIT DOWN. NO MONITOR SCREENS. NO ACCOMMODATIONS OF ANY KIND!
AND IF THIS SHIP WERE MEANT TO BE OCCUPIED, THERE WOULD HAVE TO BE ACCOMMODATIONS-- RIGHT?
I THINK WE'RE JUMPING THE GUN A LITTLE HERE. FIRST OF ALL, THERE MAY BE ACCOMMODATIONS HERE--EXCEPT THAT WE DON'T RECOGNIZE THEM AS SUCH. REMEMBER--THIS IS A RACE WE KNOW NOTHING ABOUT.
SECONDLY, WE HAVEN'T GONE VERY FAR. IT MAY BE THAT WE'LL FIND MONITORS AND THE LIKE SOMEWHERE ELSE IN THE SHIP.

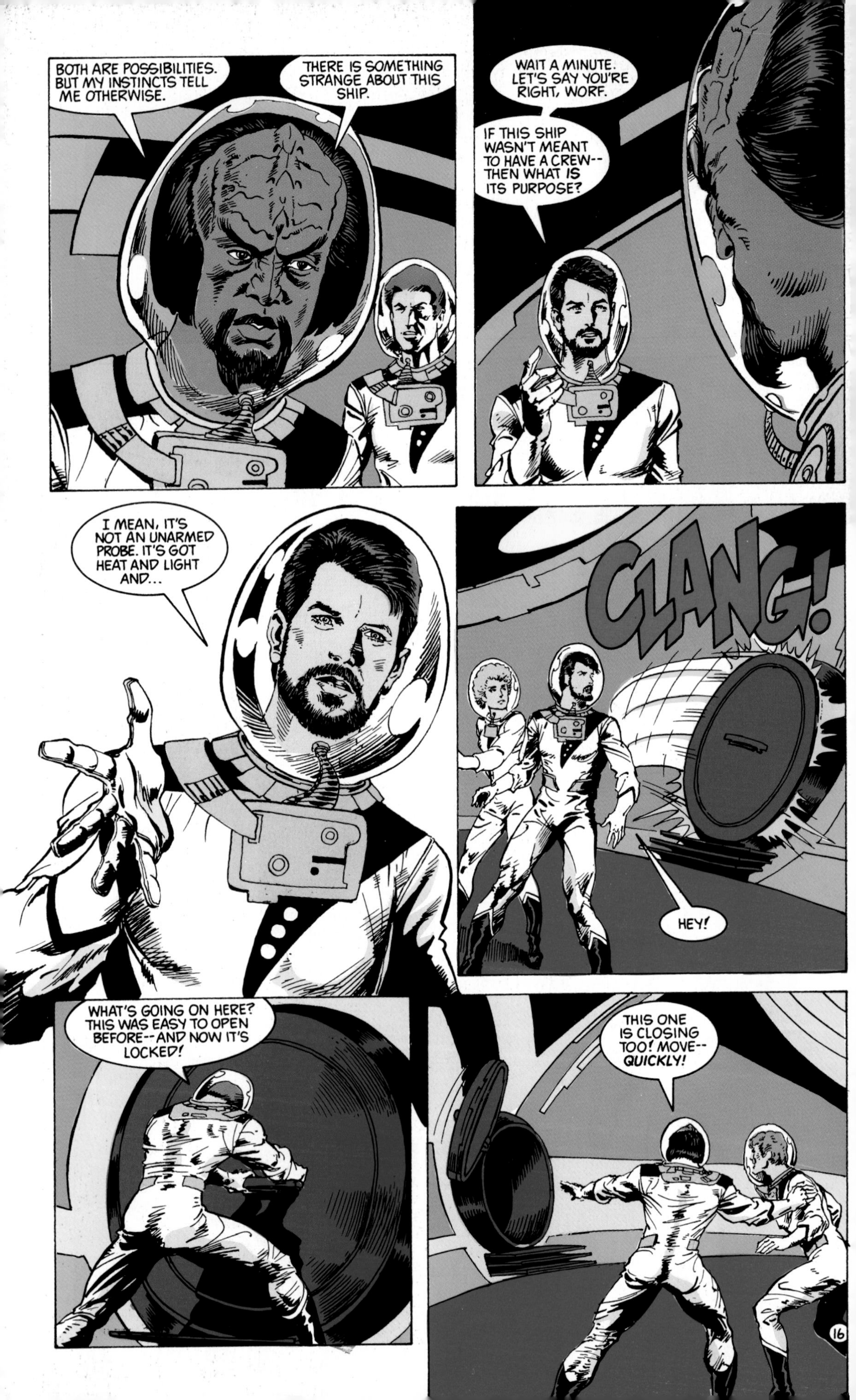
BOTH ARE POSSIBILITIES. BUT MY INSTINCTS TELL ME OTHERWISE.
THERE IS SOMETHING STRANGE ABOUT THIS SHIP.
WAIT A MINUTE. LET'S SAY YOU'RE RIGHT, WORF.
IF THIS SHIP WASN'T MEANT TO HAVE A CREW-- THEN WHAT IS ITS PURPOSE?
I MEAN, IT'S NOT AN UNARMED PROBE. IT'S GOT HEAT AND LIGHT AND...
CLANG!
HEY!
WHAT'S GOING ON HERE? THIS WAS EASY TO OPEN BEFORE--AND NOW IT'S LOCKED!
THIS ONE IS CLOSING TOO! MOVE-- QUICKLY!

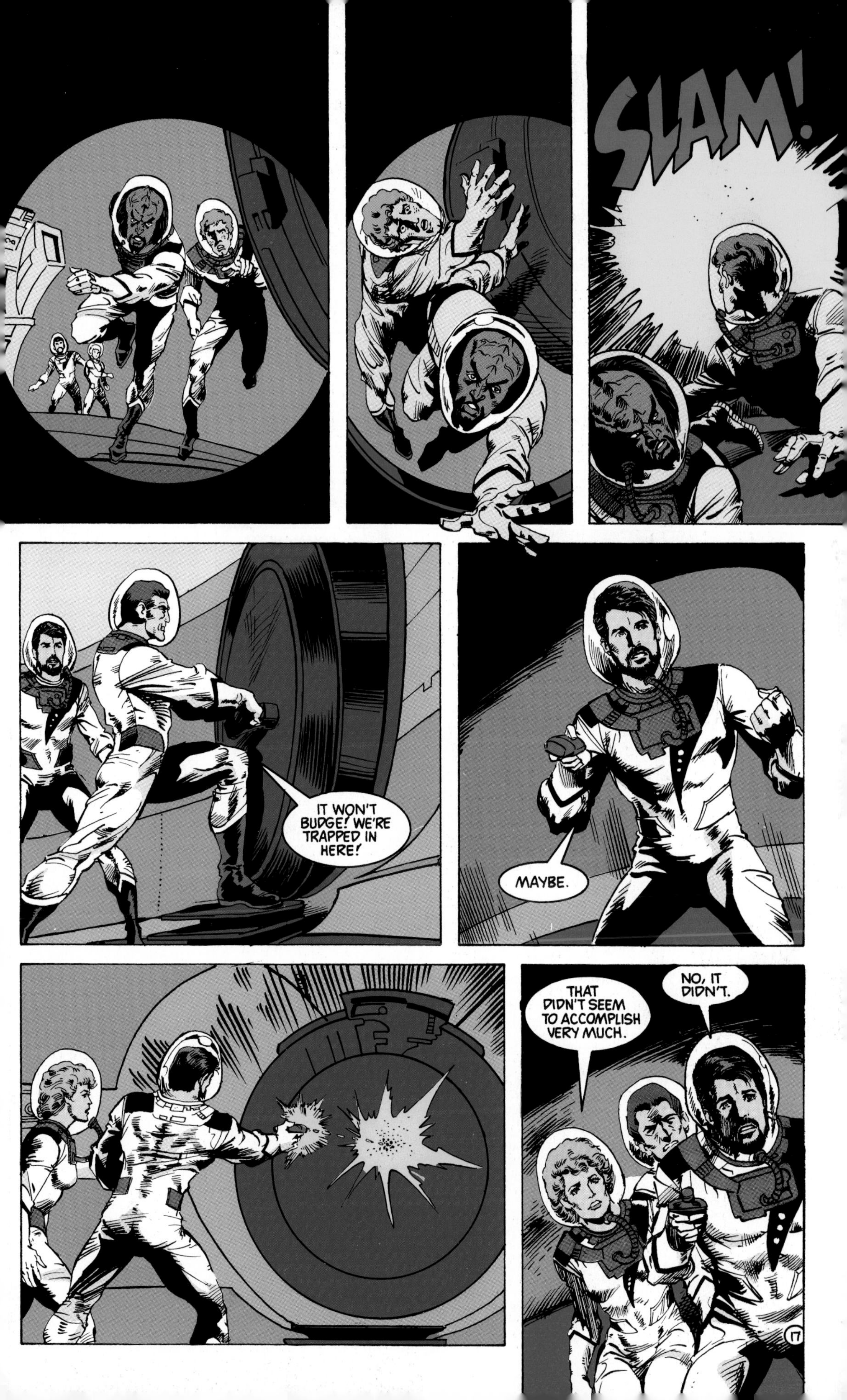
SLAM!
IT WON'T BUDGE! WE'RE TRAPPED IN HERE!
MAYBE.
THAT DIDN'T SEEM TO ACCOMPLISH VERY MUCH.
NO, IT DIDN'T.
17

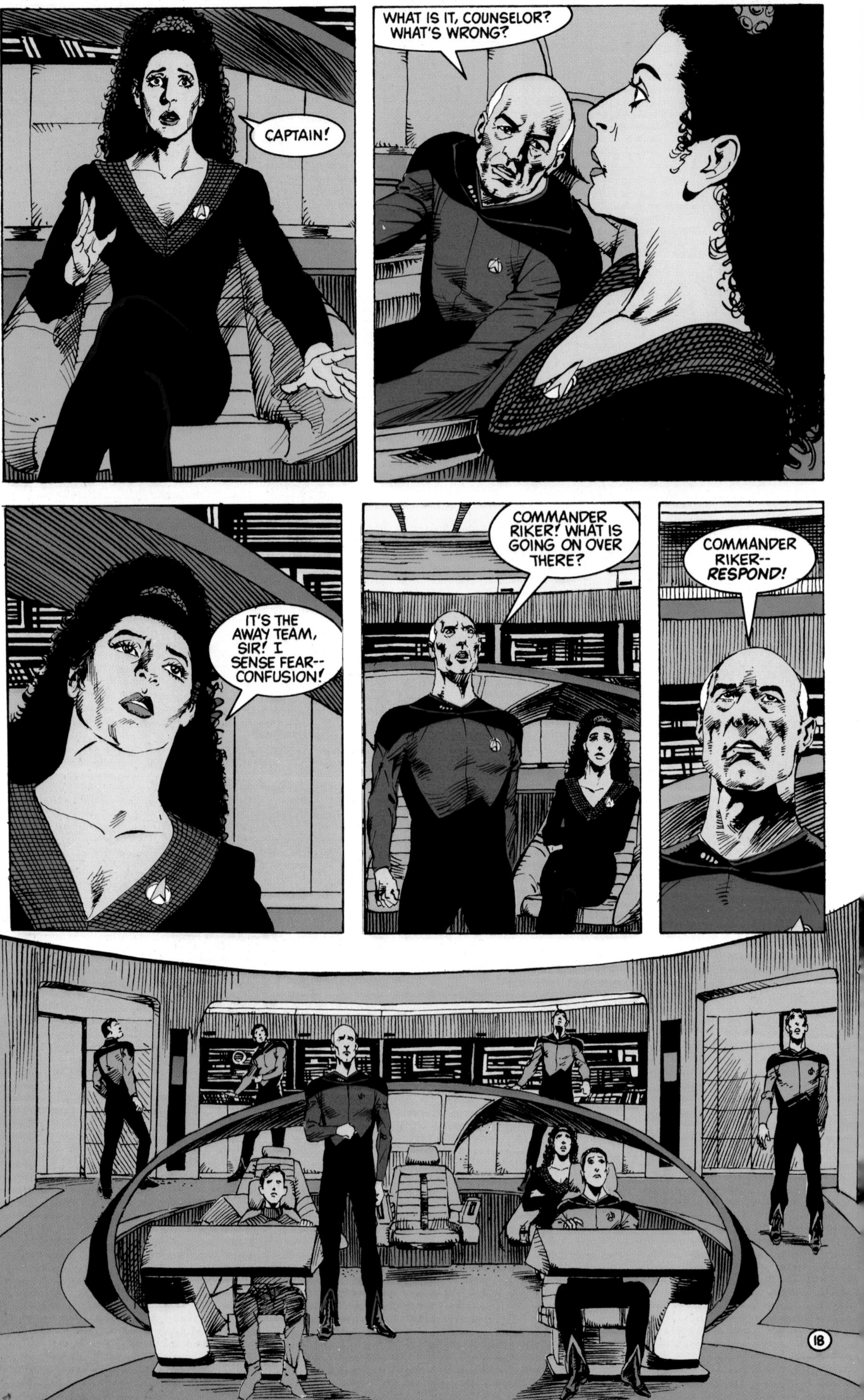
CAPTAIN!
WHAT IS IT, COUNSELOR? WHAT'S WRONG?
IT'S THE AWAY TEAM, SIR! I SENSE FEAR--CONFUSION!
COMMANDER RIKER! WHAT IS GOING ON OVER THERE?
COMMANDER RIKER--RESPOND!

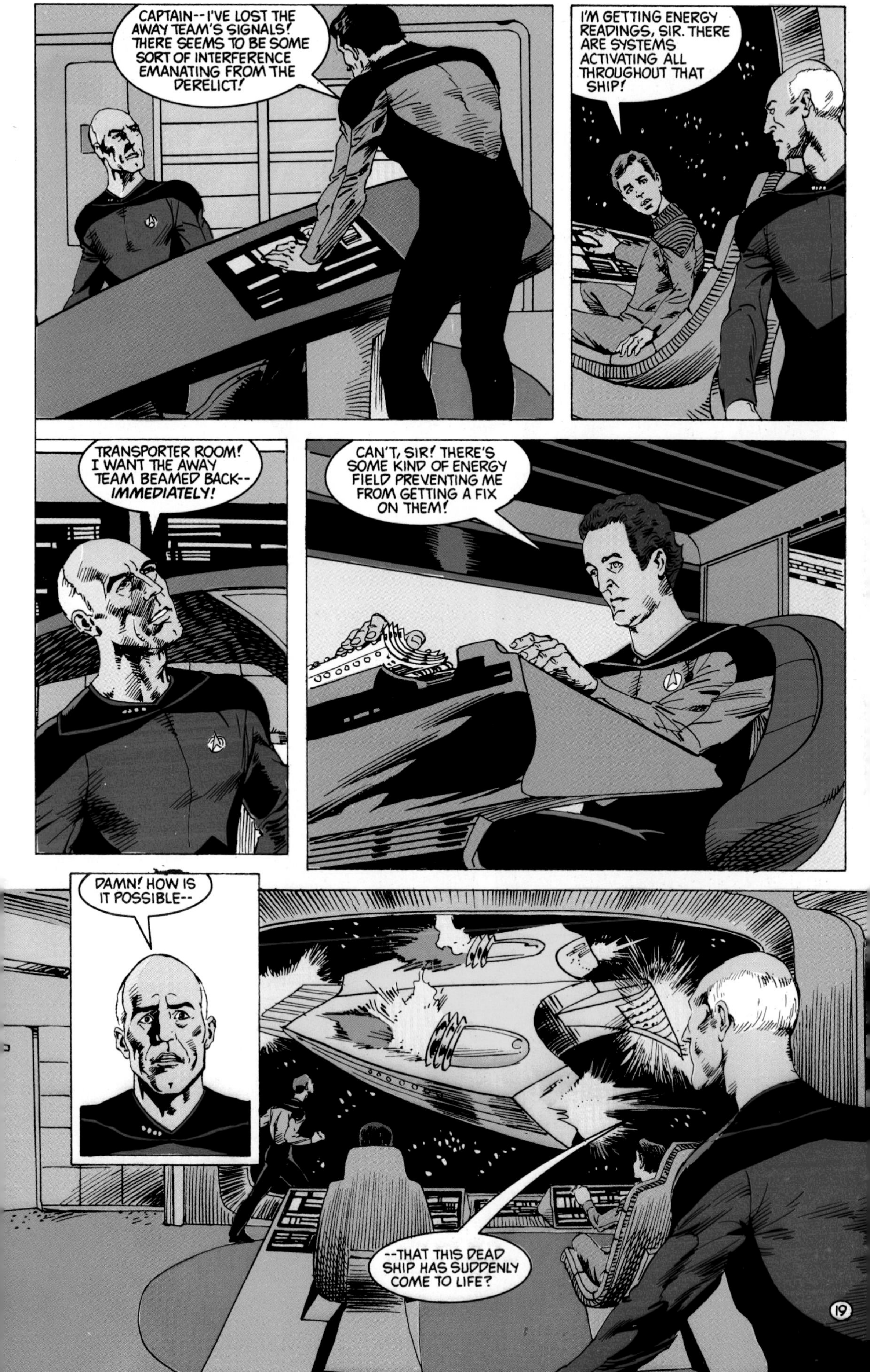
CAPTAIN--I'VE LOST THE AWAY TEAM'S SIGNALS! THERE SEEMS TO BE SOME SORT OF INTERFERENCE EMANATING FROM THE DERELICT!
I'M GETTING ENERGY READINGS, SIR. THERE ARE SYSTEMS ACTIVATING ALL THROUGHOUT THAT SHIP!
TRANSPORTER ROOM! I WANT THE AWAY TEAM BEAMED BACK-- *IMMEDIATELY!*
CAN'T, SIR! THERE'S SOME KIND OF ENERGY FIELD PREVENTING ME FROM GETTING A FIX ON THEM!
DAMN! HOW IS IT POSSIBLE--
--THAT THIS DEAD SHIP HAS SUDDENLY COME TO LIFE?

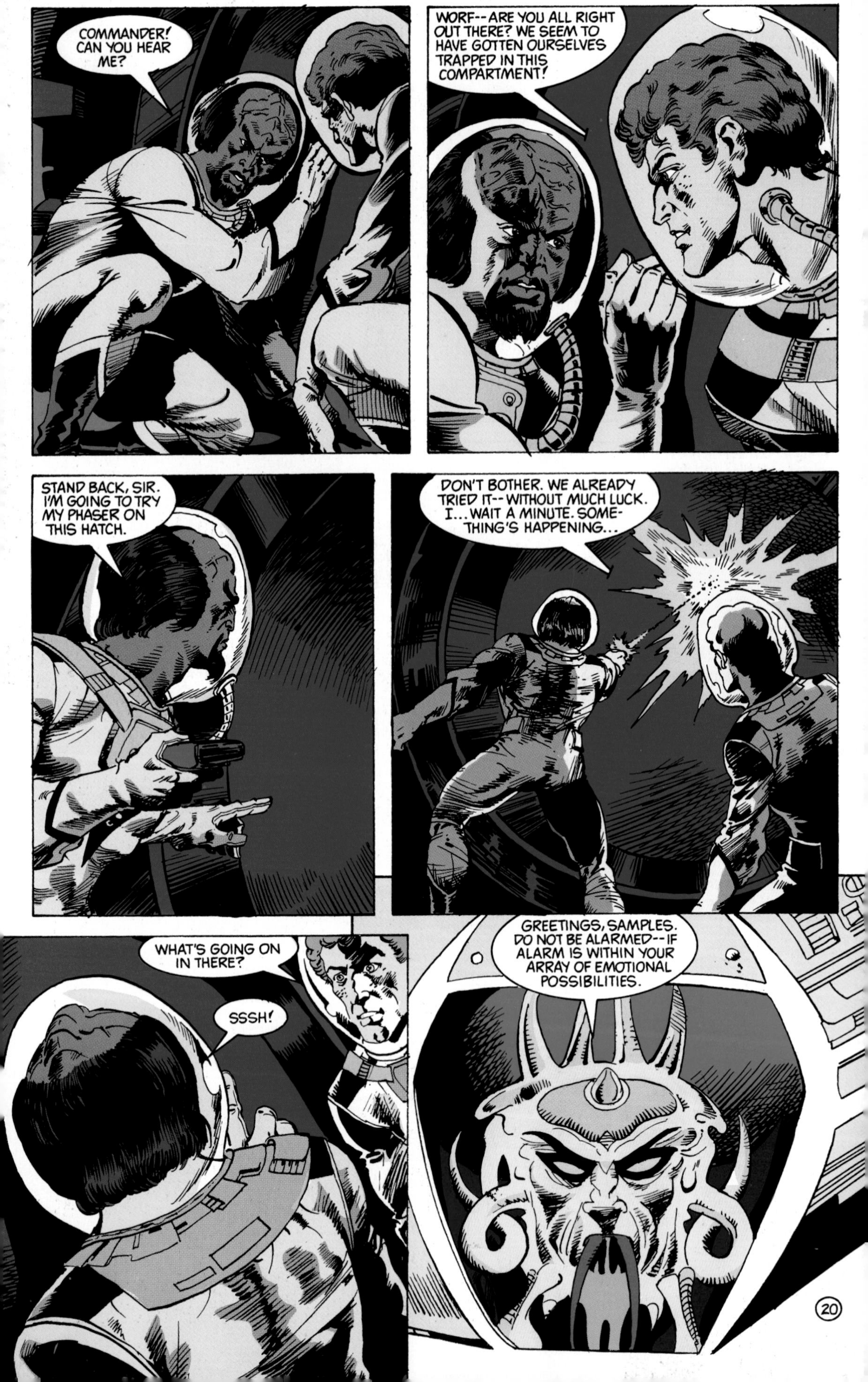
COMMANDER! CAN YOU HEAR ME?
WORF--ARE YOU ALL RIGHT OUT THERE? WE SEEM TO HAVE GOTTEN OURSELVES TRAPPED IN THIS COMPARTMENT!
STAND BACK, SIR. I'M GOING TO TRY MY PHASER ON THIS HATCH.
DON'T BOTHER. WE ALREADY TRIED IT--WITHOUT MUCH LUCK. I...WAIT A MINUTE. SOMETHING'S HAPPENING...
WHAT'S GOING ON IN THERE?
SSSH!
GREETINGS, SAMPLES. DO NOT BE ALARMED--IF ALARM IS WITHIN YOUR ARRAY OF EMOTIONAL POSSIBILITIES.

SAMPLES? WHAT DOES HE MEAN BY THAT?

LET'S LISTEN.

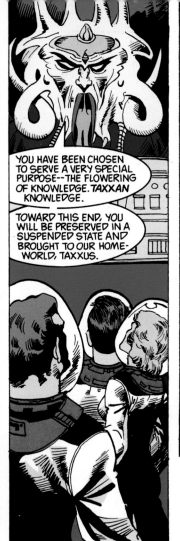

YOU HAVE BEEN CHOSEN TO SERVE A VERY SPECIAL PURPOSE--THE FLOWERING OF KNOWLEDGE. *TAXXAN* KNOWLEDGE.

TOWARD THIS END, YOU WILL BE PRESERVED IN A SUSPENDED STATE AND BROUGHT TO OUR HOME-WORLD, TAXXUS.

ONCE THERE, YOU WILL BE EXAMINED AND DISSECTED. ALL POSSIBLE CARE WILL BE TAKEN TO MAKE YOU COMFORTABLE-- FOR AS LONG AS YOU ARE ALIVE.

IN THE MEANTIME, FIND PEACE IN THE CERTAINTY THAT YOUR LIVES WILL HAVE A MEANING BEYOND ANYTHING YOU MIGHT HAVE DREAMED OF.

IN THE NEXT FEW MOMENTS, YOU WILL ACHIEVE STASIS. THE PROCESS INVOLVES NO PAIN.

FAREWELL, AND MAY YOUR JOURNEY BE UNEVENTFUL.

MY GOD.

21

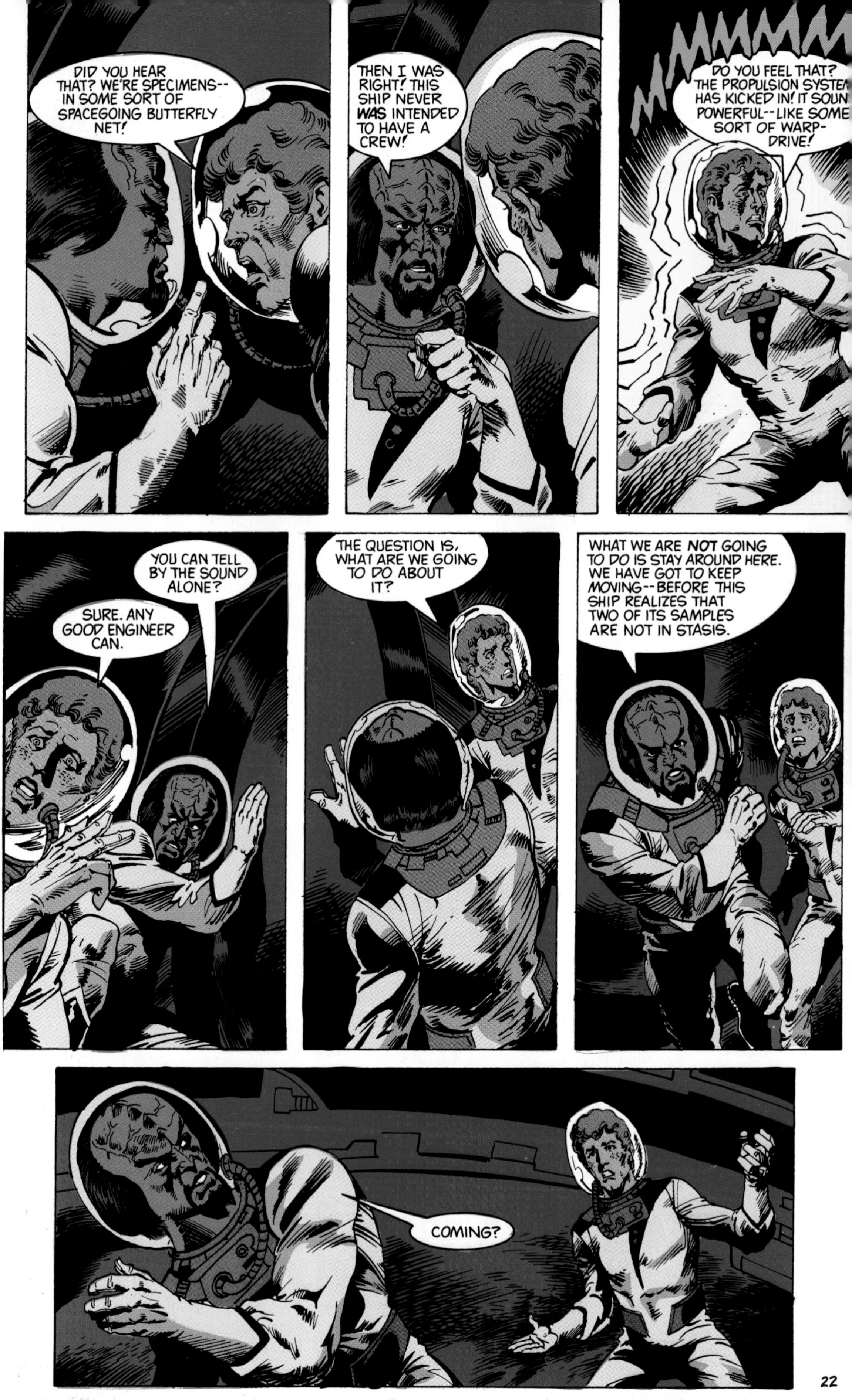
DID YOU HEAR THAT? WE'RE SPECIMENS-- IN SOME SORT OF SPACEGOING BUTTERFLY NET!
THEN I WAS RIGHT! THIS SHIP NEVER WAS INTENDED TO HAVE A CREW!
MMMMMM
DO YOU FEEL THAT? THE PROPULSION SYSTEM HAS KICKED IN! IT SOUN POWERFUL--LIKE SOME SORT OF WARP-DRIVE!
YOU CAN TELL BY THE SOUND ALONE?
SURE. ANY GOOD ENGINEER CAN.
THE QUESTION IS, WHAT ARE WE GOING TO DO ABOUT IT?
WHAT WE ARE NOT GOING TO DO IS STAY AROUND HERE. WE HAVE GOT TO KEEP MOVING--BEFORE THIS SHIP REALIZES THAT TWO OF ITS SAMPLES ARE NOT IN STASIS.
COMING?

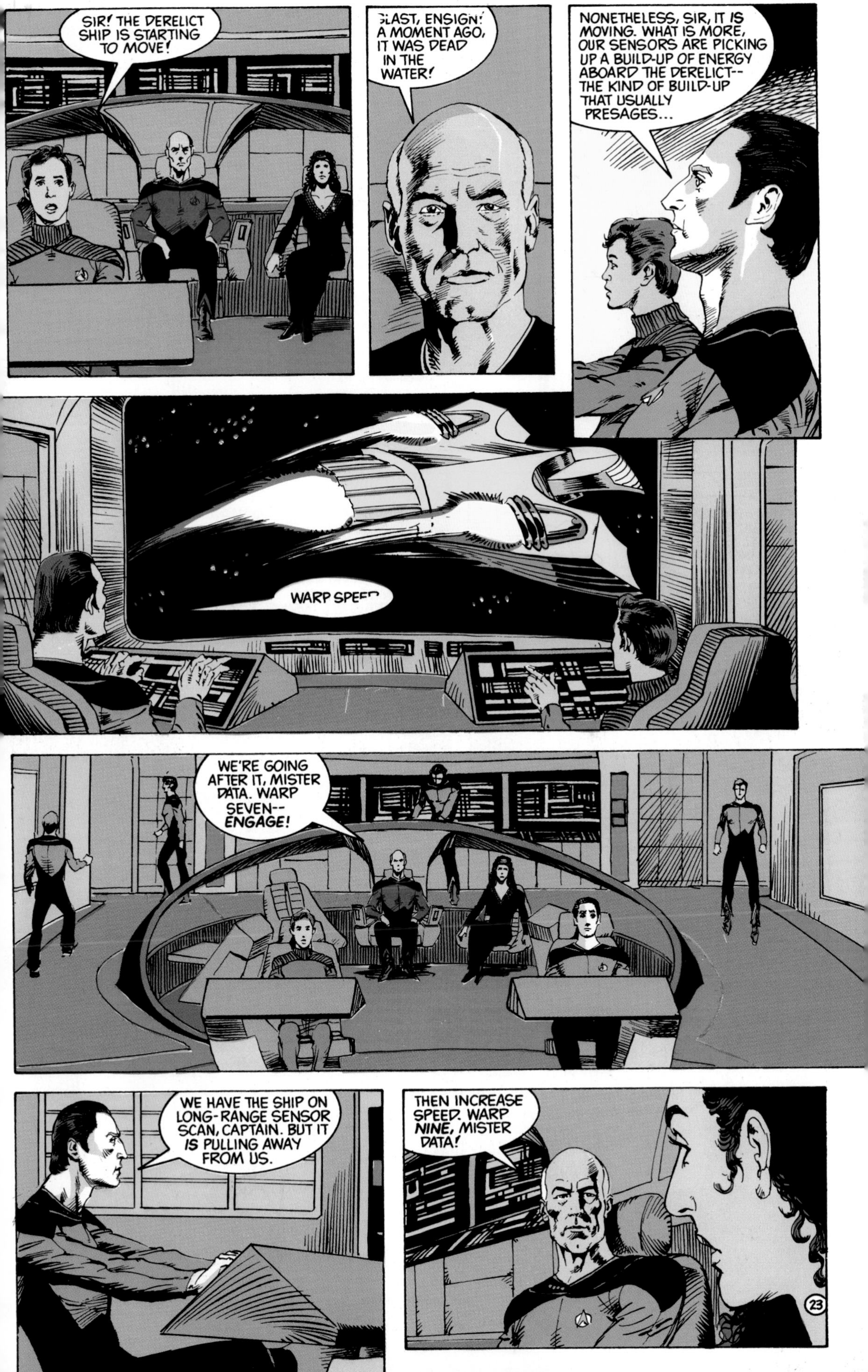
SIR! THE DERELICT SHIP IS STARTING TO MOVE!
BLAST, ENSIGN! A MOMENT AGO, IT WAS DEAD IN THE WATER!
NONETHELESS, SIR, IT IS MOVING. WHAT IS MORE, OUR SENSORS ARE PICKING UP A BUILD-UP OF ENERGY ABOARD THE DERELICT-- THE KIND OF BUILD-UP THAT USUALLY PRESAGES...
WARP SPEED
WE'RE GOING AFTER IT, MISTER DATA. WARP SEVEN-- ENGAGE!
WE HAVE THE SHIP ON LONG-RANGE SENSOR SCAN, CAPTAIN. BUT IT IS PULLING AWAY FROM US.
THEN INCREASE SPEED. WARP NINE, MISTER DATA!
23

CAPTAIN--WHAT'S GOING ON UP THERE? WE'VE GOT A DAMAGED DILITHIUM CRYSTAL-- REMEMBER?

AT MAXIMUM SPEED, YOU *COULD* BLOW THE ENGINES APART!

WE HAVE NO CHOICE, MISTER LAFORGE! THAT DERELICT SHIP HAS SUDDENLY TAKEN OFF-- ALONG WITH OUR AWAY TEAM!

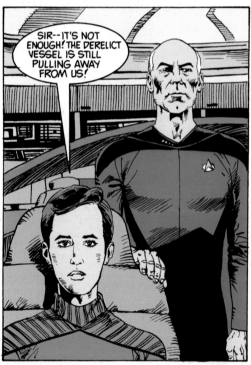

SIR--IT'S NOT ENOUGH! THE DERELICT VESSEL IS STILL PULLING AWAY FROM US!

DID YOU HEAR THAT, MISTER LAFORGE? WARP NINE--AND WE ARE *STILL* LOSING GROUND!

UNTIL WE *LOSE* THE ENGINES, LIEUTENANT, I WANT ALL THE *SPEED* WE CAN WRING OUT OF THEM IS THAT CLEAR?

AYE, SIR...

TO BE CONTINUED!

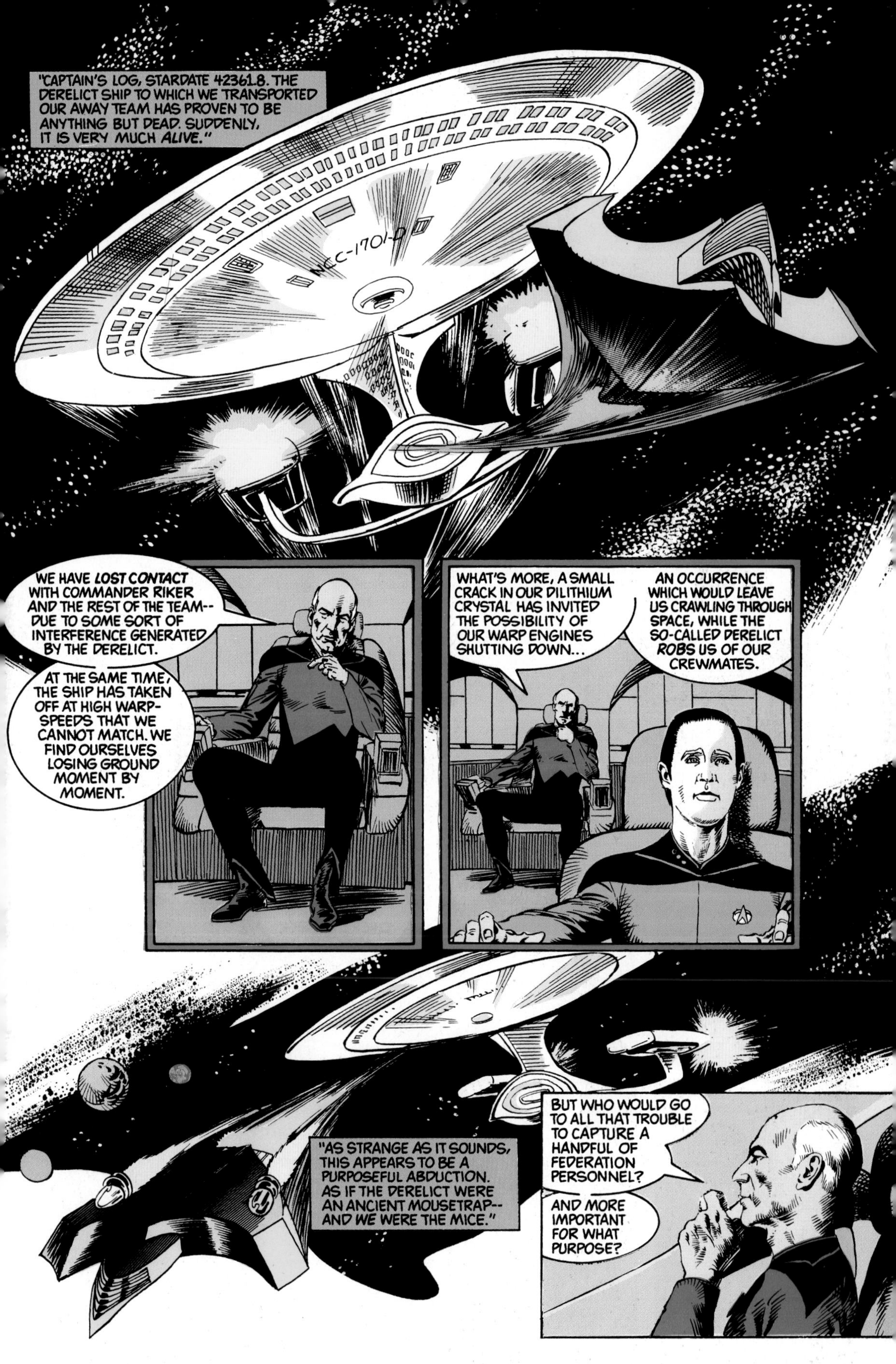
"CAPTAIN'S LOG, STARDATE 42361.8. THE DERELICT SHIP TO WHICH WE TRANSPORTED OUR AWAY TEAM HAS PROVEN TO BE ANYTHING BUT DEAD. SUDDENLY, IT IS VERY MUCH ALIVE."
NCC-1701-D
WE HAVE LOST CONTACT WITH COMMANDER RIKER AND THE REST OF THE TEAM-- DUE TO SOME SORT OF INTERFERENCE GENERATED BY THE DERELICT.
AT THE SAME TIME, THE SHIP HAS TAKEN OFF AT HIGH WARP-SPEEDS THAT WE CANNOT MATCH. WE FIND OURSELVES LOSING GROUND MOMENT BY MOMENT.
WHAT'S MORE, A SMALL CRACK IN OUR DILITHIUM CRYSTAL HAS INVITED THE POSSIBILITY OF OUR WARP ENGINES SHUTTING DOWN...
AN OCCURRENCE WHICH WOULD LEAVE US CRAWLING THROUGH SPACE, WHILE THE SO-CALLED DERELICT ROBS US OF OUR CREWMATES.
"AS STRANGE AS IT SOUNDS, THIS APPEARS TO BE A PURPOSEFUL ABDUCTION. AS IF THE DERELICT WERE AN ANCIENT MOUSETRAP-- AND WE WERE THE MICE."
BUT WHO WOULD GO TO ALL THAT TROUBLE TO CAPTURE A HANDFUL OF FEDERATION PERSONNEL?
AND MORE IMPORTANT FOR WHAT PURPOSE?

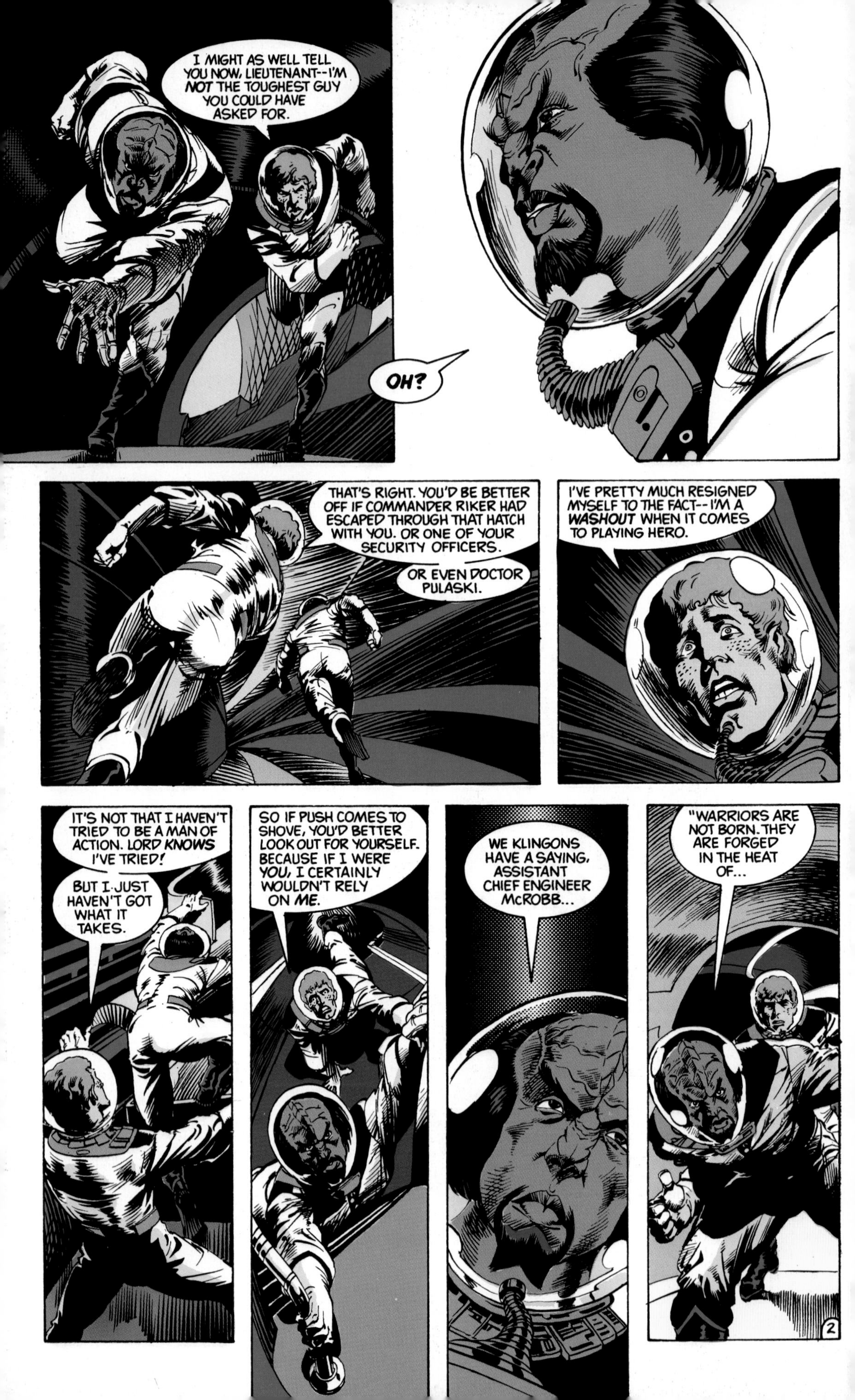
I MIGHT AS WELL TELL YOU NOW, LIEUTENANT--I'M NOT THE TOUGHEST GUY YOU COULD HAVE ASKED FOR.
OH?
THAT'S RIGHT. YOU'D BE BETTER OFF IF COMMANDER RIKER HAD ESCAPED THROUGH THAT HATCH WITH YOU. OR ONE OF YOUR SECURITY OFFICERS.
OR EVEN DOCTOR PULASKI.
I'VE PRETTY MUCH RESIGNED MYSELF TO THE FACT--I'M A WASHOUT WHEN IT COMES TO PLAYING HERO.
IT'S NOT THAT I HAVEN'T TRIED TO BE A MAN OF ACTION. LORD KNOWS I'VE TRIED!
BUT I JUST HAVEN'T GOT WHAT IT TAKES.
SO IF PUSH COMES TO SHOVE, YOU'D BETTER LOOK OUT FOR YOURSELF. BECAUSE IF I WERE YOU, I CERTAINLY WOULDN'T RELY ON ME.
WE KLINGONS HAVE A SAYING, ASSISTANT CHIEF ENGINEER McROBB...
"WARRIORS ARE NOT BORN. THEY ARE FORGED IN THE HEAT OF...
2

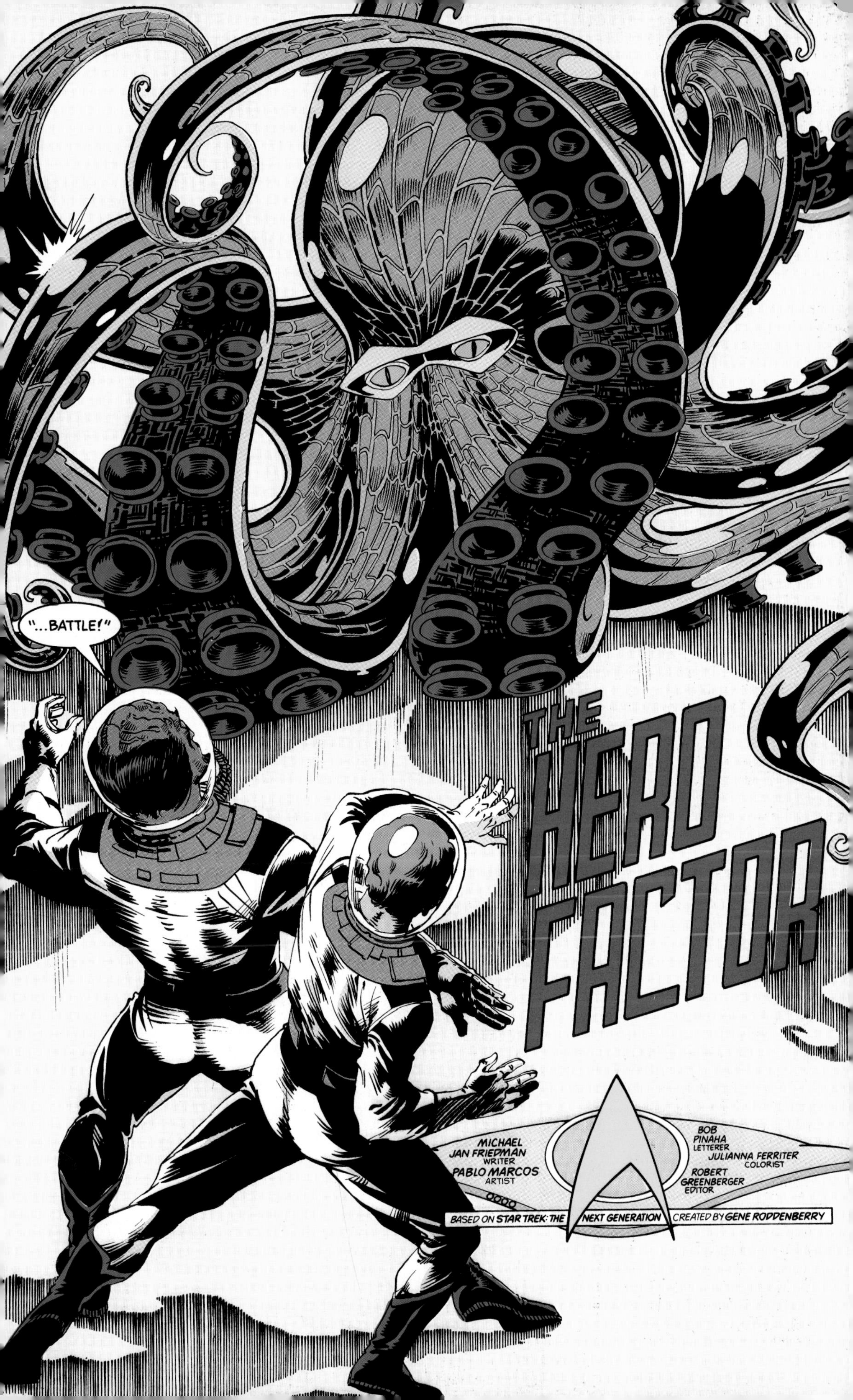
"...BATTLE!"
THE HERO FACTOR
MICHAEL JAN FRIEDMAN WRITER
PABLO MARCOS ARTIST
BOB PINAHA LETTERER
JULIANNA FERRITER COLORIST
ROBERT GREENBERGER EDITOR
BASED ON STAR TREK: THE NEXT GENERATION CREATED BY GENE RODDENBERRY

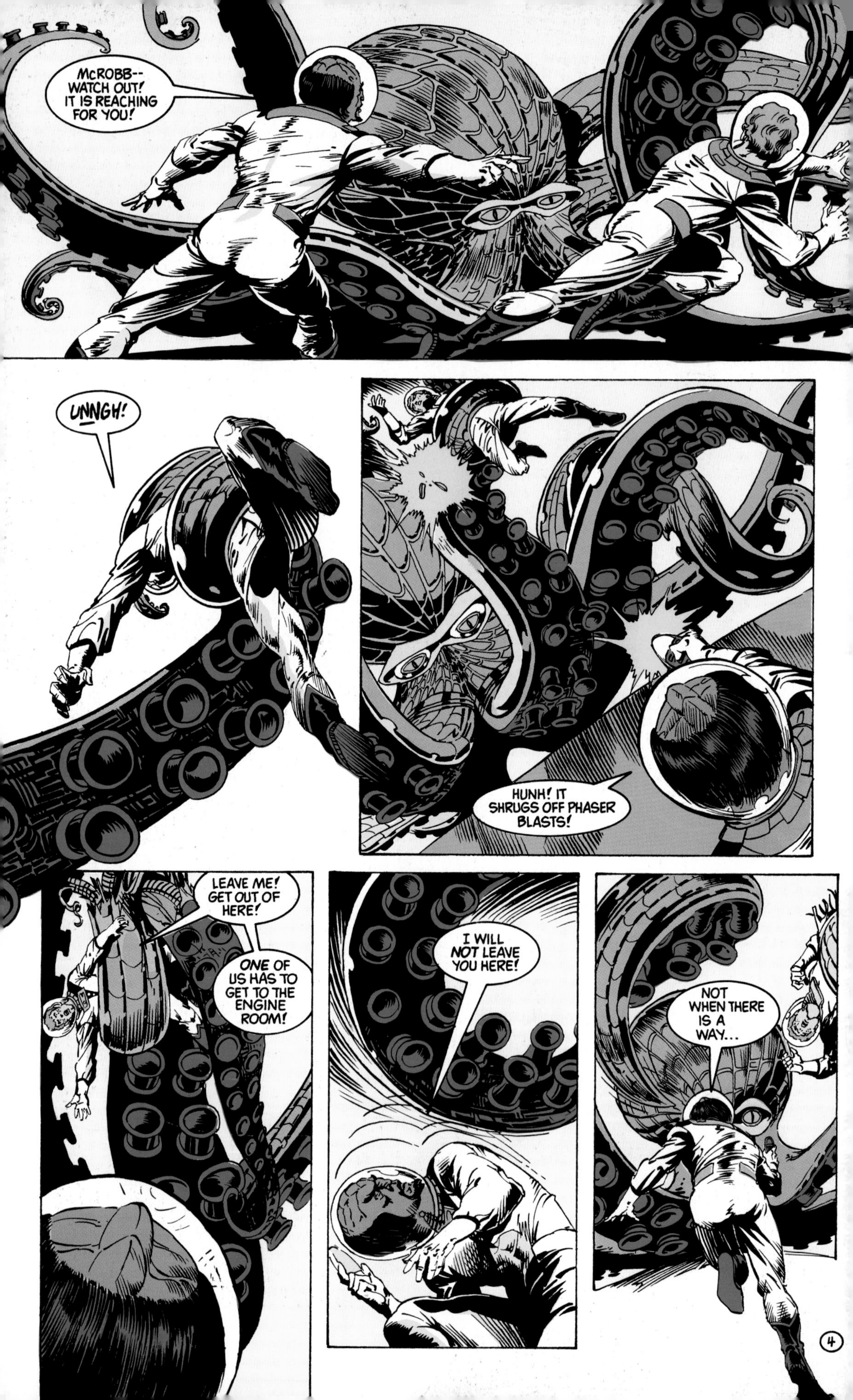
McROBB-- WATCH OUT! IT IS REACHING FOR YOU!
UNNGH!
HUNH! IT SHRUGS OFF PHASER BLASTS!
LEAVE ME! GET OUT OF HERE!
ONE OF US HAS TO GET TO THE ENGINE ROOM!
I WILL NOT LEAVE YOU HERE!
NOT WHEN THERE IS A WAY...

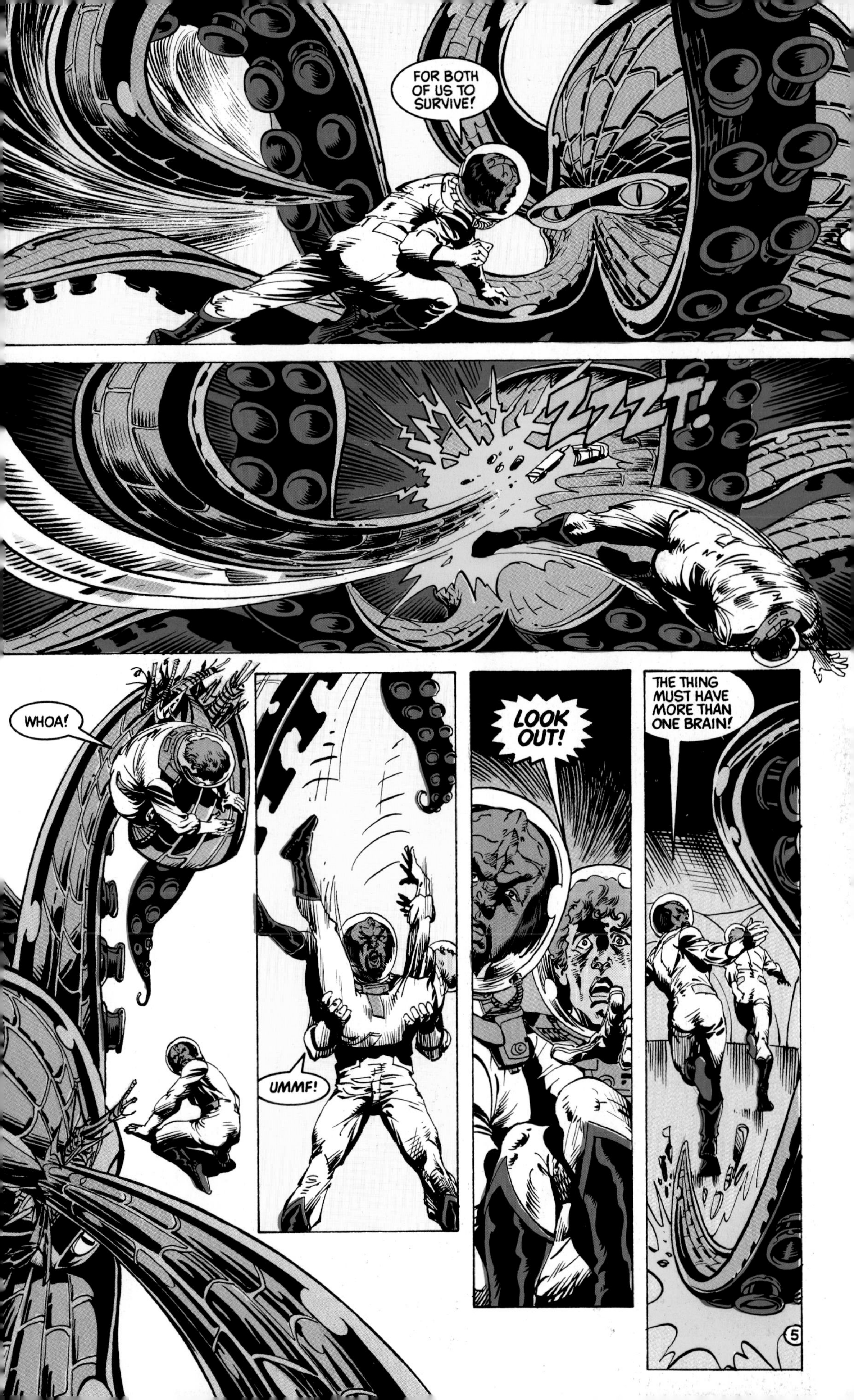
FOR BOTH OF US TO SURVIVE!
ZZZZT!
WHOA!
UMMF!
LOOK OUT!
THE THING MUST HAVE MORE THAN ONE BRAIN!
5

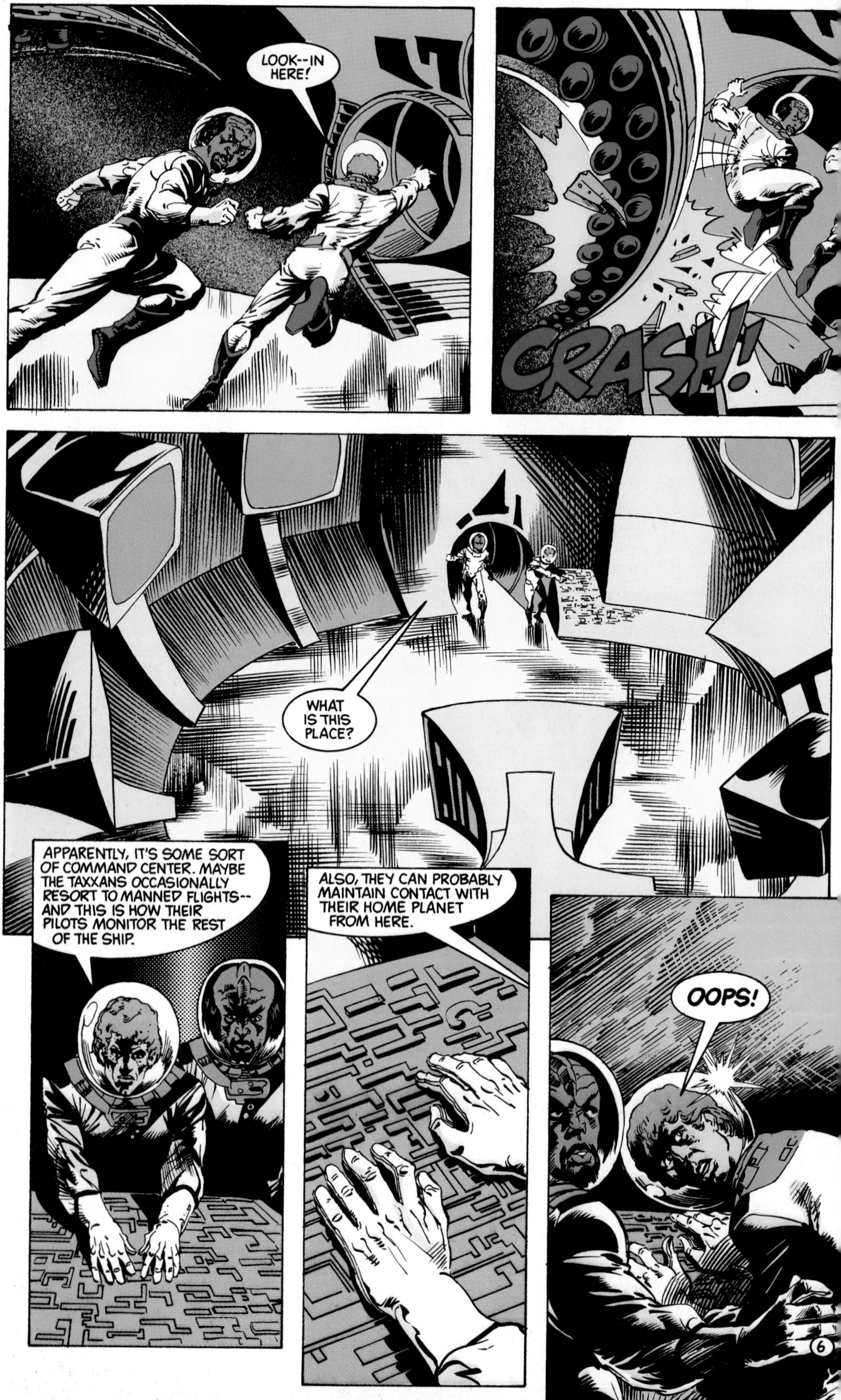

LOOK--IN HERE!
CRASH!
WHAT IS THIS PLACE?
APPARENTLY, IT'S SOME SORT OF COMMAND CENTER. MAYBE THE TAXXANS OCCASIONALLY RESORT TO MANNED FLIGHTS-- AND THIS IS HOW THEIR PILOTS MONITOR THE REST OF THE SHIP.
ALSO, THEY CAN PROBABLY MAINTAIN CONTACT WITH THEIR HOME PLANET FROM HERE.
OOPS!

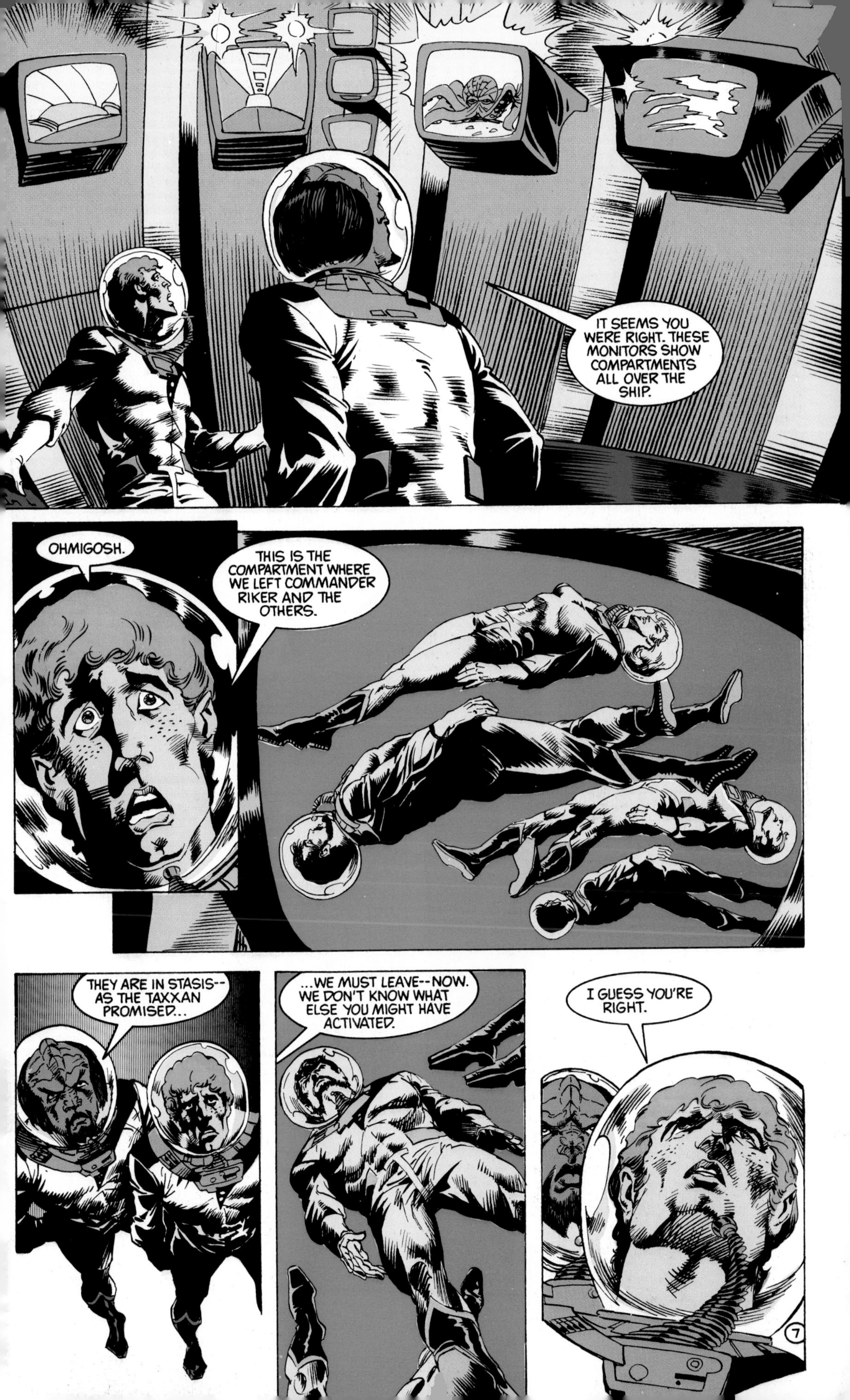
IT SEEMS YOU WERE RIGHT. THESE MONITORS SHOW COMPARTMENTS ALL OVER THE SHIP.
OHMIGOSH.
THIS IS THE COMPARTMENT WHERE WE LEFT COMMANDER RIKER AND THE OTHERS.
THEY ARE IN STASIS-- AS THE TAXXAN PROMISED...
...WE MUST LEAVE--NOW. WE DON'T KNOW WHAT ELSE YOU MIGHT HAVE ACTIVATED.
I GUESS YOU'RE RIGHT.
7

YES, LIEUTENANT. WHAT IS IT?

WE'RE REALLY TAKING CHANCES, CAPTAIN. THIS DILITHIUM CRYSTAL COULD FAIL AT ANY MOMENT.

MY INSTRUMENTS SHOW THAT THE CRACK IS SPREADING. AT WARP NINE, THE STRESS IS JUST *TOO* MUCH.

I AM AWARE OF THAT, LIEUTENANT. BUT WE WILL *NOT* SLOW DOWN--NOT UNTIL WE HAVE EXHAUSTED ALL POSSIBILITIES OF RECOVERING THE AWAY TEAM.

IS THERE ANYTHING ELSE?

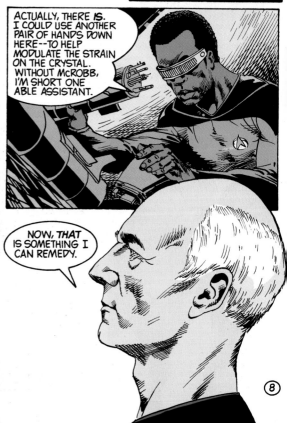

ACTUALLY, THERE *IS.* I COULD USE ANOTHER PAIR OF HANDS DOWN HERE--TO HELP MODULATE THE STRAIN ON THE CRYSTAL. WITHOUT McROBB, I'M SHORT ONE ABLE ASSISTANT.

NOW, *THAT* IS SOMETHING I CAN REMEDY.

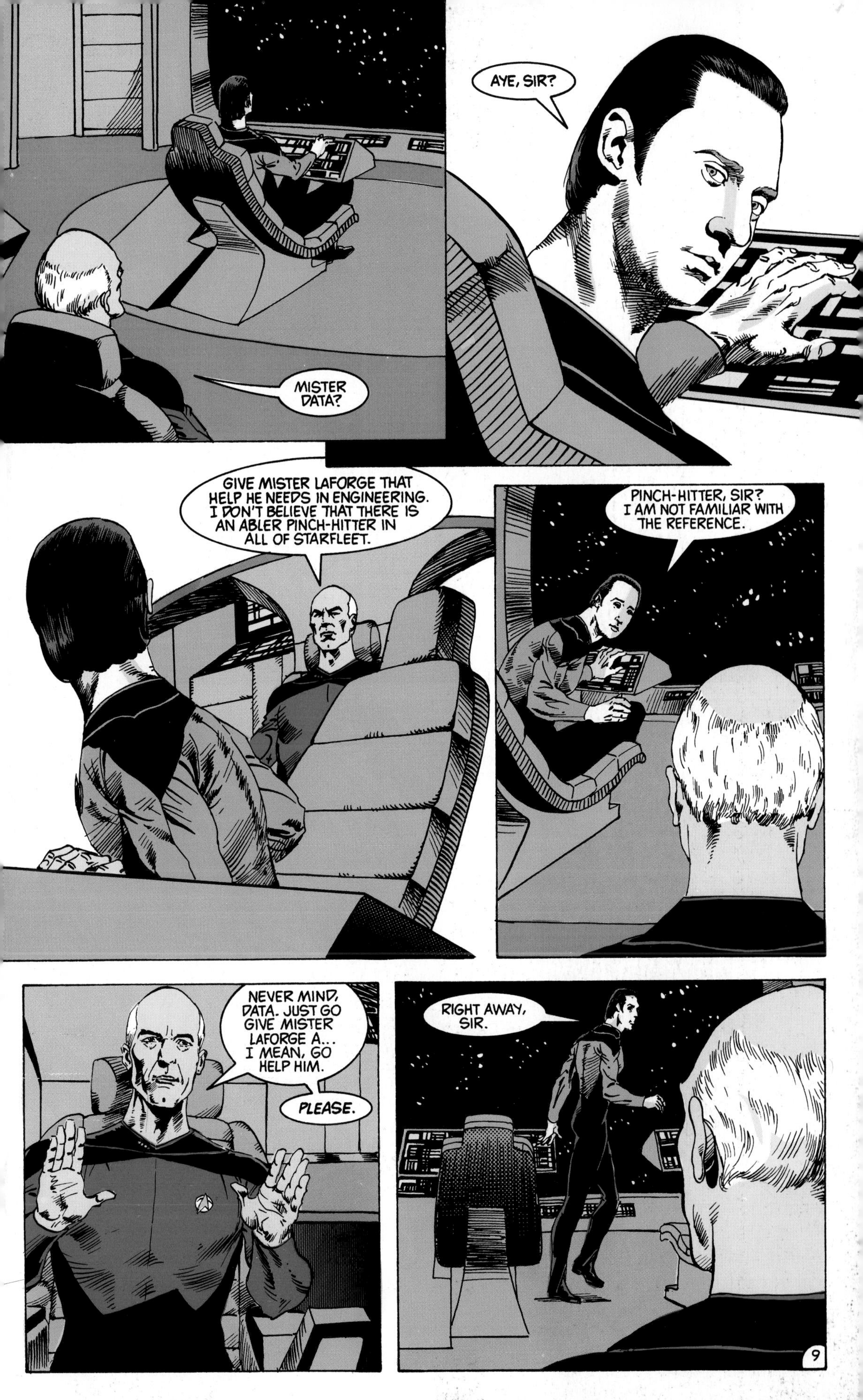
MISTER DATA?
AYE, SIR?
GIVE MISTER LAFORGE THAT HELP HE NEEDS IN ENGINEERING. I DON'T BELIEVE THAT THERE IS AN ABLER PINCH-HITTER IN ALL OF STARFLEET.
PINCH-HITTER, SIR? I AM NOT FAMILIAR WITH THE REFERENCE.
NEVER MIND, DATA. JUST GO GIVE MISTER LAFORGE A... I MEAN, GO HELP HIM.
PLEASE.
RIGHT AWAY, SIR.

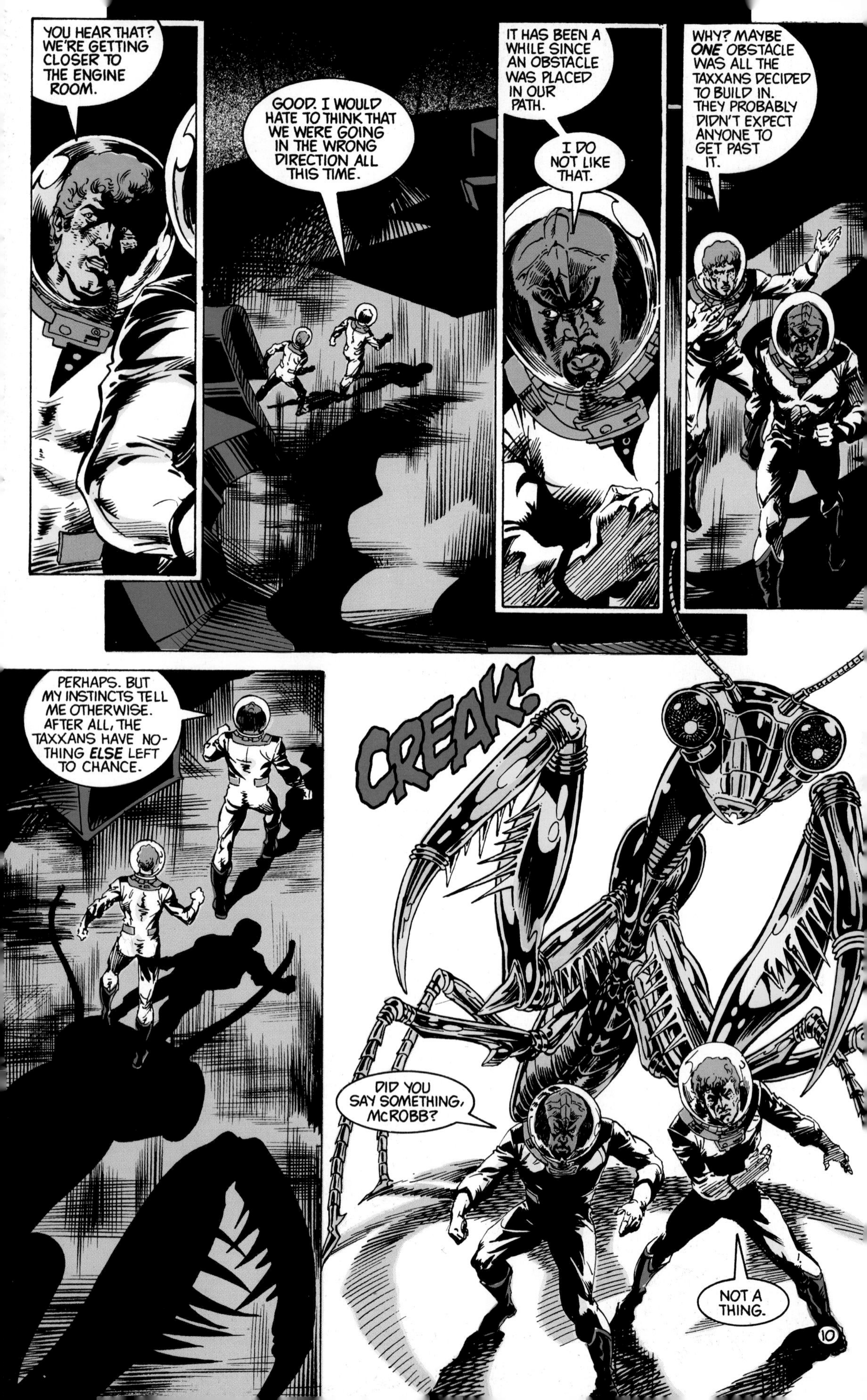
YOU HEAR THAT? WE'RE GETTING CLOSER TO THE ENGINE ROOM.
GOOD. I WOULD HATE TO THINK THAT WE WERE GOING IN THE WRONG DIRECTION ALL THIS TIME.
IT HAS BEEN A WHILE SINCE AN OBSTACLE WAS PLACED IN OUR PATH.
I DO NOT LIKE THAT.
WHY? MAYBE ONE OBSTACLE WAS ALL THE TAXXANS DECIDED TO BUILD IN. THEY PROBABLY DIDN'T EXPECT ANYONE TO GET PAST IT.
PERHAPS. BUT MY INSTINCTS TELL ME OTHERWISE. AFTER ALL, THE TAXXANS HAVE NOTHING ELSE LEFT TO CHANCE.
CREAK!
DID YOU SAY SOMETHING, McROBB?
NOT A THING.
10

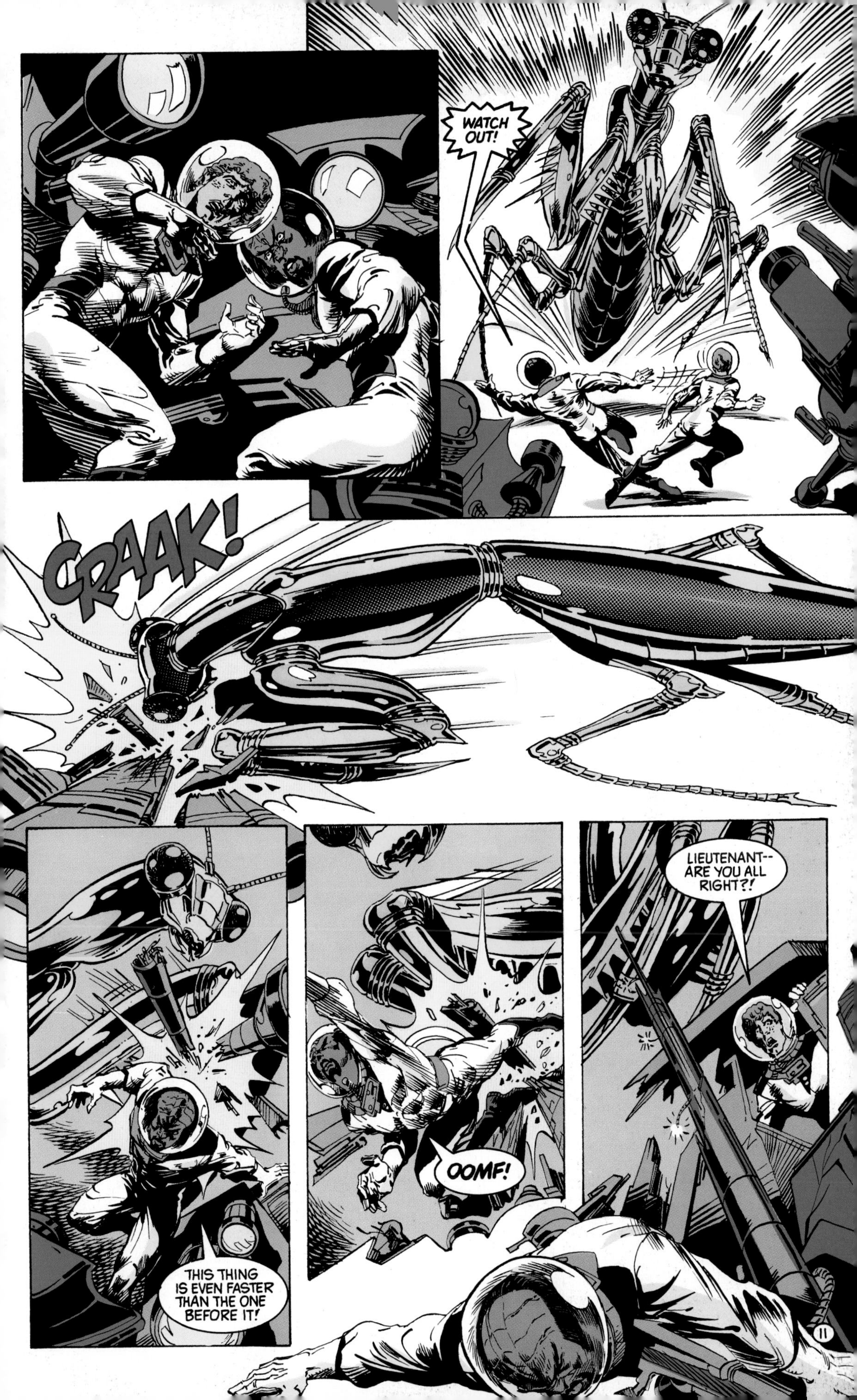
WATCH OUT!
CRAAK!
THIS THING IS EVEN FASTER THAN THE ONE BEFORE IT!
OOMF!
LIEUTENANT-- ARE YOU ALL RIGHT?!
11

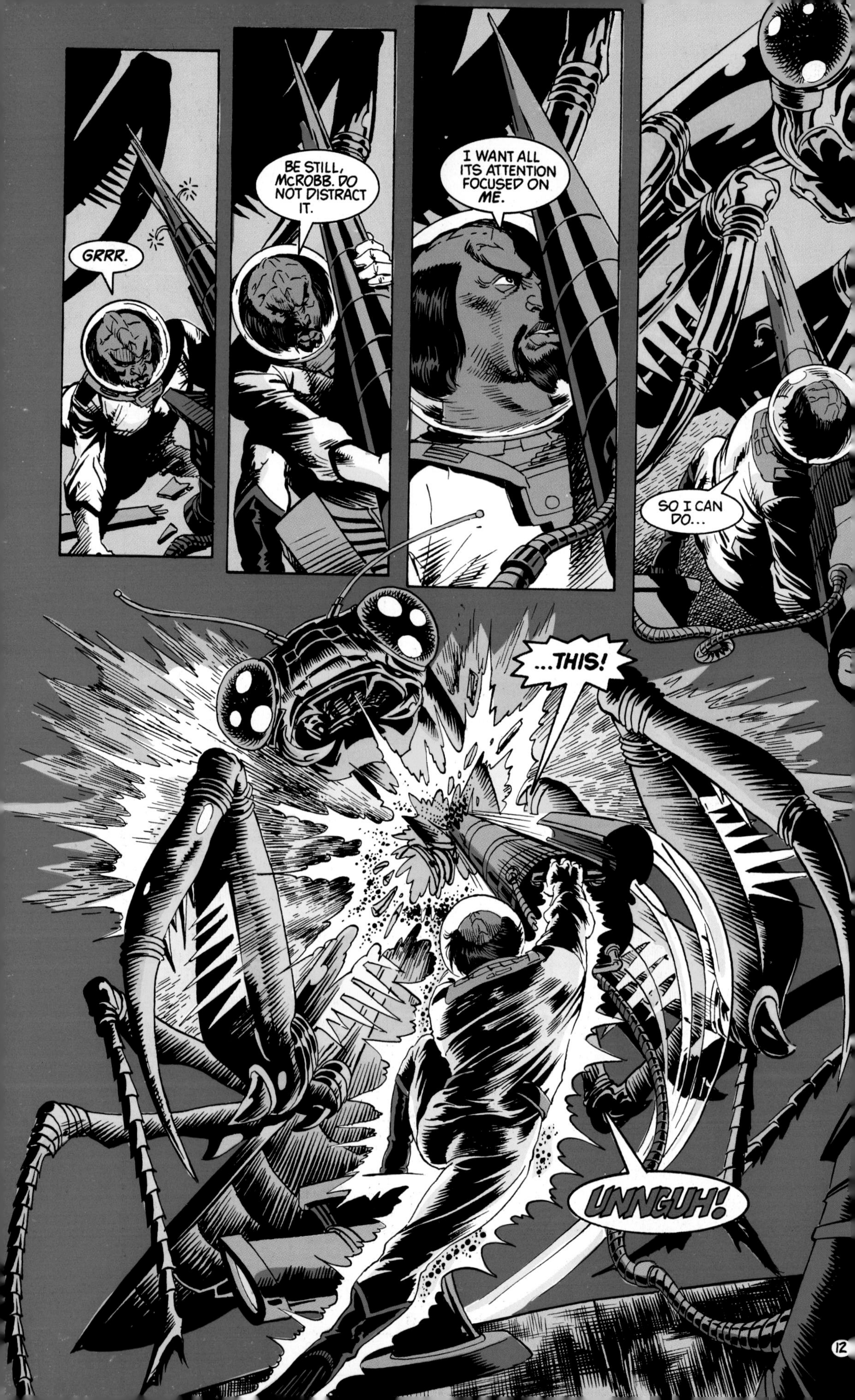
GRRR.
BE STILL, MCROBB. DO NOT DISTRACT IT.
I WANT ALL ITS ATTENTION FOCUSED ON ME.
SO I CAN DO...
...THIS!
UNNGUH!

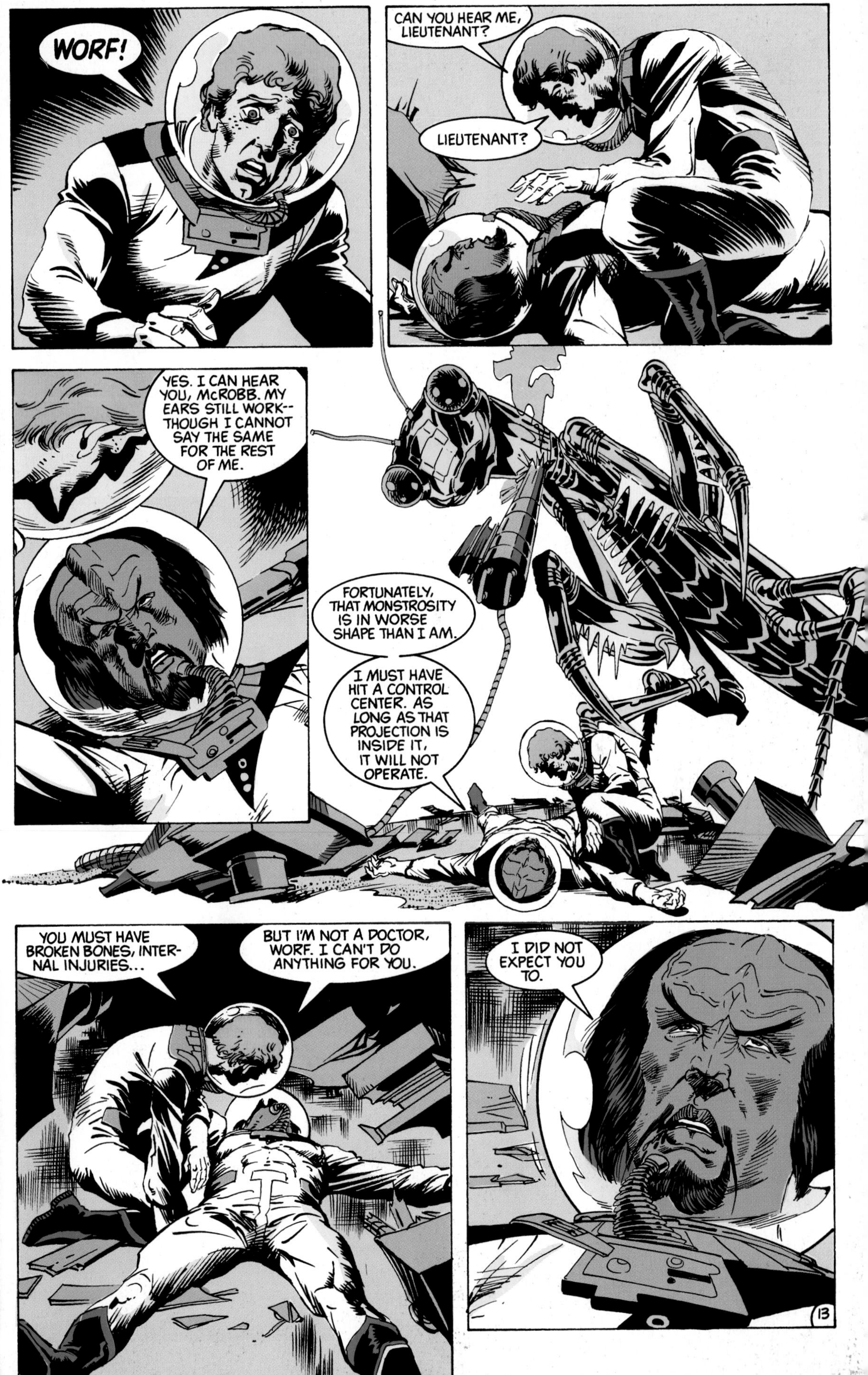
WORF!
CAN YOU HEAR ME, LIEUTENANT?
LIEUTENANT?
YES. I CAN HEAR YOU, McROBB. MY EARS STILL WORK-- THOUGH I CANNOT SAY THE SAME FOR THE REST OF ME.
FORTUNATELY, THAT MONSTROSITY IS IN WORSE SHAPE THAN I AM.
I MUST HAVE HIT A CONTROL CENTER. AS LONG AS THAT PROJECTION IS INSIDE IT, IT WILL NOT OPERATE.
YOU MUST HAVE BROKEN BONES, INTERNAL INJURIES...
BUT I'M NOT A DOCTOR, WORF. I CAN'T DO ANYTHING FOR YOU.
I DID NOT EXPECT YOU TO.
13

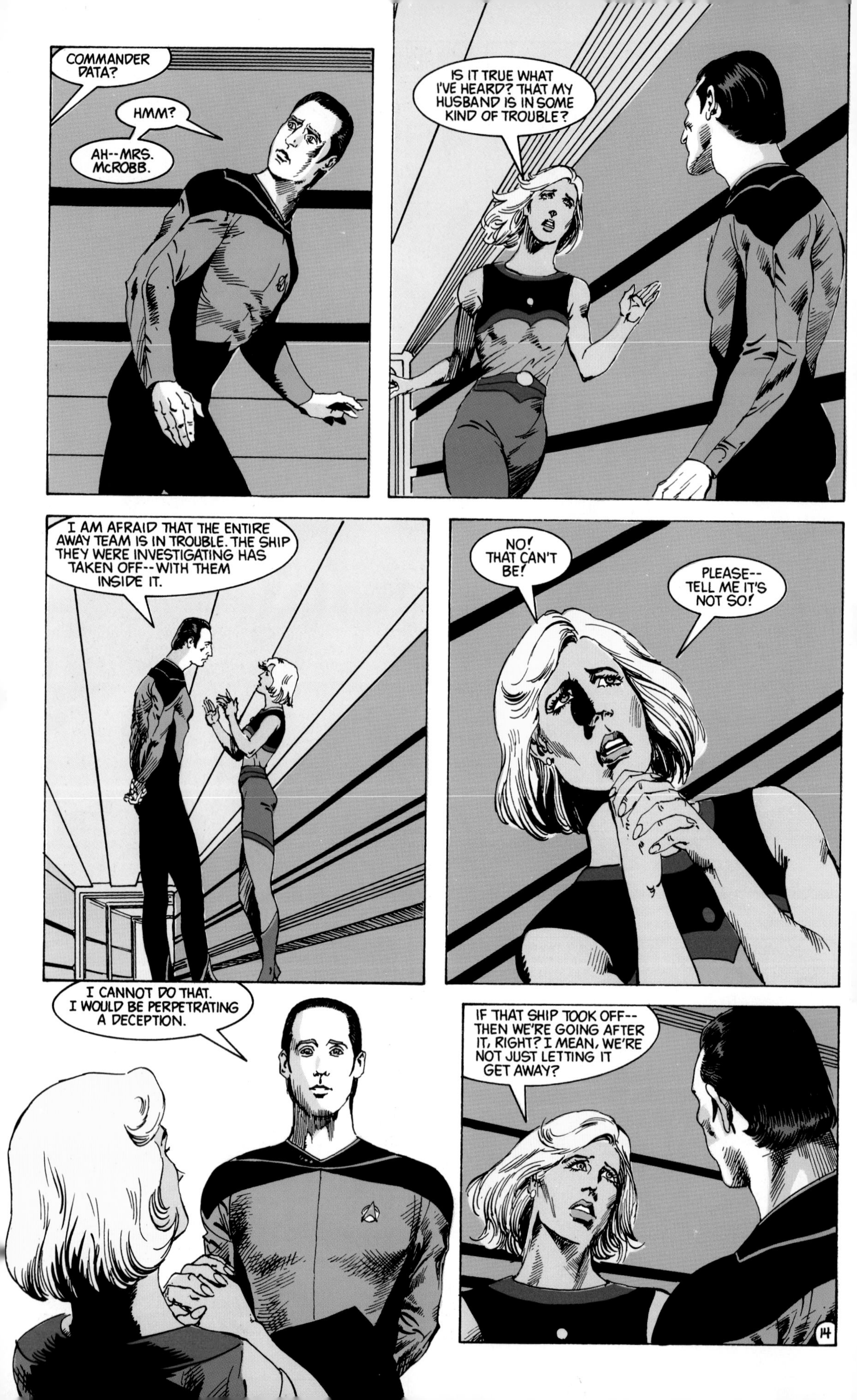

COMMANDER DATA?
HMM?
AH--MRS. McROBB.
IS IT TRUE WHAT I'VE HEARD? THAT MY HUSBAND IS IN SOME KIND OF TROUBLE?
I AM AFRAID THAT THE ENTIRE AWAY TEAM IS IN TROUBLE. THE SHIP THEY WERE INVESTIGATING HAS TAKEN OFF--WITH THEM INSIDE IT.
NO! THAT CAN'T BE!
PLEASE--TELL ME IT'S NOT SO!
I CANNOT DO THAT. I WOULD BE PERPETRATING A DECEPTION.
IF THAT SHIP TOOK OFF--THEN WE'RE GOING AFTER IT, RIGHT? I MEAN, WE'RE NOT JUST LETTING IT GET AWAY?
14

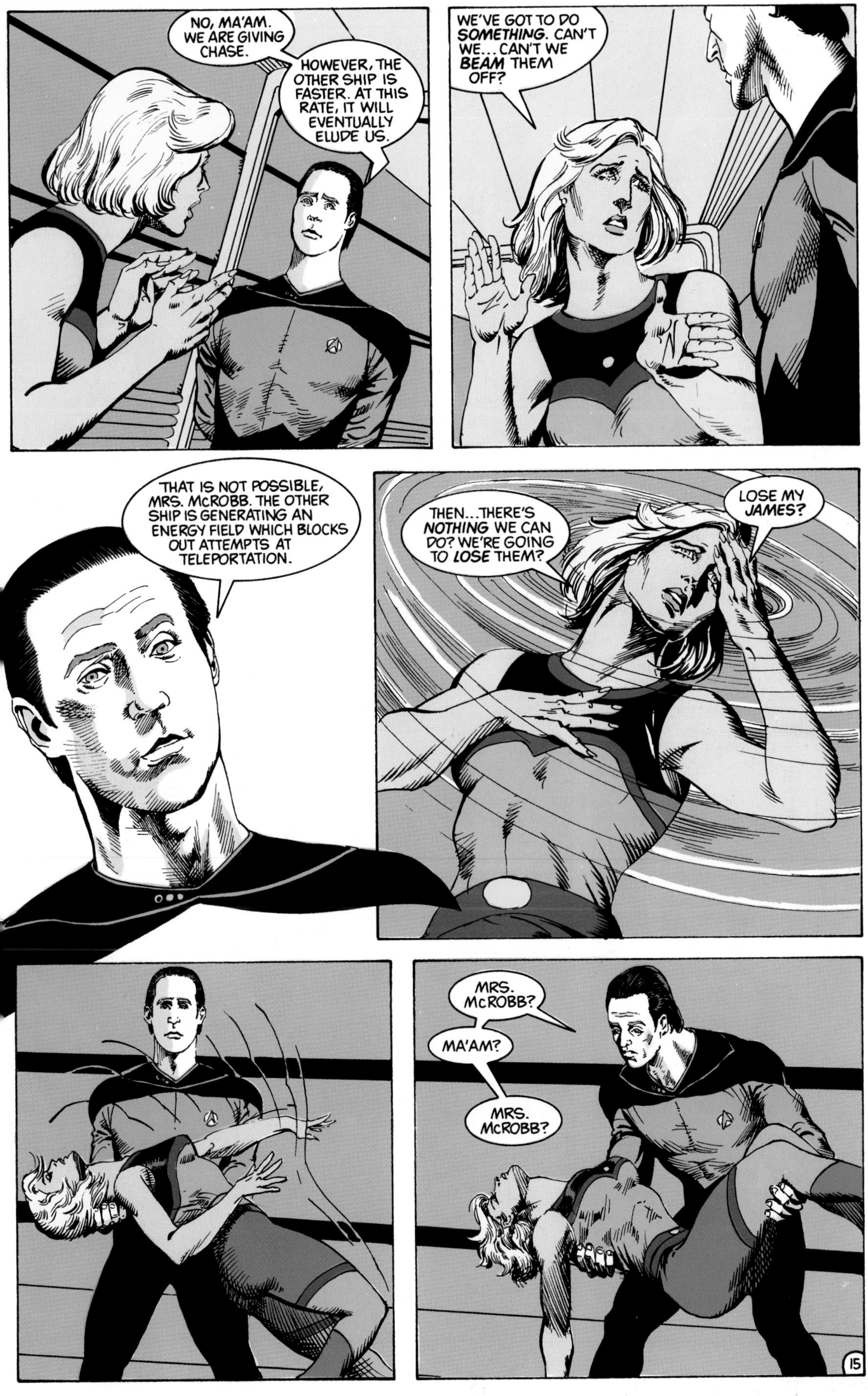

NO, MA'AM. WE ARE GIVING CHASE.
HOWEVER, THE OTHER SHIP IS FASTER. AT THIS RATE, IT WILL EVENTUALLY ELUDE US.
WE'VE GOT TO DO SOMETHING. CAN'T WE... CAN'T WE BEAM THEM OFF?
THAT IS NOT POSSIBLE, MRS. McROBB. THE OTHER SHIP IS GENERATING AN ENERGY FIELD WHICH BLOCKS OUT ATTEMPTS AT TELEPORTATION.
THEN...THERE'S NOTHING WE CAN DO? WE'RE GOING TO LOSE THEM?
LOSE MY JAMES?
MRS. McROBB?
MA'AM?
MRS. McROBB?

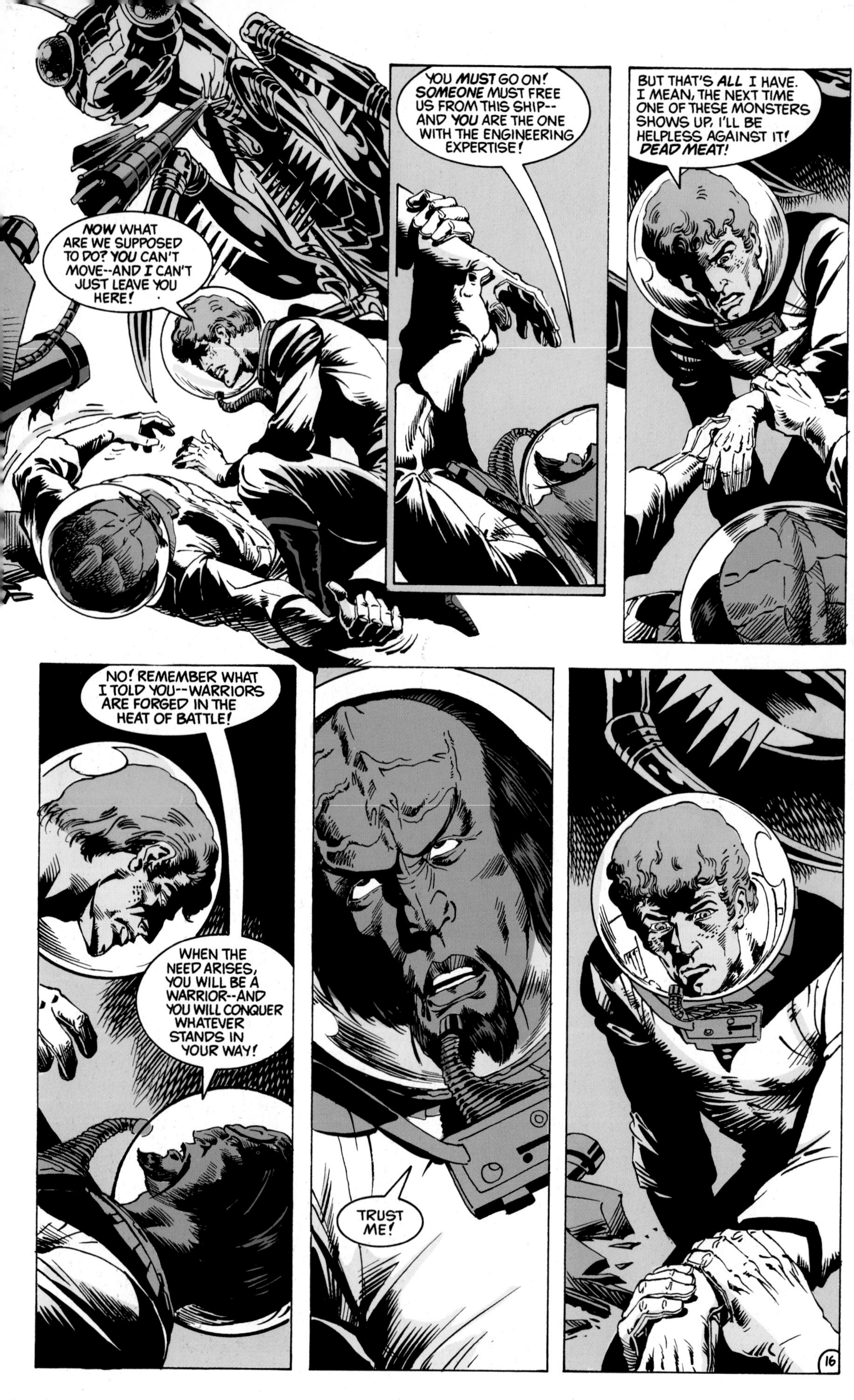
NOW WHAT ARE WE SUPPOSED TO DO? YOU CAN'T MOVE--AND I CAN'T JUST LEAVE YOU HERE!
YOU MUST GO ON! SOMEONE MUST FREE US FROM THIS SHIP--AND YOU ARE THE ONE WITH THE ENGINEERING EXPERTISE!
BUT THAT'S ALL I HAVE. I MEAN, THE NEXT TIME ONE OF THESE MONSTERS SHOWS UP, I'LL BE HELPLESS AGAINST IT! DEAD MEAT!
NO! REMEMBER WHAT I TOLD YOU--WARRIORS ARE FORGED IN THE HEAT OF BATTLE!
WHEN THE NEED ARISES, YOU WILL BE A WARRIOR--AND YOU WILL CONQUER WHATEVER STANDS IN YOUR WAY!
TRUST ME!

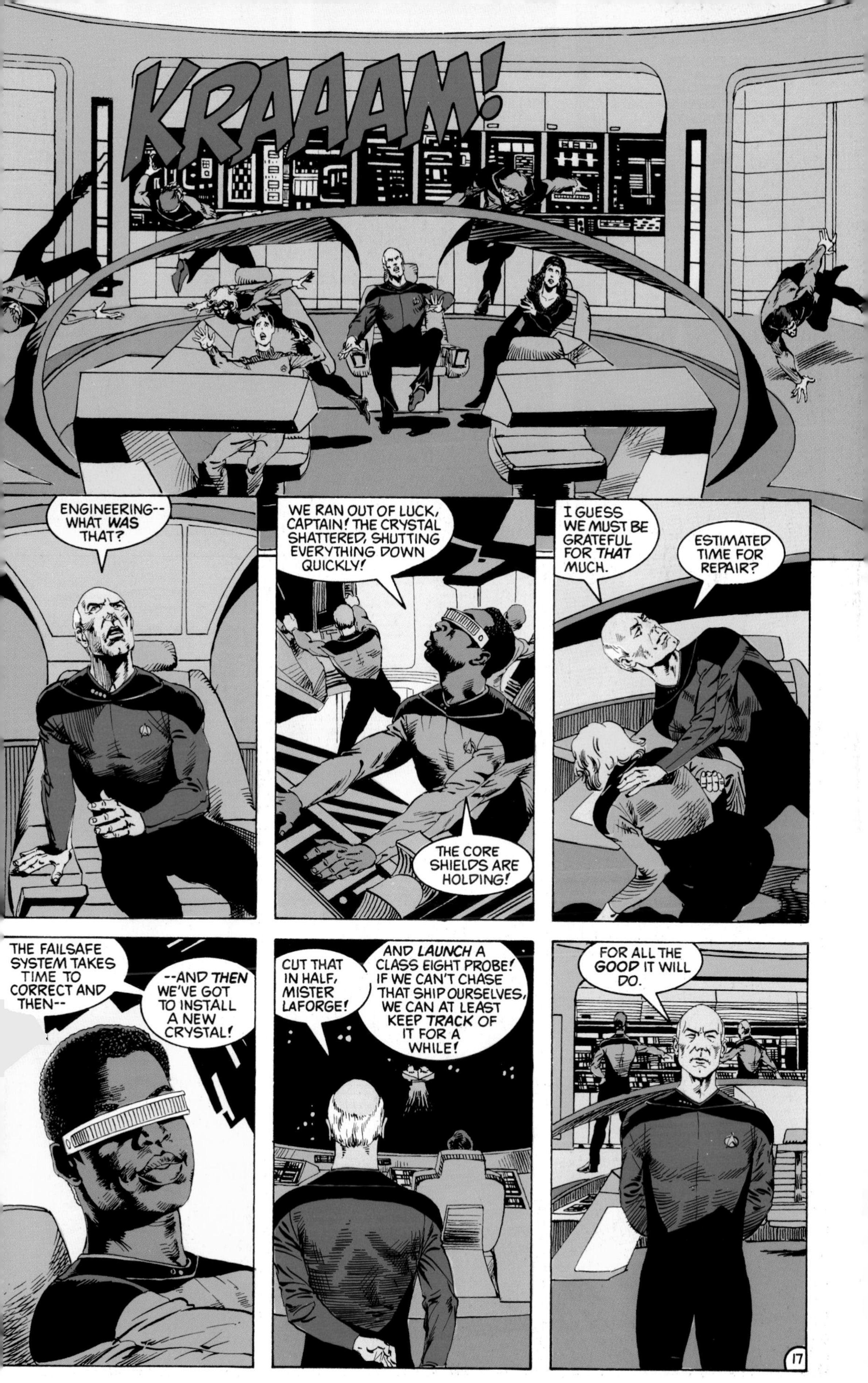
KRAAAM!
ENGINEERING-- WHAT WAS THAT?
WE RAN OUT OF LUCK, CAPTAIN! THE CRYSTAL SHATTERED, SHUTTING EVERYTHING DOWN QUICKLY!
THE CORE SHIELDS ARE HOLDING!
I GUESS WE MUST BE GRATEFUL FOR THAT MUCH.
ESTIMATED TIME FOR REPAIR?
THE FAILSAFE SYSTEM TAKES TIME TO CORRECT AND THEN--
--AND THEN WE'VE GOT TO INSTALL A NEW CRYSTAL!
CUT THAT IN HALF, MISTER LAFORGE!
AND LAUNCH A CLASS EIGHT PROBE! IF WE CAN'T CHASE THAT SHIP OURSELVES, WE CAN AT LEAST KEEP TRACK OF IT FOR A WHILE!
FOR ALL THE GOOD IT WILL DO.

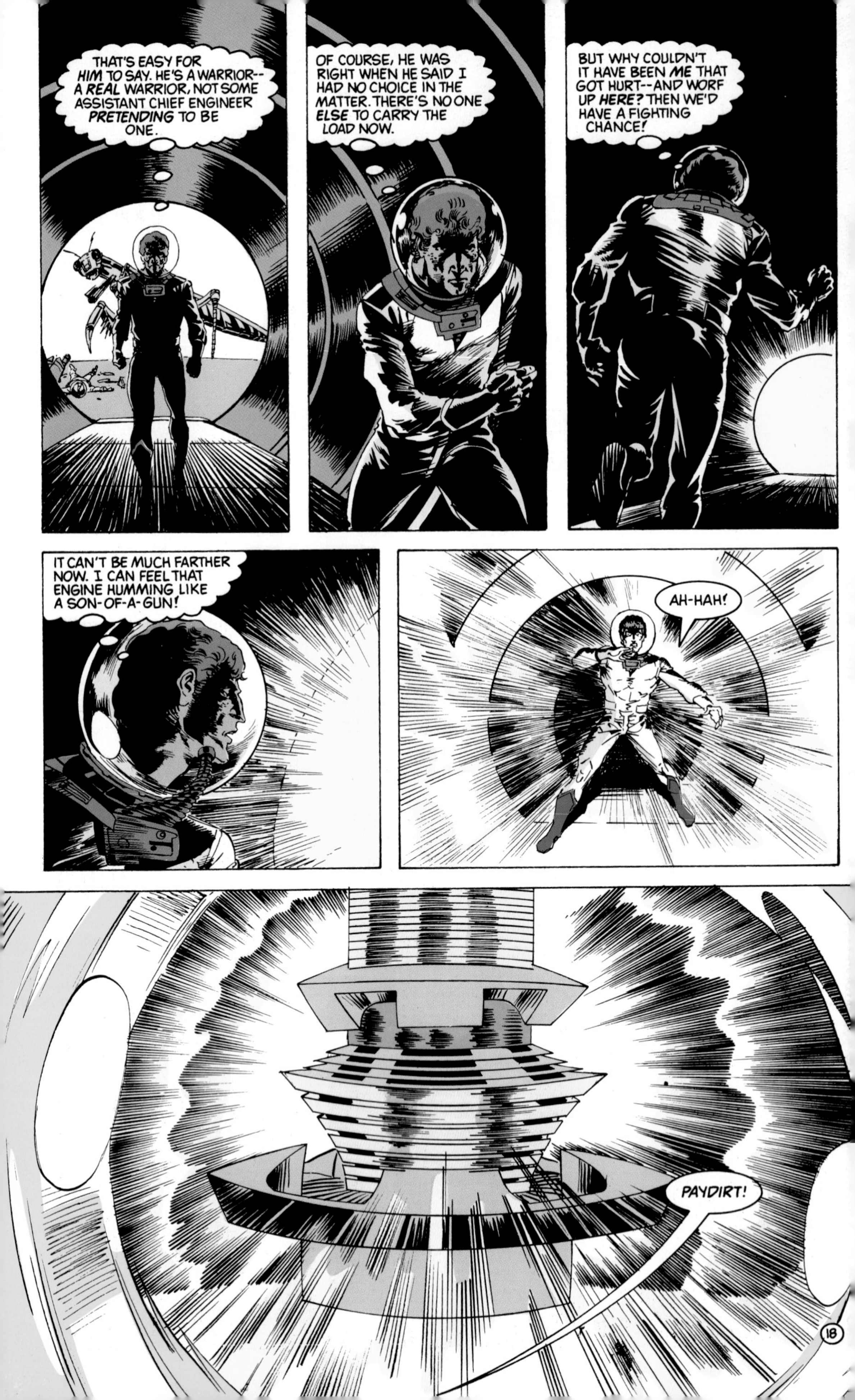
THAT'S EASY FOR HIM TO SAY. HE'S A WARRIOR-- A REAL WARRIOR, NOT SOME ASSISTANT CHIEF ENGINEER PRETENDING TO BE ONE.
OF COURSE, HE WAS RIGHT WHEN HE SAID I HAD NO CHOICE IN THE MATTER. THERE'S NO ONE ELSE TO CARRY THE LOAD NOW.
BUT WHY COULDN'T IT HAVE BEEN ME THAT GOT HURT--AND WORF UP HERE? THEN WE'D HAVE A FIGHTING CHANCE!
IT CAN'T BE MUCH FARTHER NOW. I CAN FEEL THAT ENGINE HUMMING LIKE A SON-OF-A-GUN!
AH-HAH!
PAYDIRT!

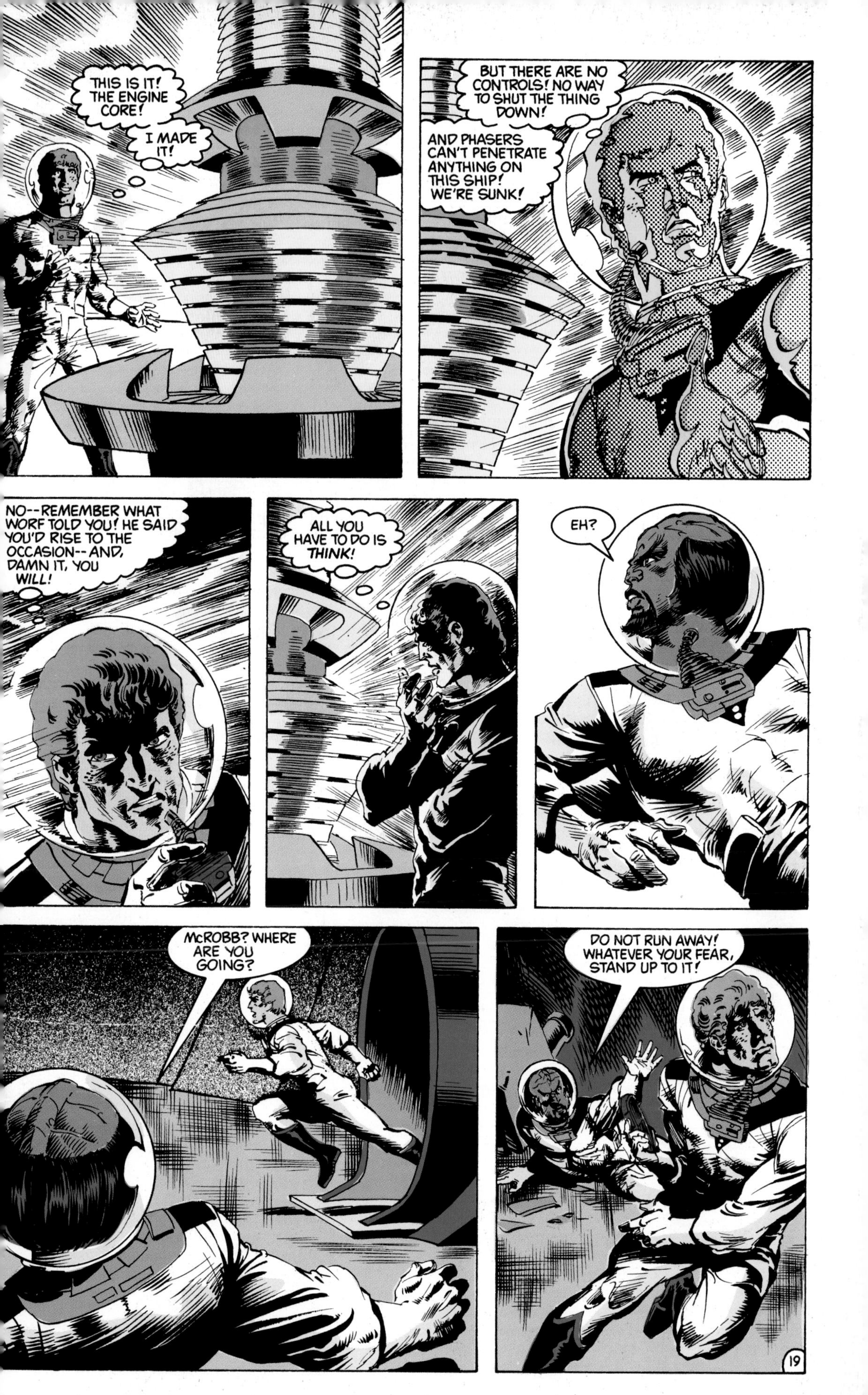
THIS IS IT! THE ENGINE CORE!
I MADE IT!
BUT THERE ARE NO CONTROLS! NO WAY TO SHUT THE THING DOWN!
AND PHASERS CAN'T PENETRATE ANYTHING ON THIS SHIP! WE'RE SUNK!
NO--REMEMBER WHAT WORF TOLD YOU! HE SAID YOU'D RISE TO THE OCCASION--AND, DAMN IT, YOU WILL!
ALL YOU HAVE TO DO IS THINK!
EH?
McROBB? WHERE ARE YOU GOING?
DO NOT RUN AWAY! WHATEVER YOUR FEAR, STAND UP TO IT!
19

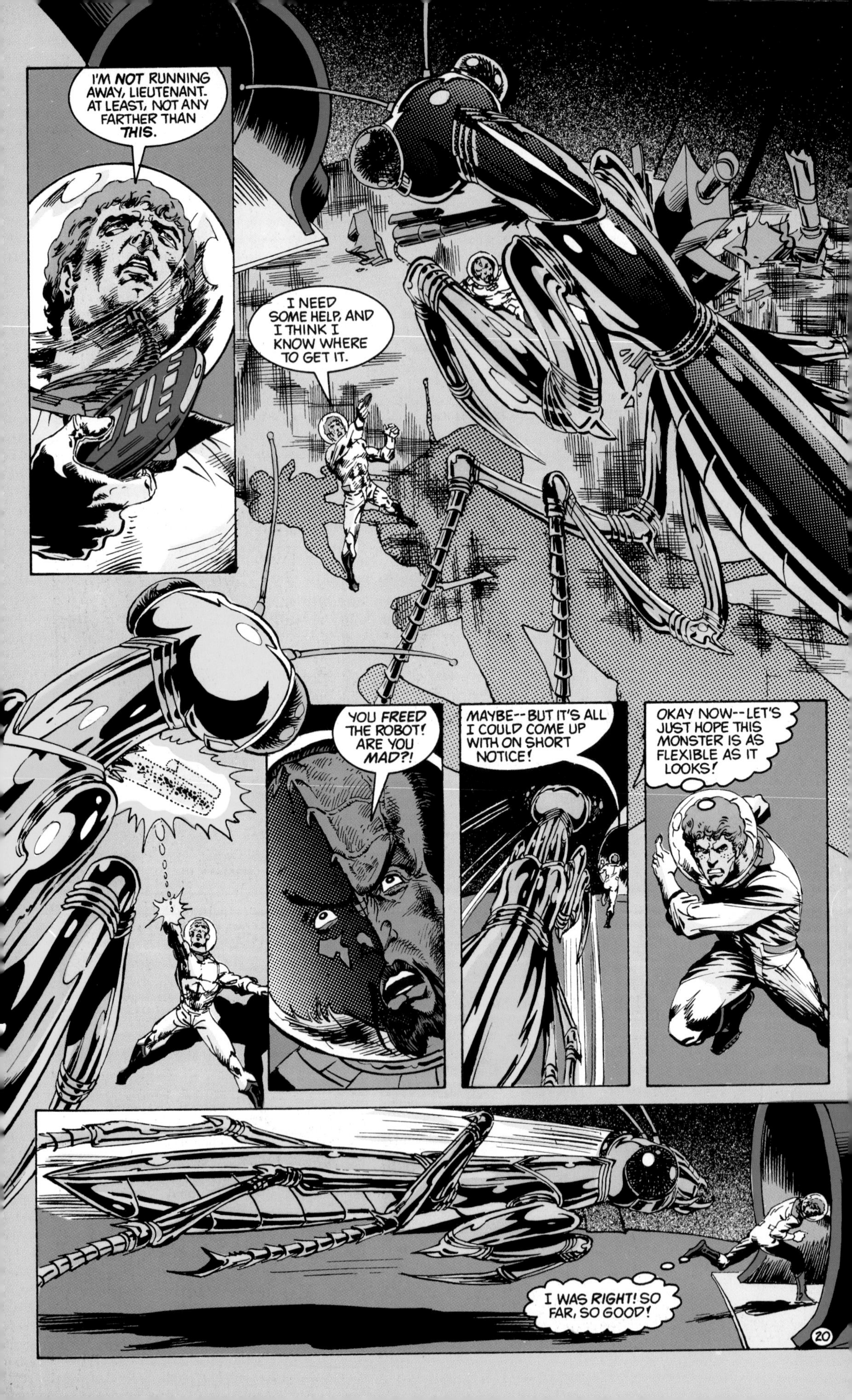
I'M NOT RUNNING AWAY, LIEUTENANT. AT LEAST, NOT ANY FARTHER THAN THIS.
I NEED SOME HELP, AND I THINK I KNOW WHERE TO GET IT.
YOU FREED THE ROBOT! ARE YOU MAD?!
MAYBE--BUT IT'S ALL I COULD COME UP WITH ON SHORT NOTICE!
OKAY NOW--LET'S JUST HOPE THIS MONSTER IS AS FLEXIBLE AS IT LOOKS!
I WAS RIGHT! SO FAR, SO GOOD!

NOW, ALL I HAVE TO DO IS STAY ONE STEP AHEAD OF IT--

--UNTIL WE GET THROUGH THIS PASSAGEWAY--

--AND INTO THE NEXT COMPARTMENT!

SLAM!

ALL RIGHT--END OF THE LINE! LET'S SEE HOW GOOD AN IDEA THIS REALLY WAS!

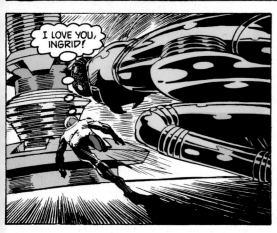

I LOVE YOU, INGRID!

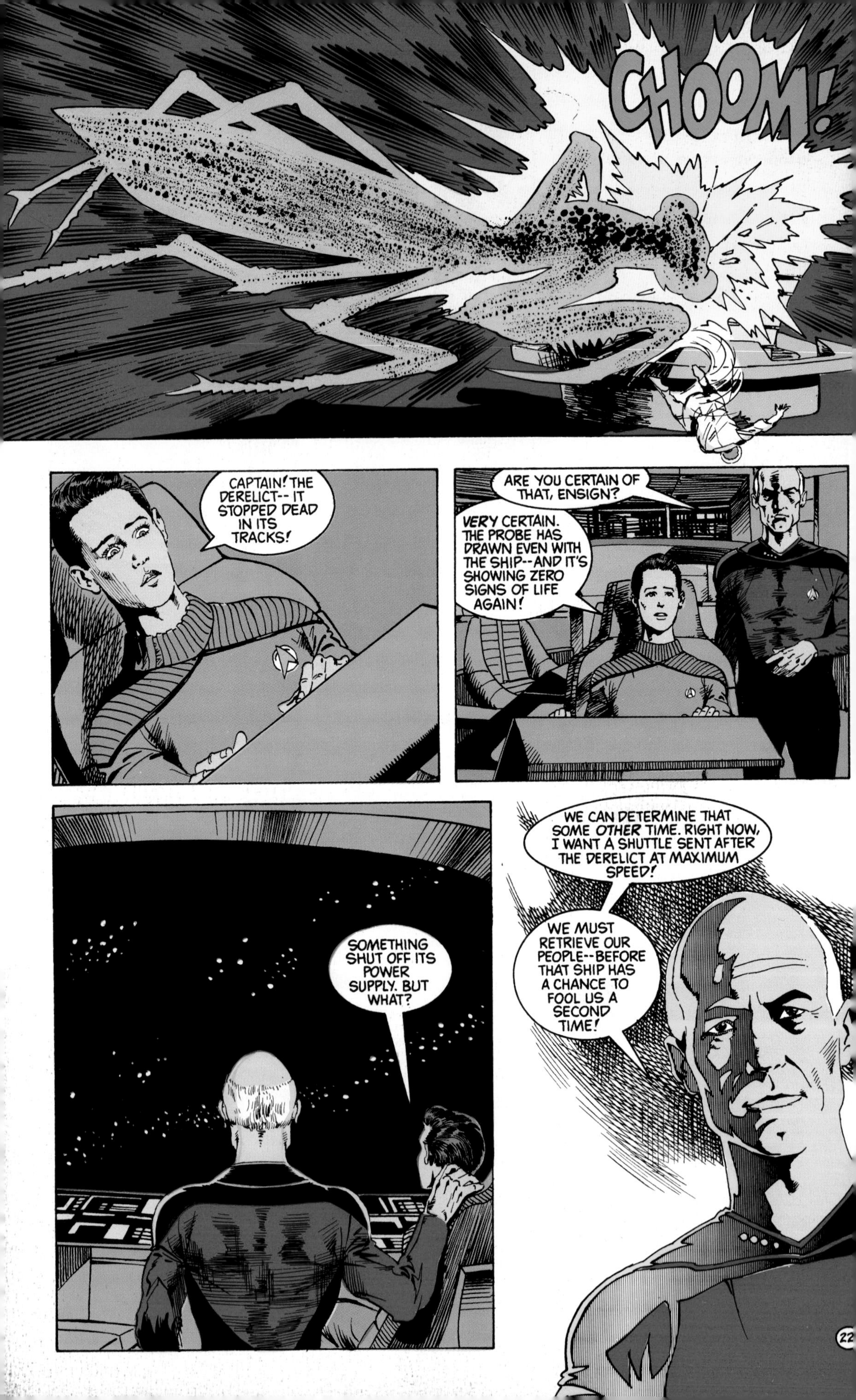
CHOOM!
CAPTAIN! THE DERELICT-- IT STOPPED DEAD IN ITS TRACKS!
ARE YOU CERTAIN OF THAT, ENSIGN?
VERY CERTAIN. THE PROBE HAS DRAWN EVEN WITH THE SHIP--AND IT'S SHOWING ZERO SIGNS OF LIFE AGAIN!
SOMETHING SHUT OFF ITS POWER SUPPLY. BUT WHAT?
WE CAN DETERMINE THAT SOME *OTHER* TIME. RIGHT NOW, I WANT A SHUTTLE SENT AFTER THE DERELICT AT MAXIMUM SPEED!
WE MUST RETRIEVE OUR PEOPLE--BEFORE THAT SHIP HAS A CHANCE TO FOOL US A SECOND TIME!

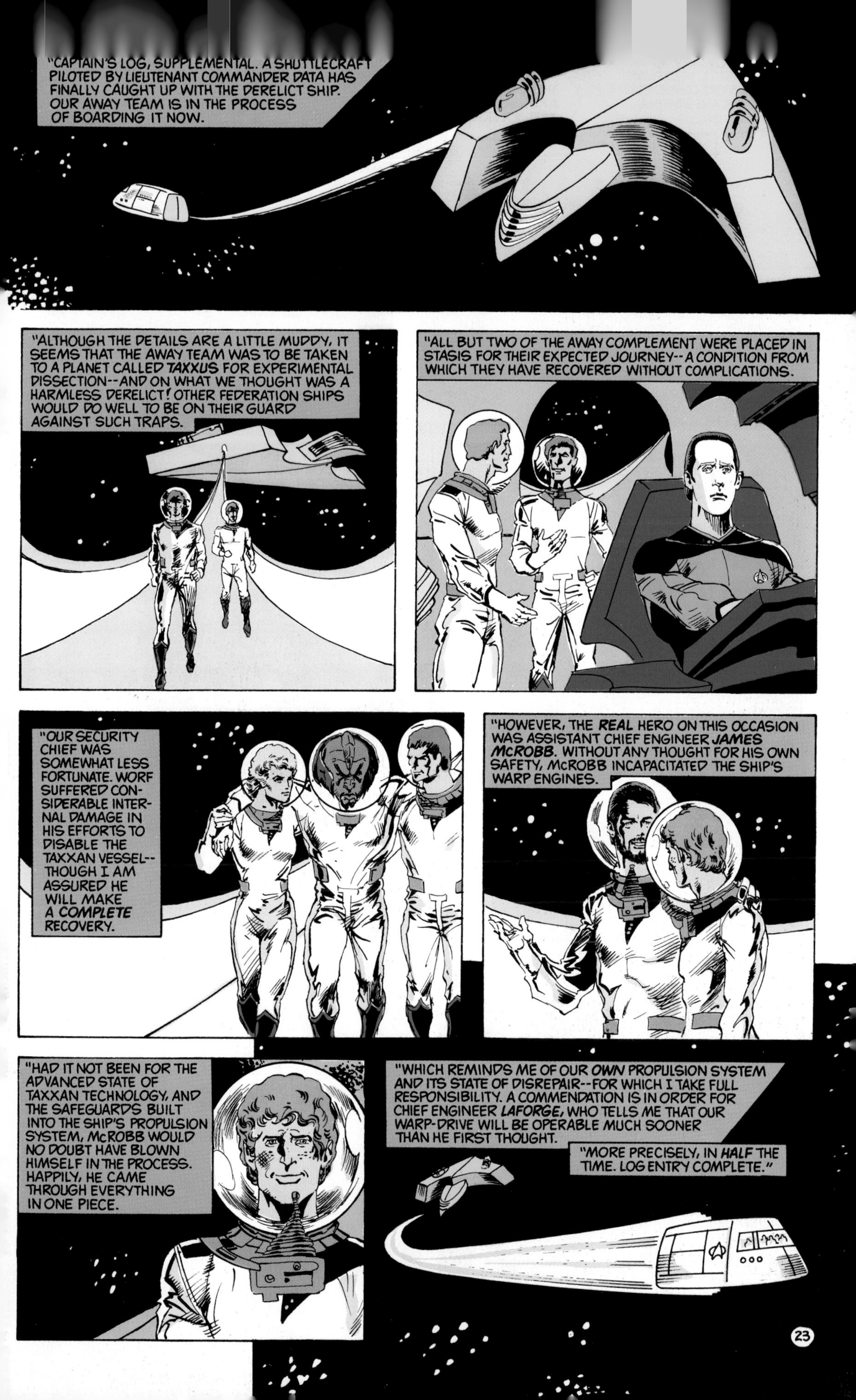
"CAPTAIN'S LOG, SUPPLEMENTAL. A SHUTTLECRAFT PILOTED BY LIEUTENANT COMMANDER DATA HAS FINALLY CAUGHT UP WITH THE DERELICT SHIP. OUR AWAY TEAM IS IN THE PROCESS OF BOARDING IT NOW.
"ALTHOUGH THE DETAILS ARE A LITTLE MUDDY, IT SEEMS THAT THE AWAY TEAM WAS TO BE TAKEN TO A PLANET CALLED TAXXUS FOR EXPERIMENTAL DISSECTION--AND ON WHAT WE THOUGHT WAS A HARMLESS DERELICT! OTHER FEDERATION SHIPS WOULD DO WELL TO BE ON THEIR GUARD AGAINST SUCH TRAPS.
"ALL BUT TWO OF THE AWAY COMPLEMENT WERE PLACED IN STASIS FOR THEIR EXPECTED JOURNEY--A CONDITION FROM WHICH THEY HAVE RECOVERED WITHOUT COMPLICATIONS.
"OUR SECURITY CHIEF WAS SOMEWHAT LESS FORTUNATE. WORF SUFFERED CONSIDERABLE INTERNAL DAMAGE IN HIS EFFORTS TO DISABLE THE TAXXAN VESSEL--THOUGH I AM ASSURED HE WILL MAKE A COMPLETE RECOVERY.
"HOWEVER, THE REAL HERO ON THIS OCCASION WAS ASSISTANT CHIEF ENGINEER JAMES McROBB. WITHOUT ANY THOUGHT FOR HIS OWN SAFETY, McROBB INCAPACITATED THE SHIP'S WARP ENGINES.
"HAD IT NOT BEEN FOR THE ADVANCED STATE OF TAXXAN TECHNOLOGY, AND THE SAFEGUARDS BUILT INTO THE SHIP'S PROPULSION SYSTEM, McROBB WOULD NO DOUBT HAVE BLOWN HIMSELF IN THE PROCESS. HAPPILY, HE CAME THROUGH EVERYTHING IN ONE PIECE.
"WHICH REMINDS ME OF OUR OWN PROPULSION SYSTEM AND ITS STATE OF DISREPAIR--FOR WHICH I TAKE FULL RESPONSIBILITY. A COMMENDATION IS IN ORDER FOR CHIEF ENGINEER LAFORGE, WHO TELLS ME THAT OUR WARP-DRIVE WILL BE OPERABLE MUCH SOONER THAN HE FIRST THOUGHT.
"MORE PRECISELY, IN HALF THE TIME. LOG ENTRY COMPLETE."

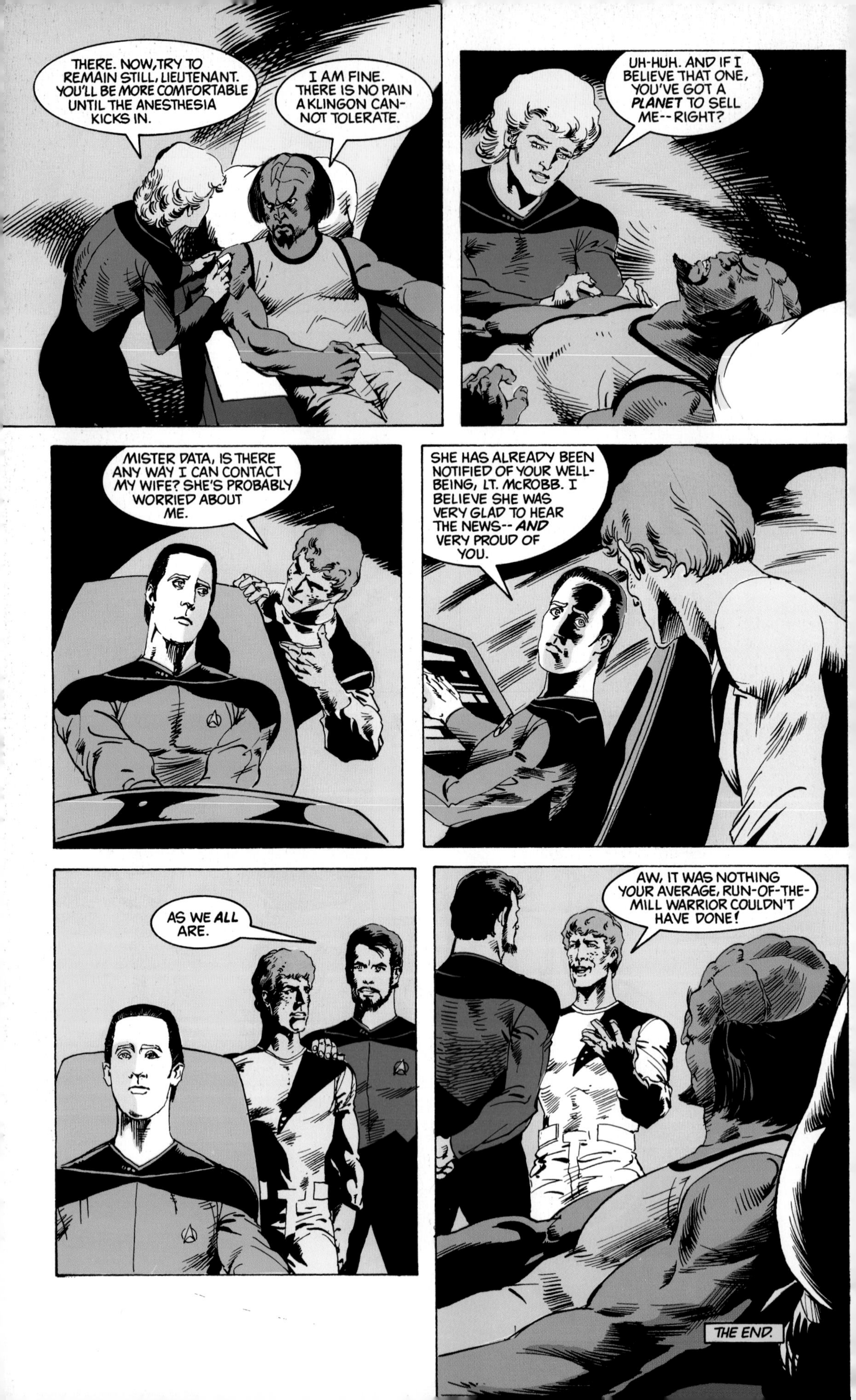
THERE. NOW, TRY TO REMAIN STILL, LIEUTENANT. YOU'LL BE MORE COMFORTABLE UNTIL THE ANESTHESIA KICKS IN.
I AM FINE. THERE IS NO PAIN A KLINGON CAN-NOT TOLERATE.
UH-HUH. AND IF I BELIEVE THAT ONE, YOU'VE GOT A PLANET TO SELL ME--RIGHT?
MISTER DATA, IS THERE ANY WAY I CAN CONTACT MY WIFE? SHE'S PROBABLY WORRIED ABOUT ME.
SHE HAS ALREADY BEEN NOTIFIED OF YOUR WELL-BEING, LT. McROBB. I BELIEVE SHE WAS VERY GLAD TO HEAR THE NEWS--AND VERY PROUD OF YOU.
AS WE ALL ARE.
AW, IT WAS NOTHING YOUR AVERAGE, RUN-OF-THE-MILL WARRIOR COULDN'T HAVE DONE!
THE END.

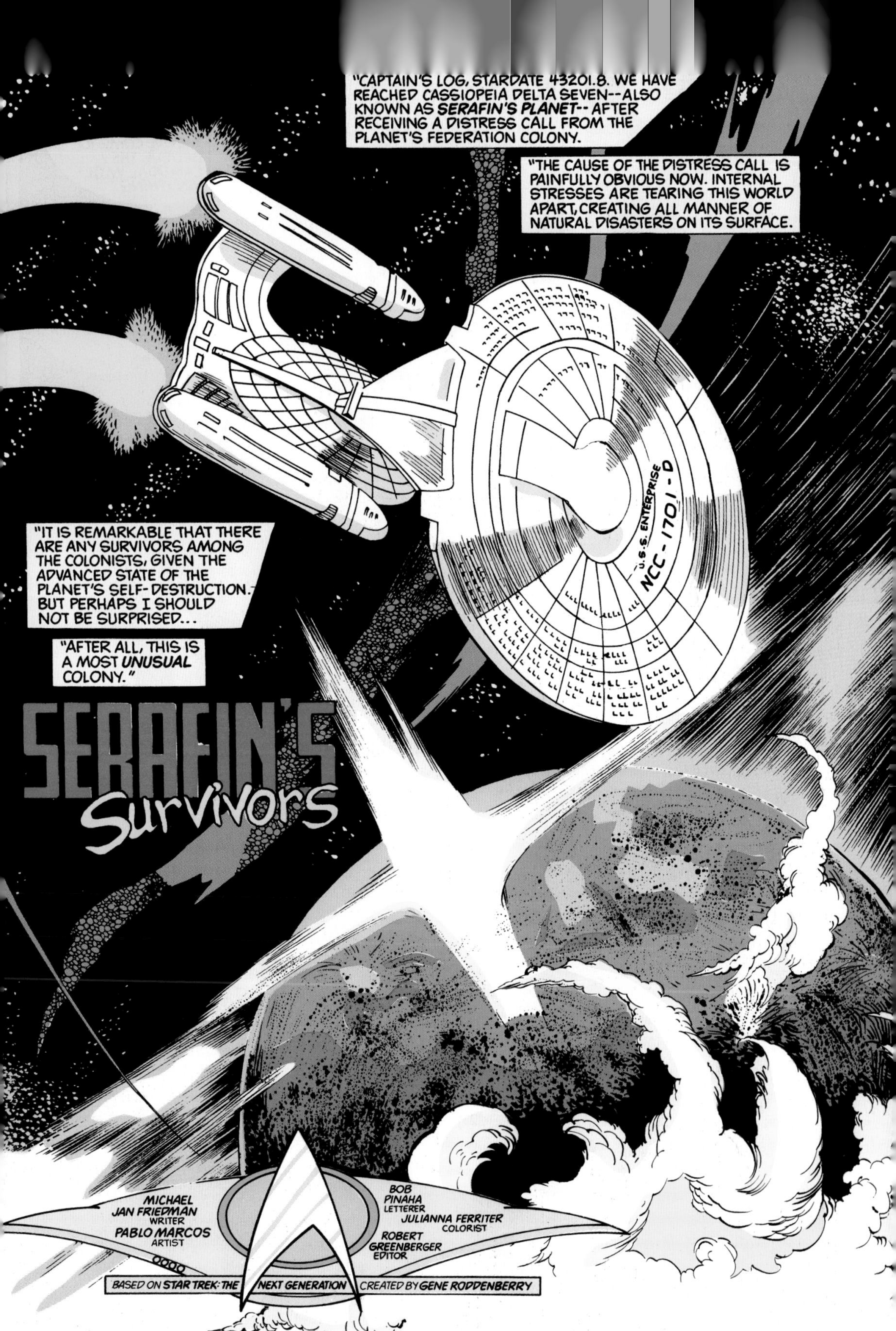
"CAPTAIN'S LOG, STARDATE 43201.8. WE HAVE REACHED CASSIOPEIA DELTA SEVEN--ALSO KNOWN AS SERAFIN'S PLANET-- AFTER RECEIVING A DISTRESS CALL FROM THE PLANET'S FEDERATION COLONY.
"THE CAUSE OF THE DISTRESS CALL IS PAINFULLY OBVIOUS NOW. INTERNAL STRESSES ARE TEARING THIS WORLD APART, CREATING ALL MANNER OF NATURAL DISASTERS ON ITS SURFACE.
U.S.S. ENTERPRISE
NCC-1701-D
"IT IS REMARKABLE THAT THERE ARE ANY SURVIVORS AMONG THE COLONISTS, GIVEN THE ADVANCED STATE OF THE PLANET'S SELF-DESTRUCTION.-BUT PERHAPS I SHOULD NOT BE SURPRISED...
"AFTER ALL, THIS IS A MOST UNUSUAL COLONY."
SERAFIN'S Survivors
MICHAEL JAN FRIEDMAN WRITER
PABLO MARCOS ARTIST
BOB PINAHA LETTERER
JULIANNA FERRITER COLORIST
ROBERT GREENBERGER EDITOR
BASED ON STAR TREK: THE NEXT GENERATION CREATED BY GENE RODDENBERRY

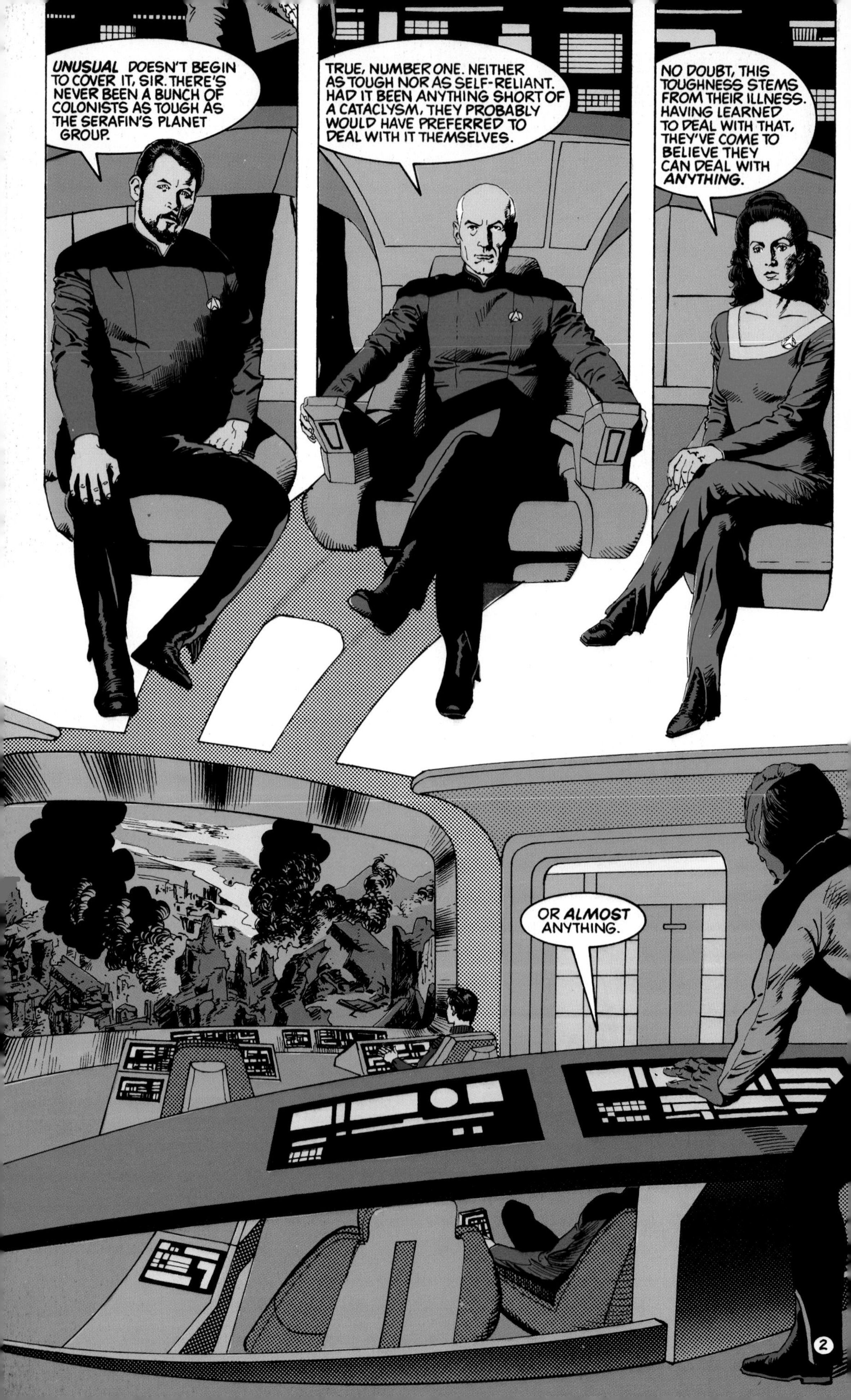

UNUSUAL DOESN'T BEGIN TO COVER IT, SIR. THERE'S NEVER BEEN A BUNCH OF COLONISTS AS TOUGH AS THE SERAFIN'S PLANET GROUP.
TRUE, NUMBER ONE. NEITHER AS TOUGH NOR AS SELF-RELIANT. HAD IT BEEN ANYTHING SHORT OF A CATACLYSM, THEY PROBABLY WOULD HAVE PREFERRED TO DEAL WITH IT THEMSELVES.
NO DOUBT, THIS TOUGHNESS STEMS FROM THEIR ILLNESS. HAVING LEARNED TO DEAL WITH THAT, THEY'VE COME TO BELIEVE THEY CAN DEAL WITH ANYTHING.
OR ALMOST ANYTHING.

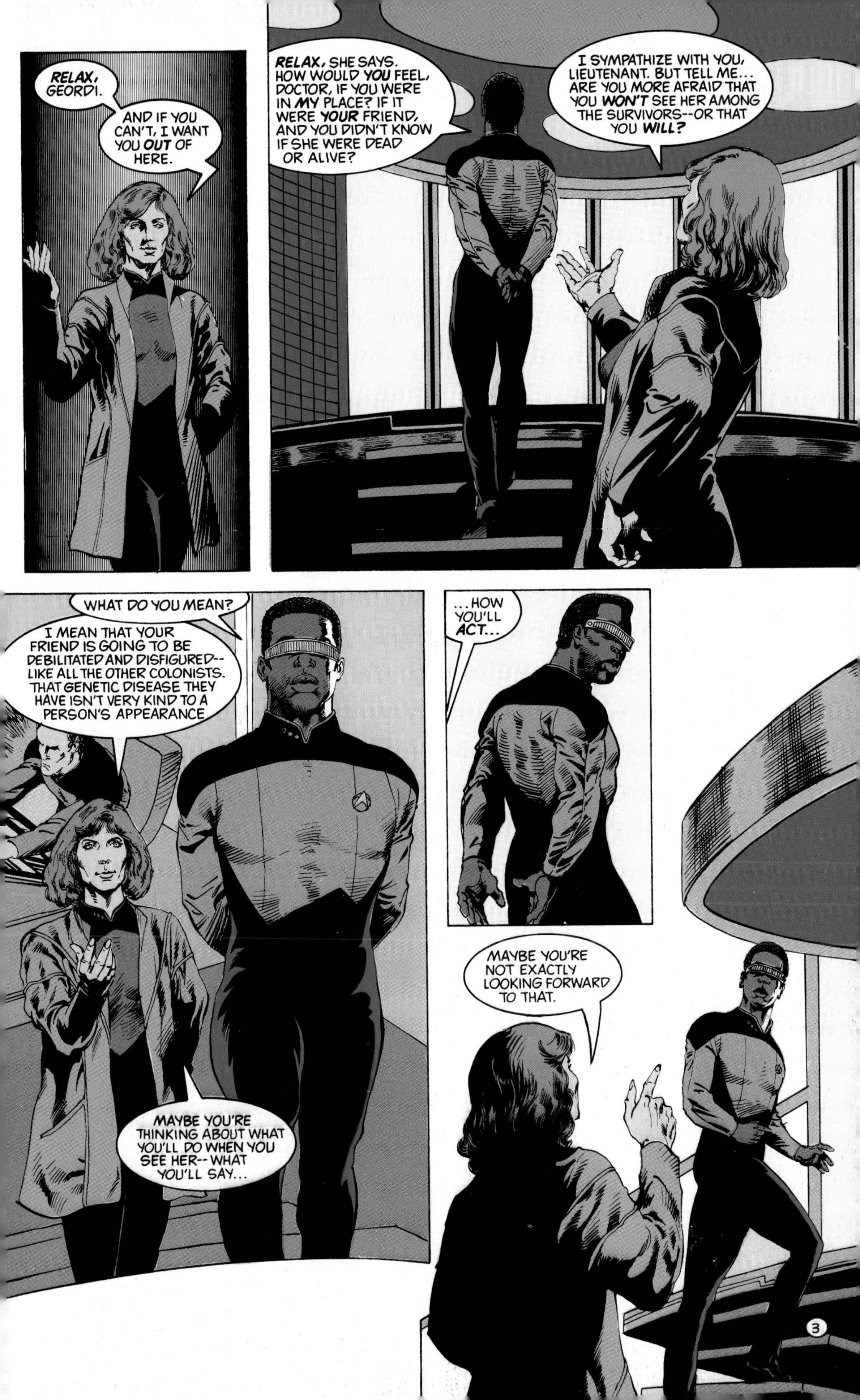
RELAX, GEORDI.
AND IF YOU CAN'T, I WANT YOU OUT OF HERE.
RELAX, SHE SAYS. HOW WOULD YOU FEEL, DOCTOR, IF YOU WERE IN MY PLACE? IF IT WERE YOUR FRIEND, AND YOU DIDN'T KNOW IF SHE WERE DEAD OR ALIVE?
I SYMPATHIZE WITH YOU, LIEUTENANT. BUT TELL ME... ARE YOU MORE AFRAID THAT YOU WON'T SEE HER AMONG THE SURVIVORS--OR THAT YOU WILL?
WHAT DO YOU MEAN?
I MEAN THAT YOUR FRIEND IS GOING TO BE DEBILITATED AND DISFIGURED--LIKE ALL THE OTHER COLONISTS. THAT GENETIC DISEASE THEY HAVE ISN'T VERY KIND TO A PERSON'S APPEARANCE
MAYBE YOU'RE THINKING ABOUT WHAT YOU'LL DO WHEN YOU SEE HER--WHAT YOU'LL SAY...
...HOW YOU'LL ACT...
MAYBE YOU'RE NOT EXACTLY LOOKING FORWARD TO THAT.

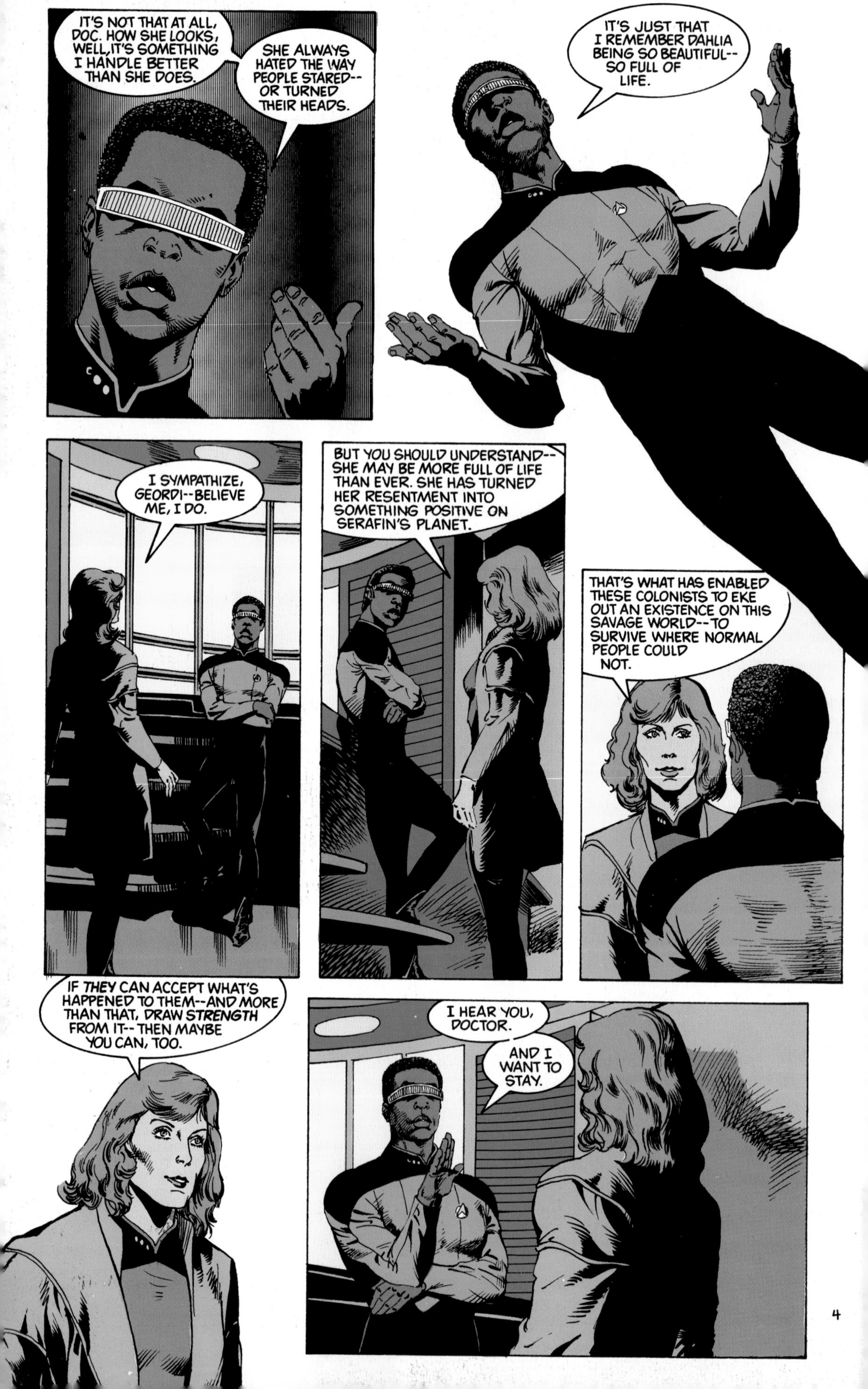

IT'S NOT THAT AT ALL, DOC. HOW SHE LOOKS, WELL, IT'S SOMETHING I HANDLE BETTER THAN SHE DOES.
SHE ALWAYS HATED THE WAY PEOPLE STARED--OR TURNED THEIR HEADS.
IT'S JUST THAT I REMEMBER DAHLIA BEING SO BEAUTIFUL--SO FULL OF LIFE.
I SYMPATHIZE, GEORDI--BELIEVE ME, I DO.
BUT YOU SHOULD UNDERSTAND--SHE MAY BE MORE FULL OF LIFE THAN EVER. SHE HAS TURNED HER RESENTMENT INTO SOMETHING POSITIVE ON SERAFIN'S PLANET.
THAT'S WHAT HAS ENABLED THESE COLONISTS TO EKE OUT AN EXISTENCE ON THIS SAVAGE WORLD--TO SURVIVE WHERE NORMAL PEOPLE COULD NOT.
IF *THEY* CAN ACCEPT WHAT'S HAPPENED TO THEM--AND MORE THAN THAT, DRAW *STRENGTH* FROM IT--THEN MAYBE *YOU* CAN, TOO.
I HEAR YOU, DOCTOR.
AND I WANT TO STAY.

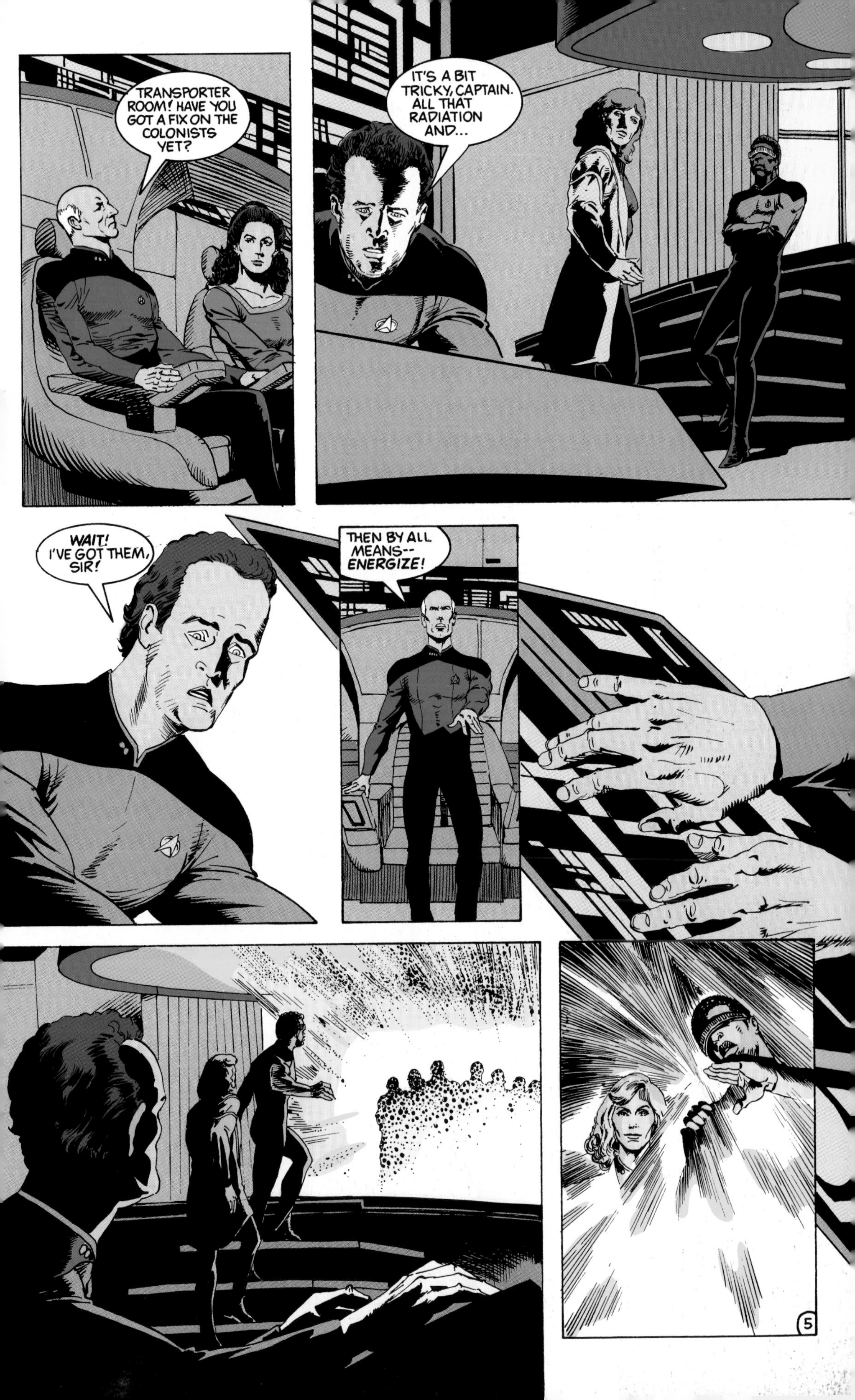
TRANSPORTER ROOM! HAVE YOU GOT A FIX ON THE COLONISTS YET?
IT'S A BIT TRICKY, CAPTAIN. ALL THAT RADIATION AND...
WAIT! I'VE GOT THEM, SIR!
THEN BY ALL MEANS-- ENERGIZE!
5

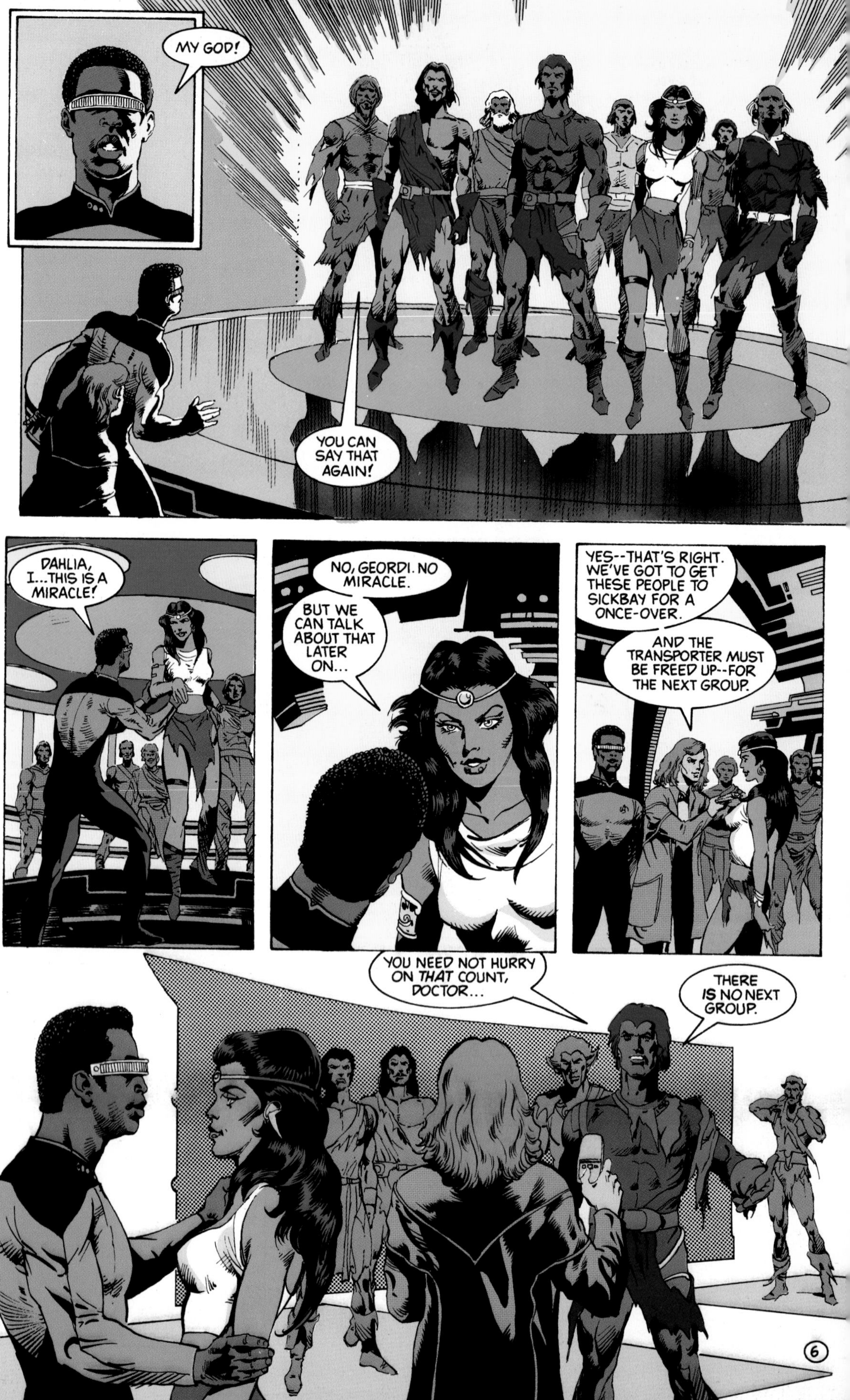
MY GOD!
YOU CAN SAY THAT AGAIN!
DAHLIA, I...THIS IS A MIRACLE!
NO, GEORDI. NO MIRACLE.
BUT WE CAN TALK ABOUT THAT LATER ON...
YES--THAT'S RIGHT. WE'VE GOT TO GET THESE PEOPLE TO SICKBAY FOR A ONCE-OVER.
AND THE TRANSPORTER MUST BE FREED UP--FOR THE NEXT GROUP.
YOU NEED NOT HURRY ON *THAT* COUNT, DOCTOR...
THERE *IS* NO NEXT GROUP.

I STILL CAN'T BELIEVE IT, DATA. IT'S LIKE A DREAM COME TRUE!

JUDGING FROM YOUR BEHAVIOR, THAT MUST BE A POSITIVE DEVELOPMENT.

OF COURSE IT'S POSITIVE! I THOUGHT I'D NEVER SEE HER AGAIN-- AND SUDDENLY, HERE SHE IS! ALL CURED AND EVERYTHING!

IF THAT'S NOT A DREAM COME TRUE, I DON'T KNOW WHAT IS!

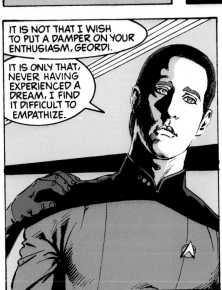

IT IS NOT THAT I WISH TO PUT A DAMPER ON YOUR ENTHUSIASM, GEORDI.

IT IS ONLY THAT, NEVER HAVING EXPERIENCED A DREAM, I FIND IT DIFFICULT TO EMPATHIZE.

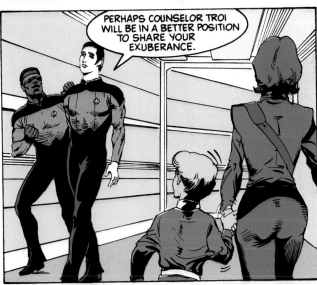

PERHAPS COUNSELOR TROI WILL BE IN A BETTER POSITION TO SHARE YOUR EXUBERANCE.

THAT'S OKAY, DATA. I'M SO HAPPY, I DON'T CARE IF NO ONE KNOWS IT--EXCEPT, OF COURSE, FOR DAHLIA!

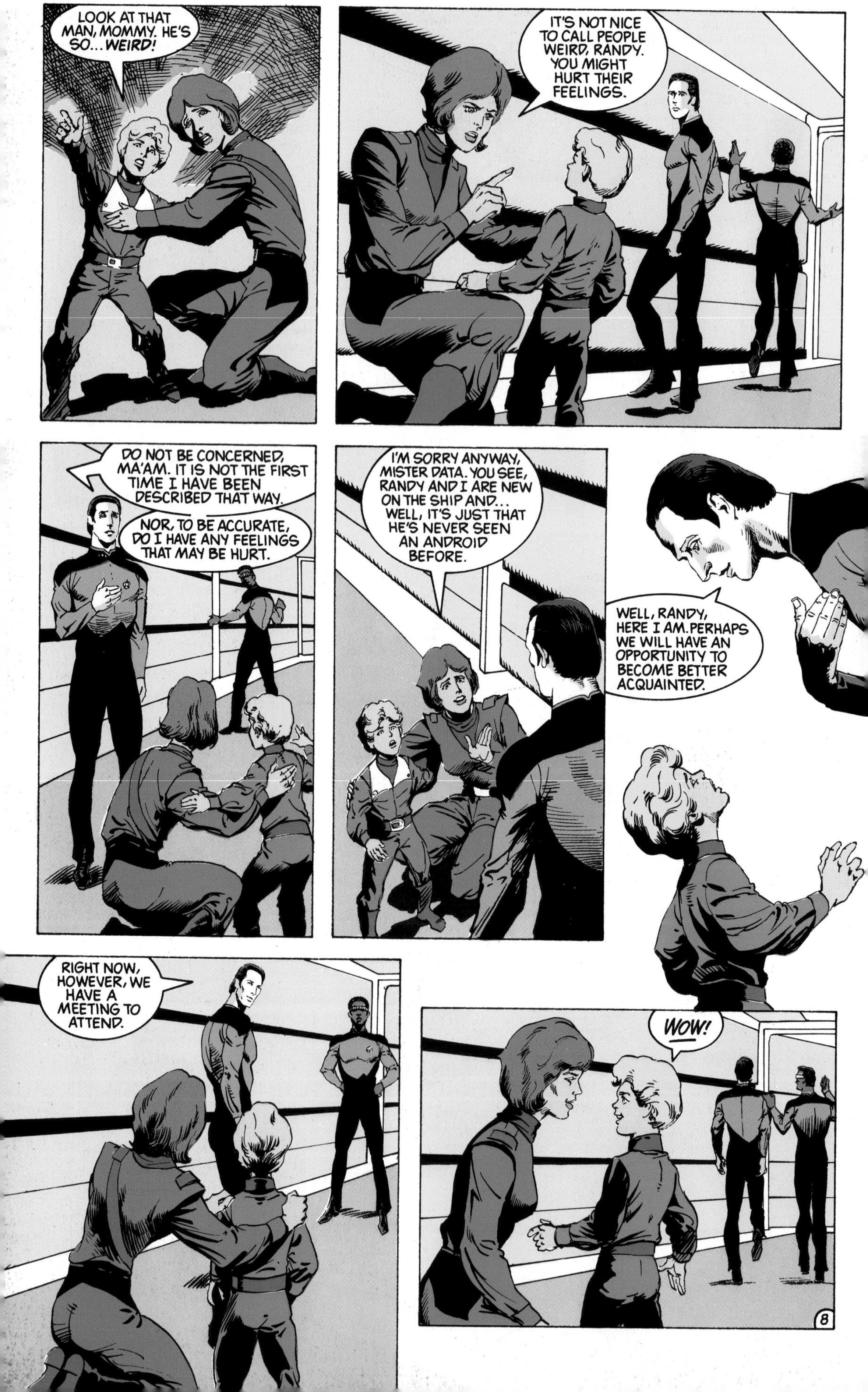
LOOK AT THAT MAN, MOMMY. HE'S SO... WEIRD!
IT'S NOT NICE TO CALL PEOPLE WEIRD, RANDY. YOU MIGHT HURT THEIR FEELINGS.
DO NOT BE CONCERNED, MA'AM. IT IS NOT THE FIRST TIME I HAVE BEEN DESCRIBED THAT WAY.
NOR, TO BE ACCURATE, DO I HAVE ANY FEELINGS THAT MAY BE HURT.
I'M SORRY ANYWAY, MISTER DATA. YOU SEE, RANDY AND I ARE NEW ON THE SHIP AND... WELL, IT'S JUST THAT HE'S NEVER SEEN AN ANDROID BEFORE.
WELL, RANDY, HERE I AM. PERHAPS WE WILL HAVE AN OPPORTUNITY TO BECOME BETTER ACQUAINTED.
RIGHT NOW, HOWEVER, WE HAVE A MEETING TO ATTEND.
WOW!
8

AH-- THERE YOU ARE, GENTLEMEN. NICE OF YOU TO JOIN US.

SORRY, SIR. WE WERE... UM, UNAVOIDABLY DETAINED.

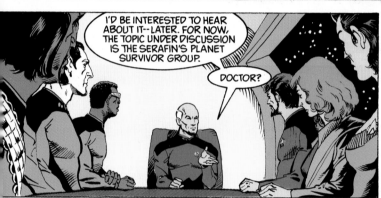

I'D BE INTERESTED TO HEAR ABOUT IT--LATER. FOR NOW, THE TOPIC UNDER DISCUSSION IS THE SERAFIN'S PLANET SURVIVOR GROUP.

DOCTOR?

PHYSICALLY, THE COLONISTS ARE ALL IN FINE SHAPE. I'M ALMOST TEMPTED TO SAY PERFECT SHAPE.

AND THERE'S ABSOLUTELY NO TRACE OF THE DISEASE THAT HAD AFFLICTED THEM.

SO FAR, HOWEVER, I CAN'T SAY WHY THEY'RE SO HEALTHY. MAYBE IT HAS SOMETHING TO DO WITH THE RADIATION THEY WERE EXPOSED TO WHEN THEIR PLANET BEGAN SPLITTING APART. MAYBE IT'S SOMETHING ELSE-- I JUST DON'T KNOW.

CAN THE COLONISTS THEMSELVES SHED ANY LIGHT ON IT?

THEY SAY IT WAS A FAIRLY RECENT DEVELOP-MENT--ONE THAT BEGAN TAKING PLACE ONLY A FEW MONTHS AGO. BUT BEYOND THAT, THEY HAVEN'T A CLUE.

9

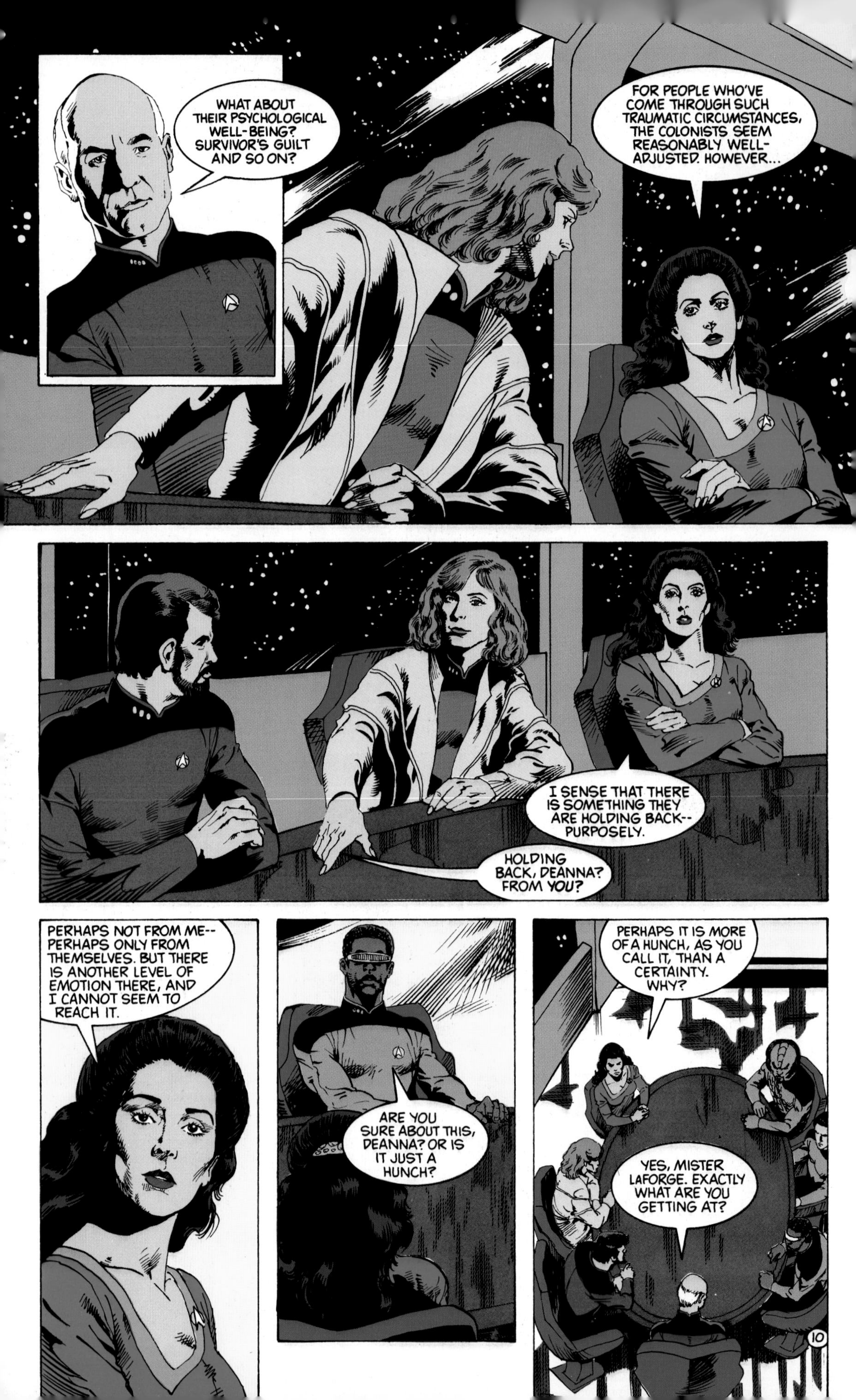
WHAT ABOUT THEIR PSYCHOLOGICAL WELL-BEING? SURVIVOR'S GUILT AND SO ON?
FOR PEOPLE WHO'VE COME THROUGH SUCH TRAUMATIC CIRCUMSTANCES, THE COLONISTS SEEM REASONABLY WELL-ADJUSTED. HOWEVER...
I SENSE THAT THERE IS SOMETHING THEY ARE HOLDING BACK-- PURPOSELY.
HOLDING BACK, DEANNA? FROM *YOU*?
PERHAPS NOT FROM ME-- PERHAPS ONLY FROM THEMSELVES. BUT THERE IS ANOTHER LEVEL OF EMOTION THERE, AND I CANNOT SEEM TO REACH IT.
ARE YOU SURE ABOUT THIS, DEANNA? OR IS IT JUST A HUNCH?
PERHAPS IT IS MORE OF A HUNCH, AS YOU CALL IT, THAN A CERTAINTY. WHY?
YES, MISTER LAFORGE. EXACTLY WHAT ARE YOU GETTING AT?
10

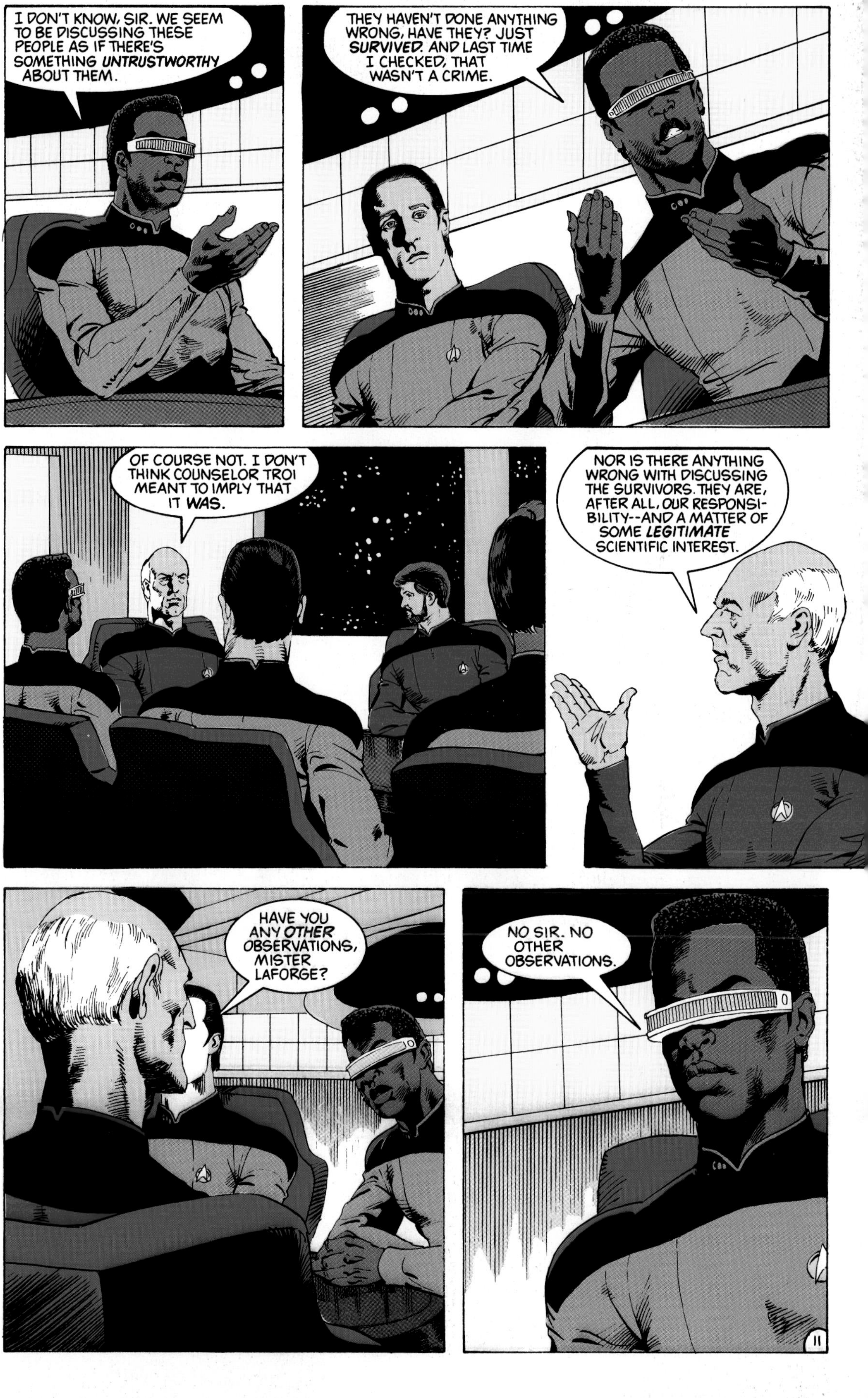
I DON'T KNOW, SIR. WE SEEM TO BE DISCUSSING THESE PEOPLE AS IF THERE'S SOMETHING *UNTRUSTWORTHY* ABOUT THEM.
THEY HAVEN'T DONE ANYTHING WRONG, HAVE THEY? JUST *SURVIVED*. AND LAST TIME I CHECKED, THAT WASN'T A CRIME.
OF COURSE NOT. I DON'T THINK COUNSELOR TROI MEANT TO IMPLY THAT IT *WAS*.
NOR IS THERE ANYTHING WRONG WITH DISCUSSING THE SURVIVORS. THEY ARE, AFTER ALL, *OUR* RESPONSIBILITY--AND A MATTER OF SOME *LEGITIMATE* SCIENTIFIC INTEREST.
HAVE YOU ANY *OTHER* OBSERVATIONS, MISTER LAFORGE?
NO SIR. NO OTHER OBSERVATIONS.
11

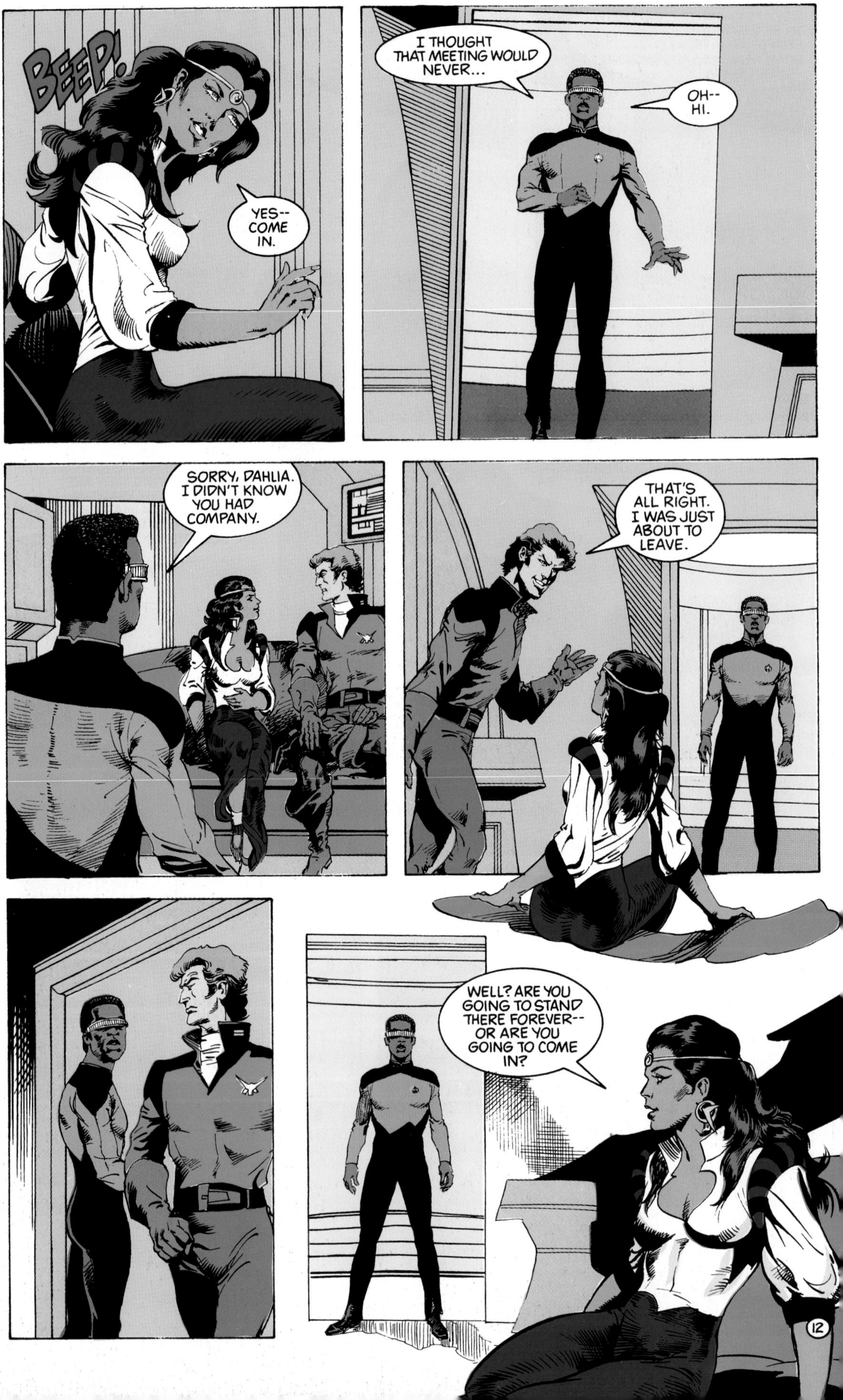
BEEP!
YES--COME IN.
I THOUGHT THAT MEETING WOULD NEVER...
OH--HI.
SORRY, DAHLIA. I DIDN'T KNOW YOU HAD COMPANY.
THAT'S ALL RIGHT. I WAS JUST ABOUT TO LEAVE.
WELL? ARE YOU GOING TO STAND THERE FOREVER--OR ARE YOU GOING TO COME IN?
12

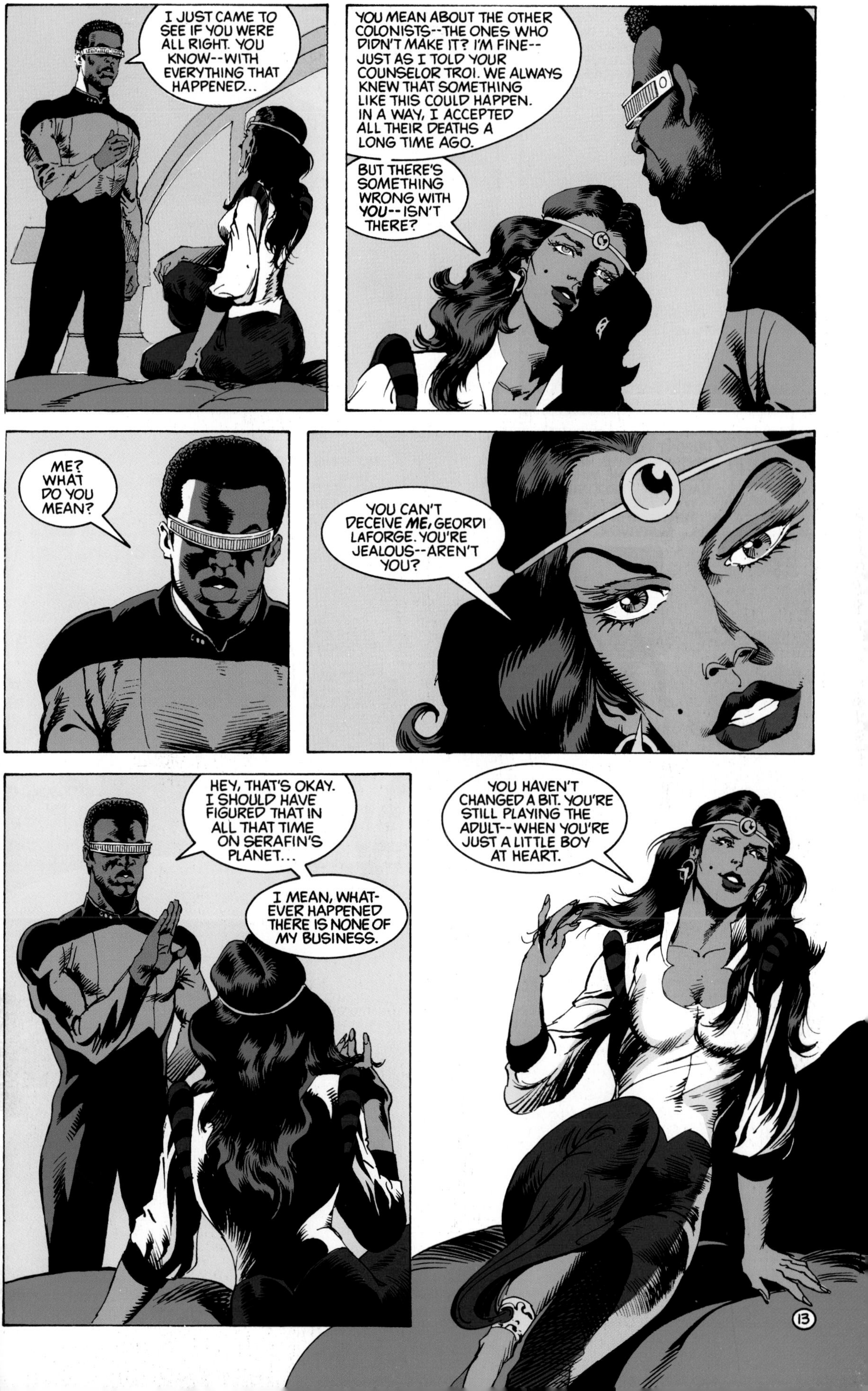
I JUST CAME TO SEE IF YOU WERE ALL RIGHT. YOU KNOW--WITH EVERYTHING THAT HAPPENED...
YOU MEAN ABOUT THE OTHER COLONISTS--THE ONES WHO DIDN'T MAKE IT? I'M FINE--JUST AS I TOLD YOUR COUNSELOR TROI. WE ALWAYS KNEW THAT SOMETHING LIKE THIS COULD HAPPEN. IN A WAY, I ACCEPTED ALL THEIR DEATHS A LONG TIME AGO.
BUT THERE'S SOMETHING WRONG WITH YOU--ISN'T THERE?
ME? WHAT DO YOU MEAN?
YOU CAN'T DECEIVE ME, GEORDI LAFORGE. YOU'RE JEALOUS--AREN'T YOU?
HEY, THAT'S OKAY. I SHOULD HAVE FIGURED THAT IN ALL THAT TIME ON SERAFIN'S PLANET...
I MEAN, WHATEVER HAPPENED THERE IS NONE OF MY BUSINESS.
YOU HAVEN'T CHANGED A BIT. YOU'RE STILL PLAYING THE ADULT--WHEN YOU'RE JUST A LITTLE BOY AT HEART.

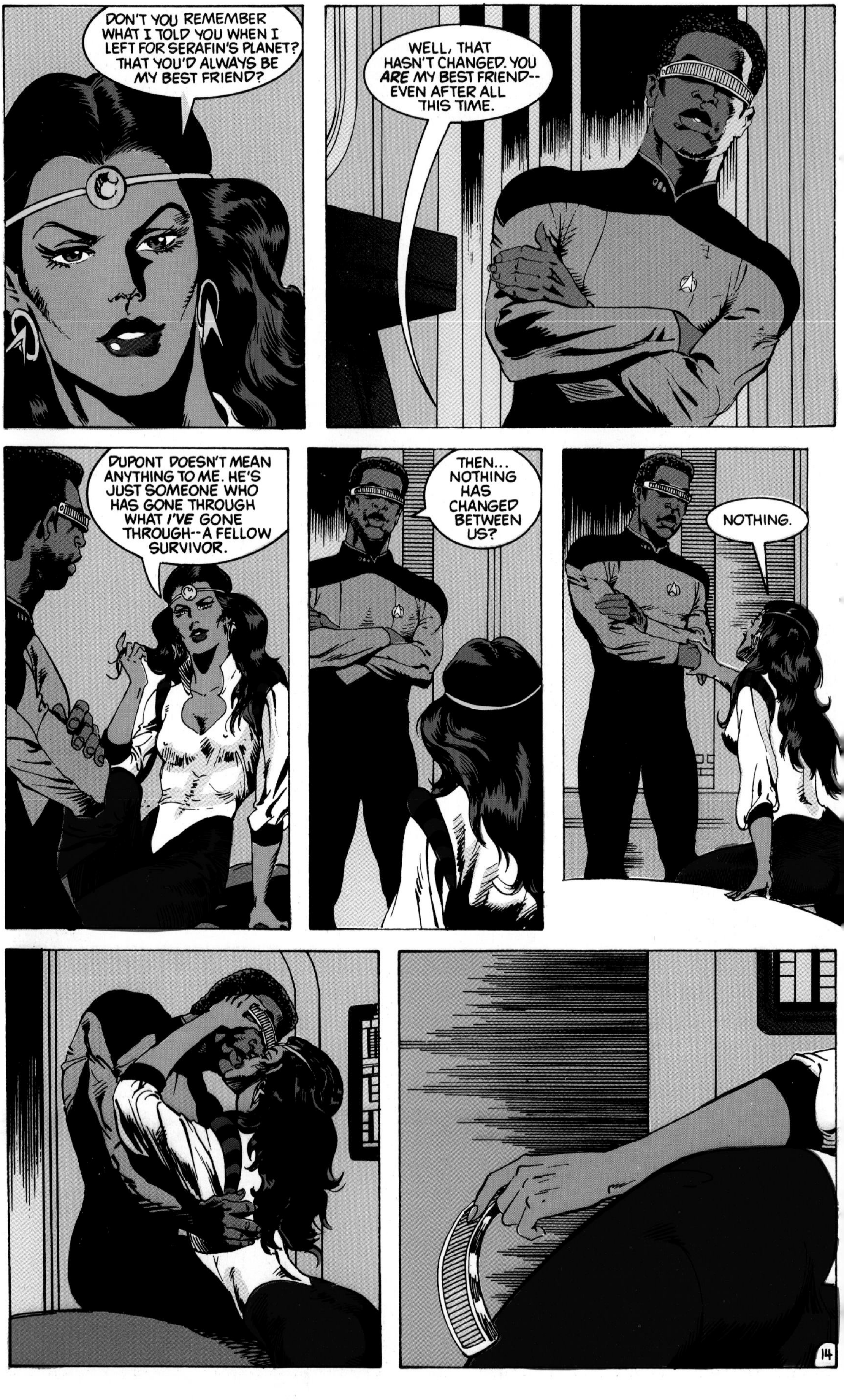
DON'T YOU REMEMBER WHAT I TOLD YOU WHEN I LEFT FOR SERAFIN'S PLANET? THAT YOU'D ALWAYS BE MY BEST FRIEND?
WELL, THAT HASN'T CHANGED. YOU ARE MY BEST FRIEND-- EVEN AFTER ALL THIS TIME.
DUPONT DOESN'T MEAN ANYTHING TO ME. HE'S JUST SOMEONE WHO HAS GONE THROUGH WHAT I'VE GONE THROUGH--A FELLOW SURVIVOR.
THEN... NOTHING HAS CHANGED BETWEEN US?
NOTHING.

...AND THEN HE SAYS, "MY MOTHER? I THOUGHT SHE WAS *YOUR* MOTHER!"

VERY GOOD, COMMANDER. I DON'T THINK I'VE EVER HEARD THAT ONE!

ALTHOUGH, AS THE ONLY MOTHER AT THE TABLE, I FEEL I MUST LODGE AN UNOFFICIAL PROTEST!

HOW INTERESTING.

WHAT IS, DATA?

YOUR JOKE, COMMANDER. I BELIEVE I GOT IT, AS ONE MIGHT SAY IN THE VERNACULAR.

YOU KNOW, DATA, WHEN ONE *GETS* A JOKE, IT'S CUSTOMARY TO *LAUGH.*

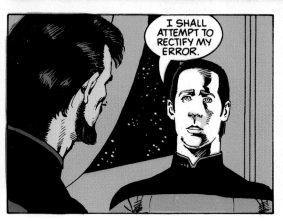

I SHALL ATTEMPT TO RECTIFY MY ERROR.

A-YUK-HO!
:giggle:
tee-hee!
HA!

15

THAT'S ENOUGH, DATA. IT WASN'T *THAT* FUNNY.

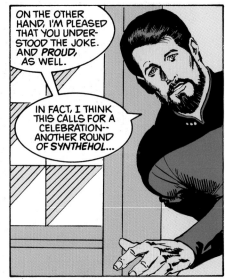

ON THE OTHER HAND, I'M PLEASED THAT YOU UNDERSTOOD THE JOKE. AND *PROUD*, AS WELL.

IN FACT, I THINK THIS CALLS FOR A CELEBRATION-- ANOTHER ROUND OF *SYNTHEHOL*...

...WHICH I'LL SEE ABOUT SECURING FORTHWITH!

HELLO, ENSIGN.

HI, COMMANDER.

HI, MOM. ER...GOT A MINUTE?

WHY, CERTAINLY, WES. WILL YOU ALL EXCUSE ME?

OF COURSE, DOCTOR. A MOTHER'S FIRST RESPONSIBILITY IS TO HER SON.

16

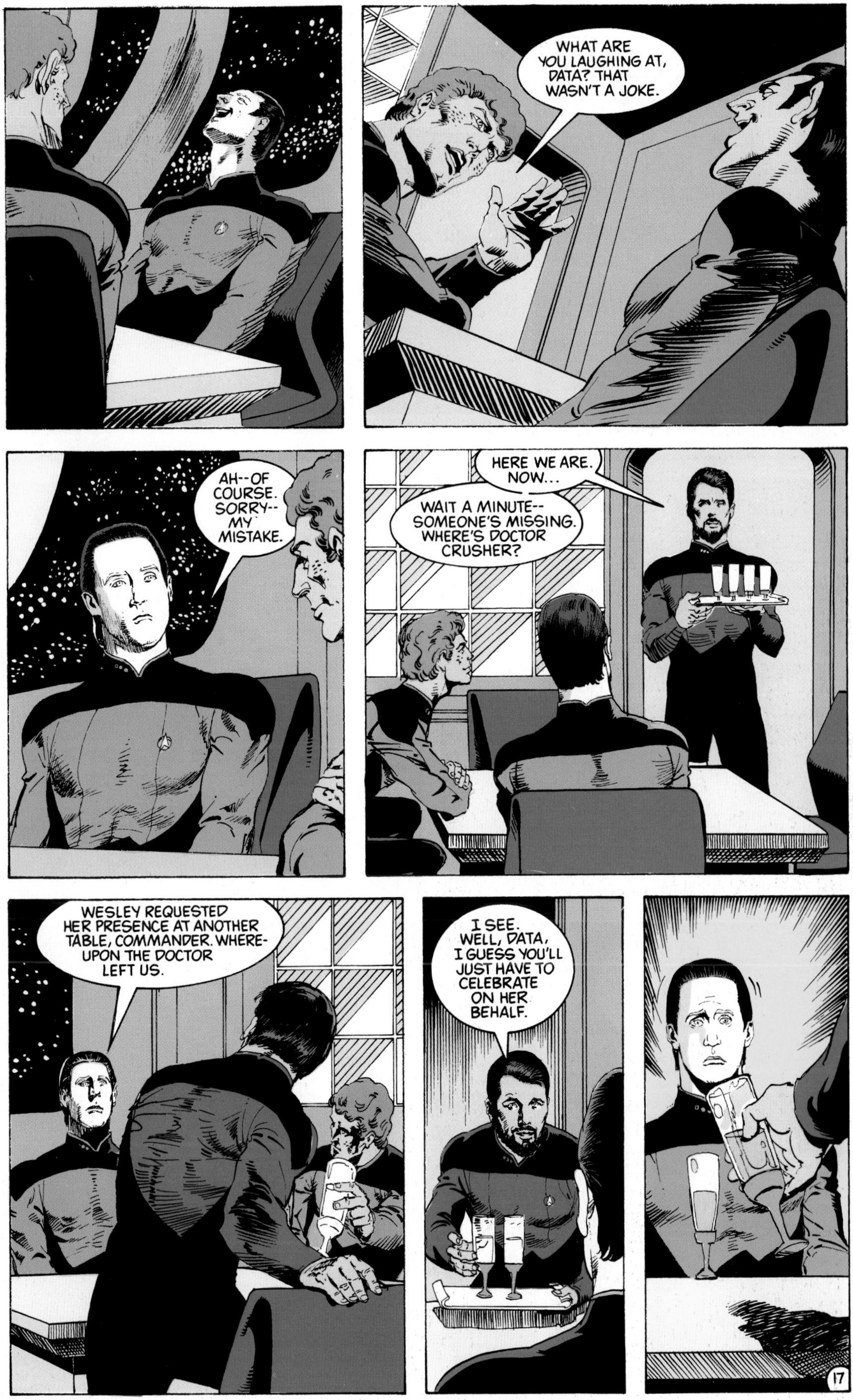
WHAT ARE YOU LAUGHING AT, DATA? THAT WASN'T A JOKE.
AH--OF COURSE. SORRY-- MY MISTAKE.
HERE WE ARE. NOW...
WAIT A MINUTE-- SOMEONE'S MISSING. WHERE'S DOCTOR CRUSHER?
WESLEY REQUESTED HER PRESENCE AT ANOTHER TABLE, COMMANDER. WHERE-UPON THE DOCTOR LEFT US.
I SEE. WELL, DATA, I GUESS YOU'LL JUST HAVE TO CELEBRATE ON HER BEHALF.

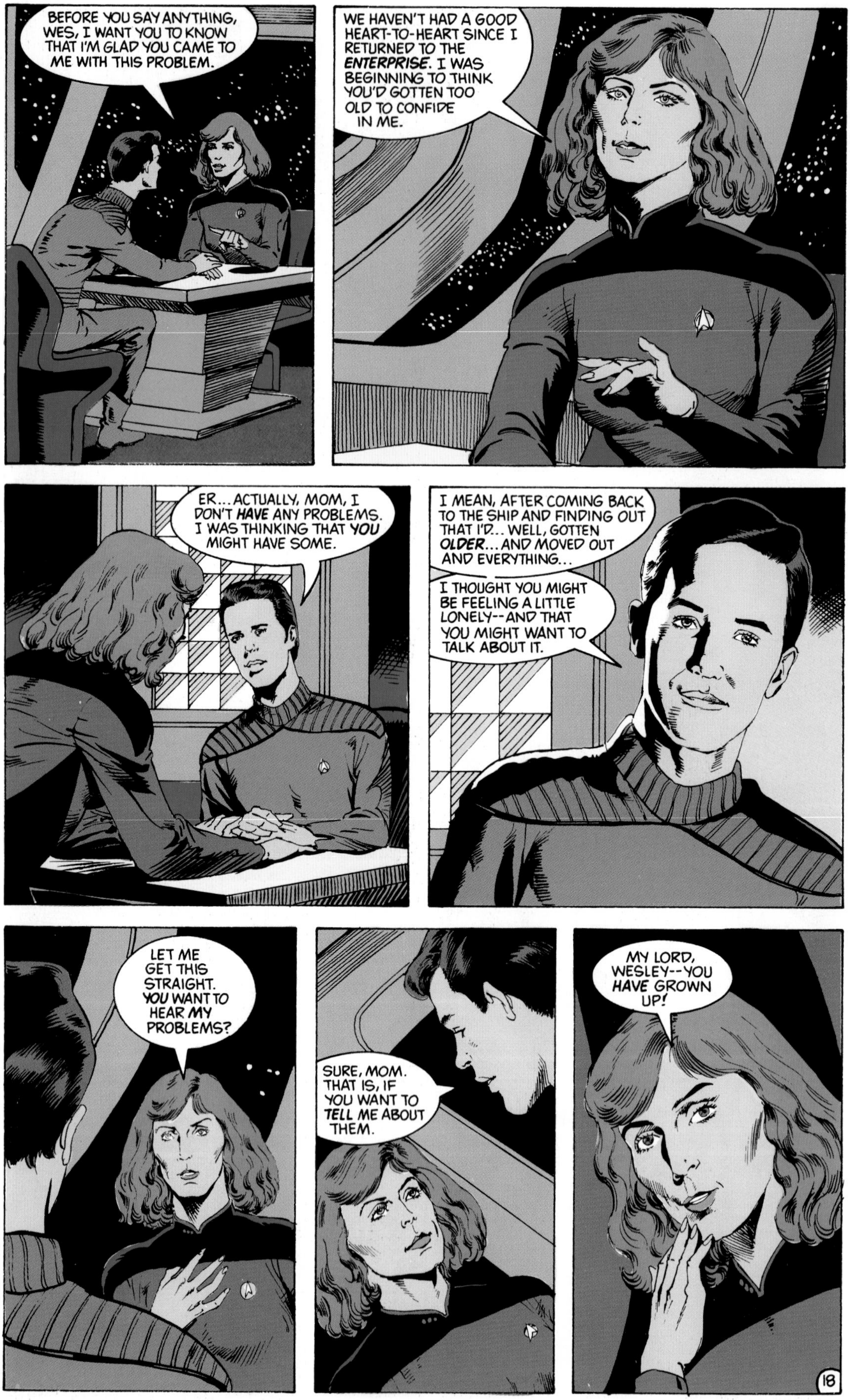

BEFORE YOU SAY ANYTHING, WES, I WANT YOU TO KNOW THAT I'M GLAD YOU CAME TO ME WITH THIS PROBLEM.
WE HAVEN'T HAD A GOOD HEART-TO-HEART SINCE I RETURNED TO THE ENTERPRISE. I WAS BEGINNING TO THINK YOU'D GOTTEN TOO OLD TO CONFIDE IN ME.
ER... ACTUALLY, MOM, I DON'T HAVE ANY PROBLEMS. I WAS THINKING THAT YOU MIGHT HAVE SOME.
I MEAN, AFTER COMING BACK TO THE SHIP AND FINDING OUT THAT I'D... WELL, GOTTEN OLDER... AND MOVED OUT AND EVERYTHING...
I THOUGHT YOU MIGHT BE FEELING A LITTLE LONELY--AND THAT YOU MIGHT WANT TO TALK ABOUT IT.
LET ME GET THIS STRAIGHT. YOU WANT TO HEAR MY PROBLEMS?
SURE, MOM. THAT IS, IF YOU WANT TO TELL ME ABOUT THEM.
MY LORD, WESLEY--YOU HAVE GROWN UP!
18

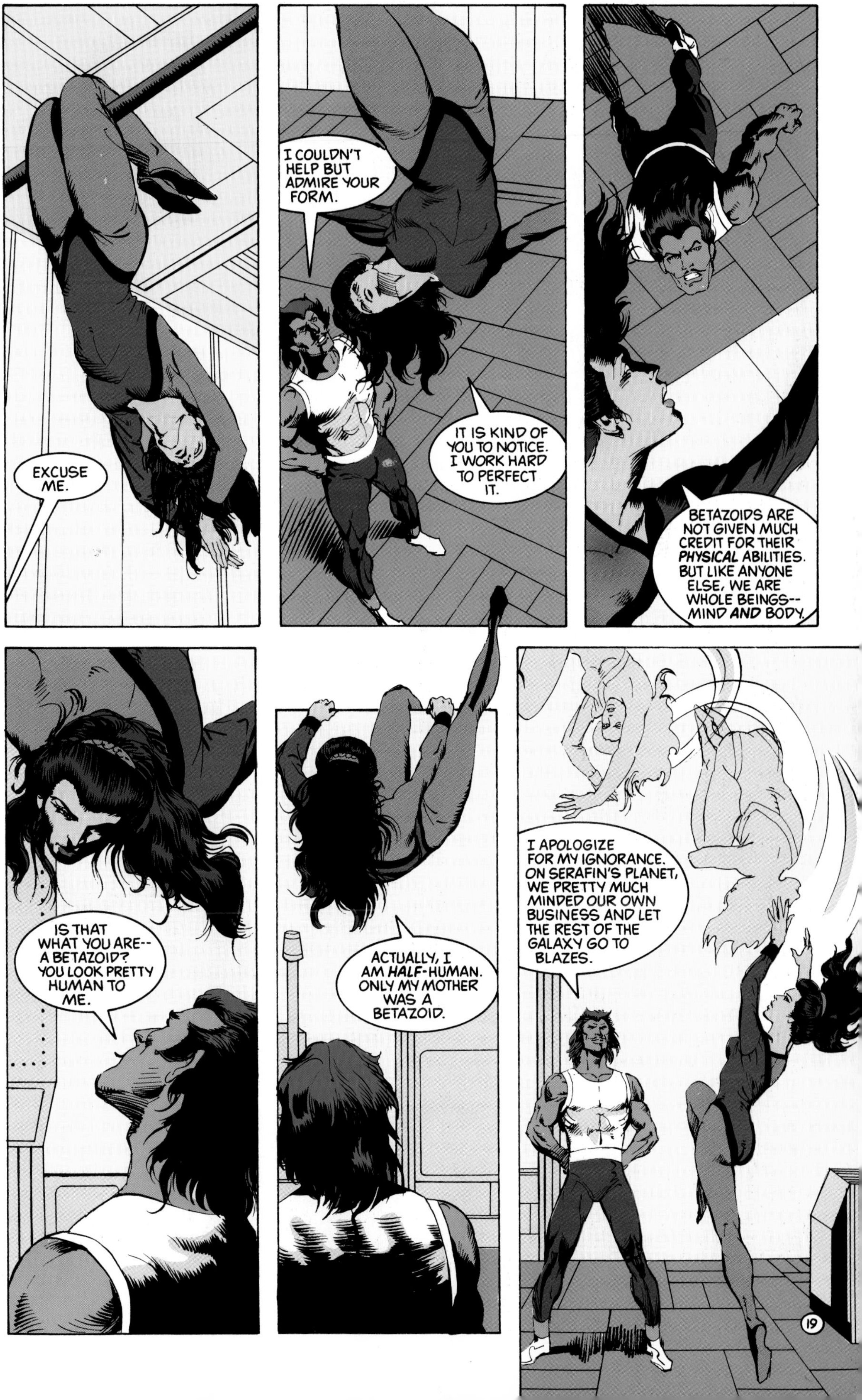
EXCUSE ME.
I COULDN'T HELP BUT ADMIRE YOUR FORM.
IT IS KIND OF YOU TO NOTICE. I WORK HARD TO PERFECT IT.
BETAZOIDS ARE NOT GIVEN MUCH CREDIT FOR THEIR PHYSICAL ABILITIES. BUT LIKE ANYONE ELSE, WE ARE WHOLE BEINGS-- MIND AND BODY.
IS THAT WHAT YOU ARE-- A BETAZOID? YOU LOOK PRETTY HUMAN TO ME.
ACTUALLY, I AM HALF-HUMAN. ONLY MY MOTHER WAS A BETAZOID.
I APOLOGIZE FOR MY IGNORANCE. ON SERAFIN'S PLANET, WE PRETTY MUCH MINDED OUR OWN BUSINESS AND LET THE REST OF THE GALAXY GO TO BLAZES.
19

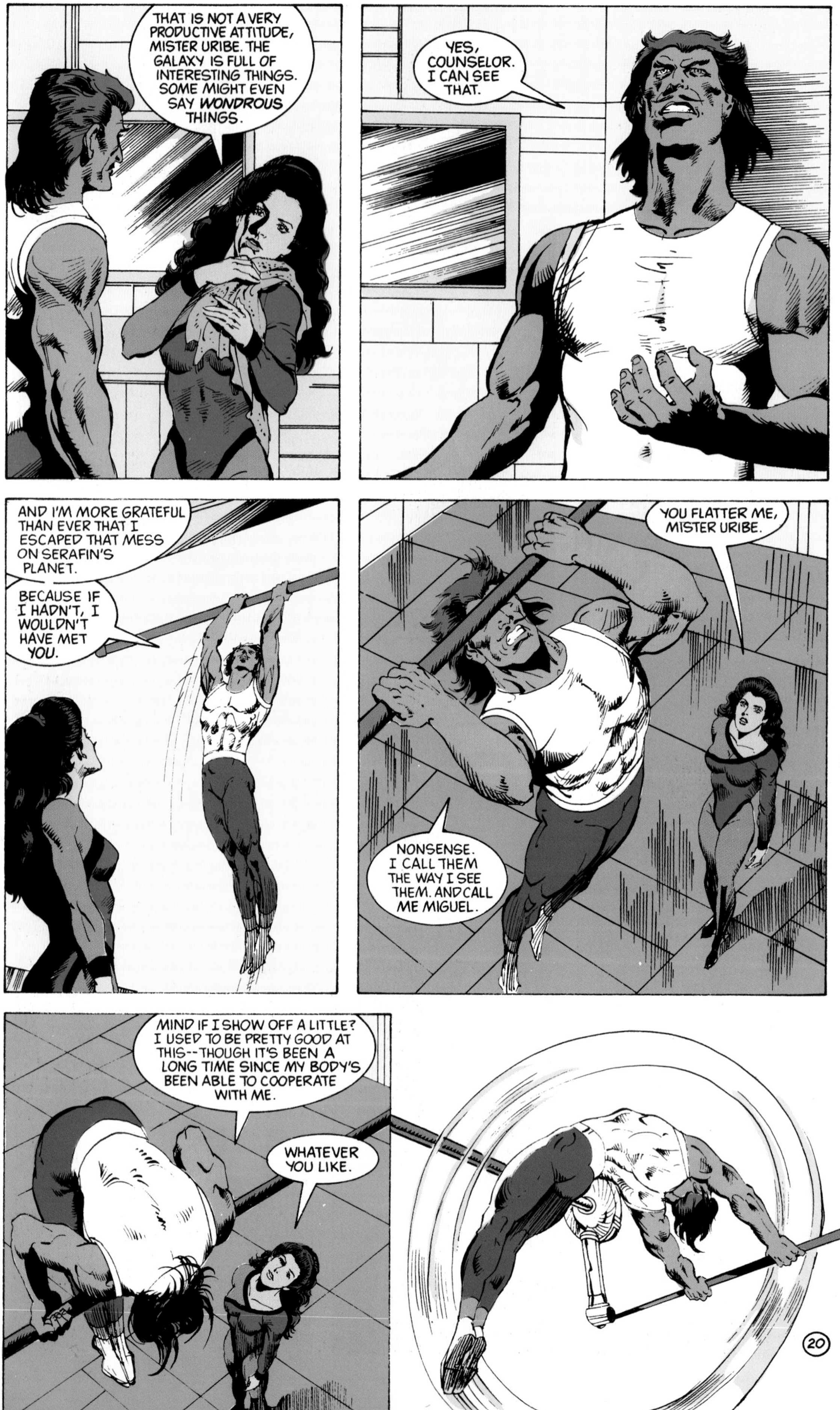
THAT IS NOT A VERY PRODUCTIVE ATTITUDE, MISTER URIBE. THE GALAXY IS FULL OF INTERESTING THINGS. SOME MIGHT EVEN SAY WONDROUS THINGS.
YES, COUNSELOR. I CAN SEE THAT.
AND I'M MORE GRATEFUL THAN EVER THAT I ESCAPED THAT MESS ON SERAFIN'S PLANET.
BECAUSE IF I HADN'T, I WOULDN'T HAVE MET YOU.
YOU FLATTER ME, MISTER URIBE.
NONSENSE. I CALL THEM THE WAY I SEE THEM. AND CALL ME MIGUEL.
MIND IF I SHOW OFF A LITTLE? I USED TO BE PRETTY GOOD AT THIS--THOUGH IT'S BEEN A LONG TIME SINCE MY BODY'S BEEN ABLE TO COOPERATE WITH ME.
WHATEVER YOU LIKE.
20

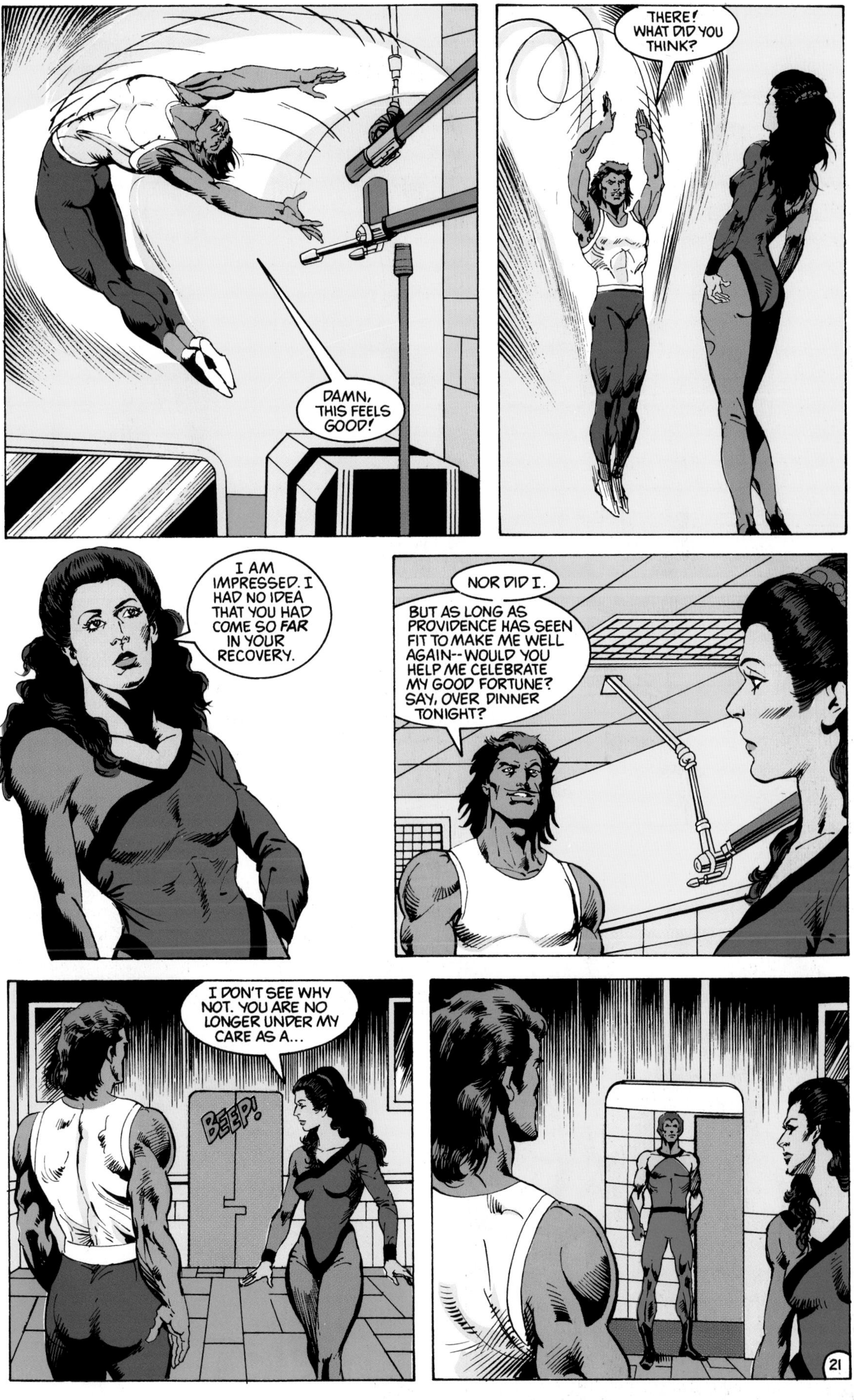
DAMN, THIS FEELS GOOD!
THERE! WHAT DID YOU THINK?
I AM IMPRESSED. I HAD NO IDEA THAT YOU HAD COME SO FAR IN YOUR RECOVERY.
NOR DID I.
BUT AS LONG AS PROVIDENCE HAS SEEN FIT TO MAKE ME WELL AGAIN--WOULD YOU HELP ME CELEBRATE MY GOOD FORTUNE? SAY, OVER DINNER TONIGHT?
I DON'T SEE WHY NOT. YOU ARE NO LONGER UNDER MY CARE AS A...
BEEP!

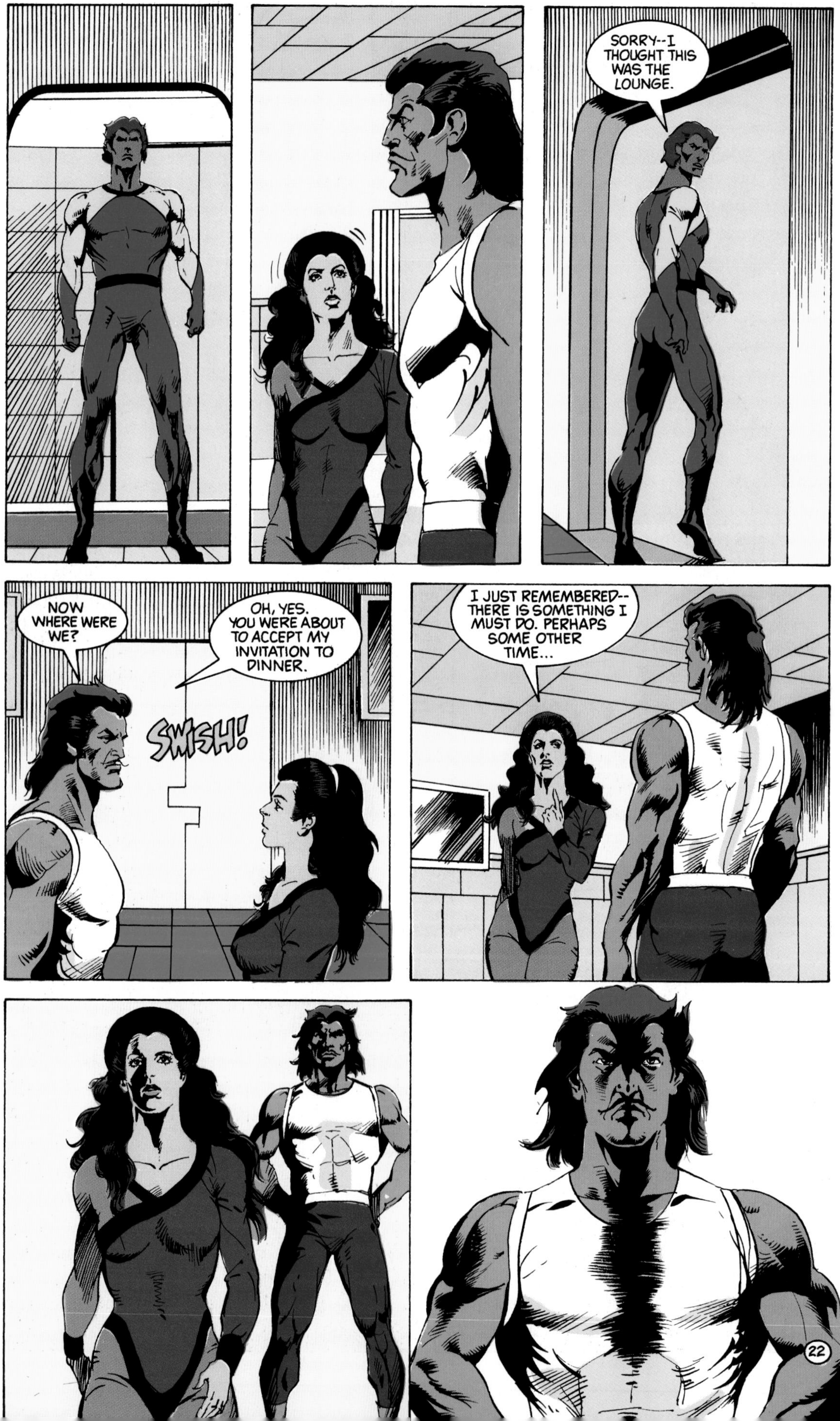
SORRY--I THOUGHT THIS WAS THE LOUNGE.
NOW WHERE WERE WE?
OH, YES. YOU WERE ABOUT TO ACCEPT MY INVITATION TO DINNER.
SWISH!
I JUST REMEMBERED-- THERE IS SOMETHING I MUST DO. PERHAPS SOME OTHER TIME...
22

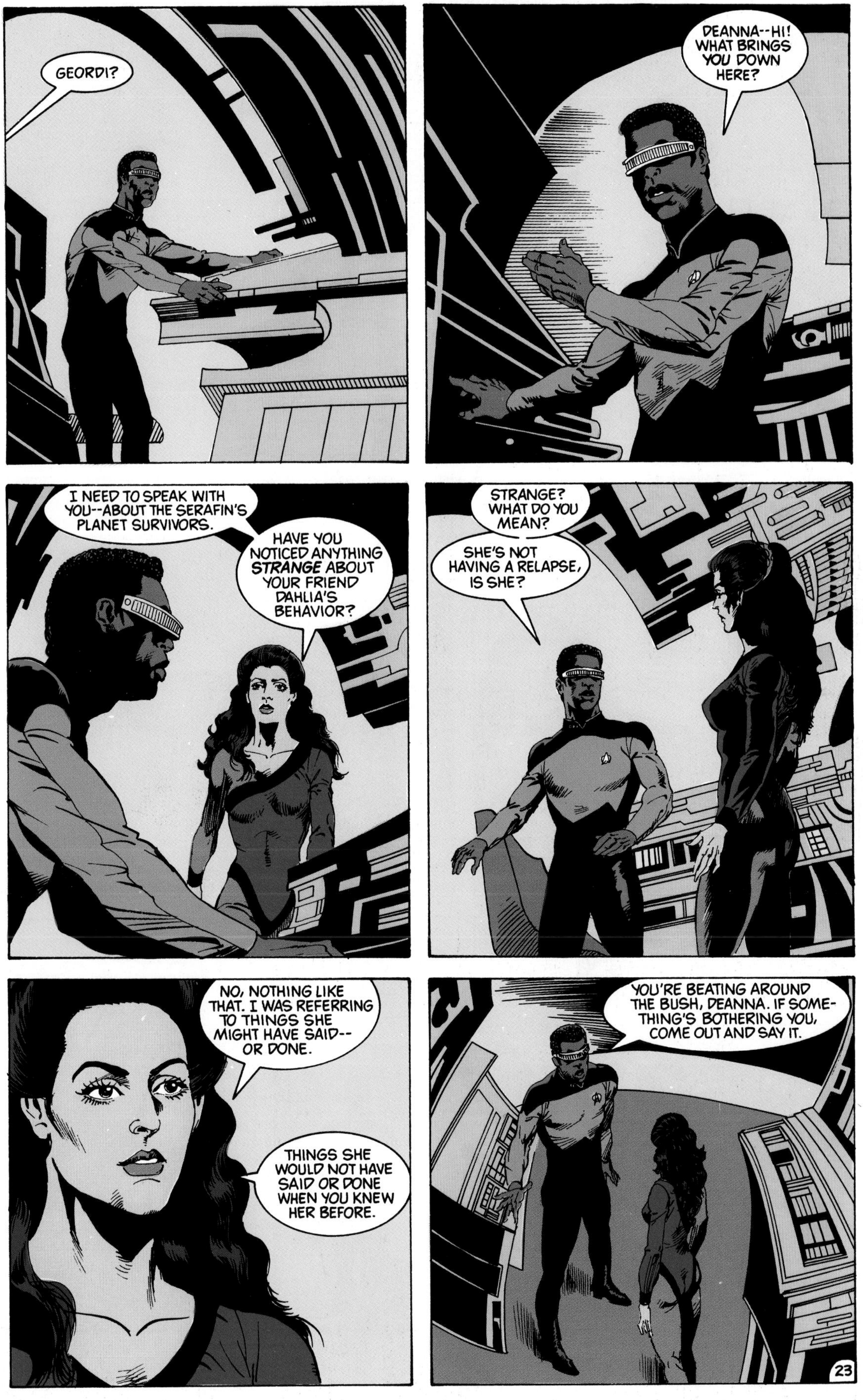

GEORDI?
DEANNA--HI! WHAT BRINGS YOU DOWN HERE?
I NEED TO SPEAK WITH YOU--ABOUT THE SERAFIN'S PLANET SURVIVORS.
HAVE YOU NOTICED ANYTHING STRANGE ABOUT YOUR FRIEND DAHLIA'S BEHAVIOR?
STRANGE? WHAT DO YOU MEAN?
SHE'S NOT HAVING A RELAPSE, IS SHE?
NO, NOTHING LIKE THAT. I WAS REFERRING TO THINGS SHE MIGHT HAVE SAID-- OR DONE.
THINGS SHE WOULD NOT HAVE SAID OR DONE WHEN YOU KNEW HER BEFORE.
YOU'RE BEATING AROUND THE BUSH, DEANNA. IF SOMETHING'S BOTHERING YOU, COME OUT AND SAY IT.

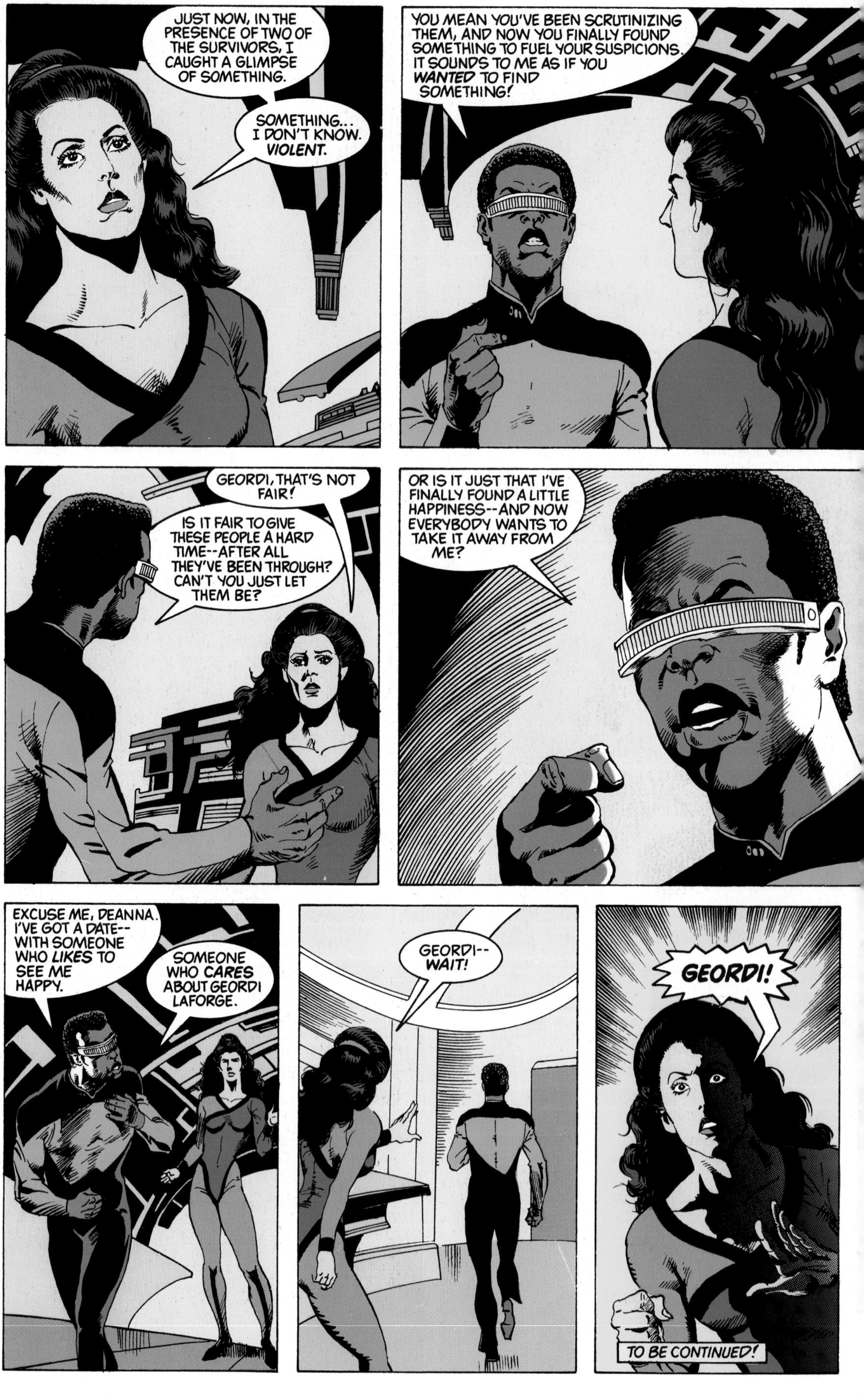
JUST NOW, IN THE PRESENCE OF TWO OF THE SURVIVORS, I CAUGHT A GLIMPSE OF SOMETHING.
SOMETHING... I DON'T KNOW. *VIOLENT*.
YOU MEAN YOU'VE BEEN SCRUTINIZING THEM, AND NOW YOU FINALLY FOUND SOMETHING TO FUEL YOUR SUSPICIONS. IT SOUNDS TO ME AS IF YOU *WANTED* TO FIND SOMETHING!
GEORDI, THAT'S NOT FAIR!
IS IT FAIR TO GIVE THESE PEOPLE A HARD TIME--AFTER ALL THEY'VE BEEN THROUGH? CAN'T YOU JUST LET THEM BE?
OR IS IT JUST THAT I'VE FINALLY FOUND A LITTLE HAPPINESS--AND NOW EVERYBODY WANTS TO TAKE IT AWAY FROM ME?
EXCUSE ME, DEANNA. I'VE GOT A DATE--WITH SOMEONE WHO *LIKES* TO SEE ME HAPPY.
SOMEONE WHO *CARES* ABOUT GEORDI LAFORGE.
GEORDI--WAIT!
GEORDI!
TO BE CONTINUED!

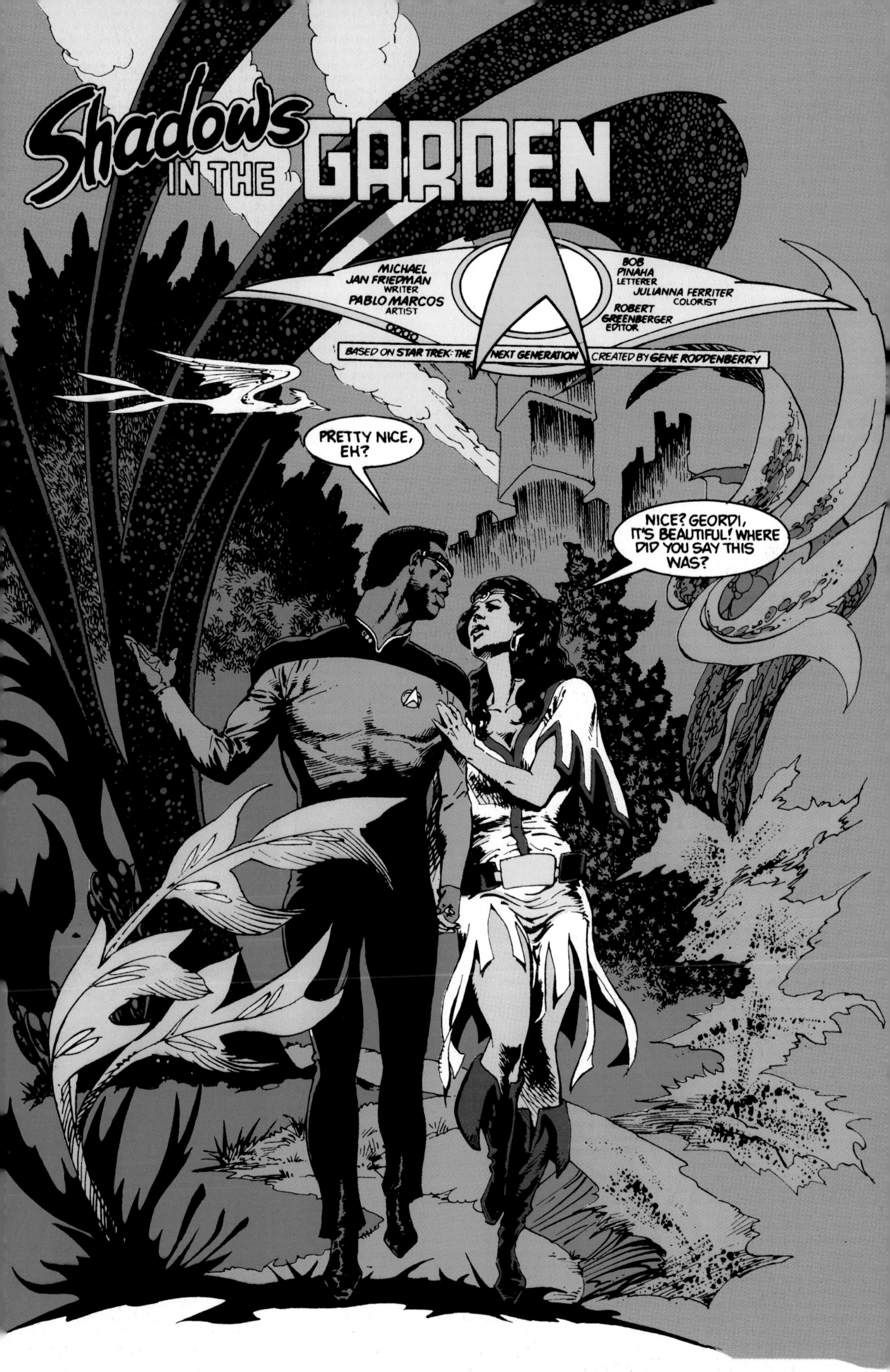
Shadows IN THE GARDEN
MICHAEL JAN FRIEDMAN WRITER
PABLO MARCOS ARTIST
BOB PINAHA LETTERER
JULIANNA FERRITER COLORIST
ROBERT GREENBERGER EDITOR
BASED ON STAR TREK: THE NEXT GENERATION CREATED BY GENE RODDENBERRY
PRETTY NICE, EH?
NICE? GEORDI, IT'S BEAUTIFUL! WHERE DID YOU SAY THIS WAS?

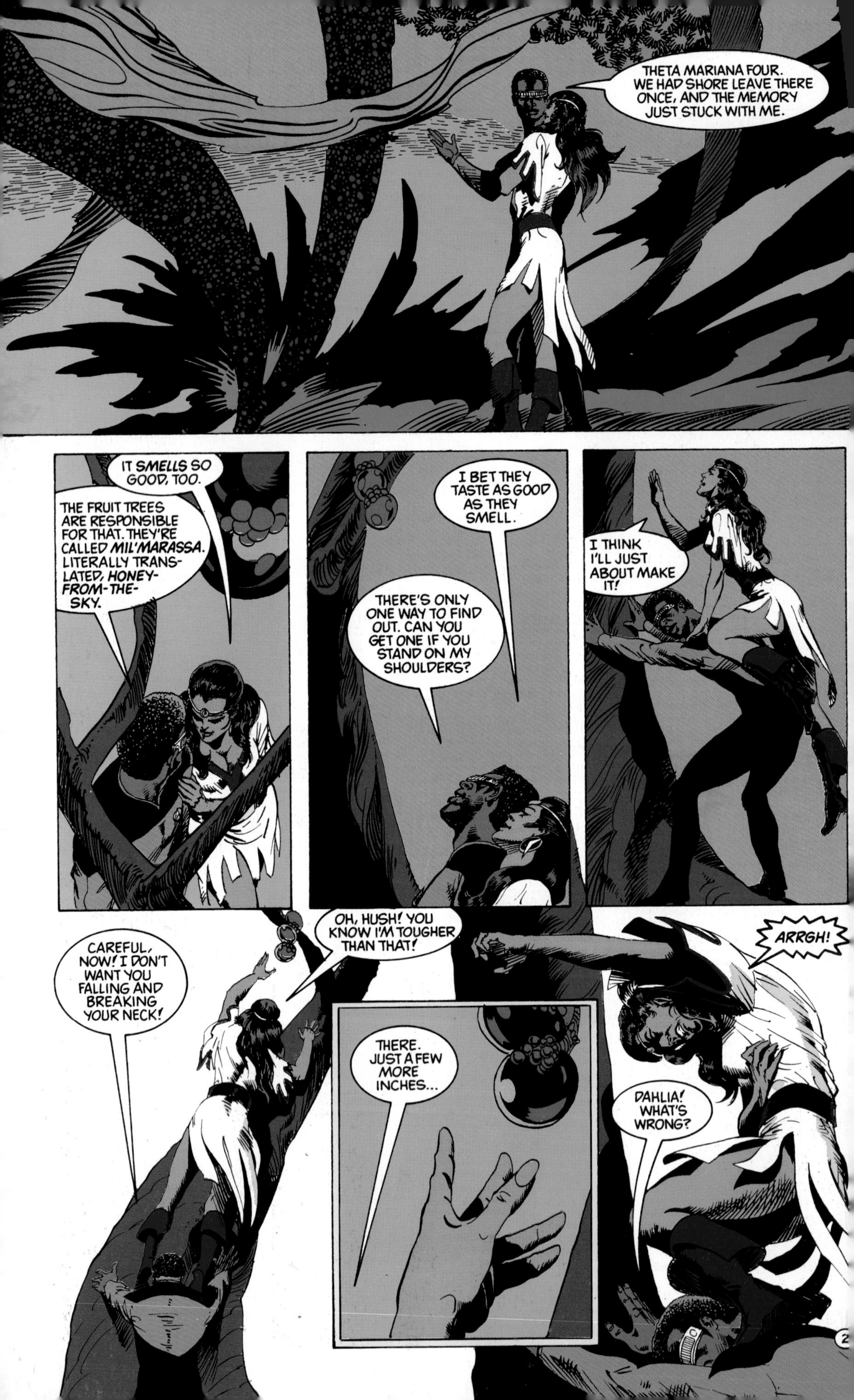
THETA MARIANA FOUR. WE HAD SHORE LEAVE THERE ONCE, AND THE MEMORY JUST STUCK WITH ME.
IT SMELLS SO GOOD, TOO.
THE FRUIT TREES ARE RESPONSIBLE FOR THAT. THEY'RE CALLED MIL'MARASSA. LITERALLY TRANSLATED, HONEY-FROM-THE-SKY.
I BET THEY TASTE AS GOOD AS THEY SMELL.
THERE'S ONLY ONE WAY TO FIND OUT. CAN YOU GET ONE IF YOU STAND ON MY SHOULDERS?
I THINK I'LL JUST ABOUT MAKE IT!
CAREFUL, NOW! I DON'T WANT YOU FALLING AND BREAKING YOUR NECK!
OH, HUSH! YOU KNOW I'M TOUGHER THAN THAT!
THERE. JUST A FEW MORE INCHES...
ARRGH!
DAHLIA! WHAT'S WRONG?

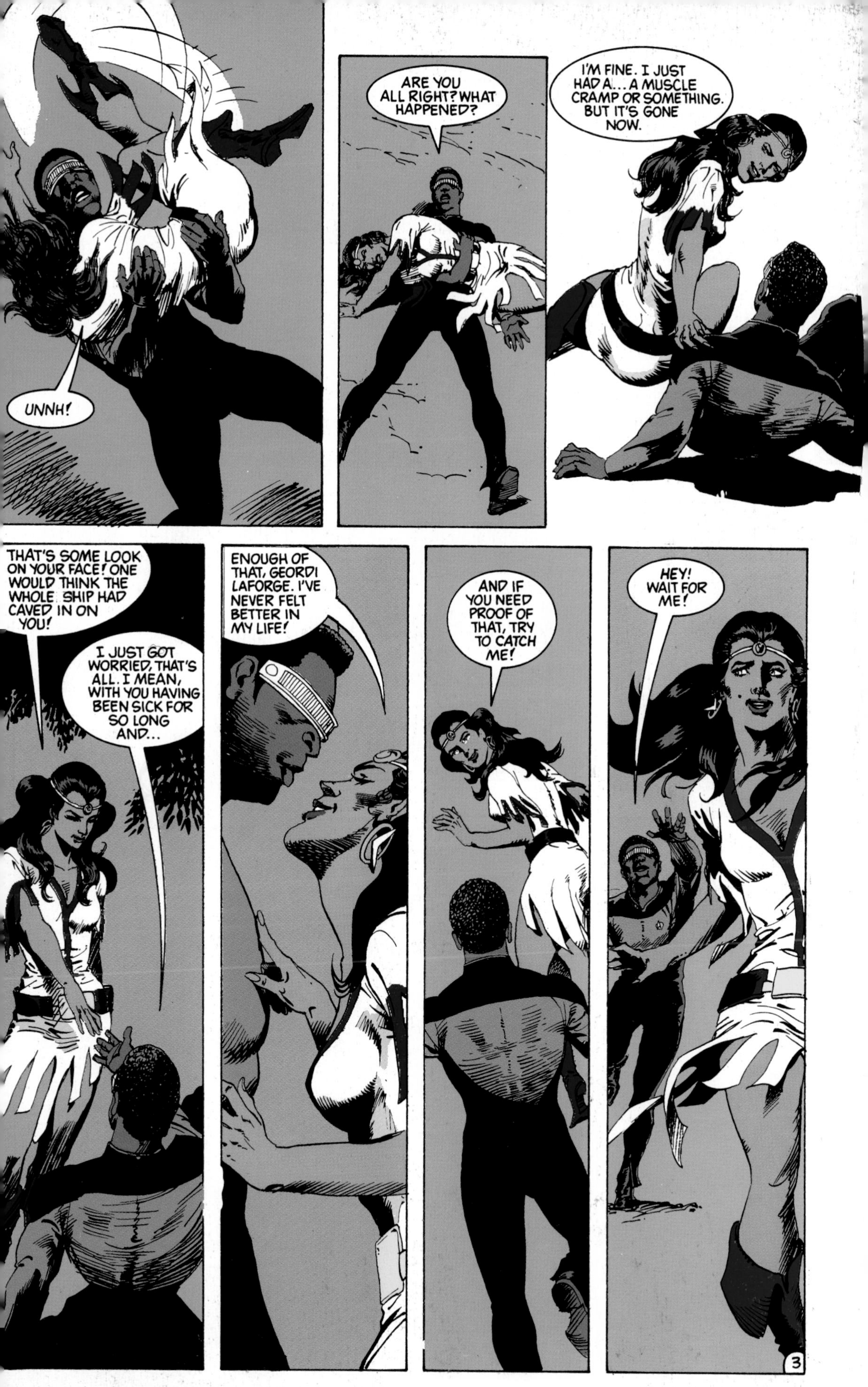
UNNH!
ARE YOU ALL RIGHT? WHAT HAPPENED?
I'M FINE. I JUST HAD A... A MUSCLE CRAMP OR SOMETHING. BUT IT'S GONE NOW.
THAT'S SOME LOOK ON YOUR FACE! ONE WOULD THINK THE WHOLE SHIP HAD CAVED IN ON YOU!
I JUST GOT WORRIED, THAT'S ALL. I MEAN, WITH YOU HAVING BEEN SICK FOR SO LONG AND...
ENOUGH OF THAT, GEORDI LAFORGE. I'VE NEVER FELT BETTER IN MY LIFE!
AND IF YOU NEED PROOF OF THAT, TRY TO CATCH ME!
HEY! WAIT FOR ME!
3

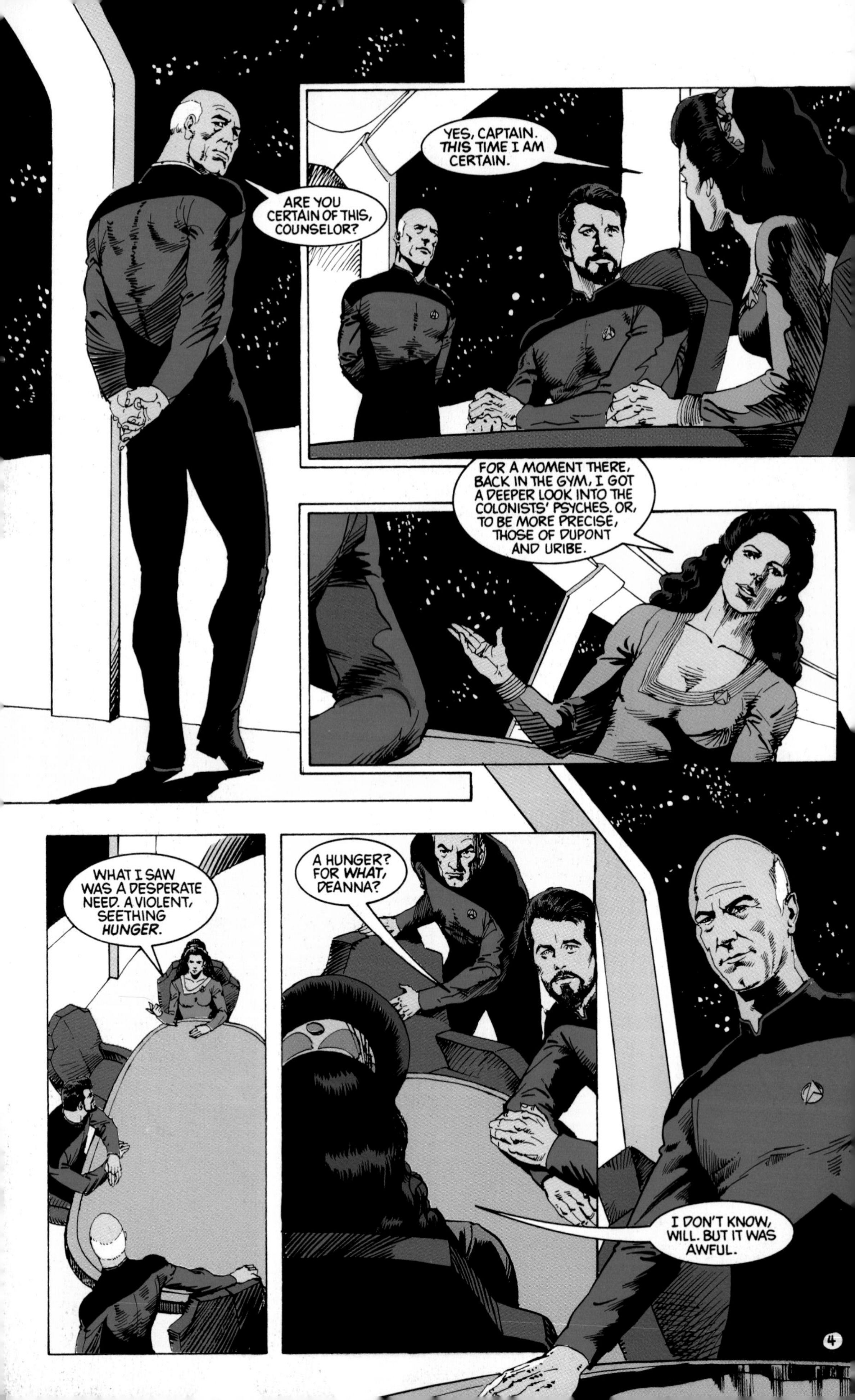
ARE YOU CERTAIN OF THIS, COUNSELOR?
YES, CAPTAIN. THIS TIME I AM CERTAIN.
FOR A MOMENT THERE, BACK IN THE GYM, I GOT A DEEPER LOOK INTO THE COLONISTS' PSYCHES. OR, TO BE MORE PRECISE, THOSE OF DUPONT AND URIBE.
WHAT I SAW WAS A DESPERATE NEED. A VIOLENT, SEETHING HUNGER.
A HUNGER? FOR WHAT, DEANNA?
I DON'T KNOW, WILL. BUT IT WAS AWFUL.

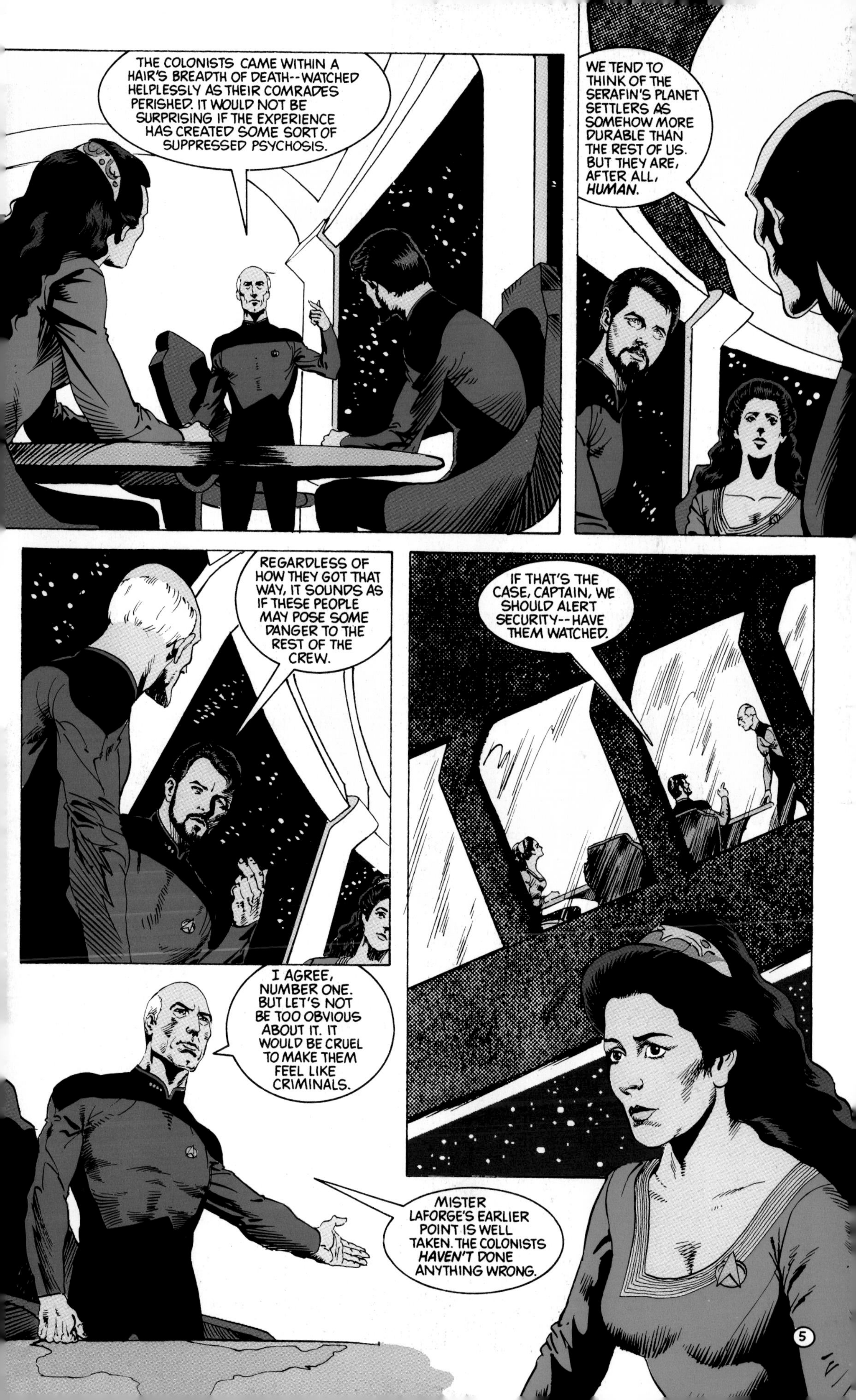
THE COLONISTS CAME WITHIN A HAIR'S BREADTH OF DEATH--WATCHED HELPLESSLY AS THEIR COMRADES PERISHED. IT WOULD NOT BE SURPRISING IF THE EXPERIENCE HAS CREATED SOME SORT OF SUPPRESSED PSYCHOSIS.
WE TEND TO THINK OF THE SERAFIN'S PLANET SETTLERS AS SOMEHOW MORE DURABLE THAN THE REST OF US. BUT THEY ARE, AFTER ALL, *HUMAN*.
REGARDLESS OF HOW THEY GOT THAT WAY, IT SOUNDS AS IF THESE PEOPLE MAY POSE SOME DANGER TO THE REST OF THE CREW.
IF THAT'S THE CASE, CAPTAIN, WE SHOULD ALERT SECURITY--HAVE THEM WATCHED.
I AGREE, NUMBER ONE. BUT LET'S NOT BE TOO OBVIOUS ABOUT IT. IT WOULD BE CRUEL TO MAKE THEM FEEL LIKE CRIMINALS.
MISTER LAFORGE'S EARLIER POINT IS WELL TAKEN. THE COLONISTS *HAVEN'T* DONE ANYTHING WRONG.

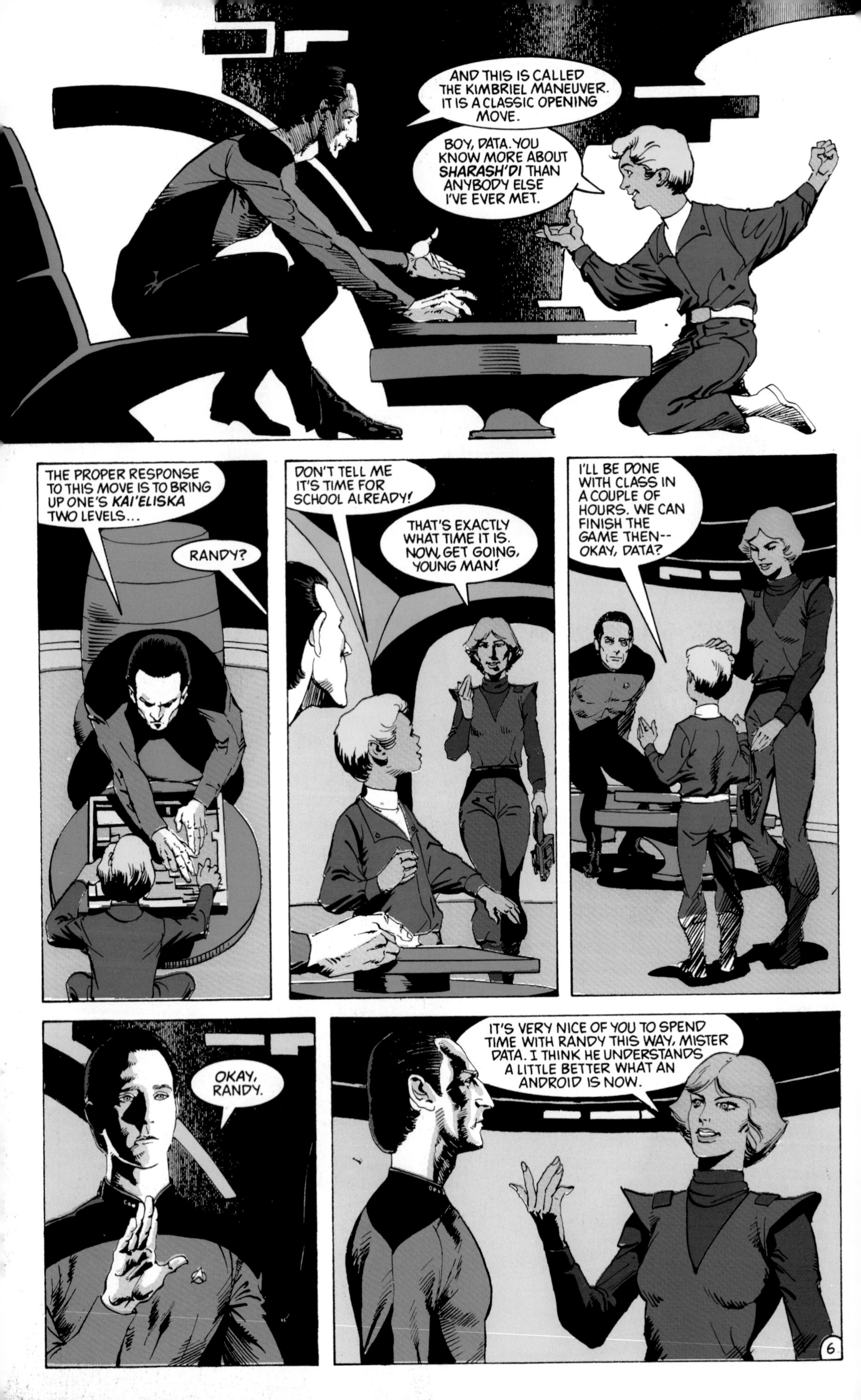
AND THIS IS CALLED THE KIMBRIEL MANEUVER. IT IS A CLASSIC OPENING MOVE.
BOY, DATA. YOU KNOW MORE ABOUT SHARASH'DI THAN ANYBODY ELSE I'VE EVER MET.
THE PROPER RESPONSE TO THIS MOVE IS TO BRING UP ONE'S KAI'ELISKA TWO LEVELS...
RANDY?
DON'T TELL ME IT'S TIME FOR SCHOOL ALREADY!
THAT'S EXACTLY WHAT TIME IT IS. NOW, GET GOING, YOUNG MAN!
I'LL BE DONE WITH CLASS IN A COUPLE OF HOURS. WE CAN FINISH THE GAME THEN-- OKAY, DATA?
OKAY, RANDY.
IT'S VERY NICE OF YOU TO SPEND TIME WITH RANDY THIS WAY, MISTER DATA. I THINK HE UNDERSTANDS A LITTLE BETTER WHAT AN ANDROID IS NOW.
6

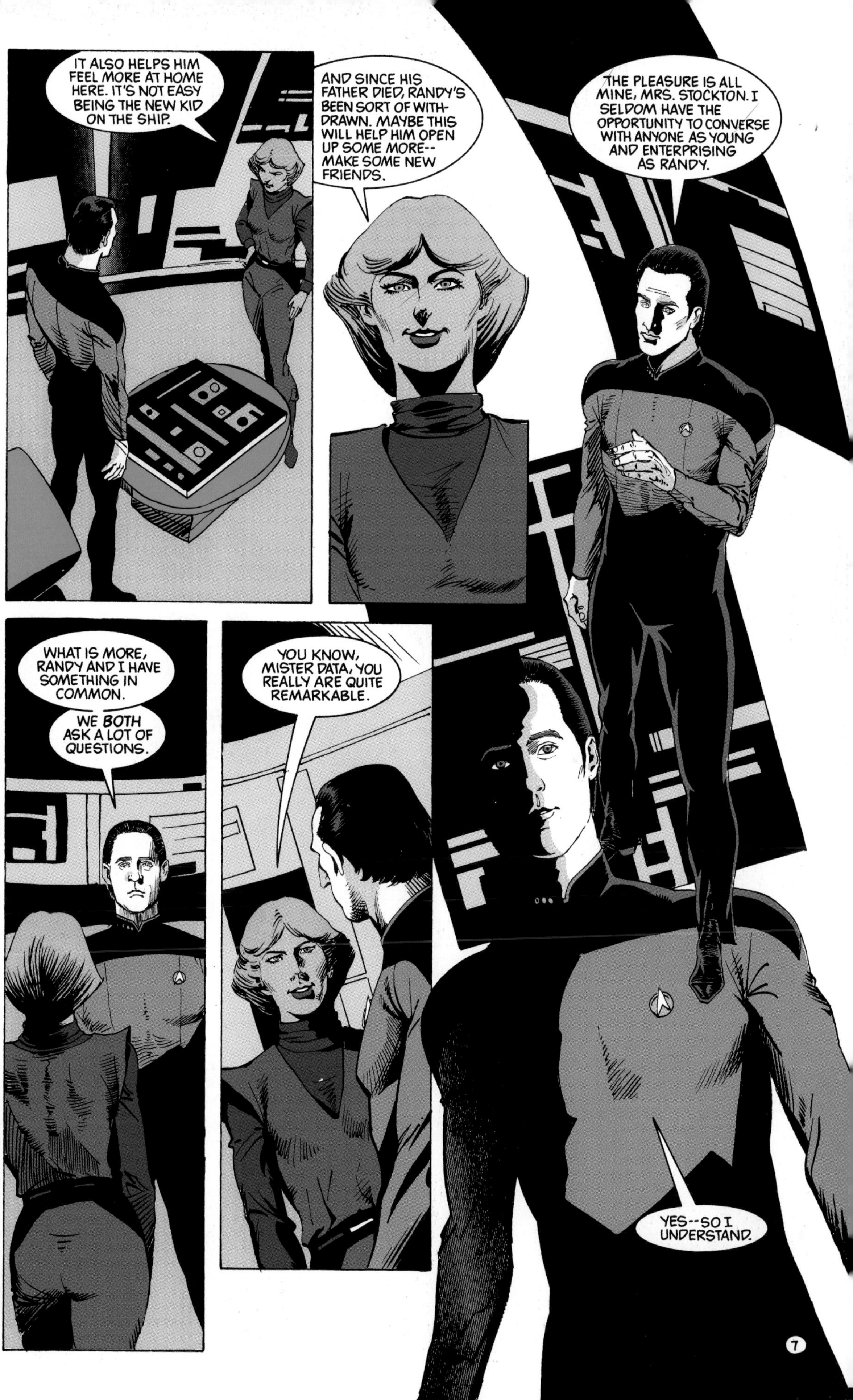
IT ALSO HELPS HIM FEEL MORE AT HOME HERE. IT'S NOT EASY BEING THE NEW KID ON THE SHIP.
AND SINCE HIS FATHER DIED, RANDY'S BEEN SORT OF WITH-DRAWN. MAYBE THIS WILL HELP HIM OPEN UP SOME MORE--MAKE SOME NEW FRIENDS.
THE PLEASURE IS ALL MINE, MRS. STOCKTON. I SELDOM HAVE THE OPPORTUNITY TO CONVERSE WITH ANYONE AS YOUNG AND ENTERPRISING AS RANDY.
WHAT IS MORE, RANDY AND I HAVE SOMETHING IN COMMON.
WE BOTH ASK A LOT OF QUESTIONS.
YOU KNOW, MISTER DATA, YOU REALLY ARE QUITE REMARKABLE.
YES--SO I UNDERSTAND.

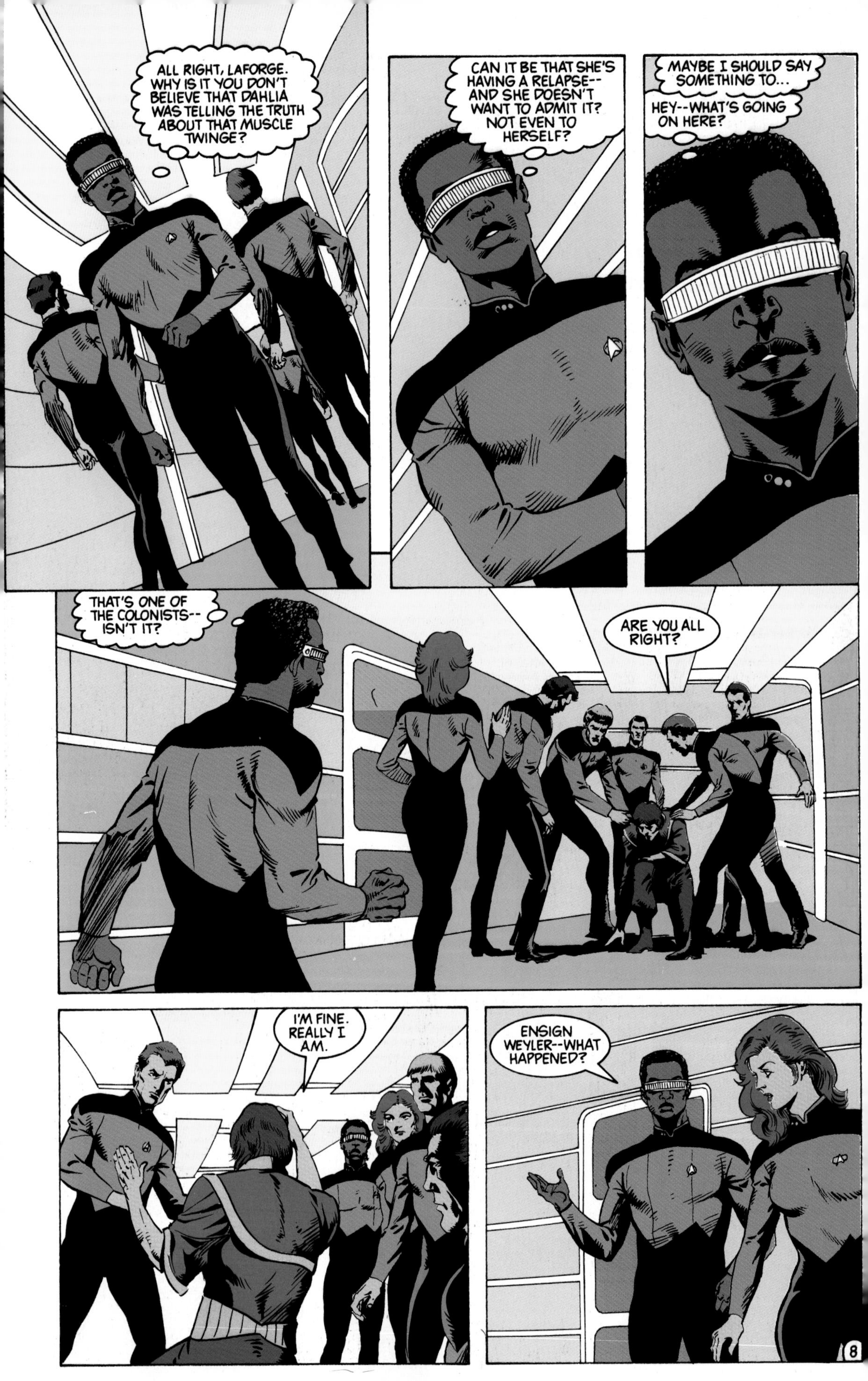
ALL RIGHT, LAFORGE. WHY IS IT YOU DON'T BELIEVE THAT DAHLIA WAS TELLING THE TRUTH ABOUT THAT MUSCLE TWINGE?
CAN IT BE THAT SHE'S HAVING A RELAPSE-- AND SHE DOESN'T WANT TO ADMIT IT? NOT EVEN TO HERSELF?
MAYBE I SHOULD SAY SOMETHING TO...
HEY--WHAT'S GOING ON HERE?
THAT'S ONE OF THE COLONISTS-- ISN'T IT?
ARE YOU ALL RIGHT?
I'M FINE. REALLY I AM.
ENSIGN WEYLER--WHAT HAPPENED?

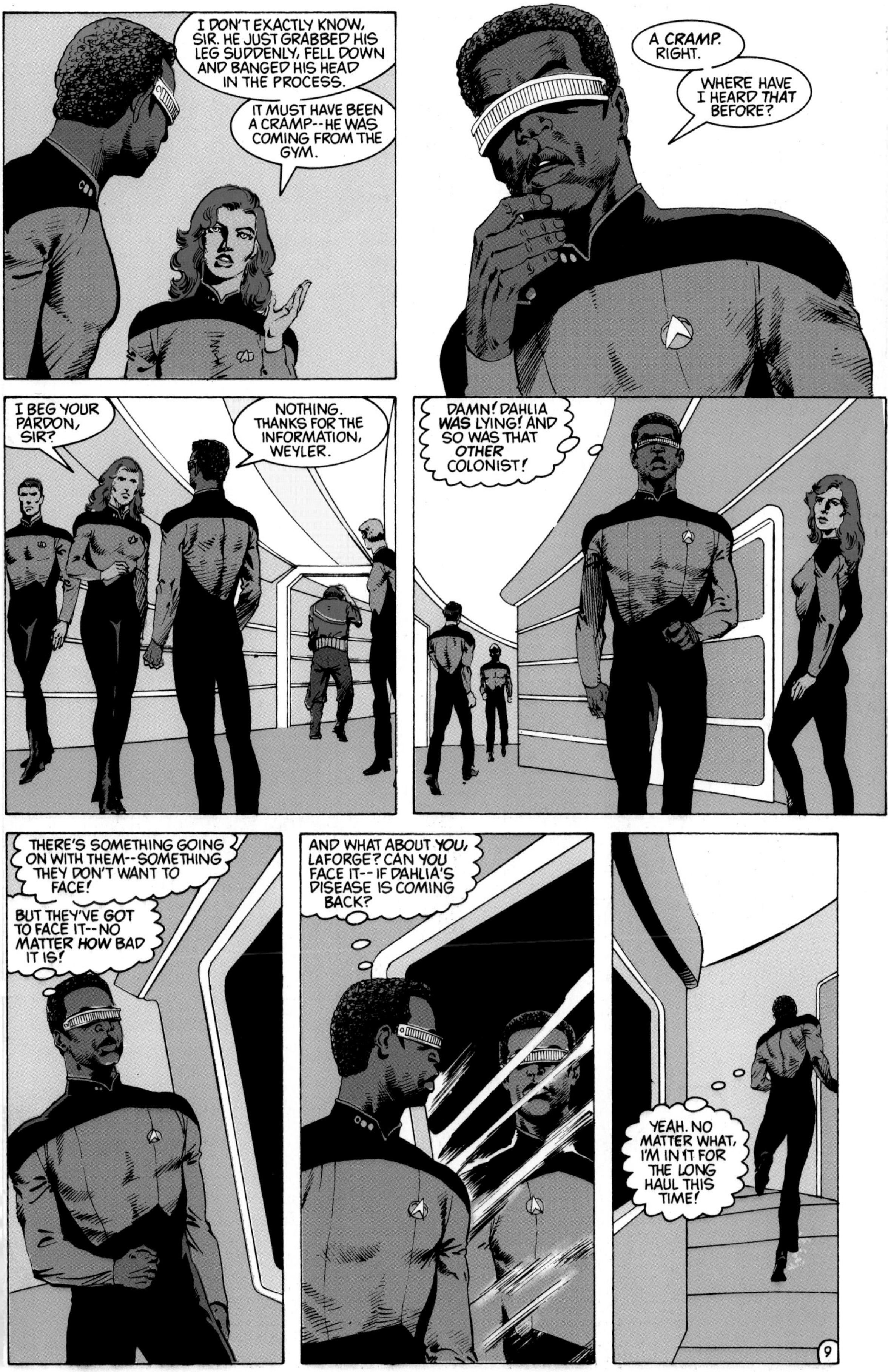
I DON'T EXACTLY KNOW, SIR. HE JUST GRABBED HIS LEG SUDDENLY, FELL DOWN AND BANGED HIS HEAD IN THE PROCESS.
IT MUST HAVE BEEN A CRAMP--HE WAS COMING FROM THE GYM.
A *CRAMP*. RIGHT.
WHERE HAVE I HEARD *THAT* BEFORE?
I BEG YOUR PARDON, SIR?
NOTHING. THANKS FOR THE INFORMATION, WEYLER.
DAMN! DAHLIA **WAS** LYING! AND SO WAS THAT ***OTHER*** COLONIST!
THERE'S SOMETHING GOING ON WITH THEM--SOMETHING THEY DON'T WANT TO FACE!
BUT THEY'VE GOT TO FACE IT--NO MATTER *HOW* BAD IT IS!
AND WHAT ABOUT *YOU*, LAFORGE? CAN *YOU* FACE IT-- IF DAHLIA'S DISEASE IS COMING BACK?
YEAH. NO MATTER WHAT, I'M IN IT FOR THE LONG HAUL THIS TIME!
9

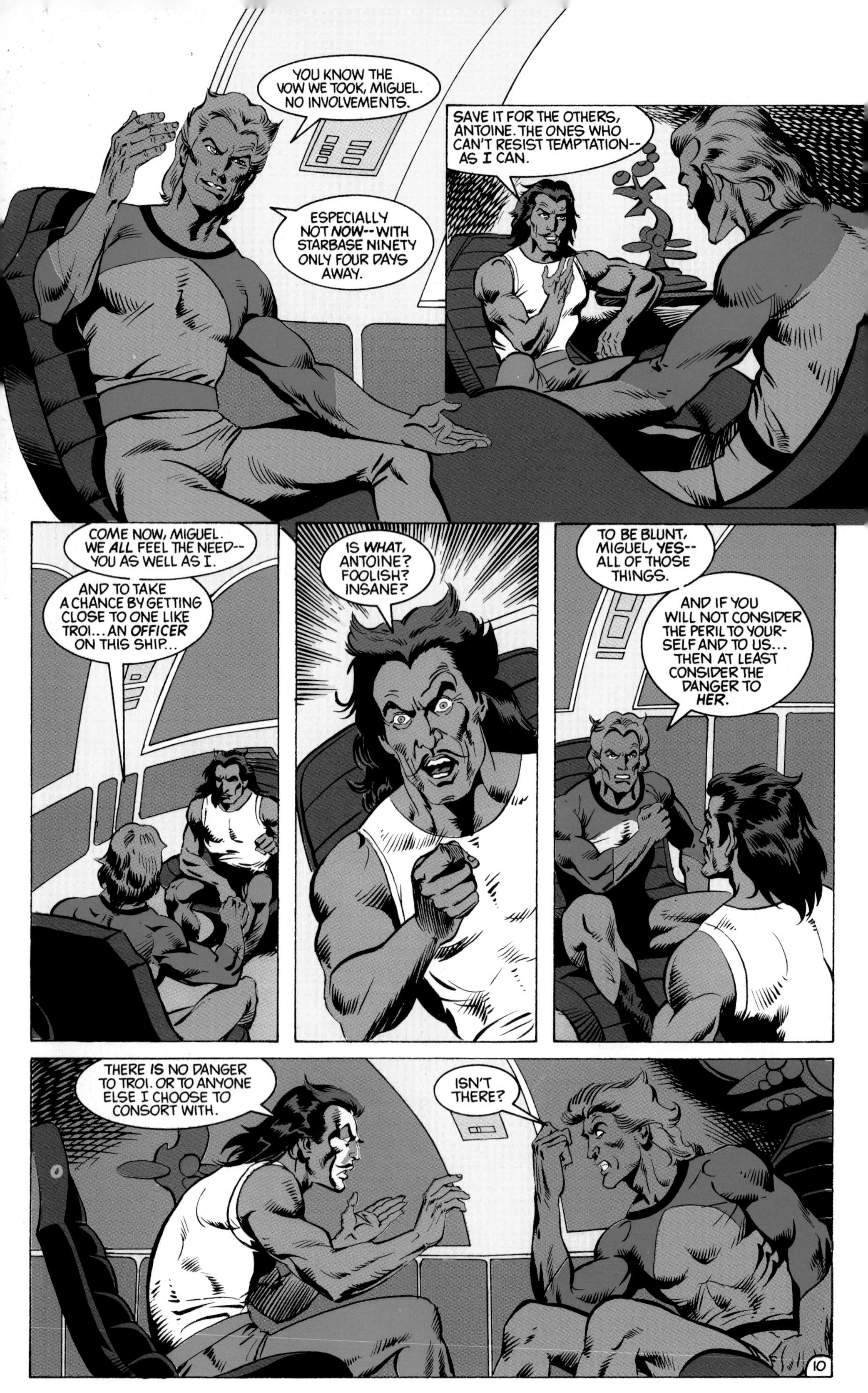
YOU KNOW THE VOW WE TOOK, MIGUEL. NO INVOLVEMENTS.
ESPECIALLY NOT NOW--WITH STARBASE NINETY ONLY FOUR DAYS AWAY.
SAVE IT FOR THE OTHERS, ANTOINE. THE ONES WHO CAN'T RESIST TEMPTATION-- AS I CAN.
COME NOW, MIGUEL. WE ALL FEEL THE NEED-- YOU AS WELL AS I.
AND TO TAKE A CHANCE BY GETTING CLOSE TO ONE LIKE TROI... AN OFFICER ON THIS SHIP...
IS WHAT, ANTOINE? FOOLISH? INSANE?
TO BE BLUNT, MIGUEL, YES-- ALL OF THOSE THINGS.
AND IF YOU WILL NOT CONSIDER THE PERIL TO YOURSELF AND TO US... THEN AT LEAST CONSIDER THE DANGER TO HER.
THERE IS NO DANGER TO TROI. OR TO ANYONE ELSE I CHOOSE TO CONSORT WITH.
ISN'T THERE?
10

HOW CAN YOU BOAST OF YOUR WILL POWER AFTER WHAT HAPPENED BACK ON SERAFIN'S PLANET?

HOW CAN *ANY* OF US MAKE THAT KIND OF BOAST?

THIS IS *DIFFERENT.* THIS IS *HERE*--NOT BACK ON THE PLANET.

WE ARE MORE EXPERIENCED NOW. WE KNOW WHAT TO EXPECT--WHAT TO AVOID. AT LEAST *I* DO.

IT'S *EASIER* NOW TO IGNORE THE NEED.

YOU'RE WRONG. IT'S NOT EASIER NOW-- IT'S *HARDER.*

COMPARED TO SERAFIN'S PLANET, THE *ENTERPRISE* IS A PARADISE. AND IN PARADISE, TEMPTATION IS MAGNIFIED.

JUST *WAIT,* MIGUEL. WAIT FOUR MORE DAYS AND WE CAN *ALL* DO WHAT WE WANT TO DO--WHAT WE *NEED* TO DO.

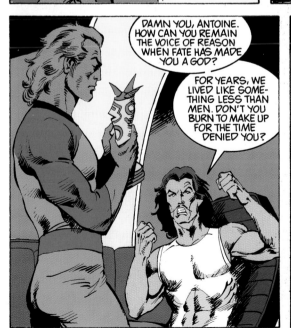

DAMN YOU, ANTOINE. HOW CAN YOU REMAIN THE VOICE OF REASON WHEN FATE HAS MADE YOU A GOD?

FOR YEARS, WE LIVED LIKE SOME-THING LESS THAN MEN. DON'T YOU BURN TO MAKE UP FOR THE TIME DENIED YOU?

YES. I DO.

BUT I CAN WAIT A LITTLE WHILE LONGER.

11

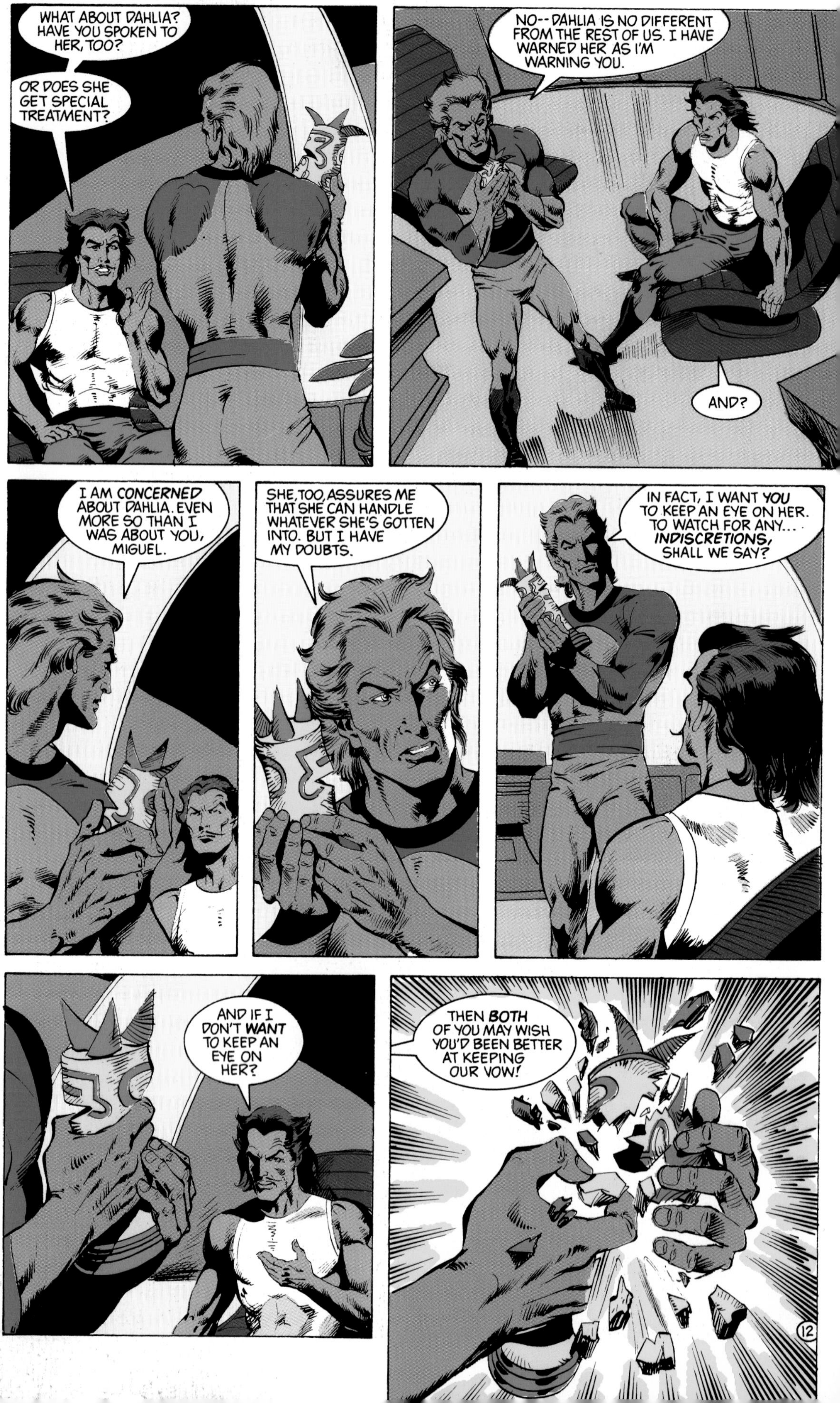
WHAT ABOUT DAHLIA? HAVE YOU SPOKEN TO HER, TOO?
OR DOES SHE GET SPECIAL TREATMENT?
NO-- DAHLIA IS NO DIFFERENT FROM THE REST OF US. I HAVE WARNED HER AS I'M WARNING YOU.
AND?
I AM CONCERNED ABOUT DAHLIA. EVEN MORE SO THAN I WAS ABOUT YOU, MIGUEL.
SHE, TOO, ASSURES ME THAT SHE CAN HANDLE WHATEVER SHE'S GOTTEN INTO. BUT I HAVE MY DOUBTS.
IN FACT, I WANT YOU TO KEEP AN EYE ON HER. TO WATCH FOR ANY... INDISCRETIONS, SHALL WE SAY?
AND IF I DON'T WANT TO KEEP AN EYE ON HER?
THEN BOTH OF YOU MAY WISH YOU'D BEEN BETTER AT KEEPING OUR VOW!
12

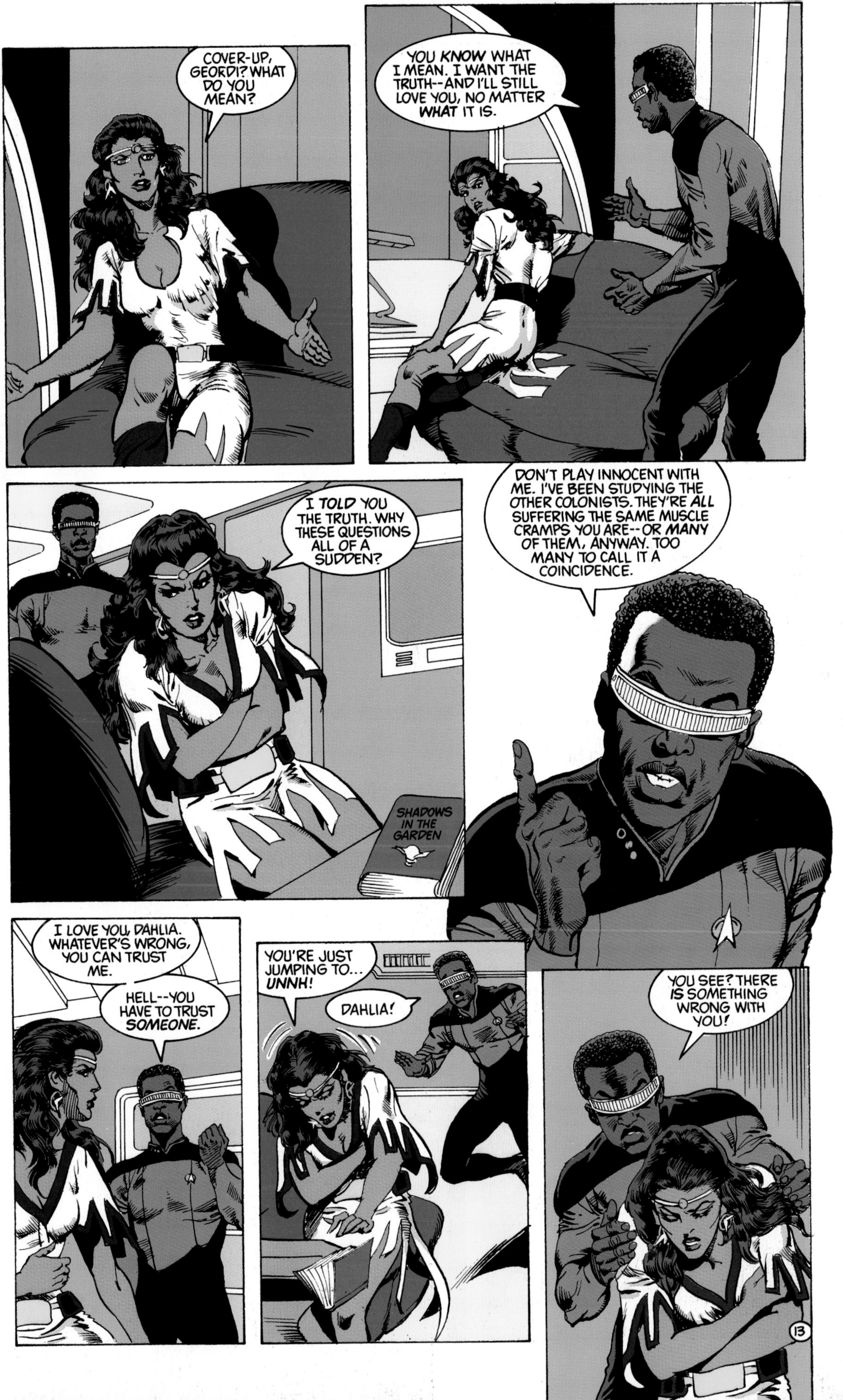
COVER-UP, GEORDI? WHAT DO YOU MEAN?
YOU KNOW WHAT I MEAN. I WANT THE TRUTH--AND I'LL STILL LOVE YOU, NO MATTER WHAT IT IS.
I TOLD YOU THE TRUTH. WHY THESE QUESTIONS ALL OF A SUDDEN?
DON'T PLAY INNOCENT WITH ME. I'VE BEEN STUDYING THE OTHER COLONISTS. THEY'RE ALL SUFFERING THE SAME MUSCLE CRAMPS YOU ARE--OR MANY OF THEM, ANYWAY. TOO MANY TO CALL IT A COINCIDENCE.
SHADOWS IN THE GARDEN
I LOVE YOU, DAHLIA. WHATEVER'S WRONG, YOU CAN TRUST ME.
HELL--YOU HAVE TO TRUST SOMEONE.
YOU'RE JUST JUMPING TO... UNNH!
DAHLIA!
YOU SEE? THERE IS SOMETHING WRONG WITH YOU!
13

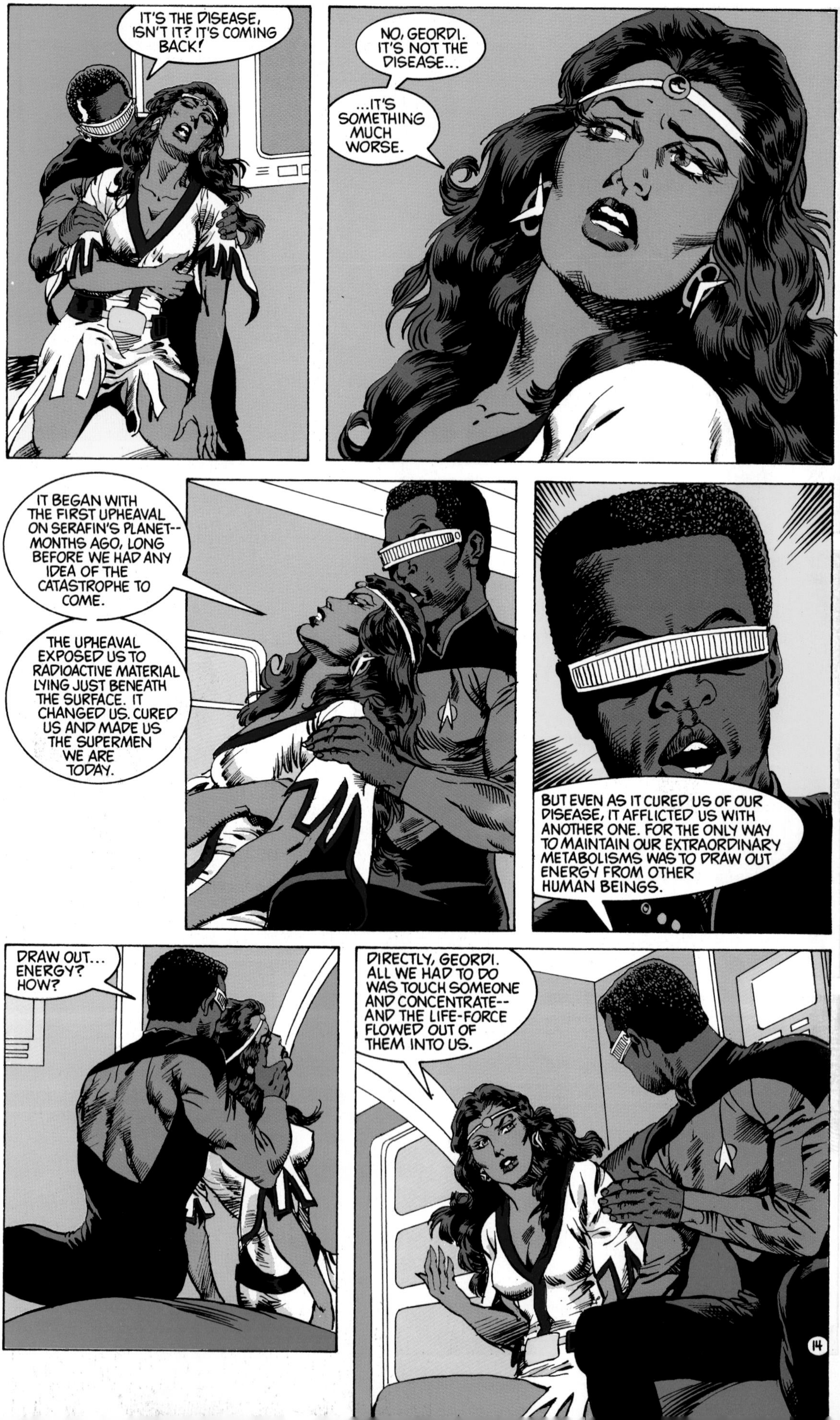
IT'S THE DISEASE, ISN'T IT? IT'S COMING BACK!
NO, GEORDI. IT'S NOT THE DISEASE...
...IT'S SOMETHING MUCH WORSE.
IT BEGAN WITH THE FIRST UPHEAVAL ON SERAFIN'S PLANET-- MONTHS AGO, LONG BEFORE WE HAD ANY IDEA OF THE CATASTROPHE TO COME.
THE UPHEAVAL EXPOSED US TO RADIOACTIVE MATERIAL LYING JUST BENEATH THE SURFACE. IT CHANGED US. CURED US AND MADE US THE SUPERMEN WE ARE TODAY.
BUT EVEN AS IT CURED US OF OUR DISEASE, IT AFFLICTED US WITH ANOTHER ONE. FOR THE ONLY WAY TO MAINTAIN OUR EXTRAORDINARY METABOLISMS WAS TO DRAW OUT ENERGY FROM OTHER HUMAN BEINGS.
DRAW OUT... ENERGY? HOW?
DIRECTLY, GEORDI. ALL WE HAD TO DO WAS TOUCH SOMEONE AND CONCENTRATE-- AND THE LIFE-FORCE FLOWED OUT OF THEM INTO US.
14

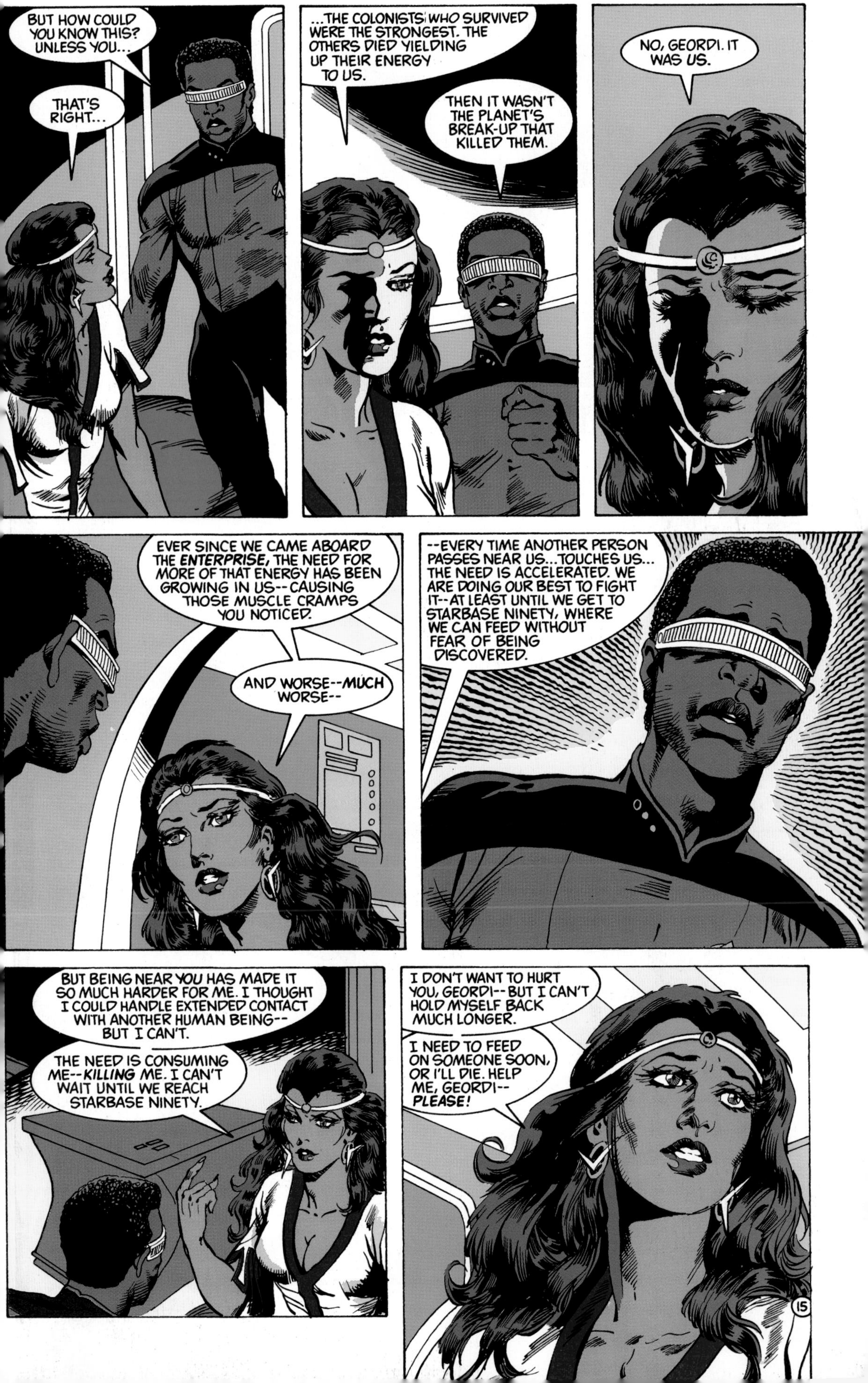
BUT HOW COULD YOU KNOW THIS? UNLESS YOU...
THAT'S RIGHT...
...THE COLONISTS WHO SURVIVED WERE THE STRONGEST. THE OTHERS DIED YIELDING UP THEIR ENERGY TO US.
THEN IT WASN'T THE PLANET'S BREAK-UP THAT KILLED THEM.
NO, GEORDI. IT WAS *US*.
EVER SINCE WE CAME ABOARD THE *ENTERPRISE*, THE NEED FOR MORE OF THAT ENERGY HAS BEEN GROWING IN US--CAUSING THOSE MUSCLE CRAMPS YOU NOTICED.
AND WORSE--*MUCH* WORSE--
--EVERY TIME ANOTHER PERSON PASSES NEAR US...TOUCHES US... THE NEED IS ACCELERATED. WE ARE DOING OUR BEST TO FIGHT IT--AT LEAST UNTIL WE GET TO STARBASE NINETY, WHERE WE CAN FEED WITHOUT FEAR OF BEING DISCOVERED.
BUT BEING NEAR *YOU* HAS MADE IT SO MUCH HARDER FOR ME. I THOUGHT I COULD HANDLE EXTENDED CONTACT WITH ANOTHER HUMAN BEING-- BUT I CAN'T.
THE NEED IS CONSUMING ME--*KILLING* ME. I CAN'T WAIT UNTIL WE REACH STARBASE NINETY.
I DON'T WANT TO HURT YOU, GEORDI--BUT I CAN'T HOLD MYSELF BACK MUCH LONGER.
I NEED TO FEED ON SOMEONE SOON, OR I'LL DIE. HELP ME, GEORDI-- *PLEASE!*

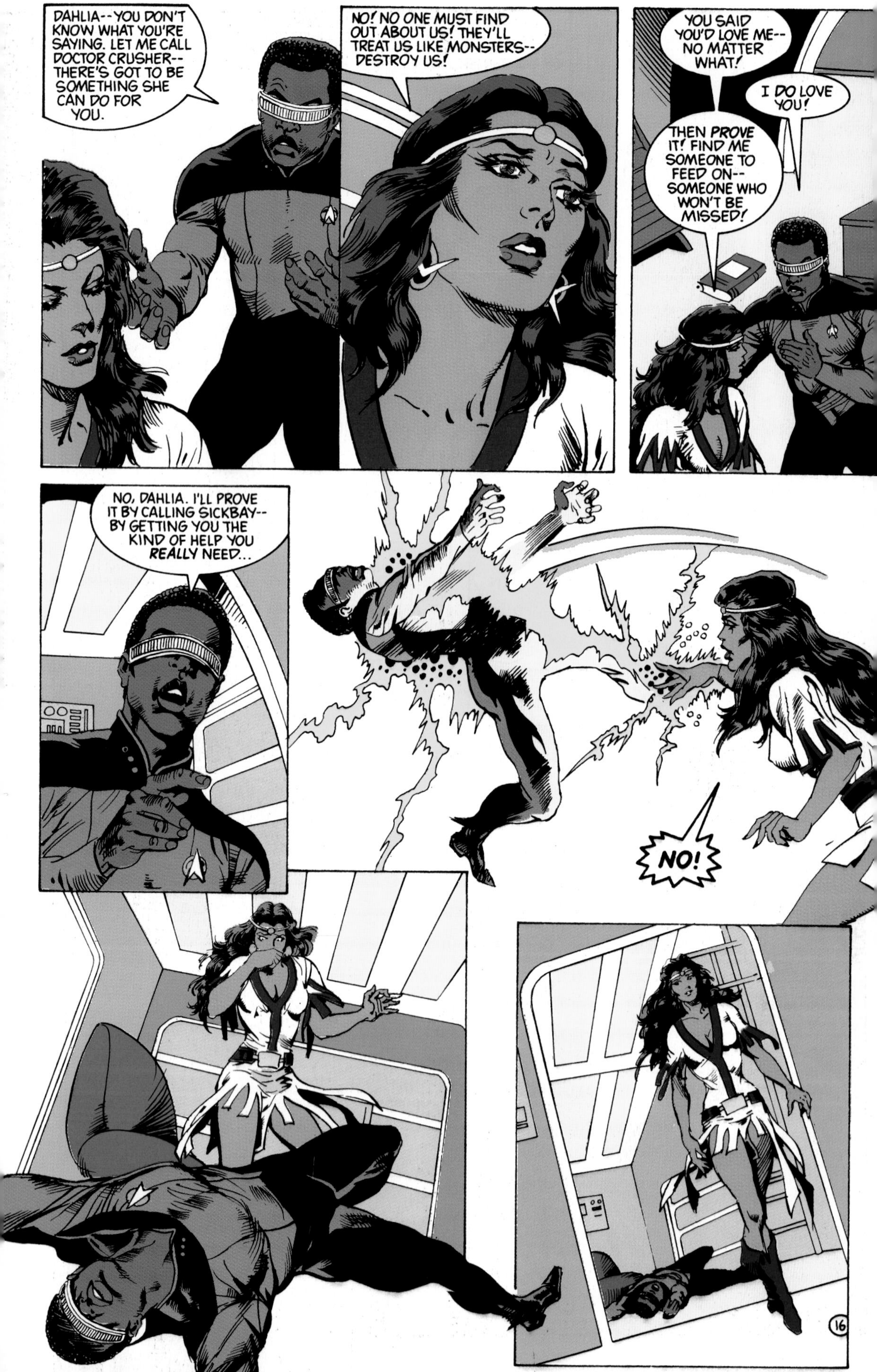
DAHLIA--YOU DON'T KNOW WHAT YOU'RE SAYING. LET ME CALL DOCTOR CRUSHER--THERE'S GOT TO BE SOMETHING SHE CAN DO FOR YOU.
NO! NO ONE MUST FIND OUT ABOUT US! THEY'LL TREAT US LIKE MONSTERS--DESTROY US!
YOU SAID YOU'D LOVE ME--NO MATTER WHAT!
I DO LOVE YOU!
THEN PROVE IT! FIND ME SOMEONE TO FEED ON--SOMEONE WHO WON'T BE MISSED!
NO, DAHLIA. I'LL PROVE IT BY CALLING SICKBAY--BY GETTING YOU THE KIND OF HELP YOU REALLY NEED...
NO!

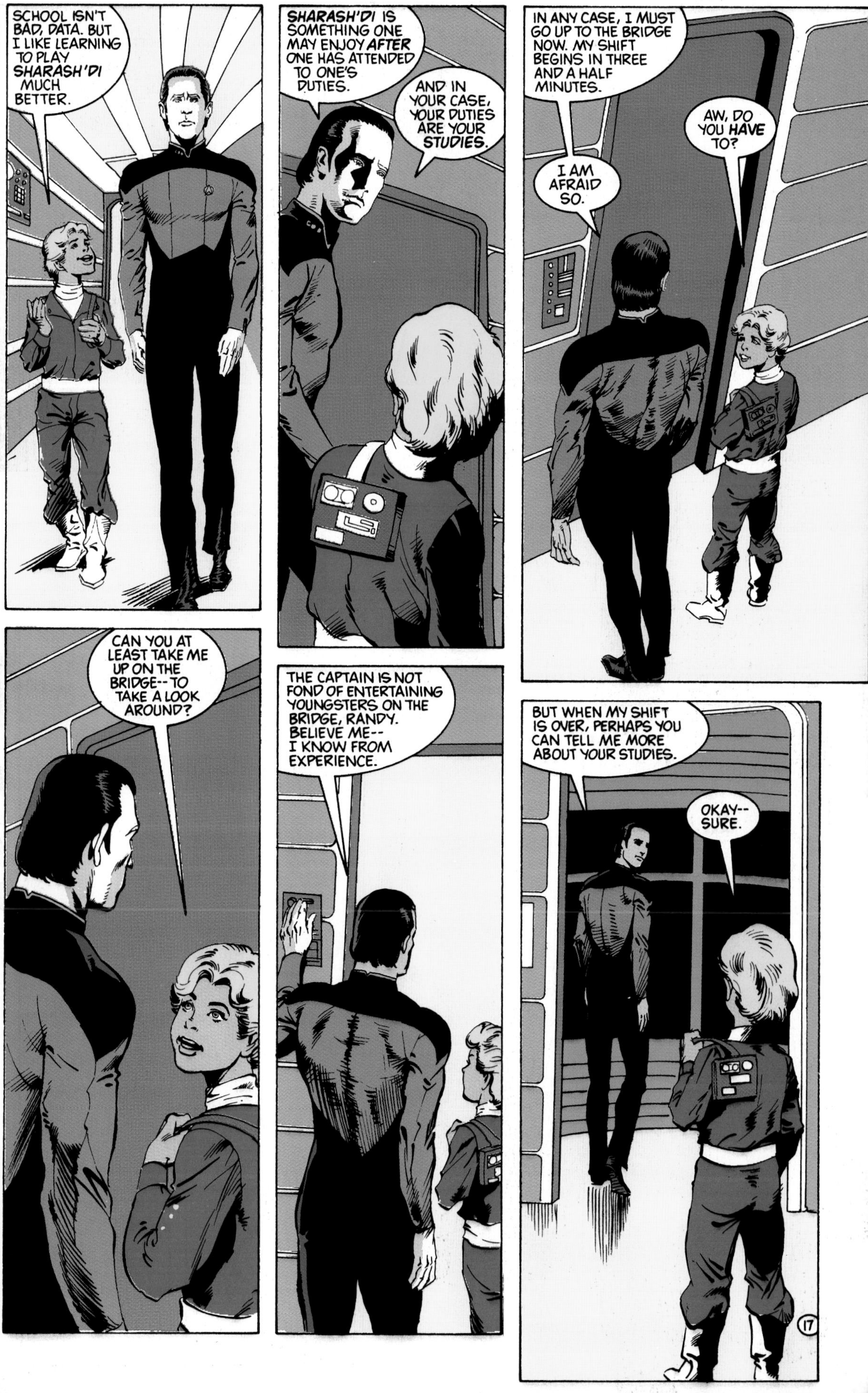
SCHOOL ISN'T BAD, DATA. BUT I LIKE LEARNING TO PLAY SHARASH'DI MUCH BETTER.
SHARASH'DI IS SOMETHING ONE MAY ENJOY AFTER ONE HAS ATTENDED TO ONE'S DUTIES.
AND IN YOUR CASE, YOUR DUTIES ARE YOUR STUDIES.
IN ANY CASE, I MUST GO UP TO THE BRIDGE NOW. MY SHIFT BEGINS IN THREE AND A HALF MINUTES.
AW, DO YOU HAVE TO?
I AM AFRAID SO.
CAN YOU AT LEAST TAKE ME UP ON THE BRIDGE--TO TAKE A LOOK AROUND?
THE CAPTAIN IS NOT FOND OF ENTERTAINING YOUNGSTERS ON THE BRIDGE, RANDY. BELIEVE ME-- I KNOW FROM EXPERIENCE.
BUT WHEN MY SHIFT IS OVER, PERHAPS YOU CAN TELL ME MORE ABOUT YOUR STUDIES.
OKAY-- SURE.
17

SEE YA LATER!

HELLO AGAIN, RANDY. IT OCCURRED TO ME THAT YOU MIGHT WANT TO ACCOMPANY ME UP TO THE BRIDGE-- IF NOT ACTUALLY *ONTO* IT. THEN YOU COULD...

AH--MISS SANTORINI. HOW ARE YOU FEELING? GEORDI MENTIONED THAT YOU HAD EXPERIENCED SOME DISCOMFORT IN...

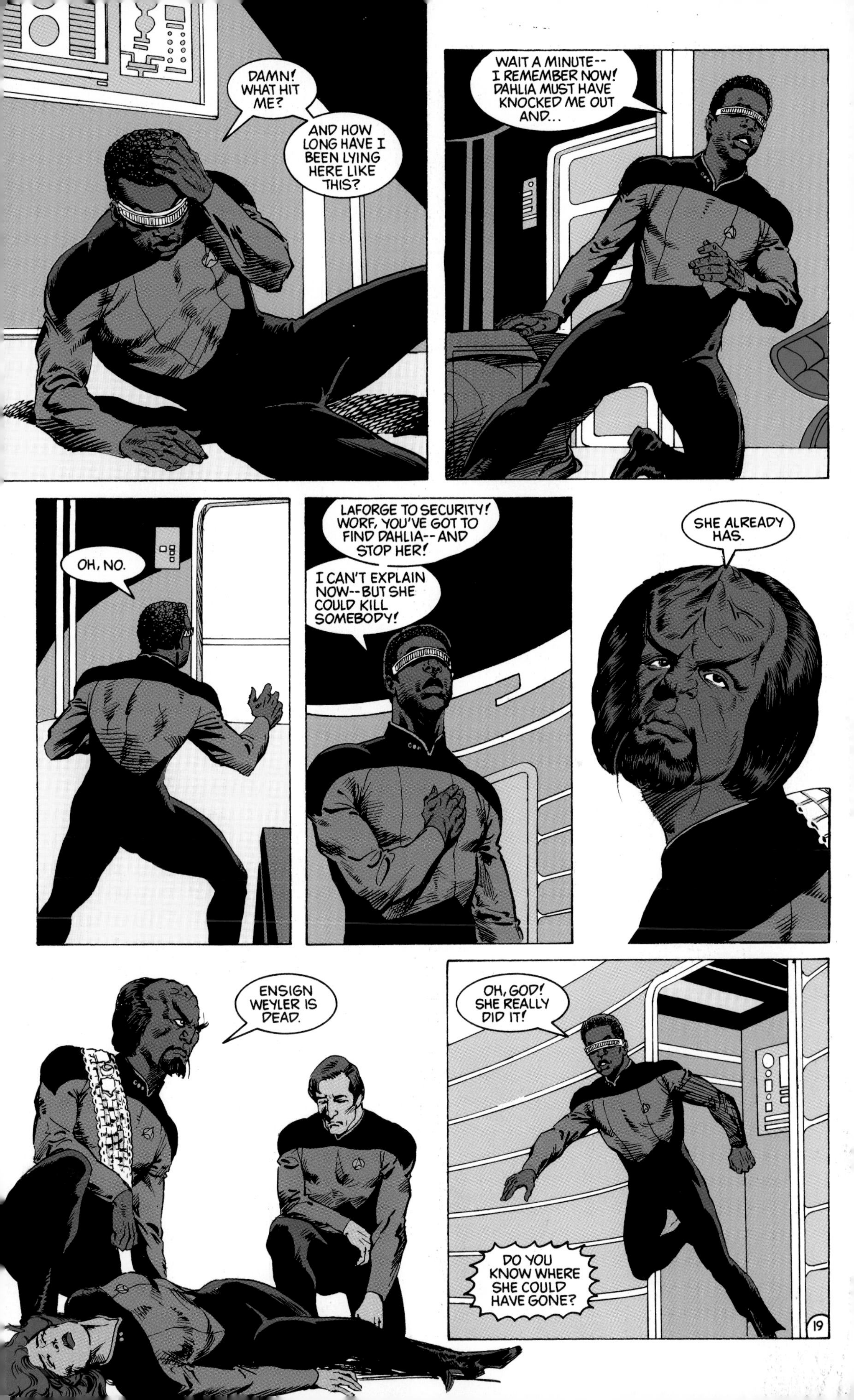
DAMN! WHAT HIT ME?
AND HOW LONG HAVE I BEEN LYING HERE LIKE THIS?
WAIT A MINUTE-- I REMEMBER NOW! DAHLIA MUST HAVE KNOCKED ME OUT AND...
OH, NO.
LAFORGE TO SECURITY! WORF, YOU'VE GOT TO FIND DAHLIA--AND STOP HER!
I CAN'T EXPLAIN NOW--BUT SHE COULD KILL SOMEBODY!
SHE ALREADY HAS.
ENSIGN WEYLER IS DEAD.
OH, GOD! SHE REALLY DID IT!
DO YOU KNOW WHERE SHE COULD HAVE GONE?
19

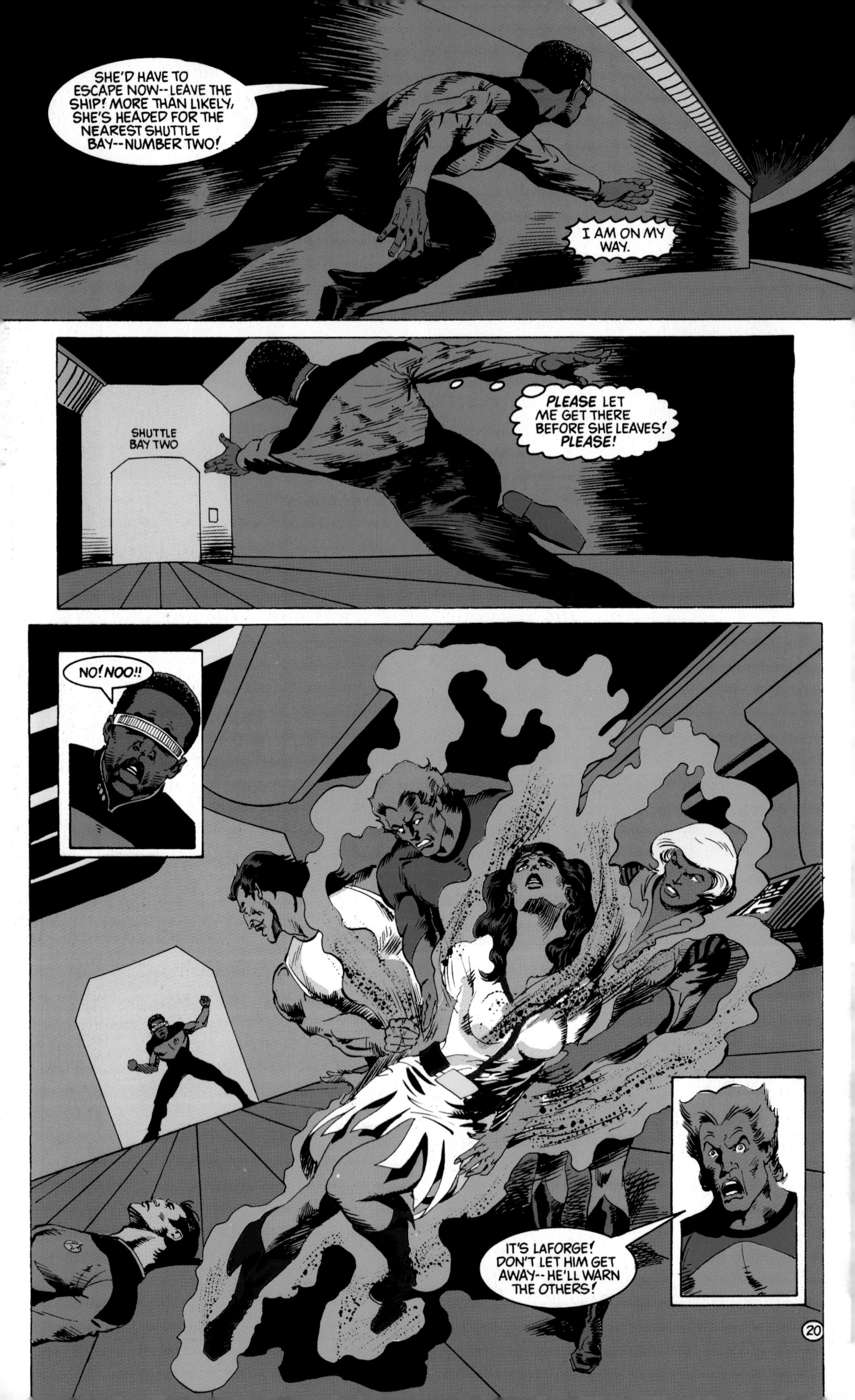

SHE'D HAVE TO ESCAPE NOW--LEAVE THE SHIP! MORE THAN LIKELY, SHE'S HEADED FOR THE NEAREST SHUTTLE BAY--NUMBER TWO!
I AM ON MY WAY.
SHUTTLE BAY TWO
PLEASE LET ME GET THERE BEFORE SHE LEAVES! PLEASE!
NO! NOO!!
IT'S LAFORGE! DON'T LET HIM GET AWAY-- HE'LL WARN THE OTHERS!

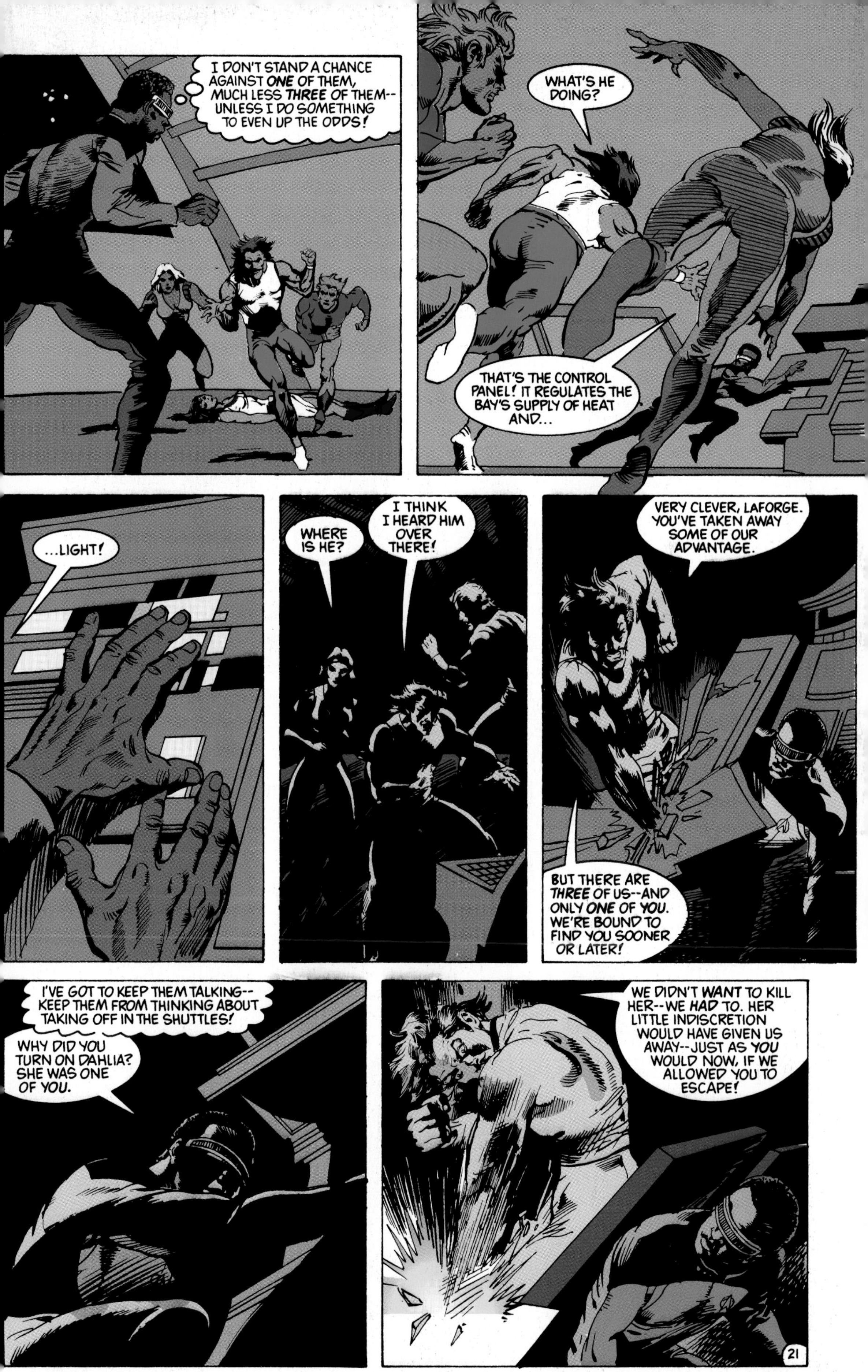
I DON'T STAND A CHANCE AGAINST ONE OF THEM, MUCH LESS THREE OF THEM--UNLESS I DO SOMETHING TO EVEN UP THE ODDS!
WHAT'S HE DOING?
THAT'S THE CONTROL PANEL! IT REGULATES THE BAY'S SUPPLY OF HEAT AND...
...LIGHT!
WHERE IS HE?
I THINK I HEARD HIM OVER THERE!
VERY CLEVER, LAFORGE. YOU'VE TAKEN AWAY SOME OF OUR ADVANTAGE.
BUT THERE ARE THREE OF US--AND ONLY ONE OF YOU. WE'RE BOUND TO FIND YOU SOONER OR LATER!
I'VE GOT TO KEEP THEM TALKING--KEEP THEM FROM THINKING ABOUT TAKING OFF IN THE SHUTTLES!
WHY DID YOU TURN ON DAHLIA? SHE WAS ONE OF YOU.
WE DIDN'T WANT TO KILL HER--WE HAD TO. HER LITTLE INDISCRETION WOULD HAVE GIVEN US AWAY--JUST AS YOU WOULD NOW, IF WE ALLOWED YOU TO ESCAPE!

BUT IF WE KILL YOU AND ARRANGE SOME SORT OF EXPLOSION--MAKE IT LOOK LIKE AN ACCIDENT--WE CAN STILL FEND OFF SUSPICION UNTIL WE REACH STARBASE NINETY.

AND THEN WE'RE HOME FREE.

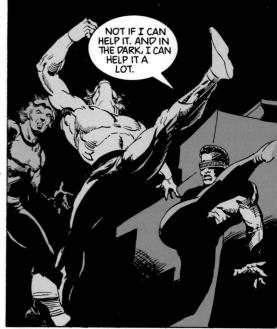

NOT IF I CAN HELP IT. AND IN THE DARK, I CAN HELP IT A LOT.

OVERCONFIDENCE CAN BE FATAL, LAFORGE! YOU SHOULD HAVE STAYED IN A CORNER SOMEWHERE AND KEPT QUIET!

COFF!

DON'T MOVE!

I TOLD YOU NOT TO MOVE.

22

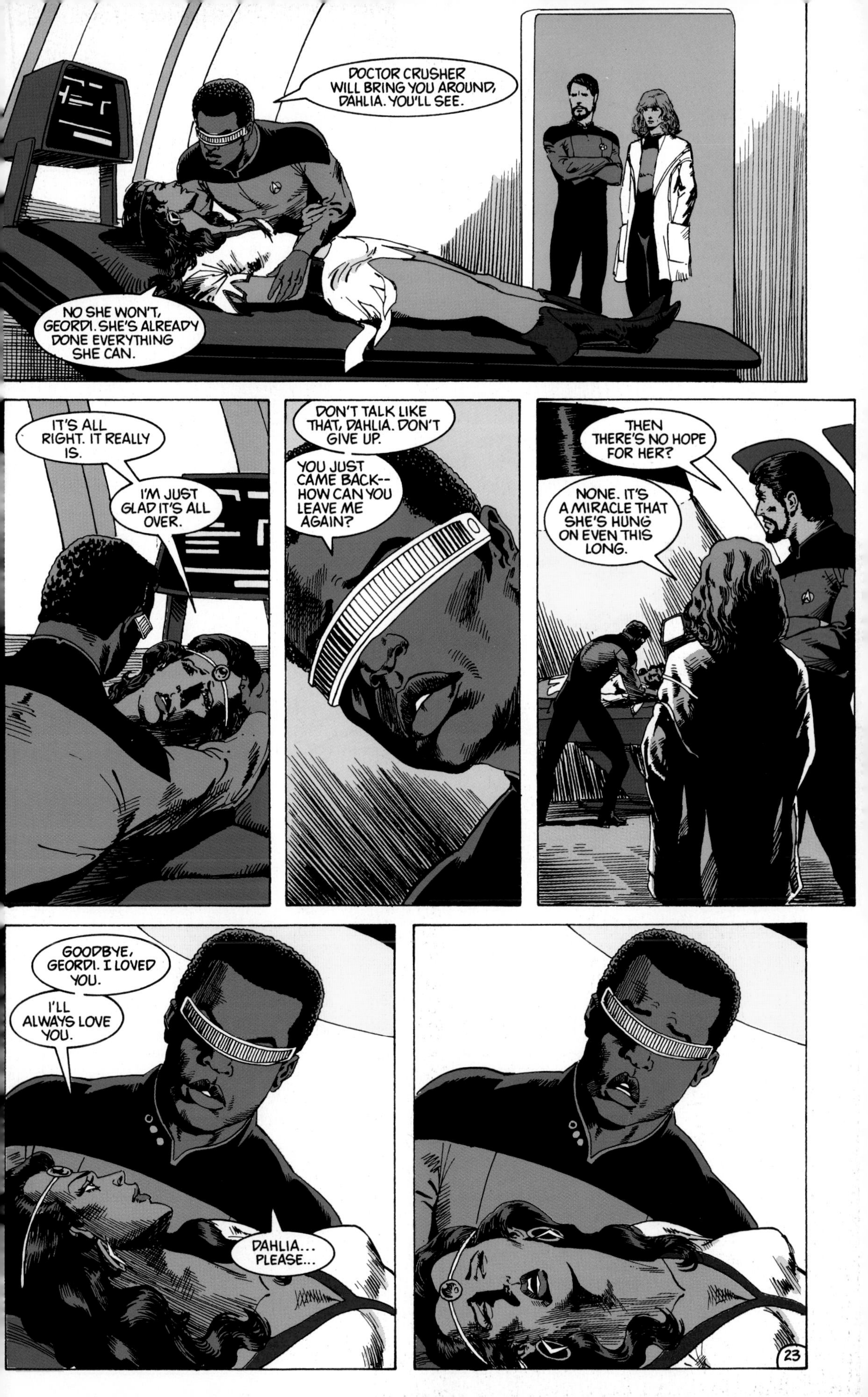
DOCTOR CRUSHER WILL BRING YOU AROUND, DAHLIA. YOU'LL SEE.
NO SHE WON'T, GEORDI. SHE'S ALREADY DONE EVERYTHING SHE CAN.
IT'S ALL RIGHT. IT REALLY IS.
I'M JUST GLAD IT'S ALL OVER.
DON'T TALK LIKE THAT, DAHLIA. DON'T GIVE UP.
YOU JUST CAME BACK-- HOW CAN YOU LEAVE ME AGAIN?
THEN THERE'S NO HOPE FOR HER?
NONE. IT'S A MIRACLE THAT SHE'S HUNG ON EVEN THIS LONG.
GOODBYE, GEORDI. I LOVED YOU.
I'LL ALWAYS LOVE YOU.
DAHLIA... PLEASE...

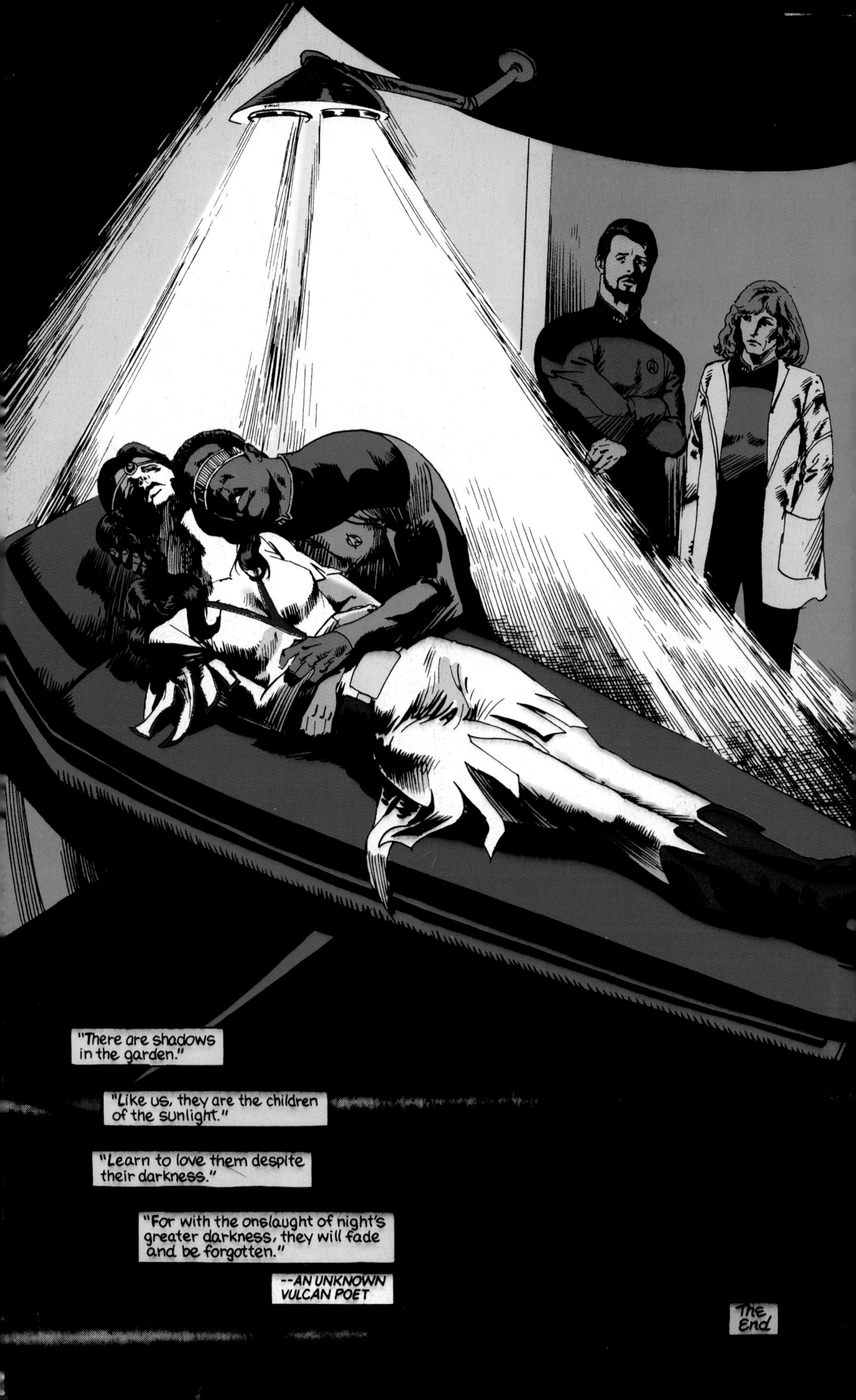
"There are shadows in the garden."
"Like us, they are the children of the sunlight."
"Learn to love them despite their darkness."
"For with the onslaught of night's greater darkness, they will fade and be forgotten."
--AN UNKNOWN VULCAN POET
THE End

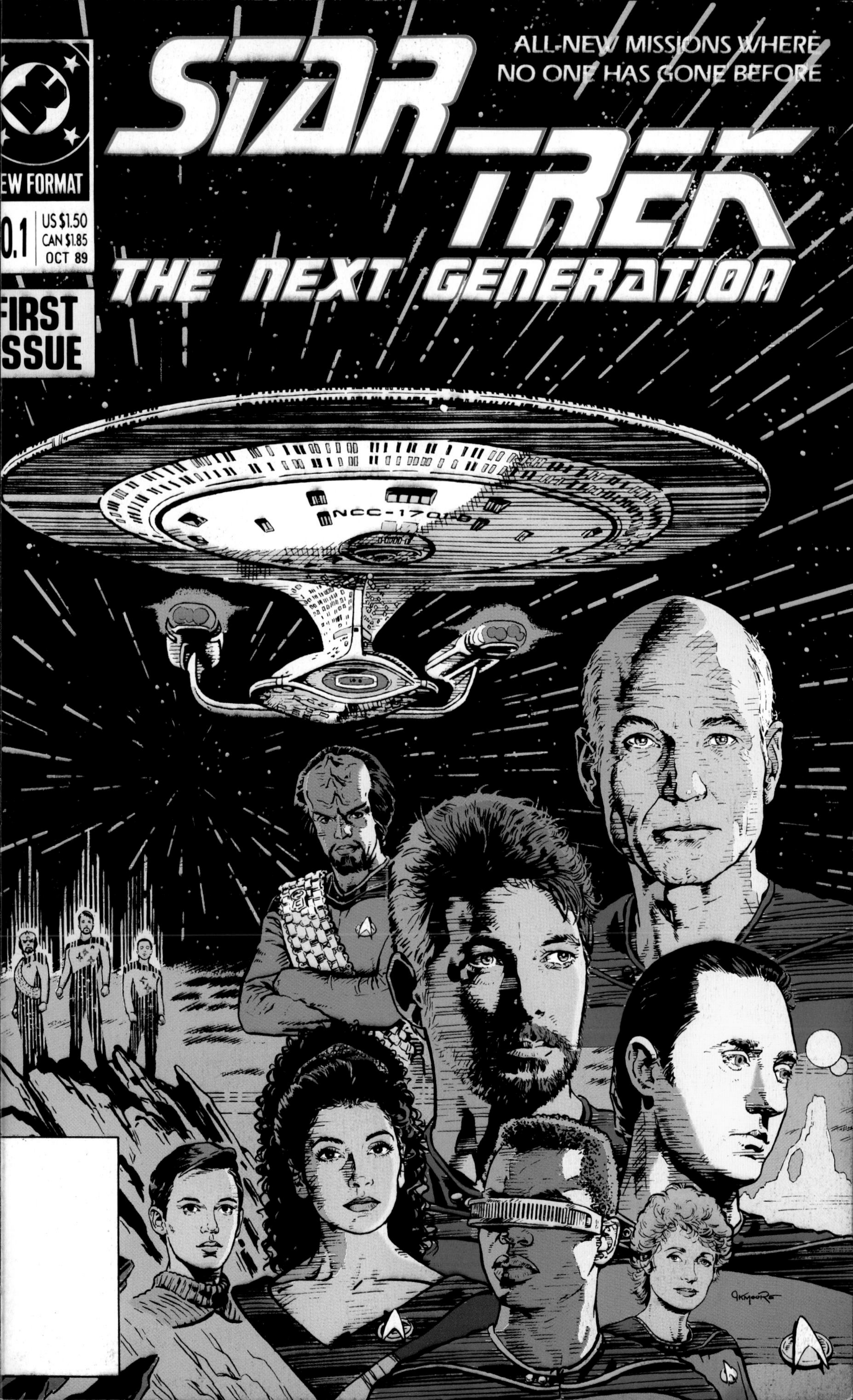

ALL-NEW MISSIONS WHERE NO ONE HAS GONE BEFORE
STAR TREK
THE NEXT GENERATION
EW FORMAT
0.1
US $1.50
CAN $1.85
OCT 89
FIRST ISSUE
NCC-1701-D

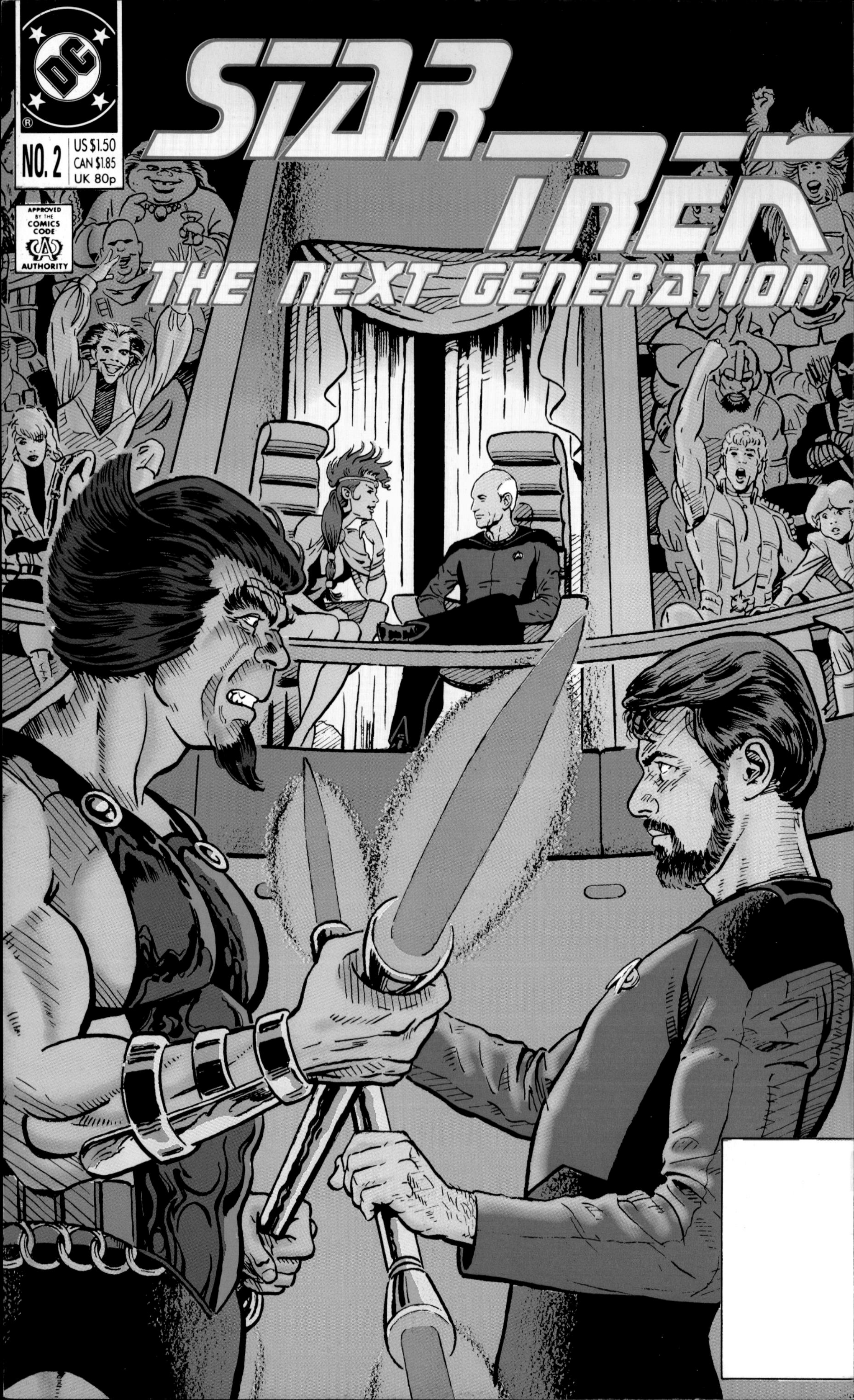

DC
NO. 2
US $1.50
CAN $1.85
UK 80p
APPROVED BY THE COMICS CODE AUTHORITY
STAR TREK
THE NEXT GENERATION

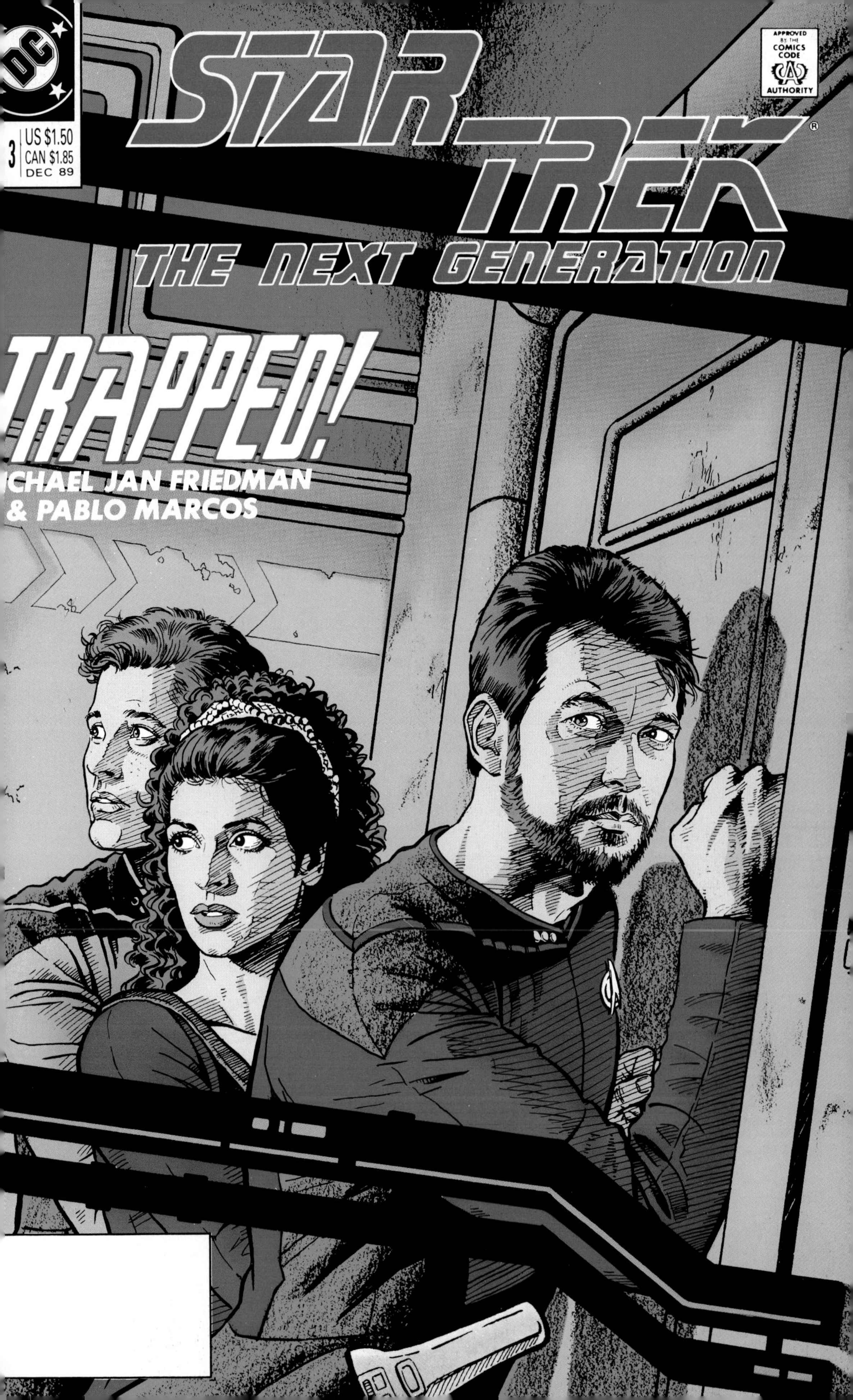
DC
US $1.50
CAN $1.85
DEC 89
3
APPROVED BY THE COMICS CODE AUTHORITY
STAR TREK
THE NEXT GENERATION
TRAPPED!
CHAEL JAN FRIEDMAN
& PABLO MARCOS

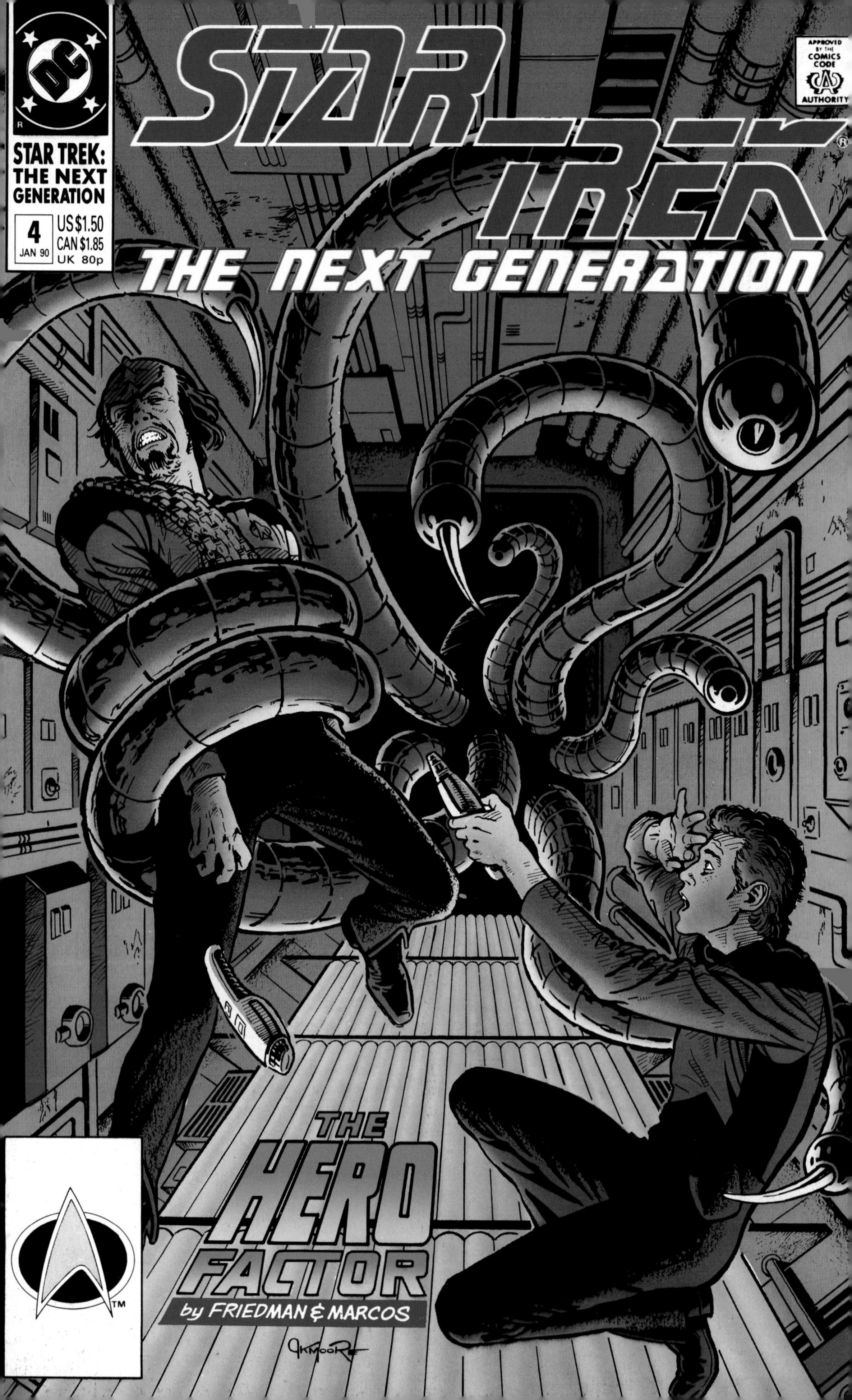
DC
STAR TREK
THE NEXT GENERATION
STAR TREK: THE NEXT GENERATION
4
JAN 90
US$1.50
CAN $1.85
UK 80p
APPROVED BY THE COMICS CODE AUTHORITY
THE HERO FACTOR
by FRIEDMAN & MARCOS

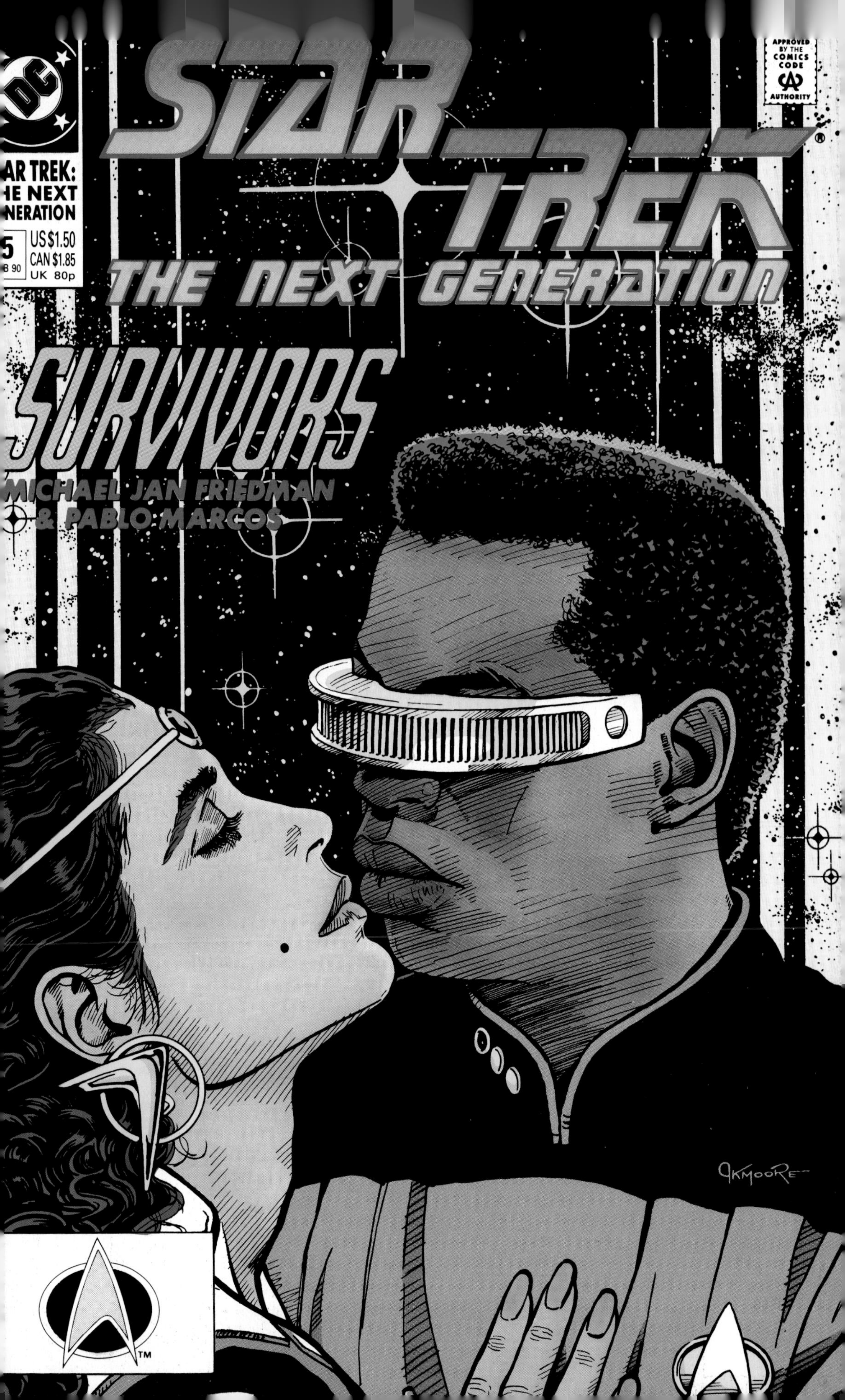
DC
STAR TREK
THE NEXT GENERATION
AR TREK:
IE NEXT
NERATION
US $1.50
CAN $1.85
UK 80p
APPROVED BY THE COMICS CODE AUTHORITY
SURVIVORS
MICHAEL JAN FRIEDMAN
& PABLO MARCOS
TM

CREATOR BIOGRAPHIES

MICHAEL JAN FRIEDMAN

is a prolific novelist within the many universes of *Star Trek*, with over 40 titles published to date. His work includes the *Stargazer* series, the original series trilogy *My Brother's Keeper*, plus *Star Trek: Deep Space Nine* and *Starfleet Academy* novels. He is also the author of the *Vidar* trilogy and has written *X-Men* and *Wishbone* novels. Friedman's non-fiction work includes the *Tomb Raider Tech Manual* and the *Star Trek Federation Travel Guide*, and other comics work includes *2099 Unlimited*, *Darkstars*, *The Flash*, *Justice League Task Force* and *Outlaws*.

PABLO MARCOS

is one of the most successful ever Peruvian comics artists, having started his career working for companies such as Marvel, DC, Atlas and Warren in the '60s. He has worked on a dazzling array of titles, including *Avengers*, *Batman*, *The Brute*, *Captain America*, *Conan*, *Fantastic Four*, *Green Arrow*, *Ironjaw*, *Jungle Action*, *Spider-Man* and *Warlord*. As an inker, Marcos has worked with industry greats including John Buscema, John Byrne and Bill Sienkiewicz.

STAR TREK
MAGAZINE

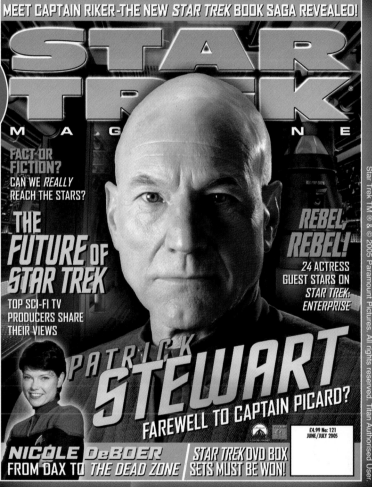

100 PAGES!

MEET CAPTAIN RIKER-THE NEW *STAR TREK* BOOK SAGA REVEALED!

STAR TREK
MAGAZINE

FACT-OR FICTION? CAN WE *REALLY* REACH THE STARS?

THE *FUTURE* OF *STAR TREK*

TOP SCI-FI TV PRODUCERS SHARE THEIR VIEWS

REBEL, REBEL! 24 ACTRESS GUEST STARS ON *STAR TREK: ENTERPRISE*

PATRICK STEWART
FAREWELL TO CAPTAIN PICARD?

NICOLE DeBOER FROM DAX TO *THE DEAD ZONE*

STAR TREK DVD BOX SETS MUST BE WON!

£4.99 No: 121 JUNE/JULY 2005

THE BUMPER 100-PAGE MAGAZINE DEVOTED TO ALL THINGS *STAR TREK*!

ON SALE AT ALL GOOD NEWSAGENTS NOW*

SUBSCRIBE TODAY and automatically become a member of **The Official UK STAR TREK Fan Club!**
Call: 0870 428 8201 or visit www.titanmagazines.co.uk

*PLEASE NOTE ONLY AVAILABLE IN THE UK

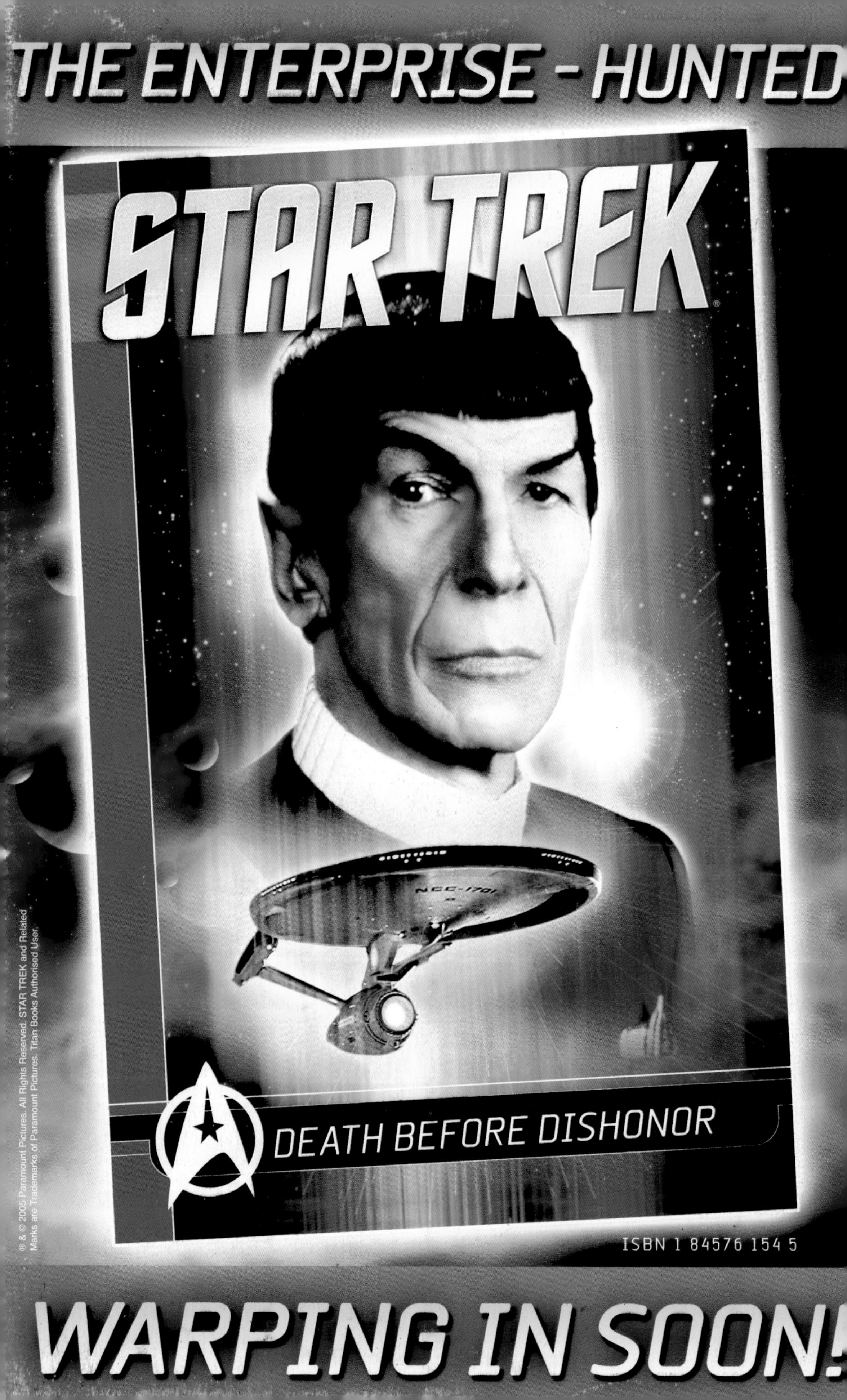
THE ENTERPRISE - HUNTED
STAR TREK®
NCC-1701
DEATH BEFORE DISHONOR
ISBN 1 84576 154 5
® & © 2005 Paramount Pictures. All Rights Reserved. STAR TREK and Related Marks are Trademarks of Paramount Pictures. Titan Books Authorised User.
WARPING IN SOON!